ELEANOR
OF
AQUITAINE

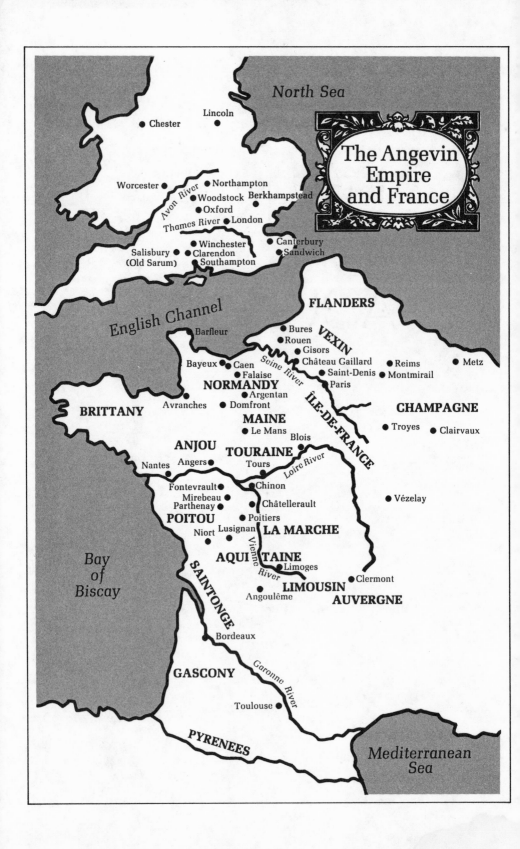

ELEANOR OF AQUITAINE

A BIOGRAPHY

MARION MEADE

HAWTHORN/DUTTON
NEW YORK

Library of Congress Catalog Card Number: 80-80014
ISBN: 0-525-48460-4
15 14 13 12 11 10 9

The proper study of mankind is woman and, by common agreement since the time of Adam, it is the most complex and arduous.

Henry Adams
Mont-Saint-Michel and Chartres

Contents

The Family of Eleanor of Aquitaine

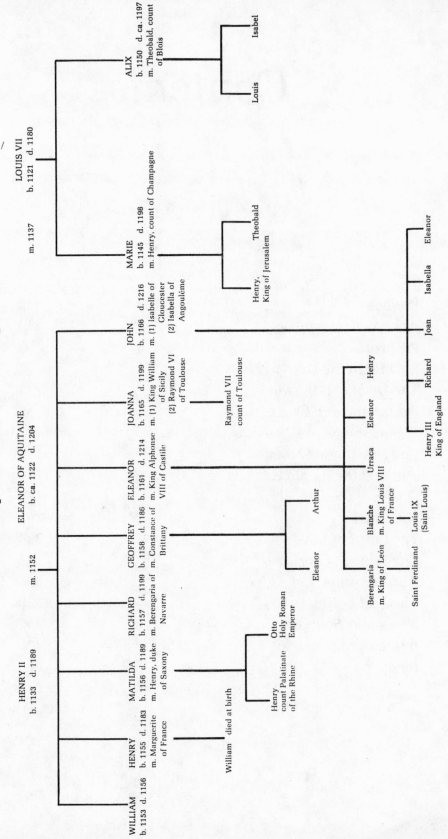

Preface

It is one of the paradoxes of history that those persons commonly believed to wield the least political power may sometimes exert the greatest force on the course of human events. Although Eleanor of Aquitaine, queen of France and later of England, lived at a time when women as individuals had few significant rights, she was nevertheless the key political figure of the twelfth century. At the age of fifteen she inherited one-quarter of modern-day France, but since women were thought unfit to rule, her land as well as her person were delegated to the custody of men. Her whole life thereafter became a struggle for the independence and political power that circumstances had denied her, although few of her contemporaries could realize this.

The historical record, written to accommodate men, has assigned women whom it could not ignore into three classic categories: wife, mother, and whore. Eleanor of Aquitaine can be found in all three, even though her life represented much more. It is true that she was the wife of King Louis VII of France and King Henry II of England, as well as the mother of one of Western civilization's great heroes, Richard Coeur de Lion, and also of one of the great villains, King John. Nevertheless, she did more than marry and bear children, and as the eminent historian Bishop William Stubbs wrote, "Few women have had less justice done them in history than Eleanor." That she has been judged a bitch, harlot, adulteress, and monster is not surprising, for she was one of those rare women who altogether refused to be bound by the rules of proper behavior for her sex; she did as she pleased, although not without agonizing personal struggle. Her admiring contemporary Richard of Devizes may have called her "an incomparable woman," but for the most part history has not agreed on how to deal with her. For Shakespeare she was a "canker'd grandam," "a monstrous injurer of heaven and earth" who should be remembered for her "sin-conceiving womb." In the *Carmina Burana*, an anonymous German scholar, haunted by a passing glimpse of Eleanor, saw her as the ultimate sex symbol:

> Were the world all mine,
> From the sea to the Rhine,
> I'd give it all
> If so be the Queen of England
> Lay in my arms.

As an aggressive woman who never willingly allowed herself to become the victim of circumstances and who exercised power over the most important men of her time, Eleanor presented an image of femininity so at variance with the accepted subordinate role ordained for her sex that people could only conclude she must be a demon. In the years immediately following her death, the remarkable length of her life-span inspired a number of legends, all of them entirely derogatory. In the thirteenth-century romance *Richard Coeur-de-Lion*, she is a beautiful demon who refuses to attend Mass or partake of the Sacrament and, when forced to do so, flies out the window. The French writer Philippe Mouskès *(Chronique Rimée)* quotes her as saying to her barons after her divorce from the pious and sexless Louis VII: "Look at me, gentlemen. Is not my body delightful? The king thought that I was the devil." To the Minstrel of Reims, she remained "a very devil," a woman so depraved that she would be capable of attempting an elopement with the Moslem ruler Saladin. The calumnies of Eleanor's contemporaries continued to pursue her throughout the centuries as balladeers used her legend to fashion popular songs: in *Queen Eleanor's Confession* she is an adulteress and the mother of an illegitimate child by William Marshal; in *The Ballad of Fair Rosamond* she becomes a murderess, while the adulteress Rosamond Clifford is cast in the role of a sweet unfortunate victim.

Apart from Eleanor's portrayal in folklore, professional historians have treated her as either a mere shadow of her husbands or as an accident among the important activities of men. The English historian John Richard Green in his *Short History of the English People* devoted forty pages to the reign of Henry II, and in these Eleanor is mentioned only four times; French historians also make short shrift of her as "a naughty wife" or the owner of valuable real estate. The fact is, she was in her own right a political person of the highest importance. Her decision to divorce the king of France and her remarriage to Henry Plantagenet overthrew the balance of power in France and England, producing a disruption that required 300 years of warfare to remedy. Her quarrels with her second husband and her subsequent support of her sons in their rebellion against Henry spread confusion and dismay throughout western Europe. Henry's death and the accession of Richard brought her to supreme power, and as Coeur de Lion's representative in England during the Third Crusade, she repressed the ambitions of John while at the same time thwarting the designs of Philip Augustus. At Richard's death, it was entirely due to her efforts that John reached the throne. Despite her association with these four kings, she struggled to retain her own identity, and it is a measure of her success that 772 years after her death she survives not as Queen Eleanor of England or Queen Eleanor of France but simply as Eleanor of Aquitaine.

Eleanor left only a few writs and charters, routine documents that are for the most part as impersonal as government orders of any period, as well as three letters that may be considered genuine. There are three additional letters that, in my opinion, have been erroneously attributed to her, although I was certainly tempted to use them, since they reveal a real living being full of intense emotions. The unfortunate fact is that Eleanor, a highly literate woman, left no intimate record of herself, no letters, diaries, or poetry that might provide insights into her inner life. Her contemporaries knew her, of course, but what they observed and understood of her as an individual was rarely included in their histories.

Of necessity I have had to base this biography on written sources from the twelfth and thirteenth centuries, knowing, however, that even these contemporary chroniclers are riddled with bias, since monks and historians—in the twelfth century one and the same—have always abhorred emancipated women. The details we would like to know about Eleanor are missing, although sometimes they provide more details than one wishes to know about the men in her life: that Louis cried a great deal and fell asleep under trees, that Henry had reddish hair and doodled in church, that Richard chose his lovers from members of his own sex, that John lay in bed with Isabella of Angoulême instead of defending his kingdom. But in the case of Eleanor, the chroniclers wrote sparingly, except to insinuate that she was a bad wife and a worse mother. They claimed that she was extraordinarily handsome, and judging by her tomb effigy at Fontevrault and by the

Cloisters' capital in New York, it is possible to confirm the accuracy of their statements. Unfortunately, they neglected to mention an ordinary detail like the color of her hair.

Given these limitations, we still know more about Eleanor than about any other woman of her era. She was a woman of enormous intelligence and titanic energy who lived in a passionate, creative age. The stage on which she moved encompassed the Crusades, the new Gothic architecture, the struggle between Church and State, the songs of the troubadours, the ideas of courtly love, and the burgeoning of a feminist movement. Nor can one overlook the stellar personalities of her century: Thomas Becket; Saint Bernard; Peter Abélard; William Marshal; and the troubadour poets, of whom her grandfather William was the first. Eleanor participated in these important movements, she knew all the personalities, and, an indefatigable traveler, she was familiar with every great city of medieval times: London, Paris, Rome, Constantinople, and Jerusalem. At twenty-five she set out for the Holy Land as a Crusader and at seventy-eight she was still on the move, journeying over the Pyrenees to Spain to fetch the granddaughter whose marriage would be, she hoped, a pledge of peace between England and France.

None of the dialogue in this biography is invented—all of it comes from the chronicles—nor did I find it necessary to fictionalize Eleanor's life. Her history, what little is known of it, is novel enough.

Acknowledgments

I should like to express my appreciation to the New York Public Library for generously granting me the privilege of working in the Frederick Lewis Allen Room. I am also grateful to the following museums and organizations for their cooperation in furnishing photographs: the Metropolitan Museum of Art, the Bibliothèque Nationale, Roger-Viollet, the French Cultural Services, Photographie Giraudon, the British Tourist Authority, the Archives de France, and the Service de Documentation Photographique de la Réunion des Musées Nationaux. Thanks is also due to the literary estate of Hubert Creekmore for permission to reprint his translation of William the Troubadour's poem on page 20; to Claude Marks and the Macmillan Company for Bernard of Ventadour's poem on page 160; and to Macmillan, London, and Russell and Russell Publishers for Kate Norgate's translation of the Richard Coeur de Lion *sirventès* on page 322.

ELEANOR OF AQUITAINE

Prologue

For generation after generation Aquitaine had been ruled by a long line of Williams. The first Duke William, born in 752, was a childhood friend and loyal companion-in-arms of the Emperor Charlemagne, as well as a great warrior in his own right. *Chansons* of later centuries would embroider his feats with brilliant threads of mythology, recounting victorious deeds against terrible Saracen giants, transforming his life into legend. In plain fact, he fought bravely, reaping riches and honors until, at the age of forty-eight, he resolutely turned his back on the world and retired to a Benedictine monastery that he had built near Montpellier. After his death and canonization his retreat became known as—and today is still called—Saint Guilhem-le-Désert.

While by and large the heirs of the saintly Duke William were capable administrators, none equaled him in piety; indeed, some fell far short. Nevertheless, his line, mercifully assured by the periodic births of male children christened William, endured for over three hundred years.

Then, in the third decade of the twelfth century, through death, carelessness, or perhaps, as some claimed, the will of God, the reigns of the Williams abruptly came to an end.

There remained only a maiden of fifteen, a member of what people then called "the lesser sex."

From that moment forward everything changed, not only for Aquitaine but for the whole of western Europe.

From their palaces in Poitiers and Bordeaux, the dukes of Aquitaine ruled, after a fashion, a domain that the chroniclers described in superlatives. "Aquitaine," wrote Ralph of Diceto, "abounding in riches of many kinds, excels other parts of the western world in such wise that it is reckoned by historians as one of the happiest and most fertile

3

among the provinces of Gaul." Enclosing the two counties of Poitou and Gascony, the duchy was impressive enough to cover much of central and southwestern France, indeed its dominions spread over one-quarter of that modern-day nation. Behind its frontiers—Anjou and Brittany on the north, the wild barricade of the Pyrenees on the south, the Atlantic on the west, and on the east the Rhone ridges of the Massif Central—lay a territory not only larger but wealthier than that of the Frankish kings.

Its countryside was a richly ornamented tapestry of blues and greens and blacks, abundant dark forests and emerald pastureland criss-crossed by the silvery river waters of the Garonne, Charente, Creuse, and Vienne. Aquitaine means "land of waters," a name dating back to the century before Christ, when the Romans pushed northward from their colony at Narbonne and conquered almost the whole of Gaul. Clustered thickly in the river valleys were villages and farms, walled cities and moat-ringed castles with their massive keeps jutting straight up to the skies. The land overflowed with fruit—cherries, plums, raspberries, the wild wood strawberry—and with acre upon uncountable acre of vineyards. In the autumn, when the oak forests turned russet, the grapes would be pressed into the ruby wines for which the region was famous, and then even the humblest peasants would drink joyously until their lips were stained carmine. Along the seaboard, the harbor towns of Bordeaux and La Rochelle did a thriving export business with the wine as well as salt, and in Bayonne fishing boats ventured forth upon the Atlantic toward the limitless horizon and returned with whale, herring, and porpoise, which would hang in salted strips in the market-places.

Despite the easy life made possible by a temperate climate and an abundance of crops, the peasants lived their lives under a blanket of anxiety, always conscious of the fact that they were expendable. Most of them, whether serf or free tenant, held their lands from a seigneur on a hereditary basis. With the social strata cemented into airtight compartments, they were born in thatched hovels and died there and were taxed and worked in the interim as the nobility deemed fit. Both men and women tilled the fields and tended the vines; they kept pigs and perhaps a goose or two, and they made cheese. Inside the village churches, they prostrated themselves on the naked stones and made their novenas to the Blessed Virgin or Saint Radegonde, beseeching these holy ladies' intercession with an awesome God; but if the Lord failed to respond, they reverted to pagan superstition and summoned fairies and witches. When war came, as it did often, for the nobility regarded fighting as their chief occupation, their huts were burned, their vines trampled, their women raped. At such times they ate chestnuts and roots, and their children were found dead along the roads, their mouths stuffed with grass. It did not matter that the lands of their lords teemed with rabbit, squirrel, and crow, for the fate of the poacher, if caught, was death by hanging.

By contrast, life for those higher up the social scale was not merely agreeable, it exuded a grandeur unique for the times. True, the local lords were a pugnacious, fiercely independent lot given to continual petty squabbling, but in the late eleventh century Aquitaine enjoyed a peace and prosperity unknown to the rest of Europe. "When they set themselves to tame the pride of their enemies, they do it in earnest; and when the labours of battle are over and they settle down to rest in peace, they give themselves up wholly to pleasure." The Aquitainians lived for pleasure; it was the ideal that they pursued, the principle for which they were willing to sacrifice nearly everything. The southern lords vied with each other to establish splendid miniature courts in their castles. Refusing to hoard their gold in coffers, they used the income from their lands to purchase luxuries and hold great feasts until they won the reputation of being lavish, ostentatious, and, a principal virtue, hospitable. To outsiders, especially to the northern barons, who were bearded, unkempt, and unwashed, the luxury and elegance of the southerners, with their shaved faces and long, parted locks, appeared effeminate. The foppery of the easygoing, free-spending Aquitainians never ceased to astonish their contemporaries, and critics in subsequent centuries would still be decrying their flamboyance. "Nowadays," scornfully wrote Geoffrey of Vigeois about 1175, "the meanest would blush to wear such clothes. Rich and precious stuffs are woven, whose colours suit each man's mood; the borders of the clothes are cut into little balls and pointed tongues, until their wearers look like devils in a painting."

If the men appeared devilish to Prior Geoffrey, the women inspired even greater horror and caused Aquitaine's sober neighbors to murmur that the whole of the duchy was no better than a huge brothel. While feudal times were not the best in which to be born female, still the position occupied by the women of Aquitaine was, everything considered, remarkably high. Perhaps because the power of the Church was relatively weak there, its customary puritanism and fierce misogyny had less influence, so that women came to expect, and receive, a place of prominence in society. Under the laws of the land they could inherit property in their own right, and some, on occasion, exercised great power as landowners. At their disposal were the means of elegance, and they took advantage of opulent fashions, cosmetics, and oriental perfumes to enhance their persons. Undoubtedly, their painted cheeks and charcoal-rimmed eyes, combined with their free and easy independence, supplied a basis for the charge that moral disorder was rife in Aquitaine. Unlike their counterparts in the northern countries, the women refused to be segregated among themselves or secluded in convents and, if discovered with a lover, they were neither shut up nor killed. While adultery in women was not actually condoned, it was not severely condemned either. In sex, sex roles, and religion, there was to be found a greater degree of tolerance in Aquitaine, a greater respect for the individual.

As the twelfth century began, a phenomenon akin to a new religion began to grow in Aquitaine, one that sprang naturally from their leisurely civilization and the flourishing position of women in their culture. The new century saw the arrival of the troubadours and, with them, the advent of love as a serious, all-consuming occupation. The poets of the southland wrote not for gain but for pleasure, not in cultured Latin but in the mellifluous vernacular of the *langue d'oc,* not for men but primarily for the women of the great castles and manors. Windy *chansons de geste,* with their lofty deeds and blood-and-guts machismo, awoke no echoes of glory in the hearts of these elegant baronesses and countesses, already semidivinized. They longed to while away their evenings with songs of love in which women were cherished, adored, and romantically seduced. Under their eager patronage, there flowered a new school of poetry that touched on subjects never before covered by verse; one day the sweet new lyrical style of the troubadours emerging from the salons of these bluestockings born before their time would culminate in Petrarch and Dante.

That such a radically different type of poetry should suddenly bud and then take firm root in the popular imagination of all classes was not at all accidental. For the very first troubadour was no low-born minstrel wandering the dusty Poitevin roads in search of a meal but the most powerful lord in the land.

A Child in the Land of Love

Duke William IX had always been an ardent lover of women. His vehemently sensual nature matured early, and he indulged his appetites with a lusty, pagan delight. It made little difference to him whether the woman was harlot or virgin, peasant or noble maiden. When William IX was fifteen, his father died, and the domain passed into his hands. If his barons believed that the amiable young man would be easy to manipulate, they soon discovered their mistake, because he quickly established himself as a lord worthy of respect. For all the lad's notoriety as a Don Juan, he was intelligent, sensitive, and possessed of a genius for writing poetry that was not to blossom for another fifteen years.

In 1088, when William was sixteen, he married the daughter of his northern neighbor, Fulk, count of Anjou, a man so disagreeable that he won the nickname "The Contrary." Fulk's daughter Ermengarde, beautiful and highly educated, appeared to be precisely the type of woman that William wanted, and not until after the wedding did he realize that she had inherited a streak of her father's sour disposition. Ermengarde, he discovered, had good periods and bad periods, her moods swinging drastically between vivacity and the most alarming sullenness, although it was possible that William's great weakness for chasing women contributed to her fits of bad temper. Moreover, she revealed a tendency to nag, a trait that thoroughly annoyed the carefree William, and the marriage got off to a bad start. After a quarrel, Ermengarde would retire to a convenient cloister, where she would sever all communication with the outside world, her husband included. But after a period of solitary retreat, she would suddenly reappear at court, magnificently dressed and smothered in jewels, behaving with a merriment that enchanted the courtiers and belied the fact that she had ever shown a sulky face. Her schizophrenic behavior soon proved too much for William, and since she had failed to conceive, he probably felt justified in sending her back to Anjou. The marriage was dissolved in 1091, and a year later Ermengarde married the duke of Brittany.

William took his time about remarrying. Not until 1094 did he hastily journey south of the Pyrenees to Aragon, where King Sancho Ramírez had just been killed in battle, leaving his twenty-year-old queen, Philippa, a widow. Serious-minded, politically astute, she was not only a formidable woman but a great heiress, and this accounted for the fact that William was not the only suitor to cross the Pyrenees in pursuit of her hand. The daughter of Count William IV of Toulouse, the county of France adjoining Aquitaine on the southeast, Philippa was one of those emancipated southern women whom circumstances threw up every so often. Her father had married twice and sired two sons, neither of whom lived. Without a male to succeed him, Count William IV realized, of course, that he would leave no heir save his daughter, a greatly disturbing fact because, even though Toulousain custom permitted women to inherit, it was considered better that they inherit a minor fief rather than the entire county itself. When Philippa was twelve, William IV sent her to Aragon to be the wife of Sancho Ramírez, a destiny of sufficient brilliance that he hoped she would have no cause for complaint. Like all the Spanish Christian kingdoms, Aragon had a sizable Moorish population, and owing to the cultural exchange between Christians and Moors, especially in architecture and poetry, the Arabized court at Aragon had attained a degree of oriental luxury foreign to European courts.

Two years after he had disposed of his daughter, Count William IV, discouraged and frustrated, suddenly resolved the crucial matter of succession by a most unusual step: He announced that he was departing for the Holy Land. In his absence—although it is perfectly clear that the count had no intention of returning—he appointed his brother, Raymond, count of Saint-Gilles, to rule in his stead. Within five years William was dead and his brother had assumed the title, despite the fact that Raymond's claim to Toulouse was highly disputable. Nevertheless, in law, as in all things, might became right. Raymond was a fifty-year-old male on the scene, the reins of power already in his hands; his niece but a nineteen-year-old female living beyond the Pyrenees.

Philippa, seething, could expect no help from her husband, since at that time he was fully occupied in a bitter campaign of reconquest against the Berber Moors, who had slowly managed to gain control of most of the Spanish peninsula. When Sancho Ramírez was killed by an arrow at the siege of Huesca, she determined to remarry as quickly as possible with the object of allying herself to a man who would help her regain her patrimony. It is not surprising that her choice fell upon Duke William of Aquitaine, a handsome man who knew how to woo a woman and who could offer a position worthy of her station in life. More important, however, William assured her that at the earliest opportunity she would get back Toulouse. He would see to it. Not that he had any intention of invading her native land; on the contrary, he greatly preferred occupations more pleasurable than war, although he always fought fearlessly when conflict could not be avoided. But momentous events beginning to take shape would enable him to make good his promise at a much earlier date than he or Philippa ever dreamed.

Since Mohammed's death in the seventh century, the banner of Islam had flown over Jerusalem. That the biblical holy places should fall into Moslem hands failed to disturb western Europe, for the Arabs, sharing Christian veneration for these places, welcomed and protected pilgrims. But in the eleventh century the barbarous Seljuk Turks, desert men mounted on camels and swift small horses, swept over the rock-strewn valleys of Jerusalem and the sepulcher of Christ; pilgrims lucky enough to return told hair-raising tales of their treatment at the hands of Islam's newest and fiercest champions, who viewed Christians as likely candidates for capture and enslavement. All of Christendom stood mute and horrified, and yet the idea of undertaking an expedition to drive out the Moslems from the Holy Land occurred to no one. Twenty-five years passed before the Christian nations decided that the scandal had become intolerable.

On a hazy day in November 1095, in a field outside the town of Clermont in the Auvergne, a tall white-robed figure slowly mounted a platform, its gold canopy billowing slightly in the misty air. Below him on the dry brown grass clustered cardinals, bishops, and black-clad monks, and behind them the cloaked laymen, pilgrims who had walked hundreds of miles over mountain and meadow, barons and knights on their richly caparisoned bays and Arabian steeds, here and there a noble dame accompanied by her maid. The vaporous breaths of men and animals rose and mingled with the odor of sour human sweat. Among the restless throng waiting to hear the words of Pope Urban II at this gathering, thereafter to be known as the Council of Clermont, was Duke William IX. He watched as the pope stood for a moment between two shimmering crosses and then moved close to the edge of the platform, his slow, level words bringing an instant hush to the crowd.

"O race of Franks, race beyond the mountains! We wish you to know what a serious matter has led us to your country, for it is the imminent peril threatening you and all the faithful that has brought us thither!

"From the confines of Jerusalem and from the city of Constantinople a grievous report has gone forth and has been brought repeatedly to our ears. . . . A race from the kingdom of the Persians, an accursed race, a race wholly alienated from God, has violently invaded the lands of those Christians and has depopulated them by pillage and fire. They have led away a part of the captives into their own country, and a part they have killed by cruel tortures.

"They have either destroyed the churches of God or appropriated them for the rites of their own religion. They destroy the altars, after having defiled them with their own uncleanness."

Muffled cries and whispers went up from the assembly as the slow, deep voice of Urban continued to describe how the invaders befouled the altars with filth from their bodies, how they circumcised Christians and poured the blood into the baptismal fonts, how they stabled their horses in the churches. The Turks were so degenerate that they ate meat on Fridays and coupled together like loathesome beasts. He called upon the girdled knights, arrogant with pride, to come to the defense of Christ. Fiercely chastizing them for their petty feuds, their habit of murdering and devouring one another in civil wars, he exhorted them to abandon their dissensions and make war against the infidel. "Enter upon the road of the Holy Sepulcher; wrest that land from the wicked race and subject it to yourselves!"

As the holy man spoke, they listened patiently, and then a shout rose from the sea of faces—*Deus lo volt!*—until the entire throng was standing, weeping, screaming a mighty roar from one throat, "God wills it!" Silencing them with uplifted arms, the pope answered, "God has drawn this cry from you. Let it be your battle cry; when you go against the enemy let this shout be raised—'God wills it!' "

Thus were kindled the fires of the First Crusade, igniting a flame that would burn for three centuries.

As night began to fall, the excited crowd melted away through the twilight, following the sound of bells summoning them to vespers. Around fires blazing in the meadow many vowed to exchange their goods for shield and lance and set out for the Holy Land with the sign of the cross on their breasts. There they would mount a thousand crosses on the walls of Jerusalem, and then they would be washed clean of their sins. Duke William IX was not among those who spoke in this manner. Sometime later during Urban's stay in Clermont William personally expressed sympathy for the pope's Crusade, but he did not commit himself. Instead he invited the pope to visit his court, and, in view of the duke's prestige and rank, Urban spent Christmas of 1095 in Limoges and the following January arrived in Poitiers, where William arranged a splendid reception in his honor. During their many meetings over the course of the next month, Urban must have sensed that, despite William's promises of support, something was amiss; while the subject of their discussions is unknown, William may have hinted of a plan beginning to form in his mind. Since the day in November when Urban spoke at Clermont, one of the first and greatest lords to respond had been Philippa's uncle, Count Raymond of Toulouse. Not only had Raymond been stirred to take the cross, but he was quickly emerging as the main organizer of the Crusade. With Raymond away, William thought, what better opportunity to advance his wife's claim to the county of Toulouse? If he mentioned this line of reasoning to Urban, he must have met with thorough disapproval, for the pope had promised that the lands and family of any Crusader would be safeguarded in his absence, that any act of aggression would be regarded as a mortal sin and the perpetrator's soul damned forever.

For the moment William did nothing. In the fall of 1096, Count Raymond rode out from Toulouse at the head of an army numbering 100,000 crossbearers and including his young wife, Elvira, and an infant son, who would die on the journey. For Raymond, it was the beginning of a new life, because he had taken an oath never to return. Aging, blind in one eye, seeking a proper ending for his years, he would remain in Outremer, the land across the sea, and establish a new dynasty. Relinquishing his claim to the countship, he nevertheless stubbornly refused to return the domain to a woman; instead he left in charge his eldest son, Bertrand.

Still William took no immediate action. Not until the spring of 1098 did he and Philippa march into her homeland, taking the city of Toulouse without a blow being struck or a life lost. Neither she nor William regarded the act as aggression—they were merely asserting a claim that they believed just and right—but others objected strenuously, and certain ecclesiastics hastened to Rome in an effort to persuade Urban that the duke should be excommunicated. The matter mushroomed to such heights that the bishop of Poitiers was forced to hurry to the papal court, where he interceded for his duke. On that occasion William escaped censure—later he would not be so fortunate—but his relations with the Church were never to be cordial again.

The year following her return to Toulouse, Philippa gave birth to a son, who would later be called William the Toulousain after the city of his birth and who would become the father of Eleanor of Aquitaine. In that same year that William X was born, news began drifting back to Europe of the capture of Jerusalem by the crusading army. The Holy Land had been regained; Count Raymond and Duke Godfrey and the other great princes were said to be living in palaces encrusted with gold and jewels, wearing sables and silky gossamer robes and lolling on Damascene couches, where Sudanese slaves served them chilled wine. So far, few of the Crusaders had returned, but the tales of glory preceding them were widely believed. Meanwhile, the twenty-seven-year-old William, undisputed master of an enviable fief, was having second thoughts about the Crusade. Although not a particularly devout man, neither was he devoid of religious feeling. Still, his suddenly kindled desire to see the Holy Land had little to do with either religion or, as was the case with some enthusiastic Crusaders, plunder; rather William burned with a feverish desire to see something of the world. The Crusade was the great adventure of his generation, and he had missed it, a mistake he resolved to remedy by organizing an army of his own. In raising funds, he preferred to avoid imposing oppressive taxation on his people and instead attempted to mortgage his domain, a not uncommon step in those crusading times, although usually done on a smaller scale. His first feeler went out to William Rufus, king of England, an offer readily acceptable to the son of William the Conqueror because he believed that the duke would never be able to redeem the pledge. Before the transaction could be closed, however, Rufus was killed in a hunting accident. William's next move must have outraged Philippa, who was happily settled—forever, she believed—in her palace at Toulouse. Her husband turned to Count Raymond's son Bertrand, the man Philippa had displaced, and offered to mortgage her lands. They would, William recklessly promised, give up all rights to Toulouse in exchange for a sum that, even though considerable, Bertrand eagerly agreed to raise. Within a few months, Philippa found herself hustled back to Poitiers, where she was to rule in William's absence, and William himself departed down the dusty white road toward the Rhine with an army of sixty thousand soldiers and pilgrims.

His expedition turned out to be anything but romantic. On September 5, 1101, near the town of Heraclea in Asia Minor, the Turks swept down and annihilated his entire army. William, standing on a nearby hill and weeping bitterly, watched his forces slaughtered before he fled with a few survivors. Behind he left only corpses and rusting armor. Ordericus Vitalis would write that when William returned from the Crusade in

1102, "He sang before the princes and the great assemblies of Christians of the miseries of his captivity among the Saracens, using rhymed verse jovially modulated." The chronicler was mistaken, for William had never been captured. After Heraclea, he sought asylum at the splendidly exotic court of Antioch. Bohemund I, prince of Antioch, was being held captive by the Moslems, but his nephew Tancred, acting as regent, gave William a warm reception and the opportunity to recover from his shocking defeat amid an atmosphere of luxury and pleasure. It was there that William familiarized himself with the Moorish songs then popular in Syria, and there is little doubt that his visit to Antioch helped to shape the poetry he would soon begin to write. In September 1102, William visited Jerusalem, where further campaigns against the Moslems were being planned by King Baldwin, but he declined to participate. War, never terribly appealing to him, certainly held no lure at this point.

At home again, his restlessness presumably purged during his eighteen months abroad, William settled down to write what would become known as the first troubadour poetry, his love poems, and those of the men and women he inspired, bringing to perfection the type of lyric that has continued in Western culture down to the present time. His poetic vision did not, however, spring full-blown from a vacuum. Although some of the influences remain a matter of conjecture, they would logically include the Latin verse of the clerics, an oriental influence from his encounters with Moors and Saracens, the cadences of Church music, and the native popular songs of wandering goliards, many of them unfrocked priests and runaway students who sang of love in Latin rhymes. Nor were the ethereal themes of courtly love, *l'amour courtois*, full-fledged in William's lyrics. Although he delighted in the beauty of women and sang the praises of love, no secularized Virgin Marys appear in his *cansos*. The duke's view of women is wholly and undisguisedly carnal, the outcome of the lover's quest physical rather than platonic. The significant departure in his sensuous poems was the egalitarian idea that a man could not demand a woman's love; she must freely consent to bestow it. The duke was a down-to-earth man whose passionate pursuit of a lady ended happily with "my hands beneath her cloak."

Over the course of the next thirteen years William's court became the center of European culture, and not the least of its attractions was the joyous song maker himself. During those years, too, the duke's family grew rapidly. Although Philippa's dream of ruling Toulouse was temporarily shattered, she dutifully fulfilled the requirements of medieval womanhood by producing, after young William, five daughters and then, a last child, another son. She seems to have successfully ignored her husband's amorous exploits, which were common knowledge, since he did not hesitate to celebrate them in verse. So widespread became the scandals that they found their way into the contemporary chronicles. William of Malmesbury related with relish that the duke erected "near the castle of Niort, certain buildings after the form of a little monastery, and used to talk idly about placing therein an abbey of prostitutes, naming several of the most abandoned courtesans, one as abbess, another as prioress; and declaring that he would fill up the rest of the offices in like manner."

This tale sounds very much like one of William's sly digs toward Philippa, because over the years, and to the duke's undisguised dismay, his wife had grown devoutly religious. She had become a convert to the teachings of a Breton reformer, Robert d'Arbrissel, who preached, among other heresies, the superiority of women. In 1099, d'Arbrissel and his followers settled at Fontevrault in the forest near the border of Anjou and built an abbey dedicated to the Virgin Mary. His abbey, however, was unique, because Fontevrault housed both monks and nuns—under the rule of an abbess. Robert d'Arbrissel believed that women were better administrators than men on account of their organizational experience gained in raising families and managing households, a view of feminine supremacy bound to attract Philippa. Her passionate devotion to d'Arbrissel and his ideas annoyed William, who, despite his obession with women, was not quite prepared to concede their supremacy. He objected to the great amount of time that his wife gave to Fontevrault and to the influence that d'Arbrissel and other ecclesiastics wielded over her, but his frank boredom with her as a wife was compounded by the fact that, now in his early forties, he had reached the dangerous age when men are apt to indulge in foolishness.

By this time, the Church heartily disapproved of William, both his affairs with women and the worldliness of his court, and he found himself constantly at odds with them over many matters. In 1114, the bishop of Poitiers had threatened to excommunicate William over an alleged infringement of the Church's tax privileges. William, furious, had stormed into the Cathedral of Saint-Pierre with sword drawn just as the prelate was about to pronounce the anathema. Flinging himself upon Bishop Peter and seizing him by the neck, he shouted, "I will kill you if you do not absolve me!" The startled bishop pretended to comply with absolution, but when at last William released him, he calmly finished reading out the excommunication. Then he thrust forward his neck and said meekly, "Strike, then. Go ahead, strike." Hesitating for a moment, the duke sheathed his sword and replied with one of the tart remarks for which he was famous. "Oh, no," he retorted. "I don't love you enough to send you to paradise."

The following year William's quarrels with the Church escalated after an incident that astonished even the blasé Aquitainians. Under the pretext of keeping Poitou obedient, he had fallen into the habit of making extensive journeys around the county; Philippa, once again in control of Toulouse, rarely accompanied him. On one of these trips he made the acquaintance of a viscountess with the provocative name of Dangereuse, the wife of Viscount Aimery of Châtellerault. This most immoderate lady formed an exuberant attachment for William who, to understate the matter, reciprocated. Later that year while Philippa was in Toulouse, William cemented his relationship with the beautiful viscountess by setting off at a gallop along the Clain River road to Châtellerault, where, the story goes, he snatched the faintly protesting lady from her bedchamber and carried her back to Poitiers.

It is unlikely that the eager viscountess protested vehemently, if at all, for she seemed quite prepared to abandon husband and children for the dashing duke. At home, William installed her in his new keep, known as the Maubergeonne Tower, which he had recently added to the ducal palace, and before long the amused Poitevins were calling his mistress La Maubergeonne. There was no question of hiding Dangereuse, nor did the lovers apparently practice discretion. Therefore, when Philippa returned from Toulouse and discovered a rival living in her own palace, her patience was sorely tried. Eyes blazing, she appealed first to her friends at court, then to the Church. With little trouble she was able to persuade the papal legate, Giraud, to speak to her husband about his imprudent behavior. But William replied jokingly to the legate, who happened to be as bald as an egg, "Curls will grow on your pate before I shall part with the viscountess." Although William's sentence of excommunication was renewed, he failed to take the matter seriously and, to Philippa's disgust, had a portrait of Dangereuse painted on his shield.

By 1116, Philippa could no longer tolerate the situation. She had wept bitterly over her husband's affair with the elegant viscountess, a woman younger and prettier than herself. For years she had been obliged to put up with his infidelities, with songs and poems of his sexual conquests, with his blithely pawning her heritage to Bertrand so that he could play the crusading hero at her expense. She had borne him seven children and managed his lands with admirable efficiency, and now, in repayment, he had mortified her by bringing a strumpet into her palace. Her heart full of rancor, gathering the remains of her shredded pride, Philippa withdrew from a situation at once ridiculous and demeaning by retreating to the Abbey of Fontevrault. William did not attempt to stop her.

Since Fontevrault's beginnings some twenty years earlier, this remarkable religious institution had become a popular mecca for aristocratic women. If its abbesses were widows plucked from the nobility, they were no less high-born than the women who came there as novices or those who merely sought a restful retreat after an active career as wife and mother. Among the women living there when Philippa arrived was, ironically, William's first wife, Ermengarde, who vacillated between the secular and the religious throughout her life. A benefactress of the Abbey of Clairvaux, she also built the monastery of Buzay near Nantes and would end her life as a nun. She and Philippa, it is said, became close friends. But despite Philippa's great dedication to the abbey and to the ideal of feminine superiority on which it was based, she was able to find little contentment living there as a rejected wife. Full of resentment and anger, she could not accept the fact that William had treated her shamefully by tossing her aside for a concubine. She soon disappeared from history, the records stating only that she died on November 28, 1118, whether from illness or wretchedness there is no way of knowing.

Little is known, too, about the viscountess of Châtellerault, except for the obvious inference: She was a woman who did as she pleased and who cared little for public opinion. At the time of her "abduction," Dangereuse had been married for about seven years and had borne three children: Aenor, Hugh, and Ralph. While her husband could not have been pleased about being openly cuckolded, nonetheless the fact remained that the incorrigible William was his liege lord, and had Viscount Aimery objected strongly—for even in Aquitaine wife stealing was a *faux pas*—there was really little that he could do to alter the situation. As time passed, it became clear to all that La Maubergeonne had come to stay, and her presence at court became more or less taken for granted.

Although Dangereuse could never become the official duchess of Aquitaine, she determined that her relationship with William be recognized in some manner. After several years, she proposed the ingenious scheme of marrying his eldest son, William, to her daughter, Aenor; if she could not be duchess, then her daughter would hold that title in her stead. And it is a tribute to her perseverance that the duke finally agreed. The marriage did not take place without opposition, however, one of the main objectors being young William himself. When Dangereuse first arrived at court, he was barely sixteen, a strapping lad who towered over his father. He had a prodigious appetite—it was later claimed that he ate enough for eight men—and already showed signs of a stubborn, quarrelsome nature. Although he had inherited his father's charming manner, the resemblance between father and son ended there. One chronicler contended that the boy, provoked beyond endurance by the injury that his father's liaison had done to his mother, revolted in a seven-year struggle that ended only with his capture by the duke. While the records flatly contradict this theory, nonetheless it must be concluded that young William did not adapt to the changes in his family life without great difficulty. Although the idea of marrying the daughter of his father's mistress may have been distasteful to him, the will of La Maubergeonne finally prevailed, and the marriage took place in 1121.

In contrast to her colorful mother, Aenor appears to have been a rather timid person who lacked the smallest semblance of forcefulness. Puppetlike, she moved through life doing the things expected of her and leaving behind no trace of an interesting or even distinct personality. Presumably her mousy character had been influenced by the unorthodox events of her early life: her abandonment as a child when her mother suddenly disappeared one day as well as the resulting stigma of being the daughter of a notorious adulteress. Perhaps Dangereuse believed that she was making up for Aenor's early deprivation by arranging a brilliant marriage, for undeniably the position into which she finagled Aenor was highly desirable; but on the other hand, there is no evidence that it brought the girl happiness. No more than fourteen and possibly younger, Aenor moved into the Poitevin court under her mother's watchful eye and set about the difficult task of trying to please a husband who must have regarded her with something less than enthusiasm. Careful to give no offense, she soon realized that her main obligation, the route by which she might gain favor, was to provide her awesome father-in-law with grandchildren. Luckily, she became pregnant within a few months.

There is a story that, a few days before Eleanor's birth, a pilgrim approached her parents with the mysterious prophecy "From you will come nothing good"; but this legend grew up afterward, and it is customary to remember prophetic statements once time has already demonstrated the course of events. Unfortunately, few details are available about Eleanor's entry into the world. She was born either in

Poitiers or at the castle of Belin near Bordeaux in the year 1122, but the month and day have not survived. She was named after her mother, "alia-Aenor" meaning "the other Aenor," but as William and his wife had passionately desired a son, their feelings about her must have been mixed. Since they could not have foreseen that one day this daughter, outshining all the Williams preceding her, would change the history of her time, they felt mildly disappointed. A year or two later Aenor gave birth to a second child, and once more it was a girl, Aelith, but always to be known as Petronilla. Soon afterward she again became pregnant, and this time she finally had the son she had wanted so desperately. With the birth of William Aigret, the duchy was assured of an heir.

Eleanor was a remarkably robust child, lively, boisterous, and headstrong. From the beginning, she radiated good health and intelligence, as well as a zest for life reminiscent of the old duke's, but like both her grandfather and Dangereuse, she possessed a certain restlessness, a lack of discipline that made it difficult for her to tolerate restrictions, an impatience that did not allow her to suffer boredom easily. Modesty did not come naturally to her; she seemed to have a knack for drawing attention to herself, a characteristic that went largely unnoticed in a family of spirited exhibitionists. No one took the trouble to put her in her place.

She could hardly help knowing that she was not ordinary. Her grandfather called himself "Duke of the Entire Monarchy of the Aquitainians," and her family tree sagged under the titled weight of counts, dukes, and conquerors. The ancestral palace at Poitiers was already many centuries old. In Merovingian times it had served as the seat of justice, and in the tenth century Duke William V remodeled it and began construction of the Great Hall. (Today, after many additions, some of them made by Eleanor herself, her ancestral home still stands in Poitiers and still serves as the Palace of Justice.) During the long sunny days of her childhood Eleanor and Petronilla must have romped together in the palace garden. At midday the shadowy passageways inside the castle might be gray and dank, but outside, the sun's rays beat down vertically from a steel-white sky and bounced off the helmets of the soldiers pacing the ramparts. In the garden she could have crawled beneath the leafy branches of trees drooping heavily with pears, peaches, lemons, pomegranates, and quince, or listened to the grasshoppers sawing harmoniously in the herb beds, where the hot air hung heavily with the smells of horehound, wild myrrh, and coriander.

In the evenings there would be entertainment in the Great Hall, and it is not difficult to conjure an image of Eleanor mesmerized by jongleur and storyteller. The hall would be decorated with flowers, the floors strewn with fresh green rushes; the ladies in their brightly colored gowns with long sleeves trailing on the ground and mantles fastened at the breast with ornate pins would wear golden bands around their hair or braids plaited with embroidered ribbons. As the air quivered with the clamor of horns and bells, there would come a procession of other-worldly creatures who could not have helped but delight the young Eleanor: acrobats jumping and twisting, marionettes dancing, jugglers tossing balls and silvery knives high into the air. Later would come the storytellers casting spells with their tales of Arthur and Charlemagne and Roland, of fair Helen and weeping Dido, of Julius Ceasar, who was so brave that he crossed the sea without invoking the name of Christ. Far into the night past matins the candles sputtered hot wax and the fire in the great hearth cast amber shadows on the jongleurs, who sang the Troubadour's verses about noble ladies graciously consenting to give their love to "gentle men." No lovesick maidens were these women but vigorous, sensual beings who freely gave and took pleasure.

Eleanor was never happier than when sitting in the Great Hall, but of course the verses were not always intelligible to her. One of her grandfather's most popular poems, a ribald tale that later formed the basis for one of Boccaccio's *Decameron* stories, told of a young man's amorous adventures while walking through the Auvergne disguised as a pilgrim. The narrator, whom one can imagine to have been William himself, stops at a castle where he meets Dame Ann and Lady Eleanor, two sisters whose husbands happen to be away. Slyly pretending to be mute, he speaks gibberish to the sisters, who decide to offer him a meal while they carefully look him over and decide if he might be shamming. After they have fed him, they further test the young man's dumbness, for if he is truly mute, "what we do will ne'er be told by him." Stripping their guest naked, they bring out a ferocious red cat with long whiskers and cruel claws, which they drag along his back. "With the anguish I turn pale," moans the narrator, but despite the dozens of wounds on his back he manages to remain silent.

"Sister," says the delighted Dame Ann, "he's mute indeed. I think we may prepare ourselves for sport and play." After preparing a hot bath for their guest, Ann and Eleanor are ready for serious business. Describing a typical male fantasy, the narrator tells us that he and the randy sisters go to bed for eight days, an experience that leaves him somewhat the worse for wear:

How much I tupped them you shall hear:
A hundred eighty-eight times or near,
So that I almost stripped my gear
And broke my equipment;
I could never list the ills I got—
Too big a shipment.

Presiding over the merriment at the ducal palace was the old troubadour himself, who no longer roamed the countryside acting out his erotic fantasies, or if he did, the chroniclers did not consider his wenching scandalous enough to record. Then in his fifties, he was forced by old age to settle down and worry about the state of his soul. After Philippa's death, his estrangement from the Church had begun, evidently, to weigh heavily enough that he made concessions in order to have the ban of excommunication lifted. In 1119, he had joined King Alfonso I of Aragon in a Crusade against the Almoravide Moors, but whether he undertook this campaign out of religious zeal or for more mundane reasons is debatable. A likely explanation is that his long-discarded first wife, Ermengarde, seemed determined to make trouble for him. At Fontevrault she had grown intimate with Philippa, and it is safe to assume that the conversations between the two cast-off ex-wives frequently focused, in the most uncomplimentary way, on the man they had in common and on his new mistress. Full of sympathy for Philippa's situation, Ermengarde took upon herself the task of avenging her unhappy friend. Philippa's death brought her storming down from the north of Poitou with the remarkable demand that she be reinstated as duchess of Aquitaine. After twenty-eight years of separation, it seems unlikely that Ermengarde actually wished to resume living with William. Clearly, however, she wished to harass the duke, as well as the viscountess of Châtellerault. In October 1119, she made an unannounced appearance at a council being held by Pope Calixtus II at Reims, petitioning the pope to personally excommunicate William and oust Dangereuse so that she, Ermengarde, might resume her rightful place. Although the pope declined to accommodate her, the reappearance of this alarming specter must have made William nervous, and at that juncture Moorish Spain must have seemed an infinitely more desirable place than Aquitaine, where there was always the possibility of an encounter with the rampaging Ermengarde.

In those last years William determined to change his ways. Convinced that he must submit to God's will, he regretfully vowed to abandon his love of debauchery. "My friends were Joy and Chivalry," he wrote, "but

I from both must parted be." His flame burning at medium-low, he seemed indifferent to currents of political unrest trickling throughout his domains. The year of Eleanor's birth, he lost Toulouse to twenty-year-old Alphonse-Jourdain, the youngest son of the Crusader Raymond of Saint-Gilles. This time he felt too weary to further pursue his dead wife's bothersome inheritance. As the year 1126 began, William's vitality began to ebb, and after an illness, he died on February 10.

The main lines of Eleanor's character were established in those early years when her grandfather's court was the center of western European culture. With his death, both the domain and the literary salon that he had created passed to Eleanor's twenty-seven-year-old father, who, lacking literary gifts of his own, had nonetheless studied music and possessed sufficient appreciation of the arts to continue drawing talented poets to the Poitevin court. If William IX had considered women—writing about them, courting and seducing them—to be his main vocation in life, he still took seriously his executive duties as duke of Aquitaine and count of Poitou. In comparison, his son William X was a weak man with a complex character that prevented him from paying strict attention to matters of importance. Like other sons of famous men, William lived all his life with memories of a brilliantly gifted father against whom he had never been able to compete. He himself was a giant in physical stature, which in the twelfth century meant that he was over six feet tall, and all accounts indicate that he possessed the grace and charm characteristic of the family. But he had failed to inherit the Troubadour's intelligence, his political acumen, and sound judgment, an unfortunate deficiency because during his reign Aquitaine no longer enjoyed the unchallenged political supremacy of previous years. The main characteristics known about William are his quick temper, his penchant for picking quarrels, and his stubbornness; he tended to make snap decisions and, once having made up his mind, adhered to his chosen course regardless of the consequences. In any case it was, ironically, this very ineffectualness in dealing with ordinary stresses of life that was to have such fateful consequences in shaping his eldest daughter's destiny.

Before Eleanor was seven, she had attained a degree of sophistication appropriate to her rank. Unlike most of her contemporaries, male and especially female, she was carefully educated. In this, her family can be counted as unusual, because generally speaking, it was thought better that women remain unlettered. Rather they should know how to spin and sew, embroider and sing, look straight ahead with unaffected quietness, and behave with neither prudery nor overfamiliarity. In these particular areas Eleanor showed little aptitude. On the other hand, she was an excellent student who had a quick intelligence and the type of mind that delighted in acquiring knowledge. At an early age she was taught to read and write, probably by the resident chaplain, who would have shown her how to hold a wax tablet on her right knee and copy with an ivory stylus the alphabet from the *Disticha Catonis,* the common beginner's reader. She would also have received instruction in the rudiments of counting, first using her fingers as an abacus and then, for higher sums, seedpods strung along a stick. She must have studied Latin literature and perhaps a little astronomy, at least enough to name the constellations.

Eleanor's mother, and undoubtedly her grandmother as well, played a significant role in her general upbringing. Following the educational system of the nobility, Aenor would have been responsible for not only Eleanor and Petronilla but also the daughters of other noble families sent to her for instruction in manners and housewifery, just as their brothers came to William for education in knighthood. The palace on the Clain undoubtedly swarmed with maidens who, under Aenor's tutelage, received instruction in embroidery and weaving, in the management of a baronial household, in singing, playing simple accompaniments on the harp, and speaking politely to their elders. Girls of the twelfth century learned to ride well and to become adept at falconry. Other skills including games of chess, checkers, and backgammon were considered important too.

As a child, Eleanor grew especially fond of her Uncle Raymond, although the big handsome boy, only eight years her senior, seemed more like a brother than an uncle. Philippa's last-born, brought forth in Toulouse that very same year that William had left her for Dangereuse, was tall, blond, and powerfully built. Landless from birth, now motherless and fatherless, he appeared indifferent to his dismal heritage. As a portionless younger son, he rightfully should have been destined for the Church, a vocation he dismissed as lacking in the proper splendor. Accomplishments such as reading and writing he disdained to learn, but he knew all the troubadours' songs and made himself respected at the palace for his immense strength. Because he could bend an iron bar, the awed children called him Hercules. Then Eleanor saw her special uncle no more. He had gone away, she learned, across a mist-shrouded channel to seek his fortune in a chilly land where the untamed natives clad themselves in wolfskins, although the king of the English had taken a liking to the boy and treated him as kindly as if he had been his own dead son. But she would never forget the laughing boy with his sensitive spirit and mighty body.

While the ancestral palace at Poitiers was home, Eleanor gradually became acquainted with the rest of her father's sunlit realm, where life was by turns impetuous and languid. Weeks and sometimes months of each year were spent on ducal progresses throughout the land, and on these migrations the family, leading a life appropriate to its exalted rank, would be surrounded by a suite large enough to people a small town: minstrels, notaries and scribes, chaplains and clerks, cooks, falconers, and scores of humbler servants. While still a small child, Eleanor had seen the grape harvest in Cognac and she had breathed the fishy breezes at Talmont, where the tiny village crowned a rocky headland and the church, teetering on the edge of the Gironde cliff, had a nave that fell into the sea. She knew a place near Poitiers on the far bank of the Clain where there was a hermit's cell carved with snakes; she knew that on a certain road near Maillezais her Aunt Agnes presided over an abbey and that at Blaye there was a forge where the armorers repaired her father's traveling gear. She came to recognize castles and keeps, knowing which castellans gave lavish banquets and patronized the finest jongleurs and which chatelaines had been immortalized in the troubadours' *cansos*. From the uplands of the Limousin to the port of Niort in the marshy, mosquito-ridden west, from the forests of Poitou to the foothills of the Pyrenees, she was beginning to put down a taproot in her homeland.

Very often one of these leisurely *chevauchées* ended at the tiled fountains and semitropical gardens of the Ombrière Palace in Bordeaux. This powerful fortress squatted at the southeast corner of the old Roman wall that girdled the city, and from its buttressed walls and stout rectangular keep Eleanor could gaze down at the silken sails rocking gently on the waters of the Garonne. Here at the Ombrière, William received his vassals, great and small, signed petitions, and heard the feuds and disputes that largely accounted for much of his administrative business. On these trips, and at the court in Poitiers, Eleanor learned a great deal about politics, although this certainly was not William's intention, nor did he take any special pains to rear her for a position of authority. Rather, she absorbed politics by a process of osmosis, just as she soaked up the literature created by Cercamon, Marcabru, and other troubadours at her father's court, and she grew up believing that affairs of state were a province not necessarily restricted to men. Scarcely a day passed that she did not hear her father inveighing against turbulent vassals who resisted his authority at the slightest opportunity. At that time, William's grand duchy was quickly being transformed into a shaky house of cards, and even though culturally it stood as the foremost land in Europe, politically and economically it was falling behind the north. Such omens of danger did not concern Eleanor, who saw only the importance of her father's position and, reflected, her own. Aware, of course, that her brother, William Aigret, took precedence, she still had, as the eldest child, a part to play in the day-to-day affairs of government. Her name first appeared in the records in July 1129, when she, along with her brother and parents, witnessed a charter deeding certain privileges to the Abbey of Montierneuf, her grandfather's burial place. A quill pen was used to make crosses after each name, except that of William Aigret whose tiny baby fingers were dipped lightly in ink and the imprint pressed upon the parchment. In March of the following year, the signatures of parents and two children appeared on another charter granting the brothers of the Church of Saint-Hilaire the right to cut firewood from the forest of Mouliere.

When Eleanor was eight, however, the quartet of signatures abruptly ceased. Tragedy swept the ducal family; within a span of a few months, both Aenor and William Aigret were dead in Talmont, leaving Eleanor the prospective heir of her father's domains. The death of Aenor did more than remove the warmth of a mother's affection; it also took away a stabilizing influence in Eleanor's life. She had always been defiant and independent, a child who took direction reluctantly. Her restless temperament, her vanities and self-centeredness, her bold flirtatious manner combined with a certain tomboyishness, kept her grandmother and ladies-in-waiting in a state of apprehension. One can imagine that there were those who said she needed a good whipping and others who ascribed, but not in Dangereuse's hearing, Eleanor's willfulness to bad blood, but the fact remained that more and more the girl was left to her own devices. That she began to develop into a strong-minded young woman thoroughly determined to behave as she pleased is not surprising, because the women she most admired had been cast from similar molds. Innumerable times she had listened to the history of her family: the story of her paternal grandmother riding into Toulouse to mount the throne that an accident of sex had denied her; from her maternal grandmother's lips she had repeatedly heard the now-inflated romantic tale of how Dangereuse had fled the castle of Châtellerault, riding into the forest of Mouliere with arms clasped around her lover's waist, defying Church, lawful spouses, and public opinion to remain proudly at her lord's side.

And if these ladies were not sufficiently heroic, there was Radegonde, one of the patron saints of Poitiers. Since Eleanor had been a small child, she had ridden down the hill to the southernmost gate of the city where Radegonde had founded a convent almost six centuries earlier, and there in the dark crypt containing the saint's coffin, she would place beside the tomb a tiny waxen heart and a lighted candle as she made her wish. In the sixth century, according to legend, Queen Radegonde had fled the Merovingian kingdom of the Franks, her brutal and licentious husband Clothaire in hot pursuit, and hidden herself in a newly sown cornfield, clutching her jewels and her two women companions. By God's mercy, the corn immediately sprang up around them, the tall stalks hiding Radegonde only minutes before Clothaire came riding by. The learned queen was consecrated as a nun and later came to Poitiers, where she established the convent of Sainte-Croix. It was there that she burned with Platonic love for the Italian poet-priest Fortunatus, "the delight of my soul," and there that she served him exquisite meals on dishes of crystal and silver. From the lives of these women Eleanor, as a small child, developed attitudes and feelings that she was never able wholly to escape: that a woman need not accept the fate men might decree, that she could take her life into her own hands and shape it to suit her heart's desire.

Meanwhile, Eleanor's father seemed to have paid scant attention to his daughter's development, since he was constantly embroiled in troubles so all-consuming that he could think of little else. In his few years as duke, he had acquired the reputation of being a hothead. Always quick to provoke a fight, he had grown increasingly obstinate after the deaths of his wife and son. In 1130, for instance, when the Chair of Peter was being claimed by two popes, he brought down a host of difficulties upon his own head by enthusiastically supporting the antipope, a cardinal who called himself Anacletus II. The fact that an important lord like the duke of Aquitaine would fail to support Innocent II, who occupied the Holy See, was serious enough to aggravate the schism in the Church at that time and bring the renowned Bernard, abbot of Clairvaux, sallying from his cloister to deal with this threat to "God's business."

No churchman of the day was more admired than Bernard. Unquestionably the most powerful single individual of the twelfth century, a maker of popes, a chastiser of kings, who listened to his advice and sometimes followed it, he had a gift for oratory that won him the name *Doctor Mellifluus*, "the honey-sweet doctor," but his contemporaries claimed that the sight of him was sufficient to persuade audiences even before he opened his lips. In 1115, the twenty-five-year-old Bernard had taken thirteen Cistercian monks and settled in a wooded place in Champagne called Valley of the Wormwood, where, emphasizing poverty and manual labor, they built the Abbey of Clairvaux while sleeping on the ground and existing on coarse barley bread and boiled beech leaves. Not surprisingly, he nurtured a grim disapproval for the black-robed monks of Cluny and deplored the pernicious influence of their gilded cathedrals and stained-glass windows. Regarded as a saint during his lifetime and canonized after his death, Bernard utterly rejected the world in favor of the austerity and silence of the cloister, but, ironically, there was no monk who lived more frequently and for longer periods outside his abbey. When he learned that Duke William of Aquitaine supported the antipope, he hurried to Poitiers for the purpose of reasoning with the duke and bringing him into the camp of Innocent II. Meeting at the Abbey of Montierneuf, the two men discussed the matter for an entire week, after which time the duke, apparently moved by Bernard's charismatic personality and his formidable powers of persuasion, expressed willingness to break with Anacletus.

Yet scarcely had Bernard left Poitiers before William resumed his militant partisanship of the antipope. In fact, he raced willy-nilly ahead and turned with even greater fury against the supporters of Innocent: The altar stone on which Bernard had said Mass was smashed, and William personally drove from Poitiers every ecclesiastic who supported Innocent and then proceeded to fill the offices with his own appointees. These actions inevitably led to his excommunication.

When Eleanor was thirteen, her father again clashed with the Church, and in that year of 1135 people said that God's patience with her father had ended and that he had reached down to rescue the duke from damnation. At the time this momentous incident took place, William was away from home at his château in Parthenay, but God, through his emissary Bernard, found him just the same. News of a miracle travels on ghostly wings of air, and before her father returned to Poitiers, Eleanor must have already heard the incredible story being whispered among her high-born ladies and spoken of openly in kitchen and stable. Once more Bernard had come all the way from Champagne to seek out the intractable duke, but when he arrived at the château, William refused to see him. At last cooler heads prevailed, and then he had listened, full of truculence, as the holy man urged him to abandon the evil Anacletus and return to God. As it took a hard man to withstand the uncompromising eloquence of Bernard of Clairvaux, William gradually began to weaken and grudgingly promised that he would acknowledge Innocent. He would not, however, reinstate the expelled bishops; as a knight he could not, for he had sworn never to permit them in his domain again. Bernard sighed and stared at the duke in his deplorably fine and precious raiment, his huge muscular body radiating good health. Once, some fifteen years earlier, he had thundered, "Wine and white bread benefit the body, not the soul. The soul is not fattened out of frying pans." If William was content to leave his soul malnourished, Bernard would find other means of fattening it.

The next morning the square outside the château was packed with people from leagues around; the lamest peasant had risen from his pallet to crowd into the Church of Notre-Dame-de-la-Couldre, where the worshipers all but mobbed the saint before he said Mass. Hardly anyone in the town was absent, including the excommunicated William, who, unable to step foot over the threshold, skulked outside on the porch, pacing fretfully to and fro as he watched Bernard at the altar. After the pax, still holding the Host upon the paten, Bernard turned around and caught sight of William in the doorway. With a sudden burst of inspiration, he slowly began to make his way down the aisle, the Host held triumphantly before him, his gaze never departing from the figure of the duke. If William could not come to God, then he would bring God to William. He called out to the duke, "We have petitioned you and you have spurned us. In the recent council, the servants of God at your footstool you have treated with contempt." Trampling each other to inch close behind Bernard, the townspeople saw their prince staring at Bernard in amazement.

Thrusting the Host toward William, Bernard challenged: "Lo, here has come forth to you the Virgin's son, the head and lord of that Church that you persecute. Your judge is present, in whose name every knee in heaven, on earth, below the earth is bowed. Do you spurn him? Do you treat him with the contempt with which you treat his servants?"

William, pale and silent, began to sway like a tree trunk, and then his whole body stiffened, and he fell face downward at the holy man's feet. When the duke's *chevaliers* ran to lift him up, he collapsed again. Afterward people could not remember all the things said by the holy man, but some swore that the duke had groaned like an epileptic and foamed at the mouth. They had been there and had seen it with their own eyes.

Bernard prodded the body at his feet, commanding William to rise. "The bishop of Poitiers whom you drove from his church is here. Go and make peace with him. Pledge yourself to him in the kiss of peace and restore him to his see. Then make satisfaction to God; render to him glory for your contempt."

Slowly William struggled to his feet and staggered toward the hated bishop to give him the kiss of peace. When he returned to Poitiers a few days later, Eleanor could see a change in him, for his heart and mind had truly been seared at Parthenay, and it took some time before he recovered. Later that year he founded, as an act of reparation, a Cistercian abbey in the diocese of Saintes. He no longer growled curses upon his enemies, at least not within people's hearing, and his face seemed sunk in melancholy lines for no apparent reason. Thinking seriously about the future for the first time since Aenor's death, he reminded himself that it was long past time when he should have remarried, not that he had ever intended to do otherwise, but, easily distracted, he had shoved the problem aside to reconsider it at some later date. Although he had two illegitimate sons, William and Joscelin, he now resolved to beget a male child to inherit his duchy. Furthermore, he turned his attention to his daughters, who had reached marriageable age. While he berated himself for foolishly neglecting their future, there was good reason why he had avoided thinking about this business of succession and the dire consequences that would result should he die without male issue.

The law was far from fixed on the subject. Even though Eleanor might legally inherit, at the same time it was believed that a woman could not properly fulfill the obligations of a vassal. For one thing, she could not undertake military service and therefore might have to step aside when the forty-days-a-year soldiering had to be rendered. For this reason, feudal domains were kept, whenever possible, in the hands of men, and William understood that there were many in his own land who would take advantage of the situation. Had not his mother been evicted from the countship of Toulouse by her uncle, Raymond of Saint-Gilles? Had not he himself a younger brother who, by ironic happenstance, was also named Raymond? Although he knew that the lad was far away in Outremer, where he had schemed his way into the lordship of the rich fief of Antioch, still it was wise to take no chances.

In 1136, in an effort to straighten out his life, William announced to Eleanor and Petronilla that soon they would have a stepmother. For some time he had been eyeing a young woman who pleased him, but unfortunately Emma, the daughter of Viscount Aymar of Limoges, was already married to Bardon of Cognac. Now, by good fortune, Emma had become a widow, and before Bardon had scarcely been laid to rest, William arranged for their betrothal. Throughout Aquitaine it was said that William had become a changed man, but if the Lord had humbled and softened the arrogant duke, he had not seen fit to give him common sense; he had selected a bride from the Limousin, where the nobility had been periodically at odds with the dukes of Aquitaine for a century or more.

The news of William's betrothal brought immediate repercussions. In the Limousin, secret councils were hastily summoned among the counts of Angoulême, the viscounts of Limoges, the lords of Lusignan, and others with cause for concern. These testy vassals had chafed under the Aquitainian yoke for generations. If Emma, a possible coheiress of Limoges, bore a son—and even if she did not—it would mean an increase in William's power over them. Clearly something must be done. For some weeks the plotting and scheming continued, and the end of it was that Count William of Angoulême volunteered to carry off the young woman and marry her himself, a decision in which Emma was not consulted. When news of Emma's abduction and marriage reached the duke, he publicly uttered no word of complaint; in fact he reacted with such good grace that suspicions were immediately aroused, and the Limousin girded itself for a blood bath. Months passed without retribution, but still there was no doubt among the Limousin chieftains as to how the matter would end. William was a man of uncertain temper, and sooner or later he would wreak vengeance.

In the meantime, William's discouragement deepened, and he longed to escape the disorders of his realm. In the summer of 1136, he received word that his northern neighbor, Count Geoffrey of Anjou, was planning an invasion of Normandy; the duke of Aquitaine, among others, was invited to aid in this ambitious enterprise. On many occasions Eleanor had heard her father speak of Geoffrey Plantagenet, although not always in complimentary terms. Geoffrey, she knew, was extraordinarily good looking. Geoffrey le Bel, people called him, "Geoffrey the Handsome." Energetic and dashing, he had a certain flair that lesser lords tried to emulate, although probably no one else could have gotten away with wearing in his cap a sprig of planta genesta, the common broom plant. Geoffrey had married well, and even though he detested his cold, haughty wife, Matilda was nonetheless the daughter of King Henry of England, and it was through her that he was able to claim Normandy. Lately William had grown to admire the stylish Geoffrey, so that when the invitation arrived, he immediately accepted, perhaps hoping that a shift of scenery in the company of the buoyant count would act as a tonic to his flagging spirits. There followed a time of enthusiastic activity as the grindstones hummed along the edges of steel swords and the forge in the smithy blazed to shape new shields and hammer out stirrups, spears, and maces. In September the new arms were ready, and William's troops rode forth on their great chargers.

To Eleanor's surprise, however, her father returned unexpectedly only a few weeks later, the campaign having been temporarily abandoned when Geoffrey received a foot wound. After William's return to Poitiers, he seemed more melancholy than ever. He would sit before the leaping fire in the Great Hall staring fitfully into the flames and leaving the wine in his goblet untouched. When he spoke, it was, as often as not, of nightmares, terrible anguished dreams filled with scattered cries, disjointed ravings, the air torn from earth to heaven by shrill, heart-rending screams. Once as immune to the inhumanity of war as any, now William felt hounded by memories of the devastation in which he had recently participated, and for the first time in his life he lost his appetite for combat, an alarming development for a medieval prince with a host of enemies.

At the beginning of that winter of 1137, he decided to make a pilgrimage to the shrine of Saint James at Santiago de Compostela, in the westernmost corner of Spain. Once and for all he would cleanse his soul and seek the Lord's guidance in sorting out his tangled life; when he returned, he would begin anew with a nubile young maiden—whom, he could not say—but she would bear him a castleful of sons. Nor would he forget his daughters, for whom he planned to arrange brilliant matches. For a change his eyes shone, and he seemed his old self. There was no question of taking Eleanor and Petronilla with him, but on the other hand he worried about leaving them behind, unprotected, in Poitiers. Owing to the unrest in his land and particularly to his recent experience with the kidnaping of Emma, he felt it wisest to take precautions lest his daughters be snatched from him as well.

At the back of his mind may have lurked another anxiety: Eleanor, exceptionally beautiful at fifteen, had matured into a saucy, hot-blooded damsel, and perhaps he feared that, unproperly chaperoned, she might grant excessive courtesies to some ardent knight. All contemporary accounts of Eleanor, even when she had grown old, emphasized a radiant loveliness that went far beyond the ordinary, but unfortunately there is not a single word about what she looked like. If she conformed to twelfth-century Europe's ideal standards of feminine beauty, which rarely varied from one romance to the next, she must have been blond, with gray or blue eyes set wide apart. Her nose would have been straight, her skin white, and she would certainly have had a long slender neck, firm breasts, and perfect teeth. Apart from the physical, there is substantial evidence pointing to the fact that she was no shy, helpless maiden; she comported herself freely, laughing and flirting with the adoring young men of the court, taking charge of any gathering with sophisticated self-possession. She was the rose of the world, and she knew it, having already been told so many times in song and verse. Witty and full of irreverent high spirits, she had a streak of mischievousness that she shared with her sister, who was her inseparable companion. In spite of the fact that noble young ladies were not encouraged to behave impertinently, the two girls liked to amuse themselves by comically aping the speech and mannerisms of pompous dignitaries. In a court where minstrel and mummer were ceded positions of importance, these talents were more admired than censured.

Whatever William's reasons, he decided to avoid trouble by taking Eleanor and Petronilla with him as far as Bordeaux, where he would deposit them in the custody of that city's archbishop, a stern but kindly man and one of the few loyal vassals remaining to William. Throughout Aquitaine, the nobility's first reaction to news of his forthcoming pilgrimage was skepticism. A quarrelsome man like the duke, they said loudly, could only be seeking Saint James's help in revenging himself on his enemies. And since he had many, the land reverberated faintly with tremors of anxiety.

Early in the spring, the warm sun began to thaw the farmland and melt away the debris of winter. Rains swelled the rivers and streams, and although the rutted roads oozed with brown mud, William left for Bordeaux before Lent with a few servingmen and his daughters. A week later, having settled the damsels in the Ombrière Palace and promising to return soon wearing a cockleshell badge, the sign of a successful pilgrimage, he donned a gray cloak of rough sackcloth and a pilgrim's hat. Clutching his walking stick, he set out on foot down the road toward Gascony with only a few knights and servants. In many ways the pilgrimage would be an arduous one, but still he looked forward to the journey and to reaching Compostela in time to celebrate Easter. In his baggage he carried the *Codex Calixtus,* a newly written guidebook for Compostela-bound pilgrims, a handy manual advising that the Gascons were hospitable, that the Basques demanded excessive tolls, and other helpful information. Along the way William fell in with other pilgrims, and the hours passed in gossip, news, and the singing of psalms. The weather was fine and warm as he began the gradual green climb into the foothills of the Pyrenees, trudging beside pastures where fat cows slouched, up the twisting and turning slopes of valleys, through the misty pass at Roncesvalles where Roland fell, past the country of the Navarrese into Pamplona. A week passed and a second and then a month or more.

On the evening of April 8, 1137, William and his weary band broke march beside an inviting stream in eager anticipation of bathing and drinking after many footsore leagues on the highway. When the duke ordered water and fish to be drawn from the stream, his men warned that the waters in that region were said to be dangerous. William, a lover of good food and wine, scoffed. He was, as usual, ravenous.

The next morning, which was Good Friday, there were gray shadows around his eyes, and his hair was drenched with sweat. Frightened, his men begged him to stop and rest, but William insisted upon rejoining the throngs on the road to Santiago, only five or six miles distant. Hour after hour, he stumbled slowly along, faintly singing, his hands folded over his chest in prayer, until he was capable of walking no farther. His men laid him by the side of the road and watched his huge body disintegrate with terrifying swiftness. Later they would say that it had been the foul water or the tainted fish, but in truth they were far from certain what had made their master sicken. Soon it was apparent, even to William, that nothing could be done; he would not recover. On the near edge of death, the maladroit duke showed more political judgment than he ever had during life. Lips swollen and dry, he whispered in halting words his last will and testament:

To his beloved daughter Eleanor, his sole heir, he bequeathed his fief, a rich and now violent legacy.

To his overlord, the king of France, he bestowed both his domains and his daughter, in the hope that the worthy Louis would guard both treasures until he had found the new duchess a suitable husband to rule over the land of love. In the meantime, the king had the right to enjoy the use of Eleanor's lands.

He insisted that his death be kept a closely guarded secret until these matters reached the ears of Louis VI, extracting promises that his men would cover the mountain leagues across the Pyrenees with all possible haste and stop at Bordeaux only long enough to notify the archbishop. The stray ends tidied at last, the plums in his keeping safely distributed to the best of his ability, William fell silent.

His men, weeping aloud, carried their dying master to the vaulted cavern of Compostela's great cathedral, where he expired "most piously" after receiving Holy Communion. There, beneath the *bota-fumeiro*, the awesome silver censer swinging in smoky arcs from its ceiling pulley, the last Duke William of Aquitaine was laid to rest at the foot of the high altar, by the side of the Galilean fisherman whom Christ turned into a fisher of men.

The Devil and the Monk

The summer promised to be torrid. In Paris the stones of the Cité Palace were white and burning in the great heat of the day, and the air hung heavy and dead. As there had been no rain recently, the odeur de merde in the streets was never absent from anyone's nostrils, and black masses of flies clung indiscriminately to refuse and human alike. To escape these discomforts, Louis VI had moved a few leagues north of the city, to the suburbs where he owned a hunting lodge. More accurately, he had been transported on a litter, because his corpulence made it virtually impossible for Louis to move himself. There at Béthizy in the waning days of May he lay immobile on a royal couch, a mound of sweating, panting flesh. If not for the sin of gluttony, which he wore like a badge, he might have been known as Louis the Great or even Louis the Practical. As it was, his people had dubbed him, with appropriate candor, Louis le Gros. Louis the Fat had not always been obese, but in recent years he could no longer mount a horse or a woman, nor could he lift his enormous bulk out of bed. He could only eat and worry.

Louis was not, however, the only apprehensive person at Béthizy. Gathered anxiously around his couch were Abbot Suger, his lifelong confidant and chief minister, and a number of barons, bishops, and priests, the latter having been summoned by Suger should an emergency suddenly arise. The king was suffering from a "flux of the bowels," an attack of the same dysentery that had struck him down two years earlier. He had recovered from the first siege, but this time his condition appeared grave. During those sultry days the smell in his room was foul and suffocating and, although medicines had been prescribed for the diarrhea and the basin near his cot was frequently emptied, his ministers choked when they approached their sovereign. For all his great fat and disease-devoured body, Louis's head remained clear, and he fretted incessantly over matters he could no longer control.

33

God had blessed him with six sons but, in his infinite wisdom, had seen fit to remove the eldest just as he was approaching maturity. As a child, Philip had been Louis's favorite, but with the passage of time Louis had to confess that the boy brought him little joy. When the heir to the throne was barely pubescent, Louis had him anointed, and the vassals of all France bent the knee in allegiance, but afterward the boy no longer listened to his father. The high standards that Louis set for him, those that he himself followed, were disdained, and scoldings had little effect. The boy, says Walter Map, "strayed from the paths of conduct traveled by his father and, by his overweening pride and tyrannical arrogance, made himself a burden to all." Philip's adolescent behavior problems, excusable in an ordinary boy but alarming in a youth destined for the Frankish throne, were abruptly solved one day in October 1131, when he and a group of companions were riding along the Seine in the market section of Paris known as the Greve. Suddenly a black pig darted out of a dung heap along the quay and tripped Philip's running horse, causing it to fall and catapult the heir over its head. The fall "so dreadfully fractured his limbs that he died on the day following" without regaining consciousness.

Louis VI's second son was cast from an entirely different mold. Mild and sweet-tempered, Louis Capet the Young had been bred for the Church, a calling that seemed made to measure for his placid nature. His life had been spent in the royal abbey of Saint-Denis, immured among the monks, and even though Philip's death briefly returned him to his father for anointing, even though he had recently received instruction befitting a knight, the musty perfume of the cloister still clung to him. His piety and humility, which no one could fail to see, did not overplease his father, who feared these qualities might be mistaken for weakness and who hoped that by the time he matured, he would develop the strengths required for kingship. Aware of the priests hovering in his antechamber, ready to administer the last rites, Louis understood only too well that his son might be denied the precious years he desperately needed.

It was in this agitated frame of mind that Louis the Fat received the couriers of the late Duke William of Aquitaine and learned that his most bullheaded vassal lay dead at Compostela since Easter. If the news of William's last will and testament did not cause a spontaneous remission of the dysentery, at least it revived the ailing king. Scarcely able to conceal his joy over this unexpected bit of good fortune, he nevertheless preserved his customary grandeur of manner by asking the Aquitainians to retire while he discussed the matter with his council. Alone with his advisers, Suger tells us, Louis burst into exclamations of ecstasy; he literally stammered with delight. Had he not spent twenty-nine years attempting to extend the boundaries of his uninspiring domain? Set against the acreage of his own paltry kingdom—a strip of land mainly confined to the Île-de-France, Orléans, and part of Berry—the young duchess's fief was a formidable one. Who better than he could realize the significance of William's golden bequest? It would bring the richest fief in Europe under the crown and extend Frankish influence beyond Louis's wildest daydreams; in fact, the addition of Aquitaine to any domain would automatically lift it to prominence among nations. This munificent prize, dropped into his palsied hands like a plump chicken into a watery broth, was not to be allowed a means of escape. Duke William had implored Louis to find his daughter a husband. Who more suitable than his son and heir, Louis? Rarely did the personal and the political coincide so neatly.

Louis the Fat lost no time. Within hours, plans were under way to secure Aquitaine to the crown, and the resourceful Abbot Suger was designated as principal organizer of the wedding arrangements. The bishop of Chartres was dispatched on a secret mission to Bordeaux, where he would ostensibly pay his respects to the duchess but, in reality, make certain of Eleanor's safety. According to the southern emissaries, the heiress was under heavy guard at the Ombrière Palace, but Louis wished to take no risks. If reports were to be believed, Aquitaine swarmed with anarchists who would not hesitate to filch their liege lady from her rightful destiny. With all the dangers menacing the roads, Louis could not expect Eleanor to travel alone to the heart of France; instead, it was necessary to make a special expedition to bring her back. Nor was it enough to simply fetch her. It had to be accomplished in a style befitting this unprecedented occasion, with a pageantry gorgeous enough to impress the frivolous Aquitainians.

On June 18, 1137, a mighty cortege threaded its way over the hills of the Parisian suburbs in the direction of Orléans. Under the blue and gold banners of the fleur-de-lis they marched, two by two, first the heralds and standard-bearers, then the commanders: Count Theobald of Champagne and Count Ralph of Vermandois, who was the king's cousin and seneschal of France. The two counts, bitter rivals who had been persuaded to bury their hostilities for the occasion, were accompanied by the man unofficially in charge, Abbot Suger. They were followed by the chivalry of France, but in addition to the noblest barons and knights in the land there was a sizable body of squires, infantry, and cavalry. Next came a train of pack animals carrying portable kitchens, tents, provisions, sacks of silver deniers, and presents for the bride. To call this procession of five hundred or more a nuptial escort would not be accurate. It was a veritable army that moved down the highroad, carefully keeping within the king's lands. In the midst of the column rode the young prince, his eyes tired and bewildered under their pale blond lashes. Ringing in his ears were his father's fervent words: "My most dear son, may the powerful hand of almighty God, by whose grace kings are enabled to reign, protect thee and thine. Because if I had the misfortune to lose thee and those I send to accompany thee, I should care neither for myself nor for my kingdom."

Louis the Fat's precious son was sixteen. Uprooted unceremoniously from his devotions, he had been washed, combed, and set on a steed facing south. It was not a matter of his questioning his destiny, because he had known for some years that his vocation would not lie in the Church after all and that he would be obliged to marry. But deep within his eyes dwelt fear. Events had moved too swiftly, and he had yet to accustom himself to the curious idea that he would have to sleep with a girl. Had the choice been his, he would have lived his entire life as chastely as the angels in heaven. Women, to him, were needed to preserve the species and provide food and drink, but at the same time they were also the gateway to the devil, in short, necessary but perilous objects. When his forthcoming marriage was spoken of, he smiled with regal good grace, but if the conversation turned coarse, he blushed and lowered his eyes. None of the Franks had seen Eleanor, but they seemed to know everything about his bride-elect: She was fair and white and pink, she had a mouth as soft as an apple blossom and she was also that rarity, a literate woman in an illiterate age. None of this information reassured Louis. Before their departure, his commonsensical father had taken him aside, lecturing him on how to behave: He must conduct himself with dignity and uphold the prestige of the monarchy; he must not arouse hostility by billeting his men in the homes of vassals or plundering their fields for supplies; he must offend no one, especially once he entered Aquitaine. But Louis the Fat had provided no sexual enlightenment.

As the column marched slowly south in the insufferable heat, its reception among the peasants and burghers was not always cordial. To the indignation of more than one town, the king had financed this expedition by a special levy, and the poor grumbled over the additional and, in their opinion, oppressive, tax so that the prince could be married in style. It was no use saying that the marriage could have been executed at far less expense or that the king could have emptied the royal purse. Nevertheless, there were many who roundly cursed the cortege as it passed.

By the time they crossed the Loire near Orléans, the heat was intense, the dust stung the riders' eyes and parched throats. To escape the glaring sky, they began resting between sunrise and sunset and instead traveling by night; perhaps for this reason they entered Eleanor's domain without fanfare. On July 1, they arrived in Limoges, just in time for the festival of Saint Martial, the patron of that province, and pitched camp along the banks of the Vienne below the walled town. A great crowd had assembled for the annual feast, among them Count Alphonse-Jourdain of Toulouse, and it was here that the duchess's friends and enemies learned, to their amazement, of Duke William's death and Eleanor's imminent marriage to the heir of France. Obviously, it would have been impossible to conceal the presence of such a sizable army indefinitely but, still, Abbot Suger felt uneasy. Already riders had sped away from Limoges to spread the news, and while Suger thought it unlikely that any of Eleanor's lawless vassals would be rash enough to cause trouble with the army only a week's ride from Bordeaux, nevertheless he immediately set about creating a reservoir of good will. Shrewdly, he arranged for young Louis to make a triumphal procession into the city to worship at the shrine of Saint Martial, and he also urged the great lords of the Limousin to attend the wedding.

On the morning of Sunday, July 11, the Capetian cavalcade arrived on the east bank of the Garonne. Had Eleanor climbed to the roof of the Ombrière's keep at earliest dawn when the air was still cool, she could have watched the troop emerge from the misty hills of Larmont and pitch their richly colored tents in the meadow along the river bank. By noon the field had been transformed into a small-town carnival, the indistinct voices and laughter of knights and the oaths of varlets wafting in tantalizing puffs across the water. Since there was no bridge, small boats plied back and forth throughout the day, ferrying the most important lords into the city, where they were lodged in the ducal palace or in the homes of distinguished burghers. Eleanor's guardian, Archbishop Geoffrey du Lauroux, had crossed the river himself to welcome Prince Louis and escort him to the archiepiscopal residence. It was on this day, or perhaps the next, that Eleanor met her betrothed for the first time.

Having been exposed to a variety of persons, ideas, and events from earliest childhood, she had developed strong opinions on most subjects; similarly her ideas on the male sex were quite decided: There was no doubt of it, her prince was not a bold cavalier. Still, he did not lack appeal. Louis, scarcely a year older than she, was said to be a virgin. He seemed gentle and courteous, and his tall, slender, blond looks were attractive enough; but clearly he was not a fighter: His overdelicate mouth and sweet, simple smile almost made him look weak-minded. Eleanor surely was not in love with him, indeed it would have been odd if she had felt such an emotion for a husband cast her way by political circumstance. Nevertheless, she would have known boys whose whispered words had made her heart pound and the blood rush into her face and, by contrast, she knew that Louis did not arouse those sensations in her. On closer inspection, he was as pretty as a girl, and yet, whatever else he lacked in the way of masculinity, he did possess a touching sort of charm.

Her reservations about the marriage, which of course were not of the slightest interest to anyone, ran far deeper than the personal qualities of Prince Louis. She had never expected to marry anyone but a high lord, in fact she demanded it as her right. In some respects, Louis satisfied these requirements, but at the same time, she must have believed that he ranked beneath her. A wider and deeper geographical barrier than the blue stream of the Loire stood between France and Aquitaine. To be sure, the Capets were anointed kings, but compared to the rich, cultured dukes of Aquitaine, they were an upstart dynasty who had come to the throne only one hundred and fifty years earlier, when the last descendant of Charlemagne died. The two lands were different worlds, peopled by different races. Between the Teutonized Celts of the north and the southern Celts, steeped in heady memories of the Romans, Goths, and Saracens, there was little community of blood, even less of speech, thought, and temper. For that reason, tensions developed between the French contingent and their southern hosts, each camp viewing the other with a certain amount of polite condescension, if not barely suppressed disdain. Owing to the delirious heat and possibly to the fact that a language barrier existed between those who spoke the langue d'oc and the langue d'oil, tempers flared.

In the days before the wedding, Eleanor rarely saw Louis alone, but as feast followed feast, she had ample opportunity to observe his reactions to her exuberant countrymen and their bold, daringly clad ladies who sang and jested and drank with merciless enthusiasm. Louis may have been reminded of the popular bon mot, "The Franks to battle, the Provençaux to table," a remark that seemed amply borne out by the tedious froth of the nuptial festivities.

Day after interminable day passed in feasting. The trestle tables in the Ombrière's great hall were packed with lords and ladies whose names added up to a roll call of southern chivalry: Thouars, Lusignan, Auvergne, Perigord, Armagnac, Châteauroux, Ventadour, Parthenay, in addition to many more from the petty nobility; there were at least a thousand guests. The banqueting would begin early in the morning and last until midafternoon. "Scarcely the tongue of Cicero could do justice to the munificence of the multiform expenditures that had been made, nor could the pen of Seneca fully describe the variety of meats and rare delicacies that were there." Such epicurean dishes as might have delighted the palate of Nero were passed among the white-clothed tables in unending succession: Swans decorated with ribbons and green leaves, ducks, geese, cranes, and peppered peacocks, basted roasts of pork hot from the turnspit; from the sea, mullet, sole, lobsters fried in half an egg, oysters, sperlings; sauces spiced with the bouquet of garlic, cumin, sage, and dittany; figs, candied fruits, rice cooked with milk of almond and powdered cinnamon, tarts and junkets. Course after course, washed down with the gifts of Bacchus, came and went until the men had loosened their belts and the ladies in anticipation of their siestas began to drowse and the water in the washing basins grew gray and oily from the dipping of so many greasy hands.

The Aquitainians could not do without entertainment, and there could be heard the sweet rhythms of tambourine and flute, rebec and lute, and throughout it all, the songs of the troubadours. It is probable that this great event drew Cercamon and Marcabru, the troubadour favorites of Duke William X, and perhaps they sang the *planhs* composed in lament for their patron. "Saint James," mourned Cercamon, "remember you that knight for whom I kneel and prayers have said." But surely sadness did not prevail for long, and there were songs of love and sex and springtime on the green. Perhaps Marcabru, that musicman who claimed that no woman had ever loved him, was there with his sweet misogynistic melodies lashing out against the chicanery of unfaithful married women, his "flaming whores," "Lady Goodand-excited," "those cunts [who] are nymphos in bed." The bawdy songs that set the southerners to clapping and laughing only succeeded in shocking the French, particularly the churchmen. "The French clerks looked upon profane and frivolous songs with contempt and condemnation, and would no more have thought of indulging in such pastimes than of consigning those futilities to precious parchment fit to serve for the transcription of lives of saints."

Certainly Louis was not a lad to disgrace himself before distinguished company, but there was no doubt that he, too, looked overwhelmed and uncomfortable. Plainly he did not have the vaguest idea of how to go about enjoying himself. Eleanor may have been amused as well as disconcerted to discover his lack of sophistication, and it must have confirmed some of her private prejudices about the land that would soon be her home. Bashfulness was not one of her weaknesses. Self-possessed, vivacious, she took charge of the proceedings with an undisputed authority garnered from years of basking in the spotlight. She had learned the art of dispensing hospitality at the courts of men famed for their largesse, and now, an ardent believer in enjoyment, her own as well as others', she presided over the high table with ease and patience, seemingly oblivious of the guests craning their heads to stare. She performed her role with style, by sending tidbits of succulent game to her viscounts with the request that they do her honor by tasting them, directing the pages to refill with claret the goblets of the ladies, asking her important barons what music they would prefer to hear. With Louis at her side, hour after hour she remained at the high table, accepting her vassals' salutations and congratulations, returning compliment with compliment.

There were whispers from the tables as many a guest, staring at Louis, murmured that he almost looked like a monk. If these remarks reached Eleanor's ears, she would have been the first to admit that her betrothed seemed as mild as a lamb. At times during the course of the festivities his grave, vulnerable eyes rested on her with a strange expression of wonderment and puppylike adoration, and Eleanor for her part was an astute enough observer of human beings to comprehend that here was a man susceptible to feminine manipulation. To her, this must have seemed fortunate because she had every intention of remodeling him to suit her specifications. As a first priority, she would make a man of him, perhaps not a warrior like her father and grandfather, for that might be too tall an order, but a man just the same, one who would scorn "a cow's death" abed. And later there would be time enough for other fantasies, because her head swam thickly with ideas to add luster to her name and the house of her forebears.

On Sunday, July 25, Eleanor and Louis rode through the cobbled streets of Bordeaux, past housefronts draped with banners and garlands, to the Cathedral of Saint André. Amid the ringing of bells, the heralding of trumpets and the shouting of her people come to do their duchess honor and have themselves a holiday, they entered the smoky dimness of the church to be married by her guardian, Archbishop Geoffrey. After the ceremony they solemnly bent their heads before him to receive the golden diadems that formally recognized the couple as duke and duchess of Aquitaine.

Despite the warm welcome Louis had received in Bordeaux, Abbot Suger felt far from tranquil. Some of Eleanor's important vassals, in particular the count of Angoulême, who had heisted Duke William's fiancée, had failed to attend the marriage celebration, and now the abbot's agents reported that other hostile barons were planning to stir up mischief. Thus, while the royal couple still knelt before the altar at Saint André, the Frankish camp across the Garonne was being hastily dismantled. Tents struck, pack animals loaded, the army stood in readiness by the road that led north to Poitiers. In the langorous heat of midafternoon, as her drunken guests were toasting her long life and the townspeople feasting on the roast meat distributed by the palace kitchens, Eleanor threw off her stifling scarlet robes and quietly crossed the river with her sister and a few members of her personal household. Before the sunlight had faded from the sky, the cavalcade had put a league or two between themselves and Bordeaux, but the scent of danger permeated the column. Abbot Suger, increasingly anxious, kept alert for an ambush, and while he avoided those roads that led past well-known hostile castles and the journey proceeded without incident, his apprehension did not contribute to lightheartedness. For the first few nights Eleanor slept, as always, with Petronilla. It was not until they had passed Saintes and arrived at Taillebourg, the rugged fortress owned by the loyal Geoffrey de Rancon, that they stopped to rest and enjoy the civilized hospitality of that great lord; it was there that Louis and Eleanor shared the same bed for the first time. That this event took place without any notable trauma seems apparent from the fact that afterward they seemed on more intimate terms than ever, despite whatever misgivings each may have had about the realities of conjugal life.

After adding military reinforcements to the cortege, they pressed on and reached Poitiers on August 1. Before they had even arrived at the city gate, news of their approach spread through the town, and the Poitevins streamed into the squares and roads to roar a raucous welcome to their lady. It was a fearfully weary and disheveled royal party that drew up into the cool courtyard at the ducal palace, thankful for surcease from the remorseless heat of the road. Suger and other older members of the party verged on collapse, but with the energy of an enthusiastic fifteen-year-old, Eleanor immediately set about organizing a proper welcome for her illustrious guests. Back in the Maubergeonne Tower, the place she felt most at home, she opened the ducal chests and showered her new husband with costly gifts. Troubadours were summoned, and the signal for resumption of the feasting given out. Plans were made for the following Sunday, when Louis would be crowned count of Poitou, a solemn occasion that Suger wished to have rival in splendor the coronations of the Frankish kings at Reims.

The days slipped by all too swiftly for Eleanor, who now began to understand that her carefree childhood had ended the day her father died. The momentous events of the past two months had left no time for reflection and scarcely a moment for mourning. But in the Maubergeonne Tower, memories of her great stubborn father must have descended on her in painful waves of nostalgia and, judging from her activities, she seems to have been determined to make the most of her last days in Poitiers. In Paris, she would be virtually a nobody, only the wife of the heir to the throne. According to Louis, whose knowledge of worldly amusements had been severely limited by his life at Saint-Denis, the king and queen did not appreciate singing and dancing; to Eleanor they could only have sounded like a dreary lot.

With no father or mother, no advisers except possibly her grandmother, Eleanor was obliged to rely on her own values and inclinations as far as behavior was concerned; in the days remaining she can be seen attempting to teach her socially backward husband that life was meant to be sucked and savored, and sometimes devoured whole. Accordingly, she organized a masculine entertainment for Louis and his knights, a hunting and fishing excursion, and she dispatched them to the seaside village of Talmont, where her father had kept a richly stocked game preserve. In a holiday mood, the men set off for the ocean, forgetting the suspicious Suger's last-minute warning about one William of Lezay, a laggard castellan who had refused to render homage to the prince and who, moreover, had appropriated both the late Duke William's castle as well as his prized white gyrfalcons from the ducal hunting ground. This sulky baron and his almost ludicrous antics troubled them so little that, en route to Talmont, the party complacently removed their chain mail and swords, sending the bulky arms on ahead with the baggage train. To their astonishment, the first knights to enter the ducal castle at Talmont were taken prisoner by Lezay, who had been hoping to bag the prince himself and hold his royal person for ransom. Within minutes, Louis experienced his first taste of hand-to-hand combat as a sword was thrust into his hand and he fought for his life. As the fracas ended, Lezay's men were all butchered, save for a few who escaped to the sea through an underground passage. Hearing about it later, Eleanor was both horrified and passionately pleased.

This incident, trivial enough in itself, reveals the direction in which Louis's character and his relationship with his wife were soon to develop, because there is no question that his derring-do, less than ordinary by standards of the day, was received with high admiration by Eleanor. Thus, the shy, hesitant husband recognized a means of winning his lady's respect; the wife fortified her lord's valor with ego-inflating praise. From that time forward, she would coax, suggest, cheer, and dangle before his meek eyes the carrot of her beauty and affection in order to transform him into a fearless warrior. Given the circumstances of feudal life, her efforts were far from misguided.

During that week when Eleanor and Louis took one another's measure in the purple Poitevin nights, a courier was burning up the road between the Île-de-France and Poitiers. On August 1, the same day that the bridal party had arrived in Eleanor's ancestral city, Louis the Fat lay dying in Paris, "excessive fevers of summer" combining with dysentery to close his days upon the earth. He preferred to die in the Abbey of Saint-Denis, but the prelates in attendance gently dissuaded him: His weight and the gravity of his condition militated against his being moved at the last hour. Resigning himself, the old king directed that a carpet be laid upon the floor and strewn with ashes in the shape of a cross. Like a helpless infant who cannot yet sit or roll over, he was lowered by the hands of others onto the cross, where he stretched out his arms and relinquished his newly expanded kingdom to a monkish youth and a maiden he had never seen.

On a day in late August, the young queen of France arrived in the capital of that land that John of Salisbury would call "of all nations the sweetest and most civilized," an evocative picture with which Eleanor would never wholly agree. Dismounting, she stepped down onto a mossy stump beside an olive tree and ascended a flight of broad stone stairs leading to the Cité Palace. Knights had been known to ride their horses up the stairway and into the hall, but this was not encouraged. Crowded on the western tip of its island in the middle of the Seine, the decaying tower, which the dynasty's founder, Hugh Capet, had inherited from the Merovingian kings, could charitably be described as cramped and drafty. In marked contrast to the Maubergeonne Tower, or even to the Ombrière Palace, the Capetian royal residence appeared uncomfortably primitive, a heap of stone that gave one the eerie feeling of living in a quarry. Little light filtered through the narrow slits that passed for windows, and it was only with the greatest difficulty that the new queen could catch a glimpse of the river below or an evening star above.

Compounding her dismay over her new home were almost instantaneous conflicts with her mother-in-law, the Dowager Queen Adelaide.

At the outset, the queen mother displayed distinct animosity toward Eleanor, indeed she may have disliked her before they met, perhaps basing her preconceptions on another southerner, Constance of Provence, who had married Hugh Capet's son Robert. Although Constance had lived a century earlier, tales of her allegedly immodest dress and language still continued to circulate among the sober Franks. In Adelaide's opinion, Eleanor was a good deal worse, and as a result the queen could not take a step without the dowager's icy disapproval: She must wear modest gowns and must cultivate demureness so as not to give offense; if she continued to entertain lavishly, the royal treasury would be depleted in no time; if she would only spend more hours at her prayers and at improving her use of the *langue d'oil,* she would have no time to think of singing and painting her face. Nothing Eleanor did was right. Adelaide's nagging reflected the fact that, contrary to her expectations, her influence over her son had fallen into blatant eclipse. Not only had Eleanor taken over management of the household, but she had no compunctions about telling Louis what to do. To Adelaide's dismay, her pious boy did not object to the secular frivolities without which Eleanor could not live, nor to the good-sized entourage of morally flabby Poitevins, who not only took up space in the already crowded palace but who insisted upon behaving as if they were still in the south. For the first time within memory, the hall of the palace rang with loud laughter and the songs of minstrel and jongleur, Eleanor having had the foresight to import several music makers as part of her baggage.

Before many weeks had passed, friction arose between mother and son, but despite Adelaide's bitter complaints to Abbot Suger, the southern high life was well enough entrenched to withstand her displeasure. Clearly the Cité Palace could not contain two women as mutually antagonistic as Adelaide and Eleanor. As a result, the old queen retired to her dower estate near Compiègne, where a few months later, in a mood so precipitate that it seemed an act of spite, she married a minor nobleman, Matthew of Montmorency.

As autumn advanced into winter, the days grew darker and shorter, and since at times night fell not long after four o'clock in the afternoon, sensible Parisians went to bed early. For Eleanor, shivering in the unaccustomed cold, there was of course the temptation to huddle beside a charcoal brazier and indulge her passion for reading, but instead she seems to have occupied herself with plans to make life at the Cité Palace more agreeable. Orders were given for remodeling her dilapidated apartments: The window openings were enlarged and fitted with shutters, construction began on a fireplace and chimney to replace the brazier. She took infinite trouble to reorganize the management of the palace, which, in her opinion, could only be called slovenly, unsanitary, and remarkably primitive. Tablecloths and napkins—common amenities in the south—were introduced, and pages were instructed to wash their hands before serving. She dismissed the cantor at the palace's chapel of Saint Nicholas, replacing him with one who could conduct a decent choir. In short, she behaved as do most young brides who are whisked to new homes in strange towns; she tried to make it her own.

Apart from the many stresses to which a new wife is subject, the life of a queen in France during the middle of the twelfth century was not always glamorous; it could be and often was fearfully dull. God's good time ticked slowly when daily activities consisted mainly of prescribed female duties of the type Eleanor had always disdained. If a queen had a faculty for ennui, she could exist more or less contentedly, hawking in fair weather, sitting indoors with her ladies in foul weather, and playing chess and blindman's buff, telling stories and guessing riddles, the sort of activities we now associate with the nursery. Neither by temperament nor experience was Eleanor equipped to play such a restricted role. Much of her behavior that was considered unorthodox by the Parisians did not result from acute ignorance of their customs; rather, it was enormously difficult for her to adjust to life in the north, and thus soon after she had settled at the Cité Palace the unhappy exile began to dream of the day when she might return to her homeland.

Initially, Eleanor had harbored hopes of transforming Louis into a gallant knight, but as time went on, she must have realized that such a metamorphosis would not take place easily, if at all. In his personal routine, Louis seemed little changed by his marriage and succession to the throne. During those first months, he resumed his monastic studies at the Church of Notre Dame and, unlike most monarchs, dressed and behaved with such unassuming simplicity that one would not have supposed him King of France. Odo de Deuil, Louis's secretary and, later, chaplain, paints a touching picture of a young man "whose entire life is a model of virtue, for when a mere boy he began to reign, worldly glory did not cause him sensual delight." He could not conceive of a greater delight than decorating his chapels, assisting at the Mass, and intoning at the reading desk. Louis VII preferred the life of a monk, and any of his subjects who wished a firsthand glimpse had only to enter Notre Dame, where they could see him singing in the choir or reading the canticles. Each day, from prime through matins, he kept the vigils and on Fridays fasted on bread and water, his scrupulous devotion to the Church, unshared by Eleanor, creating perennial difficulties between them. One of Louis's more tiresome habits was prayer. If he was not on his knees among the black and white columns of Notre Dame, he was praying in the royal bedchamber, and it is not difficult to imagine the winter nights when Eleanor shivered under the fur coverlet, eyes open, watching her husband kneel on the cold stone floor in the light of a gutted candle, with his head bowed and his lips moving fervently. In sex Louis was extremely, almost ascetically, abstemious; nevertheless, there is reason to believe that he did occasionally perform his duties because at some time during the first or second year of their union Eleanor became pregnant. She must have miscarried, however, or else the child was stillborn.

Theoretically free to do as she pleased, Eleanor dressed as she liked and spent lavishly on banquets and entertainment without her husband's interference. In practice, however, Louis's lack of polish and his failure to participate in the spirit of the merrymaking cramped her style. When he did attend the gay doings in the Great Hall, the guests would find themselves in the presence of a silent, awkward youth whose uncertain expression plainly indicated that he longed to escape as soon as possible. However, the new queen's earliest fêtes for the Parisian nobility were blighted not only by Louis's shyness but by the backward Parisians themselves, for it was painfully clear that at Paris people did not approach life with the same flair and grace as did the Aquitainians. More often than not the men were loutish and stingy, the women prudes who dressed with abominable taste.

In one respect, it is surprising that Eleanor experienced such profound boredom in her new city. As a person of education and exceptional intelligence, she might have found much to excite her imagination in the richly intellectual climate flourishing there. Paris in the 1130s was a city of nearly 200,000 persons squeezed into an area that could comfortably accommodate perhaps one-third that number. The marrow of "the city of light and immortality" was the Île-de-France, that almond-shaped island cradled in the arms of the Seine and dominated by the royal enclave at one end and the citadel of the archbishop at the other. Despite Eleanor's constant comparisons with the semi-tropical luxuriance of the south, the city had much to recommend it. At the western tip of the island was a royal garden with wooden trellises and acanthus-bordered walks; there grew a jumble of roses, lilies, mandrakes, and dozens of other blooms; beds of leeks, pumpkins, and watercress; plots of mint, rue, absinthe, and the soporific poppy. The queen could sit under a pear of Saint-Regulus tree and gaze down the broad brimming stream at willows and horse towpaths lining the banks and at the water mills squatting under the bridge arches. Low in the water, barges bearing wheat, hides, wine, and salt plied the stream, and the air rang with the cries of the boatmen and the rumble of the mill wheels. From her garden wall Eleanor could watch, 100 yards away on the Left Bank, the well-trodden field called Pré-aux-clercs, where unruly students danced and held tournaments.

When she ventured out from the royal enclave, she found herself in a noisy, reeking world of crooked streets darkened by the upper stories of houses, which leaned precariously forward. Due to poor drainage the lanes ran deep with mud and the contents of chamber pots and wash-basins pitched from upper windows. Almost drowning out the pealing bells and majestic tones of the Gregorian chants from the Romanesque bouquet of churches came the constant clatter of street cries: the menders of furs, the candlemakers, the vegetable and fruit merchants, the wine *crieurs* who walked through the streets carrying a bowl that could be sampled and shouting, "So-and-so has just opened a cask of this wine. He who wants to buy some of it will find it on the Rue _____" And everywhere on the twisting, turning streets were sold things to eat: waffles, small cakes, wafers, and, carried about by the *talemeliers* in baskets covered with white cloths, the favorite pasties, turnovers filled with chopped ham, chicken, eel, soft cheese, and egg.

The city swarmed with students from every nation in Europe: John of Salisbury; nineteen-year-old Thomas Becket, clinging to his vow of chastity; and the sons of well-born fathers who had flocked there to plunge into philosophy, theology, medicine, or feudal law and, perhaps equally important, to taste the heady delights of the flesh and the tavern. On the quays along the Seine they slogged behind the skirts of learned doctors who discoursed on Plato and Aristotle as well as writings of the church fathers. Along the Petit Pont, the upper stories of the little buildings housed brilliant teachers, such as Adam de Petit Pont, and in order to hear their lectures students eagerly crowded into the tiny rooms and if necessary sat on the rickety stairs. In this intellectual's paradise one could dip into the central controversy of medieval thought: the importance of the universal versus the particular. Were universals—the Church, humanity, divinity—more important than the particulars—churchmen, individuals, persons of the Trinity? Must one be able to comprehend the universals before one could understand the particular? Should one incline toward the Realists, who believed in universals, or the Nominalists, who upheld the importance of the particulars? In Paris, one could believe as one pleased, unless of course one happened to stray too far in the direction of heresy.

Among the remarkable array of scholars assembled only a short walk from the palace of the Capets was one who stood head and shoulders above the others. Peter Abélard blazed with a glory that caused women to stare at him from their windows and men like John of Salisbury "to sit at his feet drinking in every word that fell from his lips." His fame rested mainly on his illustrious mind but partly on his skill in the art of seduction, for some twenty years earlier he had been taken as tutor into the home of the lovely Héloïse. Books were opened, but more words of love than lessons were heard. After the birth of an illegitimate son and a subsequent marriage, Héloïse's uncle had Abélard castrated, and finally the lovers separated, each taking monastic vows. Abélard's troubles were common knowledge and in *Historia Calamitatum* he himself had written about his emasculation as well as other persecutions. By the time Eleanor arrived in Paris, the unhappy Abélard had reached his midfifties, but his sharp mind and quick tongue continued to question ideas long taken for granted. Believing that only reason and intelligence can resolve inconsistencies in matters of faith—by doubting we are led to inquire; by inquiry we perceive the truth—he presumed to understand and explain the mystery of the Trinity. To apply the hot light of reason to all things in heaven and earth was an original, if not to say dangerous, notion and one that even then was propelling him toward fresh calamities. In an open debate at Sens in May 1140, his so-called blasphemous views on the Trinity would be challenged and condemned by Bernard of Clairvaux.

A man like Peter Abélard, deprived of his manhood for love of a lady, would have appealed to a romantic like Eleanor, but the ideas he espoused would also have been examined with some care; at least she would not have rejected them out of hand the way her conservative husband did. It seems inconceivable that she would not have sampled the wisdom of the ages being imparted freely on bridge and street corner, especially since the intellectual life was not barred to females, and Abélard himself boasted that noble ladies thronged his lectures. If the queen believed it beneath her royal dignity to betake herself to one of the crammed rooms on the Petit Pont, she had more suitable opportunities to hear the masters. In warm weather, the royal garden threw open its gates to the schools, and there, from a front-row seat under a pear tree, she surely could have imbibed the rudiments of dialectic and the structure of the syllogism. Indeed, in later years, she would give ample demonstration that she had mastered the fine points of intellectual swordsmanship. Still, as a woman, especially as a queen, Eleanor could never truly enter into the sweetly tumultuous life of the scholar; she could only flit through its tantalizing atmosphere, alighting now and then to inhale its perfume. Nor did her temperament at that time allow for sustained interest in any subject requiring discipline.

Most people's lives are shaped by what they remember of childhood, and Eleanor was no different. Accustomed to the extravagant green vistas of the south, those gardens full of acid sunlight and the mellow crooning of nightingales, she was not entranced by Paris. She saw only its squalor, heard only its noise. Although she had her sister for company, she was lonely and utterly bored; she missed the sound of the *langue d'oc* and the easygoing humor of the southerners. Even Louis was perceptive enough to notice her gloom, and since he felt solicitous of his wife's happiness, he did not object when she spent frivolously on costly silks and jewels.

Along with the throne, Louis inherited Abbot Suger from his father. The royal counselor hoped for the best from the young king whom he had known and loved since infancy and whose education he had personally directed at Saint-Denis. He would always remain, for Suger, "a child, in the flower of his age and of great sweetness of temper, the hope of the good and the terror of the wicked." The queen Suger liked a great deal less, although he was forced to admit that she was *"nobilissima puella,"* a most nobly born girl, which, strictly speaking, is more a statement of fact than an expression of opinion. If any man could have herded Louis and Eleanor along the narrow path of responsibility, it was the tiny prelate whom fortune had lifted from the poor rural peasantry to be chief minister of kings, head of the royal abbey of Saint-Denis, and notable author. While still a boy, Suger had met Louis the Fat at the school for novices at Saint-Denis, where they both were students. It might be thought that the son of a peasant would have little in common with the great figures of the aristocracy, but Suger, no ordinary priest, was undeniably a man of enormous culture. "He had such a great knowledge of history that no matter what prince or king of the Franks one mentioned, he immediately and without hesitation would hasten to recount his deeds." Endowed with a prodigious memory, the abbot knew the Scriptures virtually by heart and could reply succinctly to any question put to him, and he could also recite from memory the "heathen" verses of Horatio, Ovid, Juvenal, and Terence.

By temperament, he was unsuited for a life of austerity and for many years had indulged his love of luxury with soft woolen shirts, dainty coverlets, and warm furs. In recent years, however, he had been severely criticized by Bernard of Clairvaux: "From early time yours was a noble abbey of royal dignity. . . . Without any deception or delay it rendered to Caesar his dues, but not with equal enthusiasm what was due to God. . . . They say the cloister of the monastery was often crowded with soldiers, that business was done there, that it echoed to the sound of men wrangling, and that sometimes women were to be found there. In all this hubbub how could anyone have attended to heavenly, divine, and spiritual things?''

How indeed. As a result, Suger had given up his fine horses and splendid livery and exchanged his spacious home for a tiny barren cell. However, in his most current project, the restoration of Saint-Denis, he continued to indulge his love of beautiful objects by embellishing the new church with gorgeous stained glass and precious ornaments. After 1140, he devoted his entire time to Saint-Denis; this did not reflect any lessening of his interest in affairs of state but rather his fall from favor with the young king, or, more precisely, with the young queen. Eleanor rejected the notion that her husband should be closely supervised like a schoolboy instead of relying on his own judgment. And if Louis needed advice about Aquitaine, he had only to ask his wife, for, after all, who had more practical knowledge than she? After the departure of Suger and his balancing stability, the young couple were left to their own devices.

As is often the case with weak men who wish to prove their masculinity, Louis felt compelled to meet each affront to his royal authority with a display of ferocity bordering on the brutal, but much of this stemmed indirectly from a desire to impress his wife. Constantly, he looked over his shoulder to gauge her reaction, a habit that must have simultaneously pleased and annoyed her. He would never understand her, but from the first, he had adored her in the way an inexperienced boy worships a gay, confident girl; with passionate admiration he responded to her charm, to a cleverness that he himself lacked, and he indulged her extravagantly. If she was headstrong and demanding—and unquestionably she was—he excused it as perfectly normal behavior for one of her richly endowed nature. There was, of course, another side to the story: Eleanor was anxious to control everything she regarded as hers, that is, her person, about which she was hysterically vain; her life; and her lands, which she felt, quite rightly, she knew more about than Louis or any of his royal ministers. As she repeatedly pointed out to Louis, the Aquitainians, for all their splendid qualities, were a pigheaded people who would only extend their respect to a firm ruler.

Before the death of Eleanor's father, the political situation in Aquitaine had been unsatisfactory, and by now it had grown steadily worse.

For that matter, trouble had been brewing in Louis's own domains, and only a few days after his succession he had been obliged to put down a rebellion in the town of Orléans. Some sixty years earlier there had begun the growth of the communal movement whereby a few towns, in a reaction against feudal exploitation, tried to obtain a measure of self-government by establishing collective seigneuries that would recognize their economic and political interests. In some cases, Louis the Fat had encouraged communes, because he saw them as a device to curb the power of both his barons and the Church. When, however, the proposed commune occurred on the king's land, as was the case with Orléans, it was a different story, and when the Orléans bourgeois bitterly complained about outrageous taxes and demanded a charter of rights, he refused. Within days of his death, the burghers suffered a convenient memory loss and proclaimed themselves a commune. The young king, fresh from his baptism of fire in the Talmont, marched against the town and promptly executed the conspirators who had sought to foster insurrection; then, evidently reluctant to be known as a tyrant, he abruptly reversed his position and granted most of the demanded reforms. In the future, this trait of indecision would mark most of his political actions.

The rebellion in Orléans proved to be anything but an isolated case, and a similar mutiny soon occurred in Eleanor's domains—as it happened, in her own capital city of Poitiers. In late 1137, after having had a few months to digest the changes in their political fortunes as a result of William X's death, the Poitevins exhibited reluctance to put themselves into the hands of a foreign king merely because their land happened to be part of his wife's real estate. Accordingly, they repudiated Louis's authority and boldly announced themselves a free city, a serious blow to the prestige of both Eleanor and her husband. Angry and humiliated, Louis hastily threw together an army, short on knights but well equipped with siege machines, and marched on the rebellious town. Since the surprised Poitevins had barely had time to organize their defense, the king was able to easily capture the city without a single casualty on either side. In victory, however, he was unable to handle the uprising in a diplomatic or even sensible manner, or rather he dealt with the rebels in a manner that he believed would meet with Eleanor's approval.

His demands were positively ruthless: Instead of simply disbanding the commune and letting it go at that, he vindictively insisted that the sons and daughters of leading citizens be offered as hostages and sent away into exile in France. On an appointed day, the burghers were to bring their children, with baggage, to the main square before the ducal palace. The howls of the horrified Poitevins carried far beyond the boundaries of Aquitaine all the way to the Abbey of Saint-Denis, where Suger, a more impartial judge, was summoned to Poitiers to reason with his flower child. After a long talk with Louis, Suger appeared in person to the burghers and stilled their lamentations; Louis, in seclusion, had changed his mind and would allow their heirs to go free.

In Paris, Eleanor observed this incident with irritation. Mistaking brutality for strength, she longed for Louis to assert himself so that she might feel, if not love, then respect for him. His weakness overwhelmed her. Obviously, he could not be counted on to handle a simple revolt with any sense of proportion; and then, like a clumsy child, he needed to be rescued by Suger. Furthermore, resentful of Suger's interference in a matter that she felt did not concern him, she determined that his advice would not be sought in the future.

Although Eleanor did not accompany Louis to Poitiers, she made several trips back to the south during the early years of her marriage, the first of which may have been in September 1138, when she attended the festival of Notre Dame at Puy. Generally, she was accompanied by her husband, as well as her sister, who remained her closest friend and confidante. Undoubtedly, she found her relationship with Petronilla comforting, because life in Paris was even more alien than she had ever imagined. While she had not expected marriage to bring her the lover of her dreams, presumably she had hoped to find a degree of emotional and sexual satisfaction. If she had possessed these, she might have borne the shock of her new life, but as it turned out, circumstances had not brought her loving, and therefore she determined to drink deeply of living. To her, this meant excitement and novelty. There had been, of course, special occasions, as on that first Christmas of their marriage when Louis had taken her to Bourges to be crowned queen, but these temporary diversions could not replace the pleasure she had anticipated as the wife of a great lord. She knew that her happiness had been left behind in Poitiers. Was the rest of her life to be spent permanently sealed on that dreary island, condemned to live with a submissive man who feared to look at her body and felt loath to touch her even in the dark?

Considering the fact that Louis failed to attract her physically and that she had small respect for him as a man, they were, oddly enough, compatible in less personal areas. Eleanor prided herself on taking a role in the regulation of affairs in Aquitaine, and as we shall see subsequently, she also felt herself competent to advise him in matters pertaining to the kingdom of France. Nevertheless, in this latter ambition she would prove notably unsuccessful, because during the first ten years of her reign, the documents reveal her to have been virtually powerless. Unlike previous French queens, including Queen Adelaide, who shared in executive and policy-making decisions with Louis the Fat, Eleanor's name rarely appears on her husband's charters nor is there any record of her presence in the royal curia. Beginning with Eleanor, the Capetian queens of France ceased to be working sovereigns, a curious coincidence, for Eleanor would prove to be one of the most politically astute women of the medieval era. A great deal of the credit for this break in tradition can be attributed to the domination of Abbot Suger, who regarded both Louis and Eleanor as insufficiently mature to govern wisely. While Suger may have relegated the queen to an official back-seat, he could not prevent her from wielding a wifely influence over her husband. That many of Louis's actions, whether or not on her advice it is impossible to gauge, appeared to be ill considered did not seem to trouble her, nor did his destructiveness impinge strongly upon Suger either. When, for instance, Louis finally got around to punishing William of Lezay by personally hacking off his hands, no one felt concern about the fate of an obscure baron who had stolen a few birds in faraway Talmont.

By 1141, however, a number of Louis's vassals began to suspect that there was more than met the eye to the boy king, so pious, so kind, so timid. For some time now Eleanor had been preoccupied with the idea of invading the county of Toulouse, which, in her opinion, belonged to her through her grandmother Philippa. That the domain should remain in the usurping hands of Alphonse-Jourdain riled her, and she repeatedly suggested to her husband that this wrong be remedied. To be sure, Alphonse-Jourdain had ruled Toulouse for some twenty years, and even Eleanor's father, who had signed his charters "William the Toulousain," had never seriously considered reclaiming his mother's patrimony. But for the queen, Toulouse had the appeal of an irresistible cause.

Swept along by Eleanor's enthusiasm, Louis readily understood that the acquisition of Toulouse would enhance Frankish national prestige, not to mention his own personal reputation. In the opening months of 1141, the two of them spent many excited hours mapping out their adventure. Like inexperienced children titillated by a new game but having no knowledge of the rules, they blundered along without any sense of direction and disdained to ask for advice. To some of Louis's vassals, among them the powerful Count Theobald of Champagne, the proposed expedition against Toulouse appeared to be a senseless and even unjust project, and they declined to support their overlord. Theobald had neglected to assist in the military action against the Poitiers commune, and when the time for departure arrived on June 24, he again failed to appear in person, nor did he trouble to send a contingent of troops. Louis, furious at the count, was forced to leave without him, but this second defection would not be easily forgiven.

Louis had absolutely no sense of military intuition, and Eleanor, who accompanied him as far south as Poitiers, had little to contribute in this area. As a result the army was haphazardly organized and ineptly led. Only a small amount of siege equipment had been brought along, because Louis and Eleanor apparently counted on taking the city by surprise, a tactic based more on wishful thinking than on any particular strategy. Perhaps Eleanor cherished illusions that Louis, like her grandparents, would capture Toulouse without a blow struck.

Alphonse-Jourdain, of course, had no intention of handing over his fief to the young duchess and her husband; warned of the Franks' approach long before they reached his ramparts, he had organized a thorough defense and sat waiting for them like a tomcat about to gobble up a puny mouse. Louis, reluctant to sacrifice his army on the altar of Eleanor's ambition, met the challenge by beating a hasty retreat, fleeing north into Angoulême and then rejoining his wife in Poitiers. Eleanor's private feelings about Louis's fiasco can be imagined; the qualities that she counted supreme in a man were valor, readiness for military adventure, knightly honor, and physical prowess. Everything else was merely garnish, as though a man had to be transformed into a killer before he could be loved or respected. Still, perhaps from pity, she must have managed to conceal much of her disappointment, because it was at this time that she opened the treasures of the dukes of Aquitaine and presented him with a magnificent crystal vase ornamented with pearls and precious stones.

The victory she had so ardently desired was forfeit; nevertheless, she decided to linger in Poitou for the remainder of the summer. She would make a holiday of it, and with Louis, Petronilla, and others in her retinue, she embarked on a *chevauchée* over the trails she remembered so nostalgically from her childhood: They visited the monastery of Nieuil-sur-l'Autise, where her mother was buried; granted favors to her Aunt Agnes's convent; and spent a few days by the sea in Talmont. Although she counted it a pleasant summer, the holiday was shadowed by failure.

When they returned to Paris in the autumn, Louis's mood alternated between depression and frenetic exuberance. Whatever the reason—lingering humiliation over Toulouse, possibly a desire to raise his prestige in Eleanor's eyes—he seemed determined to cast off the last vestiges of discretion. That year the archbishopric of Bourges fell vacant, and Louis, for reasons that baffled his barons, took it into his head to appoint his own candidate, a man named Carduc, who happened to be one of his chancellors. Technically, he did not actually insist on Carduc but extended the see freedom of choice, while at the same time vetoing the one suitable candidate, Peter de la Châtre. Since Carduc was singularly unfitted for office, the canons of Bourges ignored Louis's interference and proceeded to elect Peter. He was duly consecrated by Pope Innocent II and sent to Bourges to assume his duties when, to his chagrin, he discovered the city gates bolted against him.

When Innocent learned of this outrage, his suspicions were immediately aroused, and he jumped to conclusions that probably fell close to the truth. It seemed obvious to him that Louis, a mere schoolboy, an innocent who had never strayed from the path of duty to the Church, could not be responsible. The culprit must be another, and it took him no time at all to locate her. The pontiff well remembered Eleanor's family: the stubborn duke who had failed to support him and who had exiled from Poitou all ecclesiastics loyal to Innocent, filling the sees with his own candidates. Was this not clearly a case of "like father, like daughter"? The extent to which Eleanor involved herself in this matter is not clear, but it seems reasonable to assume that she did not discourage Louis from his dangerous course. Bitterly offended when he heard of the pope's condescending remark that Louis was only a child and should be taught manners, the king responded by maneuvering himself into the most awkward corner possible. In melodramatic defiance, he placed his hands upon sacred relics and took a public oath that so long as he lived Peter de la Châtre should never set foot in Bourges.

Across the Alps, Innocent hurtled his thunderbolts of excommunication and interdict, casting the young king into outer darkness. Not only was Louis excluded from all sacraments, but in any town or castle where he dwelled no bells could ring, no church services be performed, nor marriages, confessions, baptisms, or burials. In a century when heaven and hell were real and men and women worried about their souls, excommunication was a serious business. For Louis, a man with an exceptional passion for the hallowed harmony of the cloister, it was an unimaginable blow, and yet he plunged ahead furiously, his obstinacy hardening as the months passed. His anger flared even higher when it came to his attention that Peter de la Châtre was being sheltered in Champagne by a sympathetic Count Theobald.

Louis and Eleanor made a mental list of their enemies; Theobald headed the roster.

At the spinsterly age of nineteen, Eleanor's sister remained unmarried. This unusual state of affairs was the subject of considerable comment, for Petronilla, an attractive girl, owned dower property in Burgundy and simply by virtue of her relationship to the king and queen would have made an acceptable wife. But eligible lords who came courting found their attentions politely refused; the queen's sister had long been casting her eyes elsewhere. Five years earlier, at Eleanor's wedding, she had first made the acquaintance of Count Ralph of Vermandois, the king's elderly relative and seneschal of France. Ralph was over fifty, but he bore his years lightly; the fact that he was old enough to be Petronilla's father was not exactly the trouble, however. He was a married man, and moreover, his wife, Leonora, happened to be the niece of Count Theobald.

In the summer of 1141, while Eleanor and Louis were dawdling in Poitou, their retinue included Petronilla and Ralph. Although the couple's attraction to each other was scarcely news to the more observant in the royal household, on that trip it was impossible for outsiders not to notice what was happening. Petronilla had long been a source of concern for Eleanor, who, as the elder, felt responsible for her. Like Eleanor, Petronilla possessed a strong sex drive and few inhibitions; Ralph had the reputation of being a seducer of women, and according to John of Salisbury, "he was always dominated by lust." It is safe to assume that the two were hardly conducting a platonic love affair, which meant the ever-present threat of illegitimacy and scandal. While Eleanor may have wished that Petronilla had chosen a more suitable cavalier, she also understood that her sister loved the count and would have no other as a husband. Under the circumstances, a means had to be found for them to marry, and to Eleanor, with her customary simplicity of purpose, the solution seemed clear: Ralph must secure a divorce.

Late that year the matter was quietly and swiftly remedied. Louis located three friendly bishops, one of them Ralph's brother, who annulled the marriage on the ground of consanguinity and immediately united Ralph to the Lady Petronilla. When the incredulous count of Champagne was notified that he must come and collect his discarded niece and her children, he protested vigorously. For decades Ralph and

Theobald had been sworn enemies, and this latest personal injury could not help but tax the limits of Theobald's patience. With detailed care and a calculated desire for revenge, he prepared a case against Ralph and wasted no time in dispatching it to Pope Innocent: The count of Vermandois, he explained, had failed to secure papal consent for the annulment; for that matter, the annulment had been handled in a most irregular fashion and clearly was illegal; and Louis had once again interfered in matters that fell under eccesiastical rather than secular jurisdiction.

Innocent's response was icily meticulous. In June of 1142, a Church council assembled at Lagny-sur-Marne in Champagne, at which time the papal legate, Cardinal Yves, reaffirmed the validity of Ralph's first marriage and excommunicated Ralph and Petronilla, as well as the three complaisant bishops who had stretched the law in their favor.

A more secure man than Louis might have paused to examine the impossibility of the situation. But neither Louis nor Eleanor was in any mood to exercise caution. They blamed Theobald for their troubles; twice the remiss count had dodged his responsibilities as a vassal, and furthermore, he had actually dared to provoke Louis by harboring Peter de la Châtre. Their prestige at stake, the Capets refused to submit meekly to Rome nor did they intend to set a precedent that would imperil their authority in ruling their subjects. If they capitulated to the pope's ruling, Ralph would be forced to return to Leonora, and Petronilla, most likely pregnant by then, would bear a bastard; as it was, the excommunications had cast an ignominious stain on the house of Vermandois and, indirectly, on the honor of the Capets. Both Eleanor and Louis were emphatic on one point: On no account would they compromise.

Even though Louis's first flush of anger had diminished somewhat, he still boiled with indignation and an unswerving determination to prove himself a forceful monarch. Resolved to defy the pope and to humble Theobald, he had Eleanor's full approval in taking a step that pivoted a cold war into a hot one. In January 1143, he personally led an army into Champagne and laid siege to the little town of Vitry-sur-Marne. From his encampment on the La Fourche hills above the town Louis watched his troops pour down the slope and advance on a castle belonging to Theobald. The charge was answered by a volley of arrows fired from the summits of the castle's wooden towers, but within a short period of time it became apparent that its resistance would be easily crushed. Louis's archers catapulted fiery arrows over the walls, and soon the castle crackled in flames.

The townspeople of Vitry, paralyzed at suddenly finding themselves in the midst of a war, came out of their houses and stared in bewilderment at the wild-eyed soldiers swarming through their quiet lanes and brandishing swords and torches. The men and women stopped work and gathered up their children. Although a few villagers took up knives and makeshift cudgels, most had no weapons with which to beat off the king's soldiers. Beyond the control of their officers, the troops tossed torches into the doorways of wooden houses and onto thatched roofs, and soon the fire spread through the whole town. Terror-stricken, eyes smarting from smoke, the burghers of Vitry surged down the streets leading to their cathedral, the traditional place of refuge where non-combatants might find sanctuary. There, where none could lay a finger on them, they carried the sick, the elderly, the infants. Presumably it was a large church because eventually the entire population, thirteen hundred persons, it is said, managed to squeeze inside.

From the hill above Vitry, Louis saw a double wall of flame suddenly shoot up from the church in a shower of sparks. Caught by the wind, the flames began to snap and lick the walls until the cathedral was enveloped by a thousand crimson tongues. Above the noise of the flames arose cries that carried clearly to Louis's vantage point: The curses turned to piercing screams as the trapped began to trample one another, trying to beat down the barred doors. But no one emerged through the gateway of flames, for in a few minutes the timbers of the roof collapsed, burying those who a few hours earlier had been absentmindedly stirring pots of soup or sitting at their looms.

A cloud of thick black smoke rose into the blood-red sky above the roofs of Vitry until the town was nearly engulfed, but still Louis could hear the animal howls and smell the human flesh burning to a cindered crisp. The ghastly shrieks blinded him with tears, and when his aides-de-camp came to make their reports, they found a strange and terrible sight. Louis stood immobile, his face blanched and his teeth chattering. His eyes had no expression in them. When they spoke to him, he appeared not to hear, and finally, alarmed, they led him into his field tent and made him lie down.

At twilight, the acrid smoke had spread out over the valley, and the breeze carried the stench of burnt flesh up the hillside to the doorway of Louis's tent. Soldiers sitting around the campfires could still see a few coppery embers glowing through the smoke. But the king did not emerge from his tent, not that night nor the next day nor the one after that. He lay motionless on his cot, refusing to eat or drink or speak. When he closed his eyes, time stood still, and he heard the hissing and singing of the flames and screams hideous enough to cleave the sky. Waves of rose-colored light filled his vision until the whole world had shriveled to the size of a great fiery ball of flame.

Behind the Red Cross

Over the rolling hills and valleys of Champagne swept the royal army, leaving behind a carpet of ravaged fields and smoking villages, corpses pierced by lances and disemboweled horses lying in frozen raspberry pools. That winter and chilly spring the unthawed earth ran red with blood as village after terrorized village fell before the deaf and blind ardor of Louis's soldiers. Numbers of those who ordinarily earned their bread as murderers and thieves had flocked to join the king's troops, for the aroma of plunder proved a powerful lure, and Louis welcomed all who would aid his cause. Cries of fear and hatred rent the lands of Count Theobald, and still the king's men did not tire of killing and looting. It was, some said, a splendid war.

At the Cité Palace, Eleanor followed the progress of the war with understandable relish. She rejoiced for Louis's successes, although her satisfaction was moderated by an uneasy feeling that the victories were not quite as glorious as she had expected. For months at a time her husband remained in Champagne, and when they did meet, it did not escape her notice that the war had imposed a strain on his health. He was—there was no disguising the fact—ill and broken. To her consternation, he would awake in the night sobbing or stare into the unperceived distance, hiding his demonic nightmares behind a mask of indifference. It was alarming to contrast the shy, pretty youth he had been at sixteen with the haggard, woebegone man of twenty-two, though Eleanor did her best to reassure him and raise his spirits. The catastrophe at Vitry, she told him, was not his fault; if God had permitted the church to burn, that was God's business. The war against Theobald was a just one, involving the honor of both their families. Was not Ralph of his own blood, the son of his grandfather's brother? Was not Petronilla her only sister? But Louis, feeling his soul imperiled, lifted glassy eyes and whimpered that he did not care about victory over Count Theobald. Although he managed to pull himself together and return to Champagne, he continued to suffer agonies of guilt and depression, his every action horrifying and disgusting him. Alone, Eleanor pondered the fate that had tied her to a man she considered contemptible. There was something about his lamentations strongly reminiscent of her father's agitated mood before he set off for Compostela, memories she preferred to forget. She wanted a husband who, like her grandfather, could fight and kill, who would sing songs and pay compliments. Days should be gay and nights spent in the arms of a passionate lover, not with a trembling man who buried himself in her skirts with a child's sobs and whose dreams were convulsed by horrifying visions. Nevertheless, she kept her thoughts to herself and tried to quiet his madness, for she lacked the heart to reproach him.

During these woeful months, those who had ignored omens of danger during the initial years of Louis's reign were no longer able to remain engrossed in their own affairs. Public outcry against the disorders in the realm was such that it became necessary to allocate blame and responsibility for the boy king, no longer a boy. From the stillness of Clairvaux, Abbot Bernard scribbled frenzied letters to discover what had gone wrong. Why did his beloved boy insist upon heaping sin atop sin, perversely laying waste his kingdom until it seemed in danger of cracking? "All this I was able to see," he wrote to Pope Innocent, "but alas! not able to prevent."

To Louis, Bernard worded a sharp demand:

> From whom but the devil could this advice come under which you are acting, advice which causes burnings upon burnings, slaughter upon slaughter, and the voice of the poor and the groans of captives and the blood of the slain to echo once more in the ears of the Father of orphans and the Judge of widows? . . . Those who are urging you to repeat your former wrongdoing against an innocent person [he meant Count Theobald] are seeking in this not your honor but their own convenience, or rather not so much their convenience as the will of the devil; they are trying to use the power of the king to secure the mad purposes which they are not sure of being able to achieve by themselves, and are clearly the enemies of your crown and the disturbers of your realm.

Meanwhile, buoyed by the knowledge that much of Champagne had fallen into Capetian hands, an offer of peace had been tentatively submitted to Count Theobald. The terms were simple: Louis and Eleanor promised to restore his possessions on the condition that he somehow manage to get lifted the sentences of excommunication and interdict on Ralph and Petronilla. Bernard, exhibiting more of the serpent's adroitness than his customary dovelike simplicity, urged Innocent to remove the bans long enough for Louis to return Theobald's territory— and then renew it immediately afterward. "Thus artifice would be out- witted by artifice, and peace obtained without the tyrant . . . gaining anything."

Never suspecting that Innocent, nor certainly Bernard, would be capable of such a deception, Louis ingenuously withdrew his troops, at which time Innocent played his hand expertly by offering Ralph the op- portunity to give up Petronilla. When the count refused, Innocent promptly reexcommunicated the pair; Louis, hysterical, sped his army back to Champagne, wreaking such destruction that Bernard was forced to further remonstrating. "I can tell you that, provoked by the constant excesses you commit almost daily, I am beginning to regret having stupidly favored your youth more than I should have done, and I am determined that in future to the best of my limited capacity I shall expose the whole truth about you. . . . I have spoken harshly because I fear an even harsher fate for you."

On September 24, 1143, Pope Innocent died, and his successor, Celestine II, was sufficiently moved by the disturbances in France to lift the bans of excommunication and interdict against Louis, a measure of clemency that nevertheless brought the king little solace. Nor did tran- quility come quickly or easily to France. In early 1144, Suger and Ber- nard arranged a peace conference at Corbeil, only to watch Louis ex- plode into a fit of blind rage when one of the Frankish barons made a gibe to the effect that Count Ralph led him by the nose. Like a small boy in the grip of a tantrum, he angrily stormed from the parley into the con- soling arms of his wife.

The irrepressible high spirits that Eleanor had displayed during the summer when she became queen of France had now been greatly tem- pered by tragedy, frustration, and an endless procession of small unhappinesses. Her restlessness, the impression she gave of always seeking some new exhilaration, was not so much in evidence, and the delirious melancholy that enveloped her husband inevitably began to rub off on her. As in the first days after her arrival, the Cité Palace had once again assumed the atmosphere of a monastery: no dancing and feasting, no songs of the troubadours. The poets sought more receptive patrons. There was increasing tension between Eleanor and Louis. In public they were polite to each other, but alone in their chambers, it was difficult to maintain even a simple conversation. Taking refuge in impenetrable silences, Louis read his breviary, meditated, and sank deeper into his private hell. Throughout the spring of 1144, he became increasingly remote and either slept alone or shared the royal bed like a sister. Failure weighed heavily on Eleanor, who fixed unseeing eyes on the parchment pages of her books while she brooded over her not-so-secret shame: In seven years of marriage she had not been able to bear a child. After that first pregnancy, she had never conceived again.

Her barrenness was the subject of considerable speculation among the Franks, but Eleanor, starved for sexual satisfaction, needed no prophet to divine the reason for her infertility, and she could not help feeling resentment toward the disconsolate man who caressed his rosary instead of her perfumed and massaged body. Unable to recall the last time he had embraced her, she feared that if his present emotional state continued, the opportunity for conception would not come again. It had been some years since she had counted the days on her fingers and made novenas to Our Lady, or, for that matter, worried about dying in childbirth. At fifteen and sixteen she had menstruated each month without regret, but at twenty-two, she reminded herself that by her age her mother had already borne three children and lay in her tomb at Nieuil-sur-l'Autise. Still, when all was said and done, she suspected that the fault for her empty womb might lie, not with Louis, but within herself. As a queen, her prime duty was to provide the country with an heir to the throne, and the fact that she had not come close to fulfilling this obligation weighted her with humiliation and the faint suspicion that she, like Louis, had somehow offended God. It depressed her to think that the wife of the most miserable varlet could bear a dozen babies, that servingwomen had bastards to drown; even Petronilla, who had plenty of sins for which to atone, had brought forth a son. During that dreary winter, her desire to have children—strong, handsome boys—grew to almost an obsession.

Nevertheless, as it was not her nature to bear discontent tranquilly, she determined to locate an exit from the turmoil encircling the royal family. In June, spirits at the Cité Palace began to slowly levitate as the day approached for the unveiling of Suger's newly built cathedral at Saint-Denis. Louis's spiritual advisers, as concerned about his despondency as Eleanor, hoped that the king's participation in this momentous event might bolster his confidence; in fact, the dedication of the cathedral was to be combined with a second peace conference to mend the conflicts with Champagne.

Saturday, the tenth of June, was a brilliant blue day as Eleanor and Louis began the seven-mile journey to Saint-Denis. They made slow progress because the old Roman road was clogged with scores of cheerful pilgrims—parties of monks, ladies of gentle blood accompanied by their belted knights, whores, thieves, cripples, hymn chanters, and assorted folks from Paris—the whole motley host bound for the abbey to see what miracles had been wrought by Suger's stonemasons and glaziers. Owing to the slow-moving traffic on the highway, Eleanor gave herself up to the small pleasures afforded along the roadside: the tiered vineyards and ruins of an old Roman temple adorning the slopes of Montmartre, the Martyrologium, a small chapel marking the spot where Saint Denis had been martyred. Eventually, they passed into open countryside, where the road ran between ploughed fields, and then it was not long before they arrived at the stone wall and dry ditch enclosing the little town that had grown up around the abbey. As far as Eleanor could see, the fields were dotted with tents hastily thrown up to shelter the multitudes who had no access to accommodations in the local households.

The arrival of the king and queen drew shouts from the crowd and the hurried appearance of Abbot Suger, who came out to personally escort them to the abbey's guest quarters. As Louis hurried off to the cathedral, where he spent the night praying and keeping the vigils with the monks of Saint-Denis, Eleanor was left alone with her thoughts and her maids. The next morning, the feast day of Saint Barnabas, she rose at dawn to take her place in the cathedral. Abbot Suger may have exorcised his personal fascination with corrupting secular luxuries, but he could not believe that the splendor of gold and rubies would be displeasing when dedicated to God. The most expensive marble, glass, and gems had been deposited in the hands of master craftsmen from many nations to produce a symphony in stone and glass. Gone was the earthbound Romanesque style with its massive walls and rounded arches, and in its place Suger had pioneered a bold new architecture that flung pointed arches and towering vaults against the Frankish sky. Inside, vast stained-glass windows bathed his Gothic cathedral in pools of light the color of gems. There was not one altar but twenty; above the high altar glowed a magnificent twenty-foot gold cross glittering with diamonds, rubies, and pearls, the result of two years' work by the goldsmiths of Lorraine. Incense swirled like a gray haze against the altar where the relics of the saint would be placed, and the voices of the congregation surged and mingled with the soaring notes from hundreds of clerics in the choir.

As Suger had planned, Louis played a principal role in the ceremony: It was he who led the solemn procession of bishops and monks around the cathedral as they sprinkled holy water on the outside walls, he who shouldered the silver reliquary holding the bones of Saint Denis and carried it to the altar, where it was laid to rest in a blaze of spun gold and precious stones. The contrast of his gray penitent robes and rude sandals caused a stir among the crowd. "No one would have taken the king for that scourge of war who had lately destroyed so many towns, burned so many churches, shed so much blood. The spirit of penance shone in his whole aspect." By afternoon the weather had turned uncomfortably warm, and the number of worshipers jammed into the cathedral had far exceeded its capacity because there was not a single spare inch on which to stand; outside, additional thousands milled about under the open skies.

Later that day, Eleanor slipped away to a deserted chamber in the abbey, where a private interview had been arranged with Bernard of Clairvaux. It is unclear whether the idea for the meeting had originated with Louis or Bernard or even had been initiated by the queen herself, nor what its real purpose was intended to be. In any case, Eleanor did not lack for words nor did she face the saint with any particular awe. Remembering Bernard's effect on her father at Parthenay a decade earlier, she undoubtedly looked forward to the talk with some wariness and perhaps more than a touch of rancor. Whatever her feelings that evening, she concealed them by deftly launching into a well-rehearsed declaration. She intended to inform the abbot of her uppermost thoughts—and inform him she did. Her desire was to see the ban of excommunication lifted from the house of Vermandois and her sister's marriage be recognized. If the abbot would be kind enough to use his considerable influence on Pope Celestine to see these injustices rectified, then the Capets were prepared to make certain concessions in the prickly matter of Champagne and perhaps conclude a bit of old business, the recognition of Peter de la Châtre as archbishop of Bourges.

Both the content of her speech and the forthright manner in which she presented her ideas amazed and horrified the holy man. He was unaccustomed to bargaining with women and certainly not with one who spoke as boldly as a man and eyed him with shameless curiosity. At the time of this meeting, Bernard was fifty-four. As a youth he had been blond and handsome, but years of deliberate self-abuse had given him ulcers, a digestive system that could barely keep down food, and the appearance of a walking skeleton. "His whole body was meagre and emaciated. His skin itself was of the finest texture, with a slight flush of red on the cheeks. His hair was of a yellow inclining to white; his beard was auburn, sprinkled towards the end of his life with grey." He preferred filth to cleanliness and wore a hair shirt next to his skin.

Although legend maintains that he was "hot in burning love," this did not include the love of women, most assuredly not a woman like Eleanor. While he had adored his mother, nearly all other women he feared, regarding them as snares of Satan. Familiar with sexual desire, he had once, in adolescence, glanced admiringly at a girl and immediately felt such shame that he threw himself into an icy pond, remaining there until he almost froze. His hostility toward the female sex extended to his sister Hombeline, who had chosen to marry and raise a family rather than enter a convent. Once, gorgeously dressed and trailed by a huge retinue of servants, she appeared at the gates of Clairvaux, but Bernard refused to see her. He sent a message with their brother Andrew to declare her no better than a whore, a bait of the devil to lure men to destruction.

Although Eleanor and Bernard had never met before, he had once beheld her from a distance, probably in 1140 at the Sens debate with Peter Abélard. Illustrious princesses and great lords meant nothing to Bernard, so there must have been something exceptionally magnificent about Eleanor and her ladies-in-waiting to captivate his attention so thoroughly. He must have watched those exquisites for quite a time, because later he had them so well fixed in his mind that he could offer a description to the maiden Sophia "that she may never sully her virginity but attain its reward." It is ironic that the only surviving physical portrait of Eleanor comes from a man who viewed her as a Babylonian harlot:

> You see women burdened rather than adorned with ornaments of gold, silver and precious stones, and all the raiment of a court. You see them dragging long trains of most precious material behind them, stirring up clouds of dust as they go. . . . The ornaments of a queen have no beauty like to the blushes of natural modesty which color the cheeks of a virgin. . . . Silk, purple and paint have their beauty but they do not make the body beautiful. The comeliness which goes on with clothes comes off with clothes, it belongs to the clothes and not the clothed. Thus do not emulate evil-doers. . . . Consider it wholly beneath you to borrow your appearance from the furs of animals and the work of worms.

Bernard remembered the queen as one of "those daughters of Belial who put on airs, walk with heads high and, with mincing steps, got up and adorned like a temple." Still, on that summer evening at Saint-Denis, he was able to contemplate her with an appraising eye, perhaps he even managed to overlook her appalling costume, but he was hard put to conceal his dismay at her manner. He had expected contriteness, sorrow, even pleas for forgiveness, but unlike her husband, Eleanor did not approach him as a penitent; she did not mention Vitry. Instead, he heard her daring to haggle with God, speaking indelicately of bargains and adultery and influences upon the pope. By the time she had finished, he had localized to his own satisfaction the true identity of the king's "evil genius." At this point, claim the chroniclers, Bernard commanded the queen to stop meddling in affairs of state, rebuking her so harshly that Eleanor broke down and meekly excused her behavior by saying she had been embittered by her inability to have children.

Since there were no witnesses present, the details of this scene are open to question. It is impossible to say whether she was transformed by Bernard's hypnotic personality. Certainly more august personages than she had fallen at his feet. A more likely explanation was that Eleanor, above all else a pragmatist, quickly reevaluated her position. Although it must have been galling to accept, she understood that Ralph and Petronilla had become an incurably lost cause. Rightly or wrongly, she had done everything within her power to help them, and much that she had reason to regret. Now, casting aside family loyalty, she opted for her own concerns and played the heretofore unsampled role of suppliant by presenting to the miracle maker her curable sorrow, the lack of an heir.

Bernard knew her history. In his eyes, she had sprung from adulterous grandparents and an ungodly father whose stubbornness had nearly wrecked the Church. The family was a worthless lot, arrogant, self-willed, always seeking worldly thrills and plucking the beards of the clergy when they could not get their ways. Little wonder that the offspring of such people had strayed so far from the paths of righteousness. But now Bernard could not help rejoicing that the "daughter of Belial" wished to return to the fold by aspiring to the pious objective of motherhood. "My child," he allegedly said to her, "seek those things which make for peace. Cease to stir up the king against the Church and urge upon him a better course of action. If you will promise to do this, I in my turn promise to entreat the merciful Lord to grant you offspring." Bernard had disdained to negotiate with a woman, and yet, in the end, Eleanor was able to extract the bargain she most desired.

Pact completed, the saint and the queen took leave of each other. Behind the abbey, the sun had set. Dusk hid the tall windows, but row upon row of candles could be seen gleaming through the open bronze portals. Through the shadows tonsured monks softly tramped in their black robes. The scent of incense and damp grass fluttered slowly on the crest of the evening breeze as Eleanor, exultant, hurried away to find her husband.

Within weeks, peace returned to France as Louis handed over Theobald's war-torn provinces and admitted Peter de la Châtre to the archbishopric of Bourges. The papal bans on the house of Vermandois, never removed, would be ignored in time, however. Four years later, the papacy would recognize the validity of Ralph and Petronilla's marriage, but Bernard quickly declared that they would not enjoy each other for long, and that, moreover, no children of their union would bear worthy fruit. In both respects, his predictions turned out to be fairly accurate. Ralph died in 1151. Their son, Ralph, became a leper and died in his early twenties; their daughters, Isabella and Eleanor, would have four marriages between them but neither proved able to bear children.

Eleanor, faithful to her word, kept her half of the bargain she had made with Bernard; the abbot of Clairvaux, however, was less successful. The following year Eleanor gave birth, not to the manchild she had ordered but to a daughter, whom she named Marie in honor of the Queen of Heaven.

In 1145, strife shook many of the European nations: In England, the death of Henry I ten years earlier had sparked a bitter civil war between the king's chosen successor, his daughter Matilda, and his nephew Stephen, who had seized the throne; France's neighbor, the Holy Roman Empire, reeled with internal struggles; and in Rome, the anticlerical agitator Arnold of Brescia forced the new pope, Eugenius III, to flee the Holy City and take refuge at Viterbo. In France, however, there was peace. At the Cité Palace, King Louis fasted three days a week and prayed incessantly. Following the havoc of the war, cooler heads undertook to get the young king in hand, and now he allowed himself to be guided in all matters by his advisers, notably Abbot Suger, who had returned to court as chief counselor; Eleanor, who had promised Bernard that she would allow the ship of state to be navigated by male hands, behaved most cooperatively, and that autumn, when anarchy broke out in a section of Aquitaine called Aunis, she stood aside while Louis settled the dispute. The cumbersome days passed slowly, one indistinguishable from another, and although Eleanor now had a child, the care of the infant Princess Marie rested largely in the hands of nurses. The queen found it increasingly hard to live like a nun, and lacking suitable diversions, her boredom intensified. To make matters worse, the foreseeable future held no presentiment of deliverance.

During the intolerable winter evenings when king and queen sat alone in their apartment, Louis would muse fitfully about the past and future. Memories of the war still burned in his imagination, and although he no longer suffered nightmares, he had never completely recovered from the incident at Vitry. Or, as it was now called, Vitry-le-Brûlé. He had done what he could to help rebuild the burned town, he wore a hair shirt next to his pale skin and fasted until he grew weak, but still the deadly sin haunted him, and he could think of no ordeal severe enough to wipe out his transgressions. Except perhaps one: a pilgrimage to the Holy Land. The vision of such a journey had been swimming before his eyes since childhood, when his life had been dedicated to the Church, and many times he had imagined himself tramping the road to Jerusalem, spending Easter in the Holy Sepulcher. To his wife, he now confided another secret: His elder brother, Philip, had dreamed of visiting the tomb of Christ, and when he had been killed, the ten-year-old Louis had made a vow to go on the pilgrimage in his place. Eleanor listened with one ear to the monotonous litany of his guilt, for she had heard it countless times; however, she could well understand his fantasies about distant lands, for she too knew the impulse to escape.

That year of 1145 they planned to hold Christmas court at Bourges, dispatching well in advance announcements to summon their vassals. As it happened, before Christmas there appeared a divine solution to both of the Capets' maladies in the form of a papal bull. Ever since the capture of Jerusalem nearly fifty years earlier, the West had fallen into the habit of viewing Outremer as a Christian province. Then in the closing days of 1144, the renowned city of Edessa had been overrun by the Turks. It seemed that Count Joscelin had been absent from his capital, celebrating Christmas on the banks of the Euphrates, a more pleasant section of the country. In fact, lately Joscelin had been spending most of his time in extravagant dissipation on his estate at Turbessel, and consequently he had been able to ignore the activities of a Turk named Zengi. The governor of Aleppo and Mosul, Zengi was a great warrior who, rumor said, had sprung from an Amazon, the Margravine Ida of Austria, who had supposedly been captured during the First Crusade and swept away to a harem. Whatever Zengi's true heritage, he was shrewd enough to realize that Edessa, the most vulnerable of the Frankish capitals in Syria, represented an opportunity too golden to miss. The careless Joscelin had not thought to supply Edessa with a strong garrison or reserves of food, and for that reason Zengi was able to mount a siege with little difficulty. On December 26, 1144, the Turkish army swarmed into the city and massacred all the Franks, including their archbishop, as well as many of the native Christians. Naturally the reconquest of this important Christian city, so easily retrieved from its Frankish masters, strengthened Zengi's position; he had no intention of interrupting his good luck by stopping with Edessa. The whole Latin Kingdom of Jerusalem now lay exposed to the infidel, and nobody understood the threat better than Joscelin's neighbor, Prince Raymond of Antioch.

Although rumors of disturbances in the Holy Land had been filtering back to Europe throughout much of 1145, not until autumn did there arrive at the exiled papal court in Viterbo an official plea from Queen Melisende of Jerusalem urgently requesting Eugenius to preach a new Crusade. Since his accession in February, the pope had been unable to enter Rome, and he could hardly afford to further jeopardize his shaky position by traveling beyond the Alps to personally direct a movement as had Pope Urban. It was to King Louis that the pope decided to turn for aid. Although he was well aware of Louis's troubles with the Church, the king's former waywardness was not, apparently, a consideration. Rather, since Louis was king of the land from which most of the Frankish princes in Outremer had come, he seemed the obvious leader of an expedition that would relieve them. Accordingly, on December 1, 1145, Eugenius dictated a bull urging Louis and all the faithful of the kingdom of France to rescue eastern Christendom from the infidel and promised them remission for their sins, a reminder that there was more to the Crusade than purely military objectives.

The Capets—both of them—responded eagerly to the call, a development that Eugenius could scarcely have foreseen. In truth, the arrival of the papal bull catapulted Eleanor out of her malaise and suddenly opened up unlimited horizons certain to purge whatever afflictions ailed her. At Christmas court, Eleanor sat impatiently at Louis's side as he addressed the assembled barons and prelates and revealed "the secret in his heart." At once she could see that he was going about the announcement in precisely the wrong manner by stressing the idea of penance and awkwardly rambling on about his personal desire to take the cross as an expiation for his sins at Vitry. Even though Bishop Geoffrey of Langres delivered an eloquent sermon exhorting the barons of France and Aquitaine to follow their sovereign's lead, the Crusade was received with chilly indifference. Eleanor, disappointed but hardly surprised, had already spoken privately with many of her southern chieftains, and she knew that few of them cared about the possible damnation of Louis's soul. Instead, the proposal for a new Crusade only succeeded in awakening memories of the last one, that disastrous expedition led by Eleanor's grandfather. Many were of the opinion that it would be foolhardy to emulate their fathers and grandfathers, who had been in such a hurry to reach heaven that they mortgaged their lands and rushed off to be martyred many leagues before they reached Jerusalem. With that, she could not argue.

But it was not only the southerners who held back; the Franks exhibited little enthusiasm for a Crusade, too. Among those who voiced disapproval was the elder statesman of the realm, Abbot Suger: God, he said, would be best served by the efficient and peaceful administration of the kingdom; if Louis absented himself for a year or more, the country might very well lapse into widespread disorder again. If the king truly wished to fight the enemies of Christ, there were plenty of heretics he could wipe out in France. Beneath Suger's careful reasoning lay ripples of panic that were not totally irrational. The ebullient mood of the king and queen made him profoundly nervous, a feeling only increased by the information that Eleanor also planned to take the cross. From past experience, he knew that their high spirits often preceded some unfortunate incident; with Louis's immaturity, there was no telling what folly might befall a crusading army under his leadership. Furthermore, there was always the possibility that he might be killed, leaving the kingdom without a male heir. Most of these misgivings Suger did not voice, but nevertheless he strongly urged the king and queen, if not to abandon their plan, at least to delay and reflect.

Despite Suger's open opposition, Eleanor stoutly set about counteracting Louis's negative appeal. Using her influence as best she could, she moved among her Aquitainian vassals with a fiery tongue, urging them to reconsider, playing upon their pride, chastising the cowardly and encouraging the ambitious. After a number of intimate parleys in the *langue d'oc*, she was able to change a few minds but clearly not enough for her purposes. If she could rally the lords of Aquitaine to her side, they would outnumber Louis's French vassals and assure the Crusade as a viable project. Still, as the Christmas court drew to a close, the expedition hung in the balance. It was Suger, hoping to gain time as well as partisans, who suggested that the decision be postponed until March 31, 1146, when a plenary assembly was scheduled to be held at Vézelay. Meanwhile, an appeal had already gone out from Pope Eugenius to the one man in France who might sway a nation into embarking on a holy war: Bernard of Clairvaux. To Suger's dismay, Bernard readily agreed to preach the Crusade.

A weak spring sunshine covered the hills of Burgundy. For months the news that Saint Bernard would preach at Vézelay on Easter Sunday had been radiating to the far corners of the kingdom and beyond. The town bustled with the cheerful noise of a crowd on a holiday, sightseers eager to glimpse the saint and to inspect the new Cathedral of Saint Mary Magdalene, which crowned the city on the hill. As at Clermont a half century earlier, the throngs were too great to be contained under any other roof but heaven. "And since there was no place within the town which could accommodate such a large crowd, a wooden platform was erected outside in a field, so that the abbot could speak from an elevation to the people standing about." It might have been a fairground, the field rippling with wimples and skullcaps and hoods, the platform blossoming with the colorful robes of the king and queen accompanied by their retinue of counselors and noblemen, bishops and statesmen. At the sight of Bernard mounting the dais, a tense silence descended on the crowd, for the old man, emaciated from his years of fasting, appeared close to death. Nevertheless, once he began to speak, his voice trumpeted forth loud and clear, reverberating through the crowd to tear their hearts and stir their holy rage. As the sound of his voice rang over the hillside, the words seemed, to those gathered there, as music from an angel who had suddenly dropped from the clouds. His words have not been handed down; we know only that he read the papal bull calling for a holy expedition and promising absolution for all who took the cross, but to think that he would not have embellished the papal letter with his incomparable rhetoric is inconceivable. At last, unable to restrain themselves, the people broke into discordant waves of applause and shouts of "To Jerusalem" and then there was silence once more. King Louis was moving forward to speak, but after only a few words he dissolved into the tears that came so easily to him and prostrated himself before the abbot to receive the cross.

Still under Bernard's spell, Louis's vassals forgot their earlier coolness in their eagerness to receive a cross from the abbot's own wasted hands. In every dialect of Gaul, they began to cry out, "Crosses, give us crosses!" and so great was the clamor that the hills and fields and woods seemed to echo back, "Crosses!" Soon Bernard's supply was exhausted, "and when he had sowed, rather than distributed, the parcel of crosses which he had prepared beforehand, he was forced to tear his own garments and to sow them abroad." It went on until nightfall. The feudal lords had fallen into orderly ranks, and by the light of cressets and lanterns they waited their turn to approach the man of God. Private feuds forgotten, enemies standing shoulder to shoulder, that Sunday they were all brothers enlisting in the army of Christ. In the file could be seen Count Theobald's eldest son, Henry; Alphonse-Jourdain, from whom Louis and Eleanor had tried to wrest Toulouse; Louis's brother

Robert, count of Dreux; Thierry, count of Flanders; Archibald of Bourbon; Enguerrand of Coucy; the king's uncle, Count Amadeus II; the bishops of Langres, Arras, and Lisieux; and many, many others, whose names the chroniclers did not know or lacked the parchment to list.

At some point during the daylong procession, Eleanor knelt before the abbot to receive her cross. By no means was she the only woman to do so; among the noble ladies who took the cross on Easter Sunday, we know the names of Sybille of Flanders, Faydide of Toulouse, Torqueri of Bouillon, and Florine of Burgundy, and there were wives and daughters of other great lords who followed the queen's example. Later, after the newly blessed *cruciati* had returned to their homes, stories were told describing Queen Eleanor and her ladies as a troop of armed Amazons. Dressed in cherry red boots and white tunics, with the crimson cross splashed across their breasts, they had galloped on white horses over the hillside at Vézelay brandishing swords and spurring the faint-hearted to heed the call of the Almighty. Or so it was said. From what most people knew of their flamboyant queen, the tale sounded completely in character, and those who had been present at Vézelay did not bother to disillusion them, indeed they themselves may have embroidered a few of the fabulous details. The stories only added to the general excitement and, for that matter, probably stimulated recruiting.

Later, Louis would be severely censured for permitting Eleanor to accompany him. The chroniclers would claim that, mistrusting the queen out of his sight, he had been motivated by burning jealousy. William of Newburgh, writing some fifty years after Vézelay, advances the theory that the king so adored his beautiful wife that he could not bear to be separated from her. A more reasonable explanation is simply that in the spring of 1145 few, except perhaps Abbot Suger, ever thought to question Eleanor's decision to take the cross. Contrary to what is sometimes believed, there was nothing very unusual about a woman going on Crusade. During the first expedition to the Holy Land, many noble ladies accompanied their lords. Count Alphonse-Jourdain of Toulouse had been born in the East and owed his name to the fact that he had been baptized in the waters of the river Jordan. Even on the so-called People's Crusade led by Peter the Hermit, the army of the poor was not made up principally of men; there were also a great many women and children. Throughout Eleanor's childhood, she had grown accustomed to the sight of female pilgrims; in the spring and summer, the roads of Aquitaine had been thronged with travelers bound for Compostela or Rome or Jerusalem, and many of them were women.

But, of course, there was more to her decision. At the very word *crusade,* intoxicating memories moved in her mind. Despite William the Troubadour's unfortunate experiences on the road to Jerusalem, he had managed to transcend disaster by writing of it in honeyed rhyme. Creating material for jongleur and minstrel, his odyssey had been transmuted into high adventure, and Eleanor remembered his songs with inexpressible nostalgia. With her grandfather's Crusade had traveled one of the most famous beauties of her time, the Margravine Ida of Austria, who had raised a contingent of troops and rode at their head. The fact remained that the Margravine had been among those lost during the massacre, but Eleanor no doubt preferred to believe that this admirable woman had somehow escaped. That a similar fate might await women during the Second Crusade seemed absurd. By the middle of the twelfth century, pilgrimages to the Holy Land were no longer novel; in fact, they had become the medieval version of the grand tour, excursions that persons of consequence undertook for their own spiritual and cultural enrichment.

The desire to visit the Holy Land was widespread and deeply implanted in the nature of medieval men and women. To many Christians, the desire to worship Christ in Jerusalem was an overriding emotion that enabled them to endure the dangers of a medieval journey, to face slow death from starvation or sudden death by murder en route, or to risk capture and enslavement by the Moslems. The reasons for taking the cross were as varied as the Crusaders themselves. For some, like Louis, the journey held out the hope of pardon from sin; for others, it was a means of escape from a dreary existence. While Eleanor would seem to fall into the latter category, she was by no means devoid of religious zeal; however, she was most religious when her interests and God's interests happened to coincide. Bathed in extreme boredom at her drafty castle on the Seine, how she must have leaped at the opportunity to become a Crusader. What incomparable avenues opened to her, what marvels waited Beyond the Sea, where there was no rain or snow, what tales she would bring back to mesmerize her grandchildren on long winter evenings!

Her yearnings for adventure were no more suspect than Louis's. "To him, taking the cross was a mystical adventure rather than a political move. But after a half century of rule in Jerusalem, he was convinced, as King of France, that the French crown had a messianic role to play and believed that he was following in the footsteps of Charlemagne, who, according to generally accepted tradition, had made the pilgrimage to Jerusalem." Popular legend had it that a Christian monarch, perhaps a reincarnation of Charlemagne, would bring about the millenium by taking possession of Jerusalem. In those months after Vézelay, there could be found numerous "prophets" swearing that Louis was the king who would usher in the thousand years of peace preceding the final triumph of Jesus Christ.

Largely overlooked in the excitement was one crucial fact: Louis's Crusade had arisen from dire political necessity. Not only had Jerusalem's Queen Melisende sounded the alarm for help, but Prince Raymond of Antioch could also see calamity overtaking him unless reinforcements appeared from the West. Unlike Count Joscelin, he observed the dangers clearly, and it was only natural that he should think of his niece, the queen of the Franks. In September of that year, when Zengi was assassinated by a disgruntled servant, he believed his troubles to be over; to his consternation, however, he soon discovered that Zengi's son, Nureddin, was no less fierce and warlike than his father, and a religious fanatic to boot. It is certain that Raymond sent his own messengers to the Capetian court, acquainting Louis and Eleanor with the details of the Turkish threat and stressing the gravity of his plight. William of Tyre relates that the prince wooed his relatives in Paris with "noble gifts and treasures of great price in the hope of winning favor." He might have saved himself the trouble, for Eleanor and Louis needed no added inducements.

The Crusade was scheduled to depart in the spring of 1147, but in the meantime there was much to be done. More was needed than merely the approval of the pope and the promises of princes; such an enterprise would have been doomed without the support of the general populace. There is no question that Eleanor worked tirelessly to assure the success of the operation by contributing to the recruiting of soldiers and the collection of money. After returning from the stirring events at Vézelay, she immediately set off on a personal tour of Aquitaine, proclaiming tournaments to rally knights and petty castellans and renewing special privileges enjoyed by abbeys in exchange for their financial support. At Fontevrault, for instance, she guaranteed the abbey a profit of five hundred sous from a fair held in Poitiers, and similar gifts were made to Montierneuf, La Grace-Dieu, and other religious foundations. Owing to her efforts and, very likely, to her dashing example, a remarkably high proportion of the Crusaders would come from Aquitaine, among them Geoffrey de Rancon, the lord of Taillebourg castle, where she and Louis had spent their wedding night; Saldebreuil of Sanzay, whom she had made her constable; Hugh of Lusignan; and Guy of Thouars. If Bernard of Clairvaux viewed her activity as a form of backsliding from their agreement, he did not voice his objections, for at least her efforts were focused on a pious cause.

While Eleanor carried the call to arms to the southland, the indefatigable Bernard was preaching in Burgundy, Lorraine, Flanders, and finally he embarked on an extensive tour of the Rhineland. That year crops had failed in Germany, and since there was widespread famine, hunger undoubtedly moved many to take the cross in hope of winning food and riches in the East. Their emperor, Conrad of Hohenstaufen, admired Bernard, but his position in Germany remained shaky, and he had little enthusiasm for a foreign war with so many enemies in his own yard. Frail and tremulous, Bernard circled Conrad like an aging bloodhound. Time after time he petitioned the sober emperor, only to meet with polite rebuffs. Finally, at Christmas, he cornered Conrad at Speyer, and speaking as though he were Christ himself, reminded the Holy Roman emperor of all the favors heaven had showered upon him: "O man, what have I not done for thee that I ought to have done?" The next day Conrad took the cross.

Bernard had left Clairvaux in the autumn of 1146, and he would not return until spring of the following year. So spectacular were the results of his labors that he was able to write to Pope Eugenius: "You have ordered and I have obeyed, and your authority has made my obedience fruitful. I have declared and I have spoken, and they [the Crusaders] are multiplied above number. Towns and castles are emptied, one may scarcely find one man among seven women, so many women are there widowed while their husbands are still alive."

Enthusiasm for the Crusade could not have been called universal, however, if only because such a vast operation required unusually large sums of money. "For this purpose there was a general exaction levied throughout Gaul: neither sex, rank nor dignity was spared or excused from contributing aid to the king. For which reason his pilgrimage was followed by the imprecations of his subjects." Despite whisperings and anger, the expedition slowly began to mobilize. There were innumerable decisions to be made: how to arrange transportation for 100,000 persons; how to assure a supply of food for a journey of nearly unimaginable distance; how to find responsible guides to convey them through strange lands. In all these matters the king displayed an uncharacteristic amount of initiative and efficiency.

The winter came, all the more bleak and devastating because so many were dreaming about a land where the sun always shone. Thirty miles south of Paris, snow drifts blanketed the fields of Étampes on

February 16, 1147, as Louis's barons and bishops arrived for a three-day conference to discuss preparations. Icy winds pierced their cloaks, and even inside near the castle's great hearth the men shivered and the smoke-blackened tapestries billowed along the walls. Notwithstanding the weather, spirits ran exceptionally high. Louis had promised that each would have an equal voice in the planning session, a decision for which Abbot Suger and Eleanor could only feel a measure of relief. On Sunday the sixteenth, the king opened the assembly with a report on his accomplishments to date: He had received favorable responses to his requests to the Germans and Hungarians asking permission to pass through their lands and to trade at their markets. Deputies whom he had sent to the Byzantine emperor, Manuel Comnenus, and to Roger, the Norman king of Sicily, had evoked a flurry of invitations and promises, which he intended to lay before the council for discussion. This last matter occupied their attention for much of the conference because the question of route—by sea or overland through Constantinople—was of critical importance. Obsequious letters were read from Manuel Comnenus, who, despite Byzantium's unsettling experiences with Crusaders in the past, nevertheless effusively extended hospitality and support. King Roger sent special envoys offering to transport—for a price—the army by sea.

In the lively discussion that followed, there were those who strongly favored Roger's plan: A sea voyage would eliminate the difficulties of guiding an army down the Danube and across unknown territory into Asia Minor and, furthermore, would bypass the Greeks, of whose perfidy many Franks were convinced. Other barons preferred the land route, the same one transversed by the First Crusade, and they pointed out that Roger, presently at war with Byzantium, had only made the offer to strengthen his own position. Moreover, everyone knew the Normans were notorious for their wiliness, and many said frankly that Roger meant them no good. By process of open debate, the arguments were presented, the advantages and disadvantages thrashed out, until a majority agreed that the Crusade would travel by land. In the long run, it was safer and cheaper.

Once they had reached agreement on these arrangements, the council took up the question of who would govern the kingdom in Louis's absence. The choice fell on Abbot Suger and on William, count of Nevers, but the latter declined by suddenly announcing his intention to enter the monastery of Chartreuse. Suger was only slightly more enthusiastic about accepting the regency, "because he considered it a burden rather than an honor." As the meeting ended, it was decided that the Crusade would depart three months hence. The place of rendevous: Metz.

On June 11, 1147, the bells tolled until the sky above the rooftops of Saint-Denis vibrated with an endless clangor. The cathedral had been draped with flags and gonfalons, and in the blaze of thousands of candles the red crosses on pennants and tunics seemed as if they had caught fire. Pope Eugenius had crossed the Alps to officiate, and it was he who opened the small door before the high altar and, removing the silver chest containing the bones of Saint Denis, offered the precious relic for the king's kiss. When Eugenius took down the sacred banner of France, the red and gold silk oriflamme, which left the abbey only on extraordinary occasions, and placed its gilded pike in Louis's hands, the voices of the faithful sounded a triumphant roar. The sight of the crosses shimmering in the candlelight and of the sacred banner against Louis's black pilgrim's tunic made victory seem a certainty.

Throughout the long consecration ceremony Eleanor wept, but whether from emotion or fatigue it was hard to say. Standing next to her mother-in-law, who was making a rare public apperance, Eleanor felt faint from the suffocating air and longed for Eugenius to end the proceedings by bestowing on Louis the traditional pilgrim's wallet and pronouncing the blessing. "The crowds and the king's wife and his mother, who nearly perished because of their tears and the heat, could not endure the delay; but to wish to depict the grief and wailing which occurred is as foolish as it is impossible." Earlier that morning, Louis had visited a leper colony outside the gates of Paris and kissed some of its astonished inhabitants after asking their blessing, a stunt that Eleanor without doubt must have regarded as insane if not totally unnecessary. That day she had seen little of her husband, and now she watched his exhausted figure slip from the cathedral in the direction of the monk's dormitory. That evening, while Louis and his retinue dined in the refectory with the brothers, Eleanor remained in the guest quarters of the abbey and concentrated on the morrow, which she had been awaiting so eagerly. The past year had been a time of hectic activity and almost incessant work of the type she most enjoyed, and even when there had been no more men to enlist or money to solicit, she had not been idle but spent the remaining weeks attending to personal preparations. Appreciative of the hardships that the journey might entail, she wanted to be prepared for every contingency and thus took the precaution of packing all items she might conceivably require. Into chests were folded layer upon layer of clothes so that she might change frequently on the road and present a smart appearance in Constantinople and Antioch. Let no one say that the queen of the Franks had entered the sophisticated cities of the East looking like a rustic. Into the chests also went a suitable collection of jewelry, wimples, slippers, cosmetics, belts, furs to ward off the cold, and veils to prevent sunburn. As insurance against bad weather she brought several tents; for sleeping comfort she carted along pallet beds with good mattresses for herself and her maids; to prevent illness—although she had exceptionally good health—there were carpets to cover the sodden earth. Other boxes held cooking utensils, bowls, goblets, washbasins, soap, napkins, and towels. Altogether, Eleanor's personal belongings, along with those of the other noblewomen traveling on the expedition, filled a stupefying line of wagons, and some of the more experienced Crusaders found cause for complaint. They grumbled about excess baggage, about the presence of so many women with their chambermaids, and later, when mishaps occurred, they would remember those heavy wagon trains laden with feminine accoutrements.

Crossing Champagne from Saint-Denis to Metz, swaying in the chair-saddle strapped sideways on her palfrey, invisible shackles dropped from Eleanor's arms. Thanks be to God, there would be countless months before she need return to the humdrum beat of ordinary life. Each day would bring fresh sights, unimaginable wonders to delight the eye and dazzle the senses. Already she could see the glassy green waters of the Danube, the saffron-colored sunsets over the Golden Horn, the rich bazaars and domed churches of Constantinople. In Antioch she would be reunited with her Uncle Raymond, and there would be laughter and singing in the *langue d'oc* just as in the old days. By spring they would reach the Holy Land in time to celebrate Easter in the very spot where Lord Jesus had walked and the Blessed Virgin had wept. Thanks be to God, she had everything to look forward to.

Secretly Eleanor must have felt grateful that she would not be traveling with Louis, for he had surrounded himself with the most sanctimonious of sycophants: Odo de Deuil, his former secretary, would be acting as chaplain and scribbling notes for a proposed chronicle of the expedition, and Thierry Galeran, a grim-visaged eunuch who had always disliked her, had been chosen as Louis's personal bodyguard and business adviser. Both men, she knew, would be sharing her husband's tent. Under the circumstances, she preferred her own entourage, handpicked to suit her taste: knights from Aquitaine, favorite ladies cast along the same lines as herself, troubadours and jongleurs who had flocked to her side despite the Vézelay bull expressly forbidding their presence—all congenial traveling companions who knew how to laugh and sing freely and who made prayers of appropriate length.

Long before they reached Metz, the road became jammed with troops hastening for the mobilization point, and the air was filled with the thump of hoofs, with creaking wagon wheels, and with the excited voices of the crossbearers. There were nearly 100,000 of them, so many that when they had all finally pitched their tents on the banks of the Moselle, it seemed as though some great metropolis had magically erupted from the bowels of the earth overnight. At the sight of the army that she had been instrumental in bringing to life, Eleanor could not have helped but feel proud. Never could she have dreamed that seething ocean of people, horses, tents, and wagons, herds of sheep and cattle. The weather was fair, and an atmosphere of joyful liberation from all restraints of ordinary living pervaded the camp. The meadows, which had rippled with grass a few days earlier, were soon crisscrossed by ruts and whipped into a bed of mud and dung from so many men and animals. The pavilions resounded with laughter and the sound of minstrels playing lays on their viols, and everywhere people sang hymns and marching songs. The arrival of each new company— Poitevins, Normans, Bretons, Toulousains—would be greeted with boisterous cheers as kinsman, old friends, and comrades from past campaigns were reunited. People strolled from tent to tent, feverishly talking and drinking good wine, until the pandemonium drowned out the cries of the birds and the neighs of the chargers and packhorses. In the tents of the victuallers, there were wine, bread and pastries, fruit and fish, roasted birds, cakes and venison; everywhere there was plenty to buy—for those who had the means to pay.

In the dew-soaked dawn of a morning in mid-June, the army began to move at last. As the procession made its way past the walls of Metz, church bells were pealing and crowds of women, children, old men, and beggars came to witness the greatest show they would ever see: They leaned from windows and turrets decked with red banners, they sat on the tops of walls, they lined the road and clustered at crossroads to watch the column pass. At the sight of the queen, they cried out in amazement, exclaiming over her gorgeous robes embroidered with the royal fleur-de-lis and her magnificent riding horse with its silver-trimmed saddle and plaited mane. "Pray for us in Jerusalem, lady!" they called out, and "Holy Cross" and "For Christ Jesus!" They gazed with shining eyes at King Louis, off to Jerusalem on God's business, and they cheered his distinguished lords, who bore their handsome bodies stiff and upright. Down the road marched the iron men, the enamel-helmeted knights, who bore banners emblazoned with the cross and swords studded with gems and pieces of the True Cross set in the hilts, swords that had been blessed and twice-blessed by priests and bishops. Alongside the knights rode young squires leading destriers and carrying their masters' shields. And then came the foot soldiers, so many companies of them that they could not even be counted.

As the hours passed, the townsfolk grew weary of staring and cheering. There was so much to see, more than the senses could bear: horses, donkeys, and mules, leaving heaps of warm yellow dung in the road; archers with long bows and quivers slung over their shoulders; technicians who possessed the critical skills for building siege engines and battering walls; carts and wagons piled high with arms, baggage, tents, tools, and field kitchens. Brilliant as peacocks, the noble ladies moved by on horseback and litters, surrounded by their maids and minstrels; some carried falcons on their wrists and could be seen loosing them at birds circling overhead. The earth seemed to tremble with the clatter of hoofs, and still the waves of humanity rushed steadily forward down the road leading to God's Holy City: tatterdemalion pilgrims plodding on penitent feet, washerwomen, volunteer martyrs, seamstresses, bishops, criminals seeking salvation, beggars and those temporarily unemployed, vagabonds of all descriptions, concubines and free-lance whores, packs of hunting dogs and pet monkeys and hooded birds. Somewhere in that unruly torrent rode Jaufre Rudel, the prince of Blaye, that high-born Provençal troubadour who wrote passionate verse about a mysterious lady he had never seen, his "faraway love." The carts creaked and the rein chains jangled; gusts of laughter were muffled by the clanking of shields, and from time to time a flute trilled lazily in the early-summer heat.

Looking at the bright blue sky overhead, at the vast column blending into the horizon behind her, Eleanor forgot the dark lanes of the Île-de-France, forgot the infant Marie, even forgot that somewhere in that awesome procession rode her husband. Her past, those twenty-five years washed with sweetness and sorrow, lay behind. Ahead were rivers and mountains and celestial cities.

To Jerusalem

The crusading army moved at a brisk pace over central Europe toward the Rhine, often covering ten to twenty miles each day. Through wooded country, past a wealth of streams, springs, and meadows, the host sprawled out along the road as far as the eye could see and sometimes spilled over into the adjoining fields. Rolling along like an awkward thousand-legged dinosaur, it brought to a standstill the normal activities of the towns in its path and caused civilian travelers to relinquish their places on the highway until the Crusaders had moved by.

During those last days of June 1147, it was easy to forget the religious nature of their mission. Gawking like sightseers on a conducted tour, admiring castles and clucking extravagantly over each toy village, the *cruciati* swore the woods to be a lusher shade of jade than they had ever seen before, the ploughed fields moister and blacker. After a week or so, however, they became acclimated to the scenery. One mountain, after all, was not so different from another, the towns all began to look alike, and gradually they stopped staring and admiring. The indistinguishable summer days began to melt together, with the first week passing like a dream in which time has lost its ordinary meaning. In all this excitement, Eleanor did not remain untouched. Surrounded by the ladies and knights of her native land, she perhaps felt this sense of disassociation more strongly than others. Immediately, there sprang up between her and the Aquitainians an easy camaraderie that must have recalled her childhood. Days would pass when she would speak nothing but her native dialect, which is to say there were long stretches when she did not see Louis and probably rarely thought of him. Hearing the easy laughter and familiar drawling voices, she was certainly transported back in time to the warm afternoons when she rode through Poitou on one of her father's *chevauchées*. If now she laughed and flirted, conducted herself more like a giddy young girl than a twenty-five-year-old queen, presumably that was because she did not feel obliged to behave otherwise. After the restless years in Paris, a summer of happy, if temporary, distraction was much to her taste.

Her aimless days adhered, nevertheless, to a strict pattern. Each morning she awoke before dawn to hear the camp bustling to life around her, the tents being dismantled, the carts harnessed. By the time the first embers of day began to heat the sky, she had dressed, attended to her devotions, and joined the bleary-eyed throngs on the road. Not until late afternoon would the call to halt sound. Then, as the soldiers began to set up the camp for the night, fires would be lit, dusty robes changed, and for Eleanor and the other high-born ladies, baths drawn. Later, when the wind was soft, the darkness would resonate with sounds of music and laughter as Eleanor and her household gathered in torch-lit tents or outside around a fire. All types of performers, including the forbidden troubadours, provided a veritable host of festivities and merriment for the entertainment of the nobility. This is not to suggest that hilarity prevailed throughout the entire camp; indeed, it was limited almost entirely to the contingent from Aquitaine, a fact that did not fail to attract the notice of the more devout Franks, who muttered that the Crusade was quickly degenerating into a pleasure party.

On the previous Crusade, women following the cross had lived as men and endured the same conditions, neither asking for special privileges nor receiving any. This time, obviously, it was to be different. Clearly the ladies were suffering no hardships; on the contrary, they appeared to regard the expedition as a movable feast to be adjourned during the day and resumed immediately upon halting for the night. Inevitably, tongues began to wag, with scandalmongers grumbling that the loose atmosphere would only lead to demoralization and vice. Perforce, when any sexual activity came to light, when a peasant soldier crept into the woods with a chambermaid, the episode was immediately attributed to the southern influence.

All in all, it was not surprising that the gossip soon spread to include the queen herself, since it was widely known that her entourage spent their evenings debating about love and playing games of chivalry with the troubadours. Her critics in later life insinuated that she did not lead an entirely blameless life from the outset of the Crusade, but it is difficult to gauge the extent of her indiscretion if, indeed, there was any at this stage. In all likelihood, her natural exuberance had reasserted itself, and she was merely enjoying herself to the utmost. Anxious to be the center of attention, disliking any authority save her own, she would have blandly ignored suggestions that she behave more circumspectly. However much her husband must have disapproved of the revels, he did not interfere, for Louis certainly could not afford to antagonize the southerners, who made up an important sector of his army, and, in addition, his attention was now occupied by matters more pressing than the queen's amusements.

By Louis's reckoning, it would take nearly three months of unbroken marching before they completed the first stage of their journey at Constantinople, where they would stop for a brief rest and confer with the Byzantine emperor, Manuel Comnenus. Before embarking from Metz, Louis had laid down rules of conduct for the army, but by the time they reached the city of Worms on June 29, it was abundantly clear that his orders were not being observed. Odo de Deuil, chronicling the Crusade, wrote in disgust that it would be a waste of time to list the rules, for they went unheeded. But undoubtedly one of the prohibitions stated that towns through which they passed must not be plundered for food. At Worms, where a flotilla of small craft had been assembled to ferry the army across the Rhine, there occurred the first of a series of untoward incidents that underscored Louis's deficiencies as a military commander and his inability to maintain discipline. As it happened, the army had scarcely crossed over to their encampment on the German side of the river when a quarrel broke out in the marketplace near the landing quay. As the pilgrims quickly discovered, food supplies were scarce, and the money changers charged exorbitant rates; many realized that only a wealthy person was going to reach Jerusalem without starving. When a boat laden with provisions landed at the dock, it was mobbed by a band of hungry Crusaders, who threw its crew overboard and proceeded to help themselves to the cargo. This unruly act brought immediate reprisals from the city's merchants, who sprang into the fray with oars and knives, wounding several Crusaders and killing one of them.

Louis, lost in a faraway reverie, always resentful of time taken away from his prayers, seemed perplexed about how to handle the situation. Finally, almost nonchalantly, he referred the matter to his counselor Thierry Galeran, who, in turn, suggested sending the bishop of Arras to negotiate with the aggrieved citizens of Worms, who refused to sell any more food to the Crusaders; eventually, after some difficulty, the bishop persuaded the merchants to resume commerce. Louis's initial mismanagement of the food supplies, no small failure, was making it increasingly clear to the rank and file of his army that a hasty retreat, the rescue of the Holy Land notwithstanding, was their best hope of extricating themselves from a wretched situation. If the shepherd could barely feed his flock in friendly territory, what would happen when they reached the lands of the Turks? Accordingly, the cynical, the disgusted, thought it wise to abandon the Crusade while still relatively close to home.

In the brilliant days of early July, Eleanor paid scant heed to the defection of a few malcontents. Nevertheless, well acquainted as she was with Louis's shortcomings, she might well have felt forebodings as to her husband's adequacy as a commander. In any case, if intimations of future disaster disturbed her at this time, there was little that she could do. Long ago she had been barred from the policy-making sphere, chastised by the great Bernard himself for meddling, and in recent weeks it had been a relief to distance herself, both from the Frankish high command and from her husband, who cloistered himself with his favorite attendants. Resigning herself to secondhand news of Louis's actions from Geoffrey de Rancon and other southern nobles, she was willing, evidently, to accept an anonymous role, so much so that chronicler Odo does not mention her presence among the Crusaders until some weeks later.

From Worms the route lay overland through south German territories to Ratisbon, on the Danube. Waiting there, surrounded by a suite of fawning courtiers, were two ambassadors from the Byzantine emperor. This preview of Byzantium could not help but make an impression on the Franks, although the impression was not necessarily positive. Manuel's envoys addressed Louis in such obsequious terms that he blushed, while others attending the interview were hard put to smother their smiles. The bishop of Langres, his patience exhausted by the listing of Louis's virtues, finally cried out, "Brothers, do not repeat 'glory,' 'majesty,' 'wisdom' and 'piety' so often in reference to the king. He knows himself and we know him well. Just indicate your wishes more briefly and fully." Coming to the point at last, the Greeks presented two demands that in effect asked only for guarantees that Louis came in friendship. The first, that he should not take any of their cities, was readily granted. But the second—a request to return to Manuel any city or castle, captured from the Turks, that had formerly belonged to Byzantium—was considered unreasonable and deferred until the two sovereigns could discuss the matter personally.

Manuel Comnenus, despite his gross flatteries, was unhappy and resentful. Since "Byzantine perfidy" was a political byword among the

Franks, it will be useful at this point to examine the man more closely. A half century earlier, the Greek historian Anna Comnena had watched the arrival of the first Crusaders with dismay and awe, counting them as innumerable as the leaves on the trees and the stars in the skies. To the thirteen-year-old girl it seemed that the "whole of the West, with all the barbarians that live between the farther side of the Adriatic and the Pillars of Hercules, had migrated in a body, and were marching into Asia through intervening Europe, making the journey with all their household." Now all her nephew Manuel could see was the return of that very same cloud of locusts that had swarmed into the realm in 1096. In some perverse replay of history, the Crusaders were once again set to march across Byzantine territory, installing themselves on the outskirts of his imperial city and demanding help to make a war on territory that, until captured by the Turks, had belonged to Byzantium for centuries. At the same time, he suspected that the Crusaders, in a maddening display of illogic, would make no attempt to understand the political situation in the Mideast, would refuse to listen to advice, and would ignore the fact that driving the Turks out of Asia Minor concerned Byzantium as much as it did themselves. His grandfather Alexius Comnenus had been in no mood to serve the Crusaders; Manuel, busy with his own wars, his own political problems, felt exactly the same.

Unable to prevent the Crusade, his best and perhaps only hope was to somehow use the armies of the West to further his own interests and policies. In 1147, he had been emperor for only four years. Not yet thirty, a young man renowned for his brilliance (he had studied medicine), he had never expected to reach the throne for the simple reason that he had three older brothers. However, within the space of a few years, death had removed two of them, and when his father, John, was shot in a hunting accident, the dying emperor deliberately passed over an older son and set the crown on Manuel's head. Now, whether or not he was fully conscious of the fact, he was presiding over an empire in the process of disintegration. After fifty years and more of campaigns, only the coastal districts were free from Turkish invasions. Almost annually, raiding parties would sweep over his Asiatic provinces, causing the inhabitants of those frontier lands to abandon their villages and flee to the cities.

The connecting principle running through Manuel's policies was the need to play off the various Moslem princes against each other and isolate each of them in turn. The Crusade, once promulgated, had thrown askew his diplomatic maneuvers, for it was bringing together the Moslems in an inflamed united front against Christendom. Since

Manuel stood on the brink of war with a Christian power, King Roger of Sicily, he could not possibly conduct major expeditions on two fronts at once. For this reason, in the spring of 1147, he concluded a twelve-year truce with his mortal enemies, the Turks. As double-crossing as this would appear to Louis when he learned of it, Manuel had little choice, for any alternative would have placed his empire in grave risk. In the short term, it was in his interest to speed the Crusaders into Asia Minor as quickly as possible in the hopes that by feeding them into the mouths of the Turks, both groups might devour each other.

Not yet privy to the intricacies of Byzantine policy, which would always remain beyond their grasp, Louis and his Crusaders were blithely proceeding south through Hungary toward the Greek border. By this time Eleanor had received the first of several letters from Empress Irene, stating how joyfully she was looking forward to the visit. Odo, having nothing of military importance to record, was reduced to describing the Hungarian countryside: "It abounds in good things which grow of their own accord and would be suitable for other things if the region had cultivators. It is neither as flat-lying as a plain nor rugged with mountains, but is located among hills which are suitable for vines and grains, and it is watered by the very clearest springs and streams." While Odo noted agricultural trivia in his diary, Louis, too, seemed free of cares for the time being. Since Hungary offered plenty of food, there had been no problems. In a mood of self-congratulation, he wrote to Abbot Suger that "the Lord is aiding us at every turn," and "the princes of the lands meet us with rejoicing and receive us with pleasure and gladly take care of our wants and devoutly show us honor."

At the end of August, the Crusaders crossed the border into the Byzantine Empire, and for all Louis's fine talk, they immediately began to encounter trouble, although at first they were not quite sure whom to blame for their problems. Odo noted that wrongs began to arise for the first time and, moreover, to be noticed by highborn and lowborn alike. "For the other countries, which sold us supplies properly, found us entirely peaceful. The Greeks, however, closed their cities and fortresses and offered their wares by letting them down on ropes." Even allowing for Odo's hysterically anti-Greek bias, as well as his convenient memory loss about the food riot at Worms, it is clear that the Greeks felt little affection for the Crusaders. It was at this point that Eleanor must have made the enormously upsetting discovery that the Crusade might not turn out to be the grand adventure she had envisioned. She knew that the meager, overpriced rations that the Greeks lowered over their walls were not enough to feed the army, nor could she blame Louis for failing to punish those who fed themselves by plundering. Rather than blame the Greeks, whom she was prepared to like because she planned to enjoy herself once she reached the pleasure palaces of Constantinople, it was easier to assign blame to Conrad's Germans, who had passed that way a few weeks earlier. Occasionally the two armies met, that is to say, the Frankish vanguard met stragglers from the German army, the result invariably being killing and brawling. As for the Greeks, the normally astute Eleanor seems to have made no attempt at this time to analyze the curiously hostile behavior of a Christian country that had extended a warm official welcome. Instead, in some bewilderment, she surveyed the mounting disorder and may have rationalized along the same lines as did Odo when he said, "The Germans disturbed everything as they proceeded and the Greeks therefore fled our peaceful king who followed thereafter." Since everyone loathed the Germans, she could hardly blame the Greeks for similar feelings.

The only Greeks to receive them with a modicum of enthusiasm were the clergy, who emerged from their barricaded cities carrying "icons and other Greek paraphernalia" and showed Louis the reverence due a king. As Eleanor must have known, however, after the Frankish priests celebrated Mass on local altars, the Greeks would purify them with propitiary offerings and ablutions, as if they had been defiled. The Greek churches were opulently decorated with paintings and marble, and even though both Greeks and Franks were Catholics, there was such a vast difference in ritual between the two churches that the Franks could not help but regard the Greeks as heathens. "Because of this," explained Odo, "they were judged not to be Christians and the Franks considered killing them of no importance." In other words, the situation had come to this: Louis proved unequal to the task of preventing excesses, and eventually he stopped trying.

It was September now. As the summer waned, so did the party mood that had sustained Eleanor for the past months. Her troubadours had packed away their lutes, her Amazon ladies from Aquitaine no longer seemed interested in nightly chatter about the delights of love; for everyone the atmosphere had suddenly turned somber. They had only to look about them to notice that the land, once beautiful and rich, had become a charnel house with rotting bodies of dead Germans contaminating the landscape like casually discarded garbage. Apparently, as long as the German soldiers had remained in orderly formation on the road, they were safe; those, however, who had stopped to refresh themselves at the taverns and had wandered off drunk were unceremoniously hacked to death. "Since the bodies were not buried," wrote Odo, "all things were polluted, so that to the Franks who came later, less harm arose from the armed Greeks than from the dead Germans." Eleanor and her companions wrapped their veils across their faces and grimly rode on. The crusading ballads of her swashbuckling grandfather had not prepared her for the sickening stench of corpses.

On October 3, Constantinople lay only one day's march ahead. At a meeting of the Frankish high command that night, Louis's advisers counseled him to forget about Manuel as an ally and, instead, lay siege to the imperial city. Recalling Bernard's warning to attend to holy business, Louis rejected the idea, and the following day, a Sunday, he appeared at the gates of the city to find himself the object of a mighty welcoming committee. Parading out to meet the Crusaders were nobles and wealthy men, clerics and laypersons, all humbly urging him to hasten to the *basileus*, whose greatest desire was to meet the sublime king of the Franks. No doubt the size and excessive geniality of the welcoming party had been greatly enhanced by reports from Manuel's spies that just the previous day the Franks had been talking of ransacking his capital. Accompanied by a small group of intimates, including Odo de Deuil but excluding Eleanor, Louis was conducted to the Boukoleon Palace, where a smiling and affable Manuel waited for him on the portico and planted, restrainedly, the kiss of peace upon his brow.

Eight hundred years earlier a Roman emperor had moved his government to this triangular site jutting out into the Bosporus, the dark blue waters of the Marmara Sea on one side and the Golden Horn on the other, and named the city after himself: Constantinopolis, the city of Constantine. While Rome had sunk into decay, Constantine's capital— "glory of the Greeks, rich in renown and richer still in possessions"— had grown into the wealthiest city in the known world. Even though, by the time of Eleanor's visit, much of the empire's territory had fallen to the Turks and Arabs, its economic ascendancy was still unrivaled, with two-thirds of the world's wealth enclosed within the walls of Constantinople alone.

Like the humblest foot soldier, the queen of France stood outside the walls of the fabled city, gaping in amazement. A double curtain wall girdled a metropolis so large that her eyes could not comprehend it in one glance. In the harbor, the largest in the world, bobbed the masts of hundreds upon hundreds of vessels. Inside the walls, the city's squares tinkled with splashing fountains, the abundant sweet water piped into the city by aqueducts that had been cut through the walls and stored in immense underground reservoirs, some of which still exist today. More than four thousand buildings—palaces, churches, convents, tall stone houses decorated with paintings of flowers and birds—lined the spotless thoroughfares upon which the Byzantines, unlike the Franks, would not have dared urinate. These sights, however, were not seen by the majority of the Crusaders, since Manuel had not the slightest intention of permitting what he considered an undisciplined mob of savages to enter his gates. They were ordered to make camp outside the walls, among the orchards and vegetable gardens. Even Eleanor and Louis were lodged outside the walls, in the Philopation, Manuel's hunting lodge near the Golden Horn, which had been hastily refurbished after its recent occupancy by the ill-mannered Germans.

This did not mean that the royal couple were ignored during their thirteen-day state visit. Far from it; Manuel personally escorted Louis on a tour of the various shrines, especially to Constantine's Great Palace, in whose chapel resided (so the Greeks claimed) such revered holy relics as the Holy Lance, the Holy Cross, the Crown of Thorns, a nail from the Crucifixion, and the stone from Christ's tomb. In the city's basilica of Santa Sophia, immense enough that two or three ordinary churches could have fitted under its golden dome, there were so many candles that its interior looked as bright as the outdoors, its walls and pillars glittered with mosaics of precious stones, and its eunuch choir emitted heavenly sounds. Touring the Blachernae Palace, Manuel's official residence, was such an overwhelming experience that Odo de Deuil found himself virtually speechless: "Its exterior is of almost matchless beauty, but its interior surpasses anything that I can say about it. Throughout it is decorated elaborately with gold and a great variety of colors, and the floor is marble, paved with cunning workmanship."

Constantinople enchanted Eleanor, as it had countless previous Crusaders, and helped to ameliorate her earlier, unfavorable impression of the Greeks. Its wonders may have compensated for other things that disturbed her, no doubt one of these being the empress of Byzantium.

Only a series of fortunate accidents had lifted Empress Irene, née Bertha of Sulzbach, from the backwater of Bavaria to the mighty throne of

Byzantium, and now she struggled to perform her assigned duty as consort of the *basileus* without allowing justifiable insecurities to overwhelm her. The daughter of a German count, she happened to have had a sister who married the Holy Roman emperor, Conrad of Hohenstaufen, a union that conferred considerably more status than she would normally have had. In 1142, Conrad forged an alliance with John Comnenus (then the emperor of Byzantium) against their mutual enemy of Sicily; to seal the friendship he bestowed his sister-in-law on John's youngest son, Manuel. Even though the likelihood of Manuel reaching the throne seemed remote, marriage into the Comnenus family was more than Bertha had ever dreamed of. Her fortunes transformed overnight, she had been taken to the Greek court for an intensive program of grooming, and the obliteration of her Germanness had been completed with the change of her name to Irene.

When Eleanor met her in the fall of 1147, Irene had been married less than two years and had yet to produce an heir; in fact during her thirteen years as empress she would prove capable of bearing only one child and that one a daughter. Living in the lavish grandeur of the Blachernae, garlanded by ropes of pearls from the East and surrounded by slaves and eunuchs, Irene appeared to Eleanor as the possessor of a glamorous destiny, one that the queen could see herself easily fulfilling. Under Irene's flamboyant exterior, however, hid a trembling young woman, still as much Bertha as Irene. The Crusade, to which in her homesickness she had initially responded with high anticipation, was turning out to be not only an ordeal but the most painful kind of embarrassment. In early summer, before the German segment of the Crusade had reached Constantinople, they had been preceded by reports of looting, burning, and killing; her husband had been obliged to dispatch an army to "escort" Conrad and his troops through Greece so that damage to people and property might be held to a minimum. Upon Conrad's arrival in the imperial city, the heretofore friendly relations between her husband and brother-in-law took an abrupt turn for the worse.

Anxious to rid himself of an unwelcome guest, Manuel suggested that since Conrad appeared to be in a hurry to reach Jerusalem, he might prefer to cross the Hellespont immediately and thus avoid a tedious delay in Constantinople. Conrad, incensed at what he considered Manuel's lack of hospitality, refused, and he was finally escorted to the suburban palace of Philopation, which, in the course of a few days, his army managed to pillage so effectively that both the palace and its surrounding park were no longer inhabitable. It became necessary to move the German emperor across the Golden Horn to the palace of Picridium. Adding to Irene's mortification, German soldiers seemed intent on committing as many atrocities as possible against city residents, scarcely a day passing without a major skirmish between Conrad's men and Greek troops. When her husband asked Conrad for redress, the emperor shrugged off the violence as unimportant and then angrily threatened to return the next year and sack Manuel's capital.

It was only by the greatest exercise of her diplomatic talents that Irene was able to pacify the two men, and outwardly at least, amity was restored. To her enormous relief, Conrad set off toward the end of September, helpfully sped on his way across the Straits of Saint George by Manuel's navy. Her poignant recollections of her native land somewhat diminished by that time, Irene retired to her quarters, but she could not avoid the general consternation, not to mention condemnation, among the Greeks over the barbaric behavior of her countrymen, and to a large degree, she had come to share their opinion. Now, only a week later, she was called upon to grapple once again with the role of cordial hostess to another army of Crusaders, this one, unlike the German contingent, containing a queen who would expect even more personal entertainment than the coarse-grained soldiers. Conscientiously she organized sightseeing jaunts, shopping expeditions, and banquets that "afforded pleasure to ear, mouth and eye with pomp as marvelous, viands as delicate, and pastimes as pleasant as the guests were illustrious." Daily she spooned out doses of novelty: slaves whose only function was to anticipate Eleanor's wishes; visits to Santa Sophia to see a statue of the Virgin ceaselessly dripping tears from its eyes and a casket containing the three Magis' gifts to the Christ child; a trip to the tower of the Golden Gate, where Eleanor could gaze down upon caravans whose laden camels brought sandalwood, brass, and exotic silks from the East. In short, Irene carried out her duties with meticulous formality but without any note of warmth.

From the start Eleanor had genuinely mystified the empress and the other glittering females in her entourage. What puzzled them most was why any woman would wish to travel to Jerusalem when even the relatively short trip from Constantinople to Antioch was considered treacherous for a woman. Apart from the very real possibility of being massacred en route by the Turks, there were the discomforts of dusty roads, scarce water, and general lack of amenities, which would cause any true noblewoman to recoil. When the Greek women learned that Eleanor disdained a canopied litter and usually rode on horseback like a man, it only reinforced their suspicions that the Franks, Christian though they might call themselves, were truly a primitive people. In the end, they could only conclude archly that the queen had joined the Crusade because she did not trust Louis out of her sight.

Their patronization extended to yet another area. Despite Eleanor's self-image as western Europe's foremost fashionplate, the critical Greek women compared her attire to their own sartorial splendor and found her dowdy, if not outlandish. This they took for granted, not expecting elegance from the queen of an underdeveloped kingdom such as the Franks', and it was hardly likely that their superiority did not rankle Eleanor. That those controversial trunks packed with her best finery should count for less than nothing was, however, only one of the many shocks that awaited her in Constantinople. She must have been surprised to learn how little respect the Greeks had for Crusaders, and she could not fail to see their flagrant boredom, how they listened with weary smiles to the plans Louis laid before them. The Byzantines had a poor opinion of the intellectual level of the Franks, for that matter of all Latin peoples, thinking them naive and superstitious, but at the same time Manuel feared them and was willing to go to any length to humor them. Thus, he wooed them with lavish gifts, believing as did his grandfather Alexius that the Crusaders were motivated solely by greed and ambition, but also believing that any favors he did for them would not be returned, any promises extracted would be broken without a second thought. Although Eleanor had been dazzled by Byzantine luxury—this was how kings and queens should live—at times she must have felt their gorgeous pageantry a bit excessive, if only because the Greeks seemed intent on making the Latins feel inferior.

Eleanor could hardly have failed to contrast Louis with the *basileus*. The two men were about the same age and physical stature, but there the resemblance ended: Manuel appeared resplendent in his purple robes, Louis colorless in the sad cloth of his Crusader's tunic; Manuel was suave, alert, overflowing with charm, Louis solemn and awkward. No medieval sovereign had a more acute sense of his own limitless power than Manuel Comnenus, and to Eleanor, it must have been a rude jolt to notice how no courtier dared approach the *basileus* except with bowed head and bended knee, while anyone could, and did, amble up to converse with the unprepossessing Louis. All his life he would prove woefully lacking in sophistication and majesty, but as he aged, these so-called defects of his character would grow more beguiling to his contemporaries. Nevertheless, in Constantinople, it is not too difficult to understand why his wife did not appreciate his simple traits, and those thirteen days—so uplifting, so humiliating—would mark the beginning of Eleanor's extreme disenchantment with the king.

All the while, the political situation with Manuel remained heavy with ambiguity. For the time being, thoughts of attacking Constantinople had been abandoned—they needed Manuel too much—but how far they could trust him was unclear. Furthermore, it was emphatically obvious to all that they were quickly wearing out their welcome. Some of the rowdier pilgrims had burned houses, cut down olive trees, and generally acted like drunken fools. Odo tells us that "the king frequently punished offenders by cutting off their ears, hands and feet, yet he could not check the folly of the whole group. Indeed one of two things was necessary, either to kill many thousands at one time or to put up with their numerous evil deeds." One day a Fleming soldier barged into the Greek money changers' stalls and went berserk, shouting *Havo! Havo!* seizing handfuls of gold and inspiring other Crusaders in the vicinity to do likewise. "The noise and confusion increased, the stalls came falling down, the gold was trampled on and seized." Although Louis hung the Fleming in full view of the city, he also felt obliged to make restitution to the money changers, most of whom demanded greater sums than they had actually lost. Incidents like this one helped to deplete Louis's treasury, which was badly in need of succor anyway, as his letters to Suger requesting additional funds attest. Everthing considered, it was thought best to move on.

On October 16, Eleanor left Constantinople with a sense of relief. The city, for all its spendor, had brought her nothing but disquieting and exasperating thoughts, and she relinquished her perfumed chamber in the Philopation to take up residence in a tent once more. Even though their departure had been announced, Louis characteristically dawdled outside the city walls. Five days were spent on the near side of the Bosporus, the queen and her ladies whiling away their time hawking, the noblemen fulminating against Manuel. There was nothing to do but gossip and threaten. Nobody enjoyed the delay, least of all Manuel, who continued to harass Louis in the hope that it would speed him along. He badgered the king with provocative requests: to turn over any captured towns or castles to the Byzantines, to give up one of Eleanor's ladies as a bride for his nephew, and so on, but he received no acknowledgment. Finally Manuel, an intrepid schemer, suggested that the army cross the Straits of Saint George to the far coast of Asia Minor, where it might be more comfortable. Louis's delay, however, was not based on pure capriciousness; he was waiting for a small contingent of late-arriving Crusaders who had taken an Italian route under the command of his uncles, the count of Maurienne and the marquis of Montferrat. Nevertheless, on October 21, he moved the army to the coast of Asia Minor, where they lingered another five days. What Louis hoped to gain by waiting for a small detachment of men is not clear, but it turned out to be a grave error in judgment, for during the delay the Franks, in an orgy of high spirits, ate most of the food that had been set aside for the journey to Antioch.

With each passing day, Louis's actions could not but have added to Eleanor's anxieties. On October 26, the order to break camp was finally given, but at the last moment, for inexplicable reasons of his own, Louis suddenly decided to return to Constantinople for a last-minute conference with Manuel. As the army set off across the plains without him, the sky darkened with an eclipse, a phenomenon that the superstitious medieval person invariably regarded as a menacing omen. For most of the day, the sun was shaped like a half loaf of bread. No one doubted what this meant: "It was feared that the king, who above all others shone with faith, glowed with charity, and attained celestial heights because of this hope, had been deprived of some part of his light by the treachery of the Greeks." What appeared to Louis's everworshipful admirer, Odo, as celestial grandeur of soul only meant to Eleanor that the king's slow wit had led him into some fresh disaster. Later in the day, however, he caught up with the army, safe and full of elation at the good news he had just heard from Manuel: Conrad and his Germans had fought a victorious battle against the Turks.

In fact, Manuel had lied. Unknown to the *basileus*, there had been a battle that very day in the region of Dorylaeum, but nine-tenths of Conrad's army had been annihilated. "The victorious Turks, laden with spoils and enriched by countless treasure, with horses and arms even to superabundance, retired to their own fortresses. There they eagerly awaited the coming of the king of France."

The king of France, along with his queen, was skirting the peninsula of Asia Minor in the late October sunshine in a mood of heady, if short-lived optimism. The weather was still mild and fine, just mellow and brisk enough to make one feel like traveling, and they dined on good bread and wine and illusions. Manuel had sent them a bon voyage gift of victuals, but as Eleanor must have known, the provisions would not last a week. Although Manuel sent them neither enough food for a long journey nor the guides he had promised, nevertheless, at that moment, the queen may have forgotten his windy words and been having kind thoughts about the emperor. Buoyed up by the news of Conrad's victory, these disappointments did not seem so significant after all. Divine intervention had, evidently, come to their aid at last. The Turks, after their rout by Conrad, would not be in a mood to trouble them. Traveling through a part of Asia Minor rich in biblical and Crusader history, they neared the venerable Christian city of Nicaea, which had fallen into the hands of the Turks in 1080 and whose capture had been the previous crusading army's first great victory. While camping near the Nicene lake, reviewing the heroic deeds of their grandparents, they were startled by the arrival of surprising visitors, the guides that Manuel had provided for Conrad. How the Greeks satisfactorily explained their sudden abandonment of Conrad and their return to Constantinople is not clear, but they did more or less confirm Manuel's reports of victory, for different reasons. In essence, the highly seductive news they gave Louis was that yes, Conrad had defeated a Turkish army and yes, God be praised, there had been an outstanding massacre. It was, of course, precisely what Louis wanted to hear.

The next day, or perhaps the day following, the first blow of reality fell when the advance guard reported a curious sight ahead—Germans headed in their direction, Germans who in no way resembled victors. They straggled into Louis's camp, thirsty, starved, bloody, and dazed with terror. Their comrades dead, they were the lucky few, several hundred out of ten thousand, who had survived, and it took little imagination to envision the scenes they described. For Eleanor, these amounted to echoes of what she recalled of her grandfather's experiences: ambush, thousands slain, the escape of a traumatized few. In addition to the massacre of his men, the Holy Roman emperor had lost the entire contents of his camp, his horses, arms, and gold. Already the booty was finding its way to bazaars throughout the Moslem East and would eventually be sold as far away as Persia.

Eleanor, like everyone else, was totally unprepared for the German disaster, and not unnaturally her mind must have raced ahead to wonder whether she would come to a similar grisly end. Louis, nevertheless, urged his army forward, "grieved with stupefaction and stupefied with grief," in hopes of aiding other survivors and finding the remnants of German headquarters. On November 2 or 3, he encountered a nearly incapacitated Conrad, rheumy-eyed and nursing a serious head wound. The two kings consulted together in an effort to analyze what had happened and what they should do next. There were plenty of theories to explain the massacre: Some said it was the treachery of the Greek guides, who had sneaked off after they had betrayed Conrad to the Turks; some said it was the Holy Roman emperor's own fault for taking a short cut to reach Antioch more quickly; others said it was God, punishing a holy army that thought more about wine and luxurious meals than providing themselves with arms and equipment. Most likely Conrad was right when he told Louis and his nobles: "Know that I am not therefore angry at God but at myself; for God is just but I and my people are foolish." Hearing these words, Louis began to cry and invited Conrad to share his tent.

According to Conrad, there were two possible routes to northern Syria: a wide road, which could be traversed in eight days but offered little access to food, or the indirect coastal road, which he believed to be better supplied. "Although you do not fear the power of any people" he advised Louis, "yet you likewise do not have arrows which can subdue hunger."

Winter was beginning as they set out along the seacoast, threading their way down stony canyons and through gorges made by mountain torrents. Whether or not she would live to see the spring is a question Eleanor must have asked herself more than once, especially in view of Louis's continuing blunders. Once he and a group of companions left the main body of Crusaders to search for a shortcut. For three days the king remained among the missing, wandering in bewilderment over mountain crags until he became hopelessly lost. Eventually he came across mountain dwellers—"rustics," Odo calls them, "the companions of wild beasts"—who escorted the king, looking very small and tired, back to his army. With each passing day, his losses began to mount. Pack animals died, as did the dogs and falcons who had been carried for so many months by their loving mistresses. The Greek forest dwellers became rich overnight as hungry Crusaders parted with gold and silver pieces, enameled helms and shields, costly cloaks and gowns. As the year drew to a close, there was little in which Eleanor could take comfort, since it seems likely that many of her Amazon trunks had been emptied to purchase food. More worrisome to her was the incredible disintegration of the army, Louis having given up issuing even the most elemental orders. As a result, each battalion did as it pleased, with no particular order of march being maintained and men failing to obey their officers. As far as Eleanor could observe, the group had ceased to deserve the name of an army—it was a mob roaming through the wilderness, desperately in need of a Moses to lead them. When they stopped for Christmas at Ephesus, an increasingly ill Conrad decided to board a ship bound for Constantinople. "Perchance," wrote William of Tyre, "he found the arrogance of the Franks unendurable." A far more likely assumption is that he found Louis's mismanagement of the army intolerable.

On Christmas Eve, in the fertile valley of Decervion near Ephesus, they pitched their tents on the mossy banks of the river Maeander. Horses were put out to graze in the luxuriant grass, water jars filled from the river, fires lit for cooking. As black-robed monks gathered under the trees to begin Mass, a detachment of Turks, howling and shouting like demons, suddenly appeared on the opposite bank. This was the first time that Louis's Crusaders had met the enemy, and hot to avenge the Germans, they seized the nearest horses and weapons, forded the river, and raced to meet the Turkish horsemen. Perhaps astonished by the ferocity of the Franks, the Turks broke and fled for the hills, the Crusaders in exultant pursuit.

This initially successful confrontation filled the army with extravagant false confidence. They had killed many Turks and, even better, seized an enemy camp that was well-stocked with gold. "Filled with joy over the victory and the rich spoils which they had seized, the Christians passed a quiet night and, at dawn, prepared to resume the march." At daybreak, however, they awoke to find that the Levantine winter had arrived in full force. Darkened skies loosed torrential rains and sheets of sleet, the river began to overflow, and in the distance they could see mountain tops whitening with snow. Along with the downpour, which would hammer them steadily for the next four days, violent winds ripped through the camp, overturning the gay pavilions of their tent city, which had seemed so festive the previous day, and the rising waters of the Maeander began to flood the banks. Men, horses, and equipment were crushed on the rocks and drowned. The year 1147 ended bleakly, but it would have been far more dismal if the Crusaders could have seen what the new year held.

It had now been nearly seven months since they had left Metz. According to their schedule, they should be nearing Jerusalem, and Eleanor must have pondered uneasily upon the reasons why they still were floundering in the wilds of Asia Minor. Since June, Louis had been considerably less than zealous about his duties as commander. He had closeted himself with his confidants, Thierry Galeran and Odo de Deuil; written letters to Abbot Suger pleading for money; visited shrines; and prayed interminably. Under the guise of democracy, he had divided responsibility for leadership among his barons, each night designating a different commander for the next day in a kind of round-robin chain of command. As a result, everyone—and no one—was in charge, a policy that must have added to Eleanor's contempt for him. Up until this point, Louis's inadequacy had never actually imperiled the army, but now, with one misstep, anything could go wrong. As the army left the seacoast and began to push its way inland, it must have been pathetically obvious to Eleanor that Louis scarcely knew where he was, let alone how to proceed. In November, he had followed Conrad's advice, only to realize that the coastal route was devoid of the food he needed and the weather might decimate his army. Now he determined to seek the safety of Eleanor's uncle at Antioch by proceeding as the crow flies—that is, straight over the Phrygian mountains. That this was the direction being taken by Conrad when his Teutons had been massacred was a fact he carefully evaded, no doubt believing that he had no other choice.

Leaving the valley of the Maeander, they climbed to higher ground, winding up into the foothills of the Phrygian mountains toward the apostolic city of Laodicea, where Louis planned to rest and replenish his supplies. Harassed at every step by the Turks, who assaulted boldly and retreated skillfully and easily, they arrived at Laodicea on January 3, 1148, to find the city virtually deserted. The Greek inhabitants had fled, taking with them all the edibles they could carry. For over a week the Crusaders lingered at Laodicea in a mood of cockiness, for they had driven off the Turks several times by now. The route to their most immediate destination, Adalia (the modern Antalya), on the same seacoast from whence they had recently come, wound over high desolate mountains and through the rugged pass at Mount Cadmos. Lacking native guides, having in fact no clear idea of direction, they were compelled to take their bearings from the sun and hope that God would see fit to shepherd them over the mountains. At the best of times it was a treacherous journey, but for a starving, undisciplined army who had to contend with winter storms and Turks stealthily nipping at their heels, it had all the makings of a nightmare.

Toward the middle of January, under the watchful eye of the enemy, the column slowly began moving up the mountain through a landscape as still as death. The hillsides were scattered with the skeletons of entire horses; with skulls, legs, rib cages of men, many picked clean by vultures but others still covered with rotting clothes and flesh. The corpses sprawled grotesquely where they had fallen, on their knees or faces, some on their backs with eyeless sockets staring up at the sky. For Conrad's ill-fated Germans, the Crusade had terminated here.

On the day set for the crossing of Mount Cadmos, Louis took charge of the column's rear, which included the unarmed pilgrims and the baggage. Commanding the vanguard was one of Eleanor's vassals, her old friend Geoffrey de Rancon, in whose castle she and Louis had spent their wedding night. It would be said later that Eleanor was marching with Geoffrey at the head of the column, a highly unlikely and dangerous position for an important personage such as the queen of France. Nevertheless, she must have been riding closer to the front of the line than the back. At noon, Geoffrey, unencumbered by baggage, reached the mountain's windy summit, where he was supposed to make camp for the night. Disregarding his orders, he decided to advance a bit farther, for he felt that the march had been too short that day. Scouts whom he had sent ahead assured him that there was a more wholesome spot for the camp on a nearby plateau, and after consulting with Louis's uncle the count of Maurienne, de Rancon ordered the column to move on. Geoffrey's disobedience, if such a word can be applied to an action so normal in Louis's disorganized army, alarmed no one, least of all the queen. When in the past had anyone, from the highest nobleman to the common foot soldier, paid attention to Louis's edicts, especially this one, since the king had clearly misjudged the amount of time needed to cross the mountain? Little did the queen know that the seeds of carelessness that Louis had allowed to be sown during the past eight months were now about to bear fatal fruit.

By midafternoon, the rear of the column, believing, in happy ignorance, that they had almost reached the end of the day's march, began carelessly to lag behind. Soon the army was divided, some having already crossed the summit, others still loitering along the ridge, their progress impeded by falling rocks. The Turks, who had been keeping a close watch from a distance, immediately recognized the situation for what it was, and now they quickly moved in to press their advantage. Swarming over the mountain with howls of *"Allah akbar"* ("God is great"), thrusting and slashing as if with scythes among wheat, they fell upon the panicked Christians, soldiers as well as unarmed pilgrims. As the rocky paths grew slippery with blood, humans, horses, and baggage hurtled over the precipices into the canyon below. Although there was no avenue of escape, for the Turks had seized the top of the mountain, those who tried to flee were pursued and butchered, "overwhelmed among the thick-pressing enemy as if they were drowned in the sea." William of Tyre wrote that "our people were hindered by the narrow defiles, and their horses were exhausted by the enormous amount of baggage," baggage that, as everyone believed, must have belonged to the women.

Amid the clash of battle, the king escaped notice, for in his soldier's tunic he looked like everyone else, his disdain for the trappings of royalty inadvertently saving his life. His royal bodyguard exterminated in a mess of smashed skulls and severed limbs, "he nimbly and bravely scaled a rock by making use of some tree roots which God had provided for his safety" and, his back to the mountainside, defended himself until his assailants moved on. "No aid came from heaven, except that night fell."

Meanwhile, Eleanor and the others in the vanguard were unaware of the skirmish. As the afternoon wore on, however, Geoffrey de Rancon began to grow apprehensive and at dusk he sent a party of knights back to investigate. Not until nearly midnight did the search party chance to come across their king, bloody and exhausted, stumbling on foot over the mountain with a few companions.

There was to be no sleep that night. From one end of the camp to the other could be heard the sound of voices, weeping, mourning, shrieking grief. "With tremulous voice and tearful sighs," women went out to search the mountain road for sons and husbands, servants sought their masters. During the night the stragglers drifted in, those who had escaped death "rather by chance than their own wisdom" after hiding among the bushes and rocks until nightfall.

Beside herself with anxiety during that agonizing evening, Eleanor's first reactions at the sight of her husband must have been shock and relief—shock at the immensity of the disaster, relief at the knowledge that she and Louis had escaped. At that point, however, she had no assurance that they were out of danger, indeed the facts greatly pointed to the opposite conclusion, for in the morning she could see the Turks spread over the mountainside, waiting. They were gabbling in loud voices, plucking hair from their heads, and throwing it on the ground. These exaggerated gestures, she learned, meant that they would not be dislodged from their posts.

Once the first horror had subsided, the angry survivors began to cast about for someone on whom to affix the blame. The man they chose as scapegoat, interestingly enough, was Geoffrey de Rancon; he and the king's uncle had disobeyed orders and therefore should be hung, suggestions that Louis ignored. By many of the Franks, Eleanor, too, was cast in the role of leper. It was, they said, her luggage that had prevented the rear guard from overcoming the Turkish attack, her friend Geoffrey de Rancon who had disobeyed orders, her Aquitainians who had been traveling in the vanguard and thus had escaped the brunt of the massacre. That these charges were exaggerated is obvious; that the real reason for the catastrophe was, not Geoffrey's disobedience, but Louis's maladroit leadership the Franks were not willing to acknowledge. From this time on, however, resentment against the queen began to mount, and although none declared that she deserved hanging, even her women friends treated her coldly. It is against this omnipresent feeling that she had contributed to the fiasco that consequent events must be seen.

Now that the worst had happened, Louis began to behave with perfect correctness as a commander. Marshaling what remained of his forces, he ordered them to maintain an order of march, obey their officers, and stand their ground in combat until given orders to withdraw. In this way, then, they began the tortuous descent down the mountain, the Turks aware of their weakness and harassing them every foot of the way. They had little food and no water. Those sufficiently parched with thirst bled horses or asses and drank the blood, for meals they grilled dead horses, both their own and those left behind by the Turks. "With this food," we learn from Odo, "and bread baked in the ashes of campfires, even the wealthy were satisfied."

The Crusaders who emerged from the mountains on January 20 could hardly have been called an army. Many of their horses and mules had died or been eaten. Swords and equipment had been thrown away or long since sold for food. Their baggage had enriched the Turks, and what had not been captured lay at the bottom of ravines. They had raw blistered hands, cracked lips, and their filthy clothes hung in tatters. Many, including a number of bishops, had no shoes. The condition of Queen Eleanor was not recorded by Odo, but it is certain that she was in no better shape than anyone else. If they had naively harbored illusions about having finally reached a safe haven, they were quickly disabused, for the next five weeks in the Greek city of Adalia were to be as agonizing as any they had theretofore experienced. Once a delightful seaside town boasting fertile fields and orchards, Adalia was now a beleaguered city unable to cultivate its fields for fear of Turkish attacks and dependent upon food brought in by ship. What provisions the townspeople did possess they were willing to share for only the most exorbitant prices.

The unutterably traumatic events of the last two months had tempered Eleanor's bold spirit; her nerves were strained to the snapping point. Coming down the mountain, fearful that the next minute would bring a hailstorm of arrows, she had concentrated on only one thing: survival. Now it appeared that she had hoped for too much as misfortune piled on misfortune. The chilling information from the Greeks at Adalia was that Antioch, the gateway to the Holy Land, still lay a forty days' march over mountainous, Turk-infested terrain. By sea the trip took merely three days, but even supposing ships could be found on that deserted coast in midwinter, there was no money to pay the fare of four silver marks for each person.

Sleeting rain and snow accompanied by lightning and thunder lashed the few tiny tents remaining; sickness and starvation swept the camp; horses died for lack of fodder. During that first week in Adalia, the camp rumbled with dissension. Louis made his views explicit: Since they could not transport the whole group by sea, they clearly had no choice but to resume marching overland. His disgruntled barons were equally adamant about wishing to put to sea, even if it meant leaving thousands behind. "Let us," the king insisted, "follow the route of our fathers whose incomparable valor endowed them with renown on earth and glory in heaven." His head full of visions of crusading triumphs, he talked about "martyrs" and "valor," but to his barons and knights, the words conveyed only a bizarre kind of death wish that they had no desire to share, and they told him so. There is no evidence of Eleanor's reaction to all this, but with the refuge of her uncle's court only three days away, she must have been anxious to exit by any available escape hatch. If Louis wished to pursue some mad dream of martyrdom, she would leave him to his destiny, but under no circumstances would she accompany him. It is not difficult to conjecture that she was among those who, after violent debate, "forced" (the word is Odo's) the pliable king to a saner point of view.

The decision was made in the nick of time because, with each passing week, the odds increased against leaving Adalia alive. The beginnings of plague had broken out in the camp, and the size of the burial ground needed to be enlarged daily. Not until the end of February, however, did there arrive both the ordered vessels and a favorable wind. Those Crusaders who still had money and horses, or a noble name, hastened aboard the hastily convened convoy, while the rest were left to manage as best they could. Many would perish of disease or starvation outside the walls of Adalia, many would be killed or captured, and over three thousand, converted to the Moslem faith in exchange for bread, would vanish without a ripple into the lands of the Turks.

Finally there rang out the familiar cries of the master mariners, "Unfurl the sails for God's sake." In a short time, the wind filled the sails and bore Eleanor and Louis, barely on speaking terms by this time, out of sight of land. The journey, the Greeks had promised, would take three days, but they had not allowed for the unpredictability of the weather. Battered by winter storms, the convoy was carried farther from the coast of Asia Minor but no nearer Syria, and when Eleanor lay down at night, she did not know whether the morning would find her at the bottom of the sea.

Three weeks later, on March 19, 1148, the king and queen of France, ragged and seasick, sailed into the port of Saint Simeon near Antioch.

Eleanor spent only ten days in Antioch, but those days would affect the history of western Europe for the next three hundred years. Nonetheless, on that first day when she stepped, pale and exhausted in health, into the arms of Prince Raymond, no such far-reaching consequences could have been predicted. In Syria, the winter rains had ended. It was spring, and the hillsides were covered with red and blue anemones. Unlike the haughty Manuel Comnenus, Raymond had not waited in his palace for the arrival of the Crusaders but had hastened the ten miles down the Orontes River to the port, with almost the whole population of the city in his wake. To the chanting of the *Te Deum* and the cheers of the throng, he had escorted them up to his terraced city on the slopes of Mount Silpius. After the privations of the winter, Antioch must have seemed like an hallucination to Eleanor. It was more like a vast garden than a city, with green pastureland, orchards, granaries, and ancient Roman baths enclosed within its walls. Fourteen hundred years of history were layered here. Once it was the third most important city in the Roman Empire, Julius Caesar had sat in its amphitheater, Herod had paved its streets with marble, Diocletian had built its cisterns. Through its groves of parasol pines and its hanging gardens had trooped the Arabs of Harun al-Rashid, purple-mantled Byzantine emperors, the Turks, and finally the Christians. Ancient, wise, civilized, it immediately reminded Eleanor of Bordeaux and Poitiers and brought back a flood of nostalgia for her native land. But more than the physical beauty of the place made her feel that she had come home: The official language of the city was the *langue d'oc*, the knights and priests in Raymond's service were Poitevins, and several of them she had known as neighbors during her childhood. Best of all, however, there was the magnificent Raymond himself.

Like all the men of her family, the prince was handsome and virile, a hearty adventurer who combined the traits of prowess and beauty that Eleanor admired so highly in a man and that of course she had failed to find in her husband. A true son of the Troubadour, Raymond had, like his father, considerable charm—charisma we would call it now—as well as a wry sense of humor, which often colored his actions: Indeed, his life story would have made an ideal theme for one of William's poems. Thirteen years earlier, while a knight at the English court, he had been tapped by King Fulk of Jerusalem as a husband for Princess Constance, the eight-year-old heiress of Antioch. There were, nevertheless, a number of obstacles to the marriage, the most serious being Constance's mother. Acting as regent, Alice had been ruling the principality and had no intention of giving up her power. Furthermore, she seems to have disliked her daughter and planned to marry her to Manuel Comnenus, an alliance whose political implications thoroughly horrified the Frankish barons of Syria. Therefore it was with the utmost secrecy that Raymond had journeyed to the Holy Land disguised as a peddler. Once there, he dealt with Alice by asking her to marry him, a not inappropriate match, since Raymond was twenty-one and Alice not yet thirty. Flattered, she was silly enough to allow Raymond entrance to the city, going so far, in fact, as to welcome him with an excess of emotion. While preparing for the wedding, she received the news that Raymond had just married her daughter, making himself the undisputed ruler of Antioch.

Now thirty-four, the youngest son of William IX was in his prime; he was, however, also fighting for his life. Instrumental in setting the Crusade in motion, he had hoped that his good fortune at having a niece who was queen of France would ultimately rescue his kingdom from the Turks. More than hoped, he had assumed that his close relationship with the Frankish royal house would hold the key to survival. That he was perched on the edge of a volcano he must have been acutely aware, and in fact, a year later his severed head would be adorning a gate in Baghdad. If the size and strength of the life preserver now being offered was unquestionably puny, nevertheless he still regarded it as sufficient for his purposes. The crusading army that disembarked at Saint Simeon was only a shadow of its bulk at Metz, but even so, many of those slain or abandoned along the way had been pilgrims or infantry, and Louis's host remained the most formidable Christian force to appear in the Holy Land in half a century. The news of its coming had succeeded in terrifying the Moslem world to the extent "that now they not only mistrusted their own strength but even despaired of life itself," a response that Raymond wished to take advantage of. First, however, with traditional Aquitainian hospitality, he spared no expense in making his guests feel welcome.

For the next few days the Franks were treated to a dizzying round of banquets and hunting parties. Installed in Raymond's palace with its running tap water, glass windows, and perfumed candles, Eleanor was able to discard her stinking rags and bathe with the luxurious soap for which Antioch was famous. Her uncle furnished her with a new wardrobe of silken gowns so exquisitely woven by the silk makers of Antioch that only the highest ecclesiastics in France could afford them. At the fêtes, Eleanor shared a place of honor with Raymond. The entertainment—the troubadours, minstrels, and Saracen dancers—was all very gay, very ribald, very characteristic of her grandfather's court at Poitiers. At table, they drank Persian wines cooled with snow from Lebanon mountains and Mount Hermon and dined on the specialties of the land: sugar, oranges, figs, dates, quinces, and melons. Syria was famous for its white bread and apples of paradise, which we know as bananas, as well as for artichokes, asparagus, truffles, and lettuce, the latter being considered a choice dish. All of this acted as an aphrodisiac on Eleanor's sensibilities, and her natural appetite for pleasure quickly revived. Now that the journey over the mountains was receding into an anguishing memory, she threw herself almost tumultuously into living. Her affection for her uncle, and his for her, was widely noted, and though their intimacy seems natural under the circumstances, it was not received with any special favor by the Franks, who regarded his attentions to their queen as excessive. Eleanor's exuberance did not escape comment from the increasingly hostile Franks, who continued to blame the incident at Mount Cadmos on her luggage and who undoubtedly read into the racy conversations in the *langue d'oc*, which they could not fully understand, more than was actually there.

If Raymond made an inordinate fuss over the queen, he did not forget the others. "Raymond showed the king every attention on his arrival," reported William of Tyre. "He likewise displayed a similar care for the nobles and chief men in the royal retinue and gave them many proofs of his great liberality. In short, he outdid all in showing honor to each one according to his rank and handled everything with the greatest Magnificence."

But it was Eleanor with whom he spent his time. After a twenty-year separation, they had much of a personal nature to discuss, but their conversations must certainly have focused on politics, that is, Raymond's precarious position with the Turks. Aware of his niece's intelligence, he would have explained that Nureddin had established himself along the Christian frontier from Edessa to Hama and had spent the last six months methodically snatching, one by one, the Frankish fortresses east of the Orontes River. As for Count Joscelin, whose laxness had caused Edessa to fall into Turkish hands four years earlier, he could barely hold his own. If the Turks were to attack Antioch in force, Raymond would be lost. But now, with the arrival of the Crusaders, he could easily take the offensive and strike at the heart of Nureddin's power by taking his city of Aleppo. He might also reclaim his lost provinces along the Orontes, but most importantly, he could recapture Edessa, whose fall had given rise to the Crusade.

To Eleanor, his plan seemed eminently reasonable. Should the Turks succeed in overrunning northern Syria and capturing Antioch, the entire Holy Land would be threatened, and nothing would then prevent them from sweeping down to Jerusalem. Obviously the security of the Holy City would best be established by driving back the Turks in the north. If the merits of Raymond's plan were obvious to Eleanor, they were not so to Louis. To her amazement, the king refused to hear of the scheme. He said, incredibly, that his Crusader vow obliged him to visit Jerusalem before he undertook any campaign, and he had no intention of fighting anyone until he had first worshiped Jesus Christ at the Holy Sepulcher. His reasoning seemed so childish, not to say irresponsible, that Eleanor may not have believed him at first. The recapture of Edessa had been the whole purpose of the Crusade. Had he dragged thousands of people on a three-thousand-mile journey merely to pray? The idea was too bizarre to be credible. Since he was behaving irrationally, she curbed her fury and humored him like a child, counting on Raymond to bring him back to reality.

The days that followed were full of conflict. At a full meeting of the Crusader barons, Raymond formally outlined his tactics—and Louis disdainfully rejected them. When the king realized that Eleanor supported her uncle, it only strengthened his resolve to have nothing to do with Raymond's plan. His decision, he declared stubbornly, was irrevocable, and in this his barons supported him. Raymond was not only baffled at this turn of events but enraged. "When Raymond found that he could not induce the king to join him, his attitude changed. Frustrated in his ambitious designs, he began to hate the king's ways; he openly plotted against him and took means to do him injury."

Raymond's nets had been cast carefully, but they caught only the wind. Despite the beauty of Antioch, despite Raymond's gifts, Louis felt offended, as did the rest of the Franks, by what they found there. The principality did not appear in danger, indeed its people lived a life of pleasure in mosaic-tiled houses and splendid gardens with fountains and marble-tiled pools; even the common people lived more ostentatiously than any king of France. Raymond himself, far from defending the Holy Sepulcher, wore soft slippers and loose gowns like some oriental potentate. For that matter, Louis could barely distinguish the

Saracens from the Frankish Syrians, who imitated the Moslems by wearing flowing garments, beards, and turbans and who, to his horror, had even intermarried with the natives. To add to his consternation, their offspring, the Pullani, had been invited to the banquets he had attended, and failing to understand that many Moslems lived on perfectly amicable terms with the Christians, Louis deplored having to dine with his enemies. Most shocking to him, however, was the sight of mosques in Antioch; even the Christian churches, which had been decorated by Saracen artists, looked like mosques.

He was not alone in his hostility toward Raymond. The ancient enmity between the Franks and Aquitainians had been building to a crescendo ever since Mount Cadmos, and now all the Franks could read into Raymond's battle plans was that more territory would be added to the domains of a southerner. At this point, they were in no mood to add prestige to the house of Poitou. As to what the Crusaders from Aquitaine thought about all this, the record unfortunately provides no clue. Their Crusader vows, apparently, bound them to abide by the decisions of their commander.

One would get the impression from these happenings that logic played little part in their outcome. The situation was even more absurd, for underneath the welter of all the bickering and political maneuvering hid the real reason for Louis's inexplicable decision: the familiar emotion of jealousy. Put at its simplest, the king suspected that Eleanor had taken the prince as her lover.

The contradictions of Eleanor's marital life that had been curled like a worm in the center of her slumbering sensuality now erupted into full view. Circumstances had given her a throne, but since it had brought her nothing but unhappiness, she counted it worthless; marriage had brought her a king for a husband, but this king more nearly resembled a monk. While Louis had been a faithful husband, the reason for his fidelity was, ironically, that he had utterly no interest in sex. As if all this were not enough, he was incurably dull, and while she could never truly have loved a dull man, she certainly could have lived with one. What she could not live with was a fool, and since the beginning of the Crusade, Louis's stupidity, his cataclysmic insecurities, had been writ clear for all to see.

It would have been natural for a woman of Eleanor's position in the twelfth century to have had these negative feelings about her husband.

Other queens had been desperately unhappy in their marriages, but they had accepted the situation, either because the prestige made them so much better off than other women or perhaps from the feeling that husbands were lords and masters, free to treat wives as they wished. If a queen suffered, she did so in private. If her marriage ended, it was her lord's decision, and she retreated in silent humiliation to her father's castle or into a convent. But this was not Eleanor's temperament.

Toward the end of March, the queen confronted her husband with a demand for divorce. She would go no farther with his Crusade. Not only was she washing her hands of the holy expedition, she also avowed her intention, one undoubtedly encouraged by Raymond, to relinquish both the crown of France and its king. In the future, she would remain in Antioch and resume her title of duchess of Aquitaine. Her words, evidently, caught Louis unprepared, for although the signs had been everywhere for him to read, he had never anticipated such a declaration. Undoubtedly he recalled her "constant, almost continuous conversations" with Raymond, and now her decision to stay in Antioch only strengthened his suspicions about their relationship. Inhibited and ill equipped to satisfy a woman sexually, he nonetheless did not find the role of cuckold appealing. He was hurt, bewildered, and somewhat angry, but he still loved her and needed her. How Louis initially reacted to Eleanor's declaration of independence was described by John of Salisbury, who may have heard it from Louis himself the following year. The king, John reported cryptically, "made haste to tear her away." Tear her away from whom? From Raymond, who, conceivably, might have been present at the meeting? Or did Louis demand merely that she leave the prince's palace immediately?

In the final analysis, a queen throws away a crown for much the same reason that any woman ends her marriage, that is, when she reaches that point where her life with the man has become unendurable. To deny Eleanor's strong emotions about Louis's deficiencies as a husband would be to do her less than justice. And yet her stated reason for wanting a divorce sounds almost impersonal. Undoubtedly this reason had been carefully planned in advance, because it was the only one that might have carried any weight with the king. So when Louis objected to leaving her behind, "she mentioned their kinship, saying it was not lawful for them to remain together as man and wife, since they were related into the fourth and fifth degrees."

Nothing she could have said was more certain to alarm the king. As she surely would have pointed out, there had been rumors about the illegality of their marriage for many years. Five years earlier, Abbot Bernard had written a letter to the bishop of Palestrina in which he flatly stated so, and the late bishop of Laon had also taken the trouble to calculate the degrees of their kinship. Louis could not deny that two centuries earlier Adelaide, the sister of Duke William IV of Aquitaine, had married Hugh Capet, from whom the kings of France were descended. It was not certain, of course, whether the bishop of Laon's reckoning was correct, but Eleanor herself believed, or so she said, that their having only one child and no sons during eleven years proved conclusively God's displeasure with their union.

However "deeply moved" Louis must have felt, however loath to give up a prized possession, he finally agreed to the divorce on one condition: "if his counselors and the French nobility would allow it." With characteristic indecisiveness, he neatly removed the matter from his own area of responsibility and thrust it upon others. It might be argued that a royal divorce was, after all, a state concern and should be decided in committee, but a stronger man would not have dealt with such a personal matter in this haphazard way. With what frustration Eleanor must have heard his reply can be imagined without too much trouble.

Events now began to move rapidly. Hurrying back to his quarters, Louis unburdened his distress to his intimates. Odo de Deuil was certainly among those who learned of the royal quarrel, and as the king's chronicler, companion, and confessor he must have been familiar with the minutest details of the affair. But Odo, no scandalmonger, decided that it would be politic to end his chronicle with the departure from Adalia. The other person of whom Louis asked advice was his secretary, Thierry Galeran. He was, it will be remembered, the eunuch whom Eleanor detested, and at Antioch she had mocked him among her friends, doubtless pointing out the amusing implications of her monkish husband spending his time with a eunuch. As these things have a way of doing, her imitations of Galeran, so entertaining to her friends, got back to the eunuch, and now he did not pass up the opportunity for revenge. "He boldly persuaded the king not to suffer her to dally longer at Antioch because 'guilt under kinship's guise could lie concealed' and because it would be a lasting shame to the kingdom of the Franks if, in addition to all the other disasters, it was reported that the king had been deserted by his wife, or robbed of her."

Whether Galeran presented these arguments because he hated the queen—certainly he had reason—or because he genuinely believed her unfaithful is a question Eleanor's contemporaries were unable to decide. One thing is certain, however: At this point Eleanor and her uncle supplied the chief topic of gossip among the Crusaders.

The claim of Eleanor's detractors that she had an affair with Raymond is based on very shaky foundations, among them the account of William of Tyre, who wrote thirty years after the Crusade. The archbishop would say maliciously of Eleanor: "Her conduct before and after this time showed her to be, as we have said, far from circumspect. Contrary to her royal dignity, she disregarded her marriage vows and was unfaithful to her husband."

The anonymous chronicle by the Minstrel of Reims, written in the thirteenth century, calls Eleanor "a very evil woman." More historical fiction than fact, the minstrel has Eleanor about to elope with Saladin, when Louis, alerted by a serving maid, throws on his clothes and rushes off to stop her just as she is about to set sail in one of the Saracen ruler's galleys. "And there he found the queen, who was standing with one foot upon the galley. And he taketh her by the hand and leadeth her back to her chamber." When Louis asks the queen why she is running away, the author of the chronicle puts the following words into Eleanor's mouth: "In God's name, because of your own naughtiness! For ye are not worth one rotten pear! And I have heard so much good of Saladin that I love him better than you; and know ye of a truth that henceforth shall ye have no joy of keeping me!"

Such sentiments could not have been uttered by Eleanor, since in 1148 Saladin was still a child of twelve or thirteen, but they doubtless convey a faithful enough representation of Eleanor's feelings toward Louis at that time.

The exact relationship between Eleanor and her uncle will never be known exactly, but this much seems virtually certain. She adored him because he typified the masculine splendor she had worshiped in her mighty grandfather and father, and there may also have been a physical resemblance among the three men. Deprived of her father at an early age, she would have responded eagerly and affectionately to a relative who so nearly resembled him, especially one whom she had regarded as almost an older brother during her childhood. Had Raymond not been her uncle, there is reason to believe that she would have slept with him, because she longed for physical passion, and later it will be seen that her preference in men would entirely be limited to his type. In her time, sexual relations between an uncle and niece would have been regarded as incestuous, and incest was not stylish, even in liberal Aquitaine. She could no more have slept with Raymond than with her father or, if he had lived, her brother. The possibility of an affair becomes even more preposterous when Raymond's character is taken into account. In an age when male debauchery was taken for granted, Raymond was reputed to be a faithful husband to his twenty-one-year-old wife. No puritan, he was nonetheless known to be moderate in his habits; he did not eat or drink to excess, nor did he romance women. Considering that he had shown little interest in amorous exploits so far, it seems hard to believe that he would now attempt to seduce his own niece.

However improbable the gossip in Antioch, the fact that it was widely repeated and considered apt was indicative. What happened next only confirmed, however, the rumors. On March 28, Louis quietly began mobilizing his forces for departure. Sometime after midnight, when the city lay in darkness save for the fires on the watchtowers, the army began moving out through the Saint Paul Gate, an evacuation carried out with as much secrecy as was possible for a force of several thousand persons. At the last moment, in a sort of commando operation, the queen was snatched from Raymond's palace. The chronicles provide little illumination as to Eleanor's reaction except that "she was torn away and forced to leave for Jerusalem with her husband." That she would not have accompanied Louis voluntarily is clear and probably accounts for the fact that she was seized after dark. After what kind of struggle and in what state of rage she was forcibly conducted from Antioch we can only imagine. But here was tangible proof to the Franks that their captive queen had done something shockingly indiscreet. How Raymond may have figured in the secret exodus and abduction is nonrecoverable. We only know that he was unable to prevent Eleanor's undignified departure.

Louis's arrival in Syria "had been attended with pomp and glory, but fortune is fickle and his departure was ignominious," an observation that might well serve as an epitaph for the entire Crusade. By sunup, the queen was being hustled along the road to Tripoli under tight security, the hated crown still firmly atop her head.

The Unwanted Crown

When the Crusaders caught their first glimpse of Jerusalem's white walls, they prostrated themselves on the ground weeping like children and asking forgiveness for their sins. Later, unable to sleep, they kept vigil together throughout the long night. If Eleanor had once looked forward to visiting the Holy City, her spirits were now thoroughly dampened. Winding over the Pilgrim's Ladder through the mountains high above the Mediterranean, she had stared at the groves of orange trees, the thick flocks of sheep, and at Cyprus, a silver streak on the horizon, but her face appeared hard, as if sculpted in stone. With the passing days, she had foraged her mind for alternatives, and as she saw it, there were several choices: She could arrange an escape and flee back to Raymond in his kingdom above the sea; possibly she might cajole Louis into a more reasonable frame of mind and secure his consent for a divorce without the interference of his hated advisers; at worst she would have to wait until they returned to Paris before appealing her case to Abbot Bernard or the pope. In the end, Louis surely could not hold her against her will, short of resorting to imprisonment, and that would effectively rule out his chances of siring an heir by another wife. Somehow she would find a way to return, if not to Antioch, then to Poitiers, where she would put her Eastern experience to good use by creating a milieu worthy of the duchess of Aquitaine. In the meantime, there had been cypresses and olive groves to contemplate while she attempted to reconcile herself to this temporary delay in her objectives.

At the Jaffa Gate, the regent, Queen Melisende, and her eighteen-year-old son, Baldwin, led the entire population of Jerusalem in welcoming Louis with such a remarkable outpouring of fervor that one would have thought him a messenger of the Lord. Heralded by palms and olive branches, banners and hymns, the impatient Crusaders paraded through gaily decked streets to the Holy Sepulcher, which enclosed the rock of Calvary and the tomb of the Savior. There the king laid upon the holiest of all altars the oriflamme he had brought from Saint-Denis, and then he sank down on his knees as if he had no cares in the world but those of an ordinary pilgrim. Afterward, he and his nobles made a tour of the city's precious shrines, scattering alms as they went, and finally the royal party was led to its lodgings in the Tower of David. Only then did Louis consent to rest or break his fast.

What part Eleanor played in this pilgrim's progress we do not know. John of Salisbury reported that during this period the mutual anger between Eleanor and Louis festered and increased but that they hid it as best they could. No doubt on this public and historic occasion both of them masked their private feelings and performed their expected roles as if still the most cordial of husbands and wives. In any case, Eleanor had too much pride to allow herself to be carried into the city in a litter with the curtains drawn. With regal demeanor, she, like the other Crusaders, must have trod the traditional Pilgrim's Way in her tunic bearing the cross that she had received at Vézelay. In those first days in Jerusalem she was accorded the honor due a queen, but the story of her unceremonious departure from Antioch, too juicy a piece of gossip to be suppressed, certainly influenced her treatment by the Hierosolymitans, and while not actually ignored, she certainly was not made much of, as she had been in Antioch. Any attempts by Louis to prevent her moving freely about the city would have been beneath both their dignities and would have, moreover, angered Eleanor's vassals, who were already outraged by Louis's treatment of her. Nevertheless, if not closely guarded, she was placed under discreet surveillance.

During her conversations with Raymond in Antioch, Eleanor had had ample opportunity to familiarize herself with the rivalries of the Latin Kingdom. From childhood she had been an uncommonly astute student of political subtleties, and unlike the bewildered Louis, who insisted upon regarding Jerusalem as the place in need of defense, she was quick to grasp that the Holy City stood in no danger at that moment. Furthermore, everything she had personally observed so far had made her distrustful of the Frankish Christians in Palestine.

The Latin Kingdom of the mid twelfth century was a land of intrigue, corruption, and feverish competition. During the half century since the Crusaders had conquered Jerusalem, all pretense of being soldiers of Christ had disappeared in a no-holds-barred race for land and gold. Avarice and jealousy had made them suspicious of one another and equally distrustful of newcomers from the West, since immigration inevitably led to further division of spoils.

At this time, Frankish Syria was divided into four principalities: the kingdom of Jerusalem in the south; to its north, the county of Tripoli, which extended along the Mediterranean; still farther north, the principality of Antioch; and finally northeast of Antioch, the county of Edessa, which spread eastward beyond the Euphrates River. Since the announcement of the Second Crusade in 1145, the great lords of each of these areas had hoped that through the assistance of Western sovereigns they might be able to enlarge their own territories at the expense of either their Moslem or their Christian neighbors. Each was anxious about its own affairs, each eager to extend its boundaries, and it is not surprising that each sent messengers and expensive gifts to Louis, trying to enlist his aid for their individual causes. The citizens of Jerusalem, in particular, were anxious to make the most of Louis's arrival. Mindful of the ties between the house of Capet and the prince of Antioch, they feared, however, that Raymond might persuade the king to mount a campaign against Nureddin in the vicinity of Aleppo or Edessa, and the presence of Queen Eleanor on the Crusade made this all the more likely. Therefore, it was with undisguised relief that they learned of Louis's acrimonious breach with Raymond and his midnight departure from Antioch. To make certain that Louis continued south without changing his mind along the way, the Hierosolymitan barons had sent Patriarch Fulcher to intercept the king and escort him without delay into the Holy City.

In mid-May, shortly after their arrival, an assembly was convened at Acre, an impressive gathering that included Conrad, who had recently arrived by ship from Constantinople with the remnants of his German contingent, the leading prelates and barons of Jerusalem, and the nobility of Louis's army. Queen Melisende and other noblewomen were present, but Eleanor was not. She may not have been invited, although in view of her anger at Louis, it would seem more likely that she refused to attend. Also notably absent, although the implications were only dimly perceived by Louis, were representatives from the other three Latin principalities.

Eleanor's uncle had of course abstained from any further dealings with the Crusaders, and in any case, he could hardly afford to leave his principality for some vague adventure in the south, nor was Count Joscelin of Edessa able to abandon his beleaguered territory. As for Count Raymond of Tripoli, his absence was due to an unfortunate incident that tells us much about the acrimony existing between the Frankish Syrian states. Among the Crusaders to take the cross at Vézelay had been Alphonse-Jourdain, count of Toulouse and Eleanor's old archenemy. With his wife and children he had traveled by sea and arrived at Acre a few days after Conrad. The son of the old Crusader Raymond of Toulouse, Alphonse-Jourdain had been born in the Holy Land, and his arrival at his birthplace caused a good deal of embarrassment to the reigning count of Tripoli, the grandson of his father's bastard son, Bernard. Should Alphonse-Jourdain claim the county, and apparently he had talked about doing so, his right would be hard to deny. A few days after he stepped ashore, Alphonse-Jourdain died suddenly at Caesarea. Since he had been in excellent health the previous day, there was talk of poison. It is possible that his death was accidental, but if so, no one believed it, and naturally suspicion pointed to Count Raymond of Tripoli. Whatever the truth, Raymond professed great indignation at the charges and angrily boycotted the Crusade. For the canny barons of Jerusalem, the fact that three out of four heads of the Frankish states were missing at Acre was something they took for granted; for Louis, uninformed, pulled this way and that on the swampy soil of Holy Land politics, the situation grew increasingly bewildering.

During the course of the assembly, the necessity of presenting some achievement to Christendom became overriding, and bit by bit, a plan, though foolish, began to take shape. After some token opposition, it was unanimously resolved to attack Damascus. This was, to put it mildly, a decision of immense stupidity, because of all the Moslem states, the kingdom of Damascus alone was eager to maintain friendly relations with the Franks, and like the Westerners, its emir was at odds with Nureddin. To attack Damascus, which asked nothing better than peace, would prove to be the fastest way to throw its rulers into the arms of Nureddin and a political blunder of monumental proportions. But for some time the barons of Jerusalem had been greedily eyeing the fertile lands of the Damascenes, and to the visiting Crusaders, who knew nothing of the local situation and to whom all Moslems looked alike, the idea of rescuing from the infidel a hallowed Christian city like Damascus had an irresistible appeal.

On Saturday, July 24, the Christian army pitched its tents amid the orchards and vegetable gardens on the outskirts of Damascus. These orchards, stretching like "a dense gloomy forest" for more than five miles around the northern and western sides of the city, were crisscrossed by paths wide enough only to allow the gardeners to pass through with their pack animals. Therefore, the emir of Damascus, who at first had refused to take the threat seriously, was surprised to see the army approach from the northwest, because the walls on that side of the city were the most heavily fortified. Despite a constant downpour of arrows, the Christians were able, nevertheless, to move up quickly to the city walls, and by Monday they had successfully occupied the orchard. At this point, the terrified citizens of Damascus began to lose hope; during the weekend some had already fled the city, and now others began to barricade the streets for a last desperate struggle, while the emir was forced to dispatch a messenger to Nureddin with a request for aid and reinforcements.

On Tuesday, however, the besieged Damascenes watched in astonishment as the Crusaders struck camp in what appeared to be a retreat. Actually they were not retreating but shifting from their present winning position in the orchards to the eastern side of the city, a site that, incidentally, lacked food and water. The reason for this decision was not wholly understood even by those who participated in it, and many of the Franks believed that certain Hierosolymitan barons had been bribed by the emir of Damascus to give up the siege. Later, in fact, it would be fairly well ascertained that money did change hands. While murmurs of treachery swept through the army, its leaders began to snarl openly over the division of Damascus once it would be captured. On Wednesday, July 28, Louis, unable to follow the subtle bickering much less surmount it, ordered the retreat. In confusion and fear, the army struck out for Jerusalem with Damascene horsemen in pursuit. Arab historian ibn-al-Qalanisi, an eyewitness to the retreat, describes how the Moslems "showered them with arrows and killed many of their rearguard in this way, and horses and pack animals as well. Innumerable corpses of men and their splendid mounts were found in the bivouacs and along the route of their flight, the bodies stinking so powerfully that the birds almost fell out of the sky."

The Moslem world could scarcely contain its glee. Since the First Crusade fifty years earlier, they had been obliged to contend with the legend of the invincible knights from the West, but now this image seemed to be effectively smashed. That this ferocious army, heralded as a scourge of Allah, should have abandoned its one and only campaign after four days and retreated ingloriously acted as an anodyne on their spirits. There was, they felt, nothing more to fear from intervention by the Europeans, at least not for a long time to come. In this, they proved correct. The next Western army they would have reason to fear would be led, ironically enough, by *"Malik Ric,"* the lion-hearted son of Eleanor of Aquitaine, but in the interim, the Moslems would have recovered Jerusalem.

Although it was abundantly clear that the prestige of the Franks had sunk to a mortifying low, it was by no means certain how this disaster had come about; Syrians and Crusaders hurled recriminations, each blasting the other for the abortive expedition. They had come thousands of miles, the Franks declared, and lost thousands of men to no avail; the Syrians were greedy, ungodly, and—a calculated insult—less courageous than the Moslems. The local Christians, equally eager to assign blame, charged that the Westerners, who lived comfortably in safe Christian lands, had the temerity to accuse them of cowardice; the constant danger of Palestine had made them realize the worth of life, and they had no taste for useless martyrdom. On both sides, some blamed Raymond of Antioch for sabotaging the Damascus siege, claiming that "he prevailed on some of the nobles in the army to manage affairs in such a way that the king was compelled to abandon the project and retire ingloriously."

What Eleanor thought about the expedition is not hard to imagine. She was accustomed to associating failure with any enterprise undertaken by her husband, and she had little respect for the Syrian Franks, whose jealousy and petty bickering had disillusioned her beyond measure. Still, she must have felt keenly the ignominy of that weary retreat from Damascus, which had signaled the crumbling of the Crusade, her sadness compounded by depression over her own uncertain future.

During the autumn, there was much talk of ships and sailing; even the most hardened knights had become homesick and longed for the cool breezes of the Seine and the Loire. Slowly the crusading army began to melt away: On September 8, Conrad sailed for Constantinople, and Louis's forces, "impelled by want," also wished to go home. Somehow, passage money was found for all who wished to leave. Eleanor, too, her chests packed with perfume and damask and other souvenirs of bitterness, fully expected to take ship any day, but eventually she could see that Louis was making no effort to stir. How impatiently she must have chafed at his delays and postponements. For a person who was happiest when she could fling herself into work, the enforced idleness of Jerusalem, the debilitating glare of the noonday sun, the evenings with an unwanted spouse must have caused her enormous frustration. The wounds that she and Louis had inflicted on each other, say the chronicles, did not heal during this time. The weeks dragged; winds rose suddenly off the desert, wrapping the city in a haze of hot parched air laden with fine sand; Christmas came and went; the year became 1149; and still Louis refused to move.

Many times Abbot Suger wrote reproachful letters demanding to know why Louis did not return. The country needed him, he warned; the people were bitterly lamenting their dead relatives, the churches complaining about the dissipation of their treasure, those gold and silver vessels that had been sold for food in Hungary and Asia Minor. Louis's brother Robert was threatening an armed uprising, contending that the king was unfit for kingship and should join their brother Henry as a monk in the Abbey of Clairvaux. And, briefly, Suger mentioned more personal matters. Shortly after the army had left Antioch in the spring of 1148, Louis had poured out his troubles with Eleanor to the abbot. His letter has been lost, but Suger's reply remains. Thinly disguised can be seen his annoyance with Louis: "Concerning the Queen, your wife," wrote Suger, "I suggest you conceal the rancor of your spirit, if there is any, until you have returned to your kingdom, when you may attend to both these and other things."

Suger's advice notwithstanding, the rancor had not abated, but had in fact increased. All winter the battle of wills raged, although at times Louis may have appeared to have been impressed with Eleanor's arguments. Nevertheless, he made his own feelings perfectly clear: There was nothing he would not readily grant her, except what she most desired. Unable to draw much comfort from such discussions, Eleanor grew increasingly resentful and bored, and the continuing presence of Thierry Galeran in the royal party did not help. During the summer while the Crusaders had been occupied in Damascus, she had been left to her own devices in Jerusalem. At first the celestial city had held countless wonders, but over the months it had become a city like any other. By now she had grown accustomed to the arcaded courts and narrow, stepped streets, to the stalls of the Armenian merchants in the bazaars, to the Moslem scribes and the Jews and the black slaves, and to the swaying camel caravans bearing sacks of Indian spices and musk from Tibet. Countless times she had made the pilgrimage along the most famous of all Jerusalem's streets, the Via Dolorosa, the Way of the Cross, to hear Mass in the Holy Sepulcher. "O eternal God, who has willed to declare to us by the mouth of the prophets that in the glorious sepulchre of thine only begotten Son his flesh should not see corruptions. . . ."

Nevertheless, for Eleanor, Jerusalem had become a city of waiting, a spoiled city where even the landmarks finally lost their fascination. She had seen the cell, roofed with one stone, where Solomon had written the book of wisdom; the pine groves on Mount Zion, where tradition said that the Last Supper had taken place; the site of the pool of Bethesda, where Jesus had healed the paralytic. She had climbed the Mount of Olives, its grassy slopes white with asphodel, and toured "the village called Gethsemane and, close by, across the torrent of the Kedron, the

Garden where Judas had betrayed Jesus." For years she had listened to tales about Outremer, heard minstrels croon her grandfather's songs, and like every pilgrim who entered Jerusalem's gates, she had expected it to be the most miraculous event of her life. But one could not sustain oneself forever with ruins, no matter how holy. Now, weary and restless, she was ready to go home and set her life in order.

Shifting perspective, it is possible to intuit Louis's state of mind in Jerusalem. Behind his reluctance to return to France, his confusion and aimless loitering, lay a number of ordinary human emotions. During that troubled winter and spring when his kingdom sat kingless, fear and humiliation warred with a desperate need to salvage some remnant of a life that now resembled a cracking ice floe. Afraid to look back and equally hesitant to set his feet toward the future, he was able to effectively stop the clock in Jerusalem, a place that, admittedly, seemed admirably suited to his monkish nature. One can be sure that much of his time was spent in prayer and religious sightseeing. There is less certainty of the exact nature of his relationship with Eleanor. It may well be that, alone, they heaved recriminations at each other, she berating him for his desertion of Raymond and the indignities that he had imposed on her at Antioch, he abusing her for indiscretions that provoked him into such unchivalrous behavior.

Given Louis's limitations, he had conducted the Crusade to the best of his ability, however little credit that may be to allot him. It took courage to go home, where unpleasant postmortems were already being conducted in an effort to explain his failures. It was recalled, for example, that early in 1148 the pope had been celebrating Mass when one of his assistants spilled consecrated wine on the carpet before the altar. "Many thinking men were deeply alarmed, for the prevailing belief was that such a thing could never happen in any church unless some serious evil threatened it. And indeed this belief did not err." Less charitable chroniclers decided to ignore the Crusade, only noting that Louis "was not able to do anything useful, anything worthy of mention, or actually anything worthy of France." Even Odo de Deuil had abruptly ended his history of the Crusade midway because he had nothing more to say. There was no avoiding the enormously troubling fact that thousands of lives had been lost for nothing; not one foot of ground had been won. Even so, at that time what must have agitated Louis even more than his failure to the Church was the imminent loss of his queen. The issue of divorce was both puzzling and agonizing to Louis, for his marriage truly did seem to be cursed, with only one daughter in a dozen years. To a king who desperately needed a son, this was virtually the same as being childless, and his conscience trembled that he had transgressed God's laws by living in sin with a third cousin. Nevertheless, Eleanor's determination to separate constantly warred with his own unremitting desire to keep her, for, as John of Salisbury tells us, "he loved the queen almost beyond reason." His ego terribly buffeted by military fiasco, he must have sought to restore a semblance of normality in his domestic affairs by going out of his way to regain Eleanor's affection. As subsequent events will show, he fought for her with more zeal than he had waged any military campaign.

Apart from everything else was the matter of his pride. Should he meet Eleanor's demands for divorce, if he accepted her theory that consanguinity had irrevocably tainted their marriage, then he must return empty-handed to France, having lost not only a war but his wife and that portion of his kingdom that belonged to her. From whom could he expect moral support? Bernard had declared their relationship within the forbidden degree, and for all Louis knew, Pope Eugenius might very well concur. His only recourse at this time was procrastination in the hope that time might resolve his problems and, perhaps, soften Eleanor's implacable anger.

Toward the end of April, after the Easter celebrations had been completed, Eleanor and Louis sailed from Acre. With them were less than three hundred persons, all that remained of the mighty Crusade that had set out from Metz nearly two years earlier. Only two vessels were needed to accommodate the entire party and its baggage. That the coolness between the royal couple had continued is evidenced by the fact that Eleanor and her ladies sailed in one ship, Louis with Thierry Galeran and Odo in the other. Not only did Eleanor seem eager to avoid her husband on the voyage, but she also had no desire for the company of men whom she regarded as enemies. Despite her excitement and relief at leaving Palestine, the discomforts and boredom of a long sea trip made it far from an unmitigated pleasure. To add to this, the spring of 1149 was not the safest time to be making a voyage through the eastern Mediterranean, for Sicily and Byzantium were still at war, and squadrons of both powers regularly patrolled those waters. While Eleanor and Louis were passengers aboard Sicilian ships, they may have believed that, as neutrals, they had nothing to fear. Without incident, they passed Cyprus and Rhodes and, by early summer, were rounding the Peloponnese, probably in the vicinity of Cape Malea, when they were suddenly accosted by Manuel Comnenus's navy. Louis hurriedly ordered the

Frankish flag run up on his ship, a tactic that did not succeed in deter-
ring the Greeks, who had orders to capture the royal pair and escort
them to Constantinople. "The King was appealed to to return to his Byzantine brother and friend, and force was being brought to bear on him,
when the galleys of the king of Sicily came to the rescue." Before long
the Sicilian counterattack proved successful in routing the Greeks, and
the king and queen were able to continue on their way toward Sicily,
the unpleasant incident forgotten.

Sometime in the following days, however, the two vessels lost sight of
each other with adverse winds, perhaps a storm, driving Eleanor's ship
off its course and carrying it as far south as the Barbary Coast. For the
next two months nothing was heard of the queen of France or, for that
matter, her husband. Of this period we know nothing. Whatever adventures she had, if indeed she spent time with the Berbers of North Africa
during her "circuits of land and sea," her ordeals never found their way
into the chronicles. Not until mid-July, more dead than alive, did she
wash up at the port of Palermo in eastern Sicily, only to learn that both
she and Louis had been given up for dead. Of Louis's whereabouts, no
one was able to enlighten her. Too ill to give proper attention to the implications of that information, she was taken in hand by emissaries of
King Roger and given lodgings where she might rest and regain her
strength.

Two weeks later Louis's ship appeared on the shore of Calabria near
Brindisi, where his first concern after disembarking seemed to be for his
wife. Somewhat surprisingly, he did not rush to Eleanor's side but settled down in Calabria to wait for her to join him. Writing to Suger some
weeks later, he offered Eleanor as one of his excuses for delay. "After
we were welcomed, devotedly and reverently, by the men of our most
beloved Roger, King of Sicily, and honored magnificently by letters
from him as well as messengers, we awaited the arrival of the Queen
almost three weeks." His wife, he goes on to add, "hurried to us with all
safety and joy." Nothing is said of Eleanor's misadventures and ill
health, which, evidently, he did not think Suger would consider as important as "the very serious illness of the Bishop of Langres, wavering
between life and death" and which he offered as a second excuse for his
tardiness.

Despite Louis's reports to Suger about Eleanor's "joy" in their reunion, nothing had changed, neither his fantasies of reconciliation nor
her determination to separate. She had been relieved to hear of his safe
arrival in Sicily but not to the extent of entertaining second thoughts
about a divorce. In late August, reunited for the moment, they began

journeying eastward across the ankle of the Italian boot to Potenza, where they paid a courtesy call on King Roger. It was there at the Sicilian court that Eleanor must have first learned the news about Raymond of Antioch, news that would utterly blast any hope of reconciliation.

From his father Raymond had inherited charm and joviality, but unlike him, he also possessed a tendency toward fits of temporary rage that robbed him of all reason. His maddening encounter with Louis Capet sparked one of these aberrations, which, as it turned out, was far from temporary. Raymond believed, probably correctly, that Louis's army could have crushed Nureddin, but at the same time, he could hardly have been unaware that his own forces were inadequate for such a task. While Louis had been dawdling beneath the walls of Damascus, Raymond had enjoyed some success in chasing Nureddin's army out of Antioch, but the Turks returned the following spring. At that point, Raymond, like his neighbor Joscelin of Edessa, might have secured a truce with the Turkish leader. He did not. In an act of sheer bravado, as if to prove that he alone could fight an enemy that the Crusaders had refused to attack, he launched an offensive with only a few hundred knights and a thousand foot soldiers.

At first Nureddin, unable to believe that Raymond would have the effrontery to attack with such a feeble force, thought that this might be the advance guard of a much larger army, but his disbelief quickly turned to amusement when he discovered that Raymond had no reinforcements. Contemporary Christian historians were also at a loss in explaining the prince's action, which they regarded as clearly suicidal. As William of Tyre pointed out, Raymond carelessly "exposed himself to the wiles of the enemy."

On June 27, two months after Eleanor's departure from the Holy Land, Raymond and his army were surrounded at the Fountain of Murad. Evidently Raymond made no attempt to save himself. "Wearied by killing and exhausted in spirit, he was slain by a stroke of the sword." His death was celebrated as a great victory throughout Moslem Syria. His head and right arm had been cut off and carried to Nureddin, who sent the skull in a silver box to the caliph of Baghdad as proof that Allah's most formidable enemy was truly dead.

Eleanor's grief, the horror she felt over Raymond's demise, her aching certainty that Louis's refusal to help had cost the prince his life, made her turn on the king in bitter, impotent fury. Whatever deep hostility she had felt during the past eighteen months, disguised or repressed for the sake of royal dignity, could be held in check no longer. Her anger at being dragged from Antioch by armed knights was nothing compared to her fury at Raymond's needless death and brought the marital discontentment to a head. Now she would have her divorce; nothing could shake her resolve.

Contemporary commentators do not indicate which direction Eleanor and Louis had intended to take after leaving Roger's court at Potenza, but in view of Suger's insistent letters asking Louis to make haste and the king's replies such as might be made by a tardy schoolboy, their intention was probably to sail from Naples to Marseille. If so, these plans were now suddenly discarded and their arrival in Paris postponed still further, for the couple decided to seek the opinion of Pope Eugenius, who, driven from Rome five months earlier, now resided south of Rome in the town of Tusculum. Ultimately, the decision as to the legality of their marriage would rest with the pope, and being close by, they decided to consult him immediately. For both Eleanor and Louis, the decision to visit Eugenius was a gamble, but keeping in mind Louis's tendency toward procrastination and Eleanor's impulsiveness, it seems more likely that the queen was the one who pressed for an immediate opinion.

With Eleanor immersed in her personal sorrow, they began the journey north accompanied by an escort provided by Roger. According to one of Louis's letters, she showed signs of being "seriously ill" shortly after they left Potenza, although Louis must have been aware of the precarious state of her health before they set out. Arriving at Monte Cassino on October 4, Eleanor collapsed, and they were obliged to stop at a Benedictine monastery. It would be presumptuous to attempt to diagnose an illness that occurred some eight hundred years ago, about which there are no medical records, much less a hint of the physical symptoms. But taking into consideration Eleanor's state of mind at that time, it is possible to make some reasonably educated guesses. There was, to begin with, her growing distress during the year that she and Louis had spent in Jerusalem, the terrible uncertainty over her inability to take command of her own life, and the realization that, for the present at least, she was trapped. Her harrowing months at sea had, of course, weakened her physically, and although Eleanor would prove remarkably healthy during her entire life, she had not fully recovered when she received Louis's summons to Brindisi. Adding to her unsettled state had come the news of Raymond's death, and these various elements no doubt coalesced into a mental and physical breakdown.

It is, however, an indication of Eleanor's extraordinary resilience and her determination to see her future settled that she was able to pull herself together sufficiently to resume the journey three days later. On October 9, they arrived at Tusculum, where Eugenius greeted Louis "with such tenderness and reverence that one would have said he was welcoming an angel of the Lord rather than a mortal man." Considering that Louis was in disgrace all over Europe at this time, Eugenius behaved with immense understanding. It was not in his character to make needless reproaches, but despite what he may have privately thought of this unprecedented, impromptu visit by a king who had lately bungled the Church's affairs beyond imagination and a queen come to plead for a divorce, he received them with equanimity. At once it was made clear that the purpose of their visit was not to discuss the Crusade, although undoubtedly the subject arose, but rather to have the pope act in the capacity of a marriage counselor, a role that he had been called upon to undertake in the past.

During that fall of 1149, John of Salisbury was a secretary at the papal court, and in his *Historia Pontificalis,* written four years later, he describes the two-day visit of the Frankish king and queen from his ringside observation post. John might have warned Eleanor of the reception she would receive from Eugenius, although it is quite unlikely that he would have intruded on her at that moment with anecdotes. Nevertheless, he recalled for his readers a similar visit to the court by a Count Hugh of Apulia. After a thorough investigation of the case, Eugenius denied the requested annulment, and then, to the astonishment of the court, he leaped down from his throne in tears and "in sight of all, great man though he was, lay at the feet of the count so that his mitre rolled in the dust." From between the count's feet he urged him to take back his wife and presented him with one of his own rings.

Eugenius, needless to add, was a staunch believer in marriage. If Eleanor was aware of this, it failed to deter her. Nothing in her background had bred any particular reverence for the mighty of the Church, but in her twenties, she must have felt obliged to mask any disrespectful feelings, especially on those occasions when she wanted something. Despite her emotional distress and the obvious fact that she was in no condition to take command of the situation, she understood the importance of gaining Eugenius's sympathy.

The pontiff, adhering to the best twentieth-century counseling practices, heard each party's grievances in separate interviews. It is unlikely that Eleanor expressed frankly the real sources of her discontentment with Louis. Contempt is a complicated emotion to fully explain in one session, which is all Eleanor had. Similarly, sexual frustration can be hinted at, but it would not have been a subject that Eleanor, a woman, could describe in any great detail to Eugenius, a man and a celibate man at that. In any case, either of these reasons for discarding a husband would have been interpreted as feminine caprice, and Eleanor knew it. Instead, she concentrated on what she believed the most legitimate of her grievances, that is, the fact that their invalid marriage had displeased God and prevented her from bearing an heir to the throne. In truth, Eleanor cared nothing about consanguinity—freedom, not morality, preoccupied her now—nor at this point did she desire more children by Louis. She simply could think of no better excuse. Always the pragmatist, she counted on this "sin," a popular one in divorce actions, to impress the pope, and she confidently awaited a favorable verdict.

In his interview, Louis went over similar ground but, of course, from his own viewpoint: the troubles in Antioch, the queen's coldness and resentment, her penchant for playing at life, his qualms about the illegality of their union. No mention was made of adultery; on the contrary, he gave the unmistakable impression that he desperately wanted to keep his wife, and as very often happens in such cases, the specter of loss looming on the horizon only imbued Eleanor with greater desirability. With piety, sincerity, and probably tears, Louis firmly impressed the pope that "he loved the queen passionately, in an almost childish way."

From the beginning Eleanor's chances were blighted, for she had failed to reckon with the biases of a pope who considered himself a conciliator rather than a judge. Since consanguinity seemed to be the issue troubling Eleanor's conscience, he would be happy to banish that fear from her mind at once. Both orally and in writing, he unhesitatingly confirmed her marriage, and should that not be strong enough, "he commanded under pain of anathema that no word should be spoken against it and that it should not be dissolved under any pretext whatever." This ruling, which "plainly delighted" Louis, must have plainly horrified Eleanor. But Eugenius did not stop there; during the two-day visit he harped at them every waking hour, striving, reported John of Salisbury, "by friendly converse to restore love between them." Obviously, John was not referring to the restoration of Louis's love. It was Eleanor on whom the pope exerted exceptionally strong pressure, but, taking into account her subsequent actions, it seems equally certain that he made little headway. Although she felt no love, indeed no positive emotion whatsoever for her husband, it was necessary, nonetheless, to smile, to dissemble, then to pretend she had accepted the pope's reassurances.

On the final evening of their visit, Eugenius administered the coup de grace. If the queen wished to have another child—and it must have been apparent to the old man that physical love had vanished from the marriage—then he would be delighted to arrange that as well. With the satisfaction of a person who has left no stone unturned, he prepared a special bed for the Capets, and decking it with priceless hangings from his own chamber, he personally escorted them to it. In the graphic words of John of Salisbury, "the Pope made them sleep in the same bed." Short of spending the night with them, Eugenius could not have done a more thorough job. Marriage counselor, sex therapist, well-meaning meddler par excellence, he prepared the stage for this charade, and Eleanor, hoisted on her own petard, had no choice but to perform her assigned role. That night the marriage was reconsummated. If there was ever a man incapable of raping a woman, it was Louis Capet, whose most confident couplings were those specifically endorsed and blessed by abbot or pope. In what state of despair Eleanor submitted will never be known, but technically at least, the act was against her will.

On their departure the next morning, the pope burst into tears. After loading their baggage with gifts, he effusively blessed them and the kingdom of the Franks "which was higher in his esteem than all the kingdoms of the world" and sent them on their way with an escort of cardinals. If Eleanor and Louis had arrived in Tusculum in a state of open antagonism, they left it in a far more unsettled mood. To all appearances, however, they seemed to be on good terms, at least Louis attempted to behave so. Scarcely had they traveled a few miles when a delegation of senators and noblemen from Rome came galloping toward them with the "keys" to the city. Louis, never happier than when being fussed over by a reverent crowd, was in his element. Upon reaching the outskirts of the city, the throngs of cheering Romans grew denser, and the king, followed by "nuns and boys" shouting "blessed is he that cometh in the name of the Lord," was prevailed upon to spend the day touring the city's shrines and holy places. His marriage mended, his wife restored to him, he may have overlooked the fact that Eleanor moved from shrine to shrine in the manner of a catatonic.

The hosannas over, they slipped quietly out of Rome the next day and began a series of forced marches into northern Italy and up over the Alps through the Jural Alpine pass. Some miles southeast of Paris, at Auxerre, they were met by Abbot Suger in response to a panicky note from the king imploring Suger to meet him secretly so that he might be informed of all plots and "how we must conduct ourselves toward all." It was a silent, morose group that made its way toward the Île-de-

France in the early days of November. The woodlands along the Seine were barren and damp under the autumn sun, but no one felt the chilly breath of approaching winter more deeply than Eleanor. As unsatisfactory as their papal visit had been, there existed no question in her mind that the final word on the divorce had not been spoken in Tusculum. Still, at that point, her future must have looked hopeless indeed.

The damp gray walls of the Cité Palace closed around Eleanor like a metaphorical dungeon from which there is no hope of escape. From the moment of their arrival, and for several months afterward, the Capets were the focus of whispers, rumors, and plots. Any popular rejoicing over their return was drowned by recriminations and angry mumblings of a decidedly seditious nature. There were demands for explanations, questions for which there could be no reasonable answers. The Church harked back to the inscrutable ways of the Almighty by pointing out that God's judgments never erred and lessons could be learned from even the greatest of calamities. What appeared, for instance, to Abbot Bernard as "evil times" ordained by Heaven, others were not willing to accept so fatalistically, and they looked to the earthly plane for causes. Blame was freely attributed, with Manuel Comnenus, the barons of Jerusalem, Raymond of Antioch, Geoffrey de Rancon, and even the queen herself bearing a share. Criticism fell most heavily, however, on Louis. While still in Palestine, he had quarreled with his brother Robert, who had rushed home after Damascus with plans to depose the king. Like Eleanor, Robert was angered by Louis's monkish posturings and decided, not without justification, that his brother might be happier at the Abbey of Clairvaux than upon the throne of France. It took all of Abbot Suger's considerable acumen to suppress the rebellion and preserve the king's birthright until he made up his mind to come home. Even so, there remained in the realm an atmosphere of sullenness that could not be dispelled by the feeble attempts of a few patriots to defend their sovereign. Surely, some Parisians suggested, ordinary decency, if not national pride, demanded that the Crusade and the king's safe return be honored in some way. Probably prompted by Suger, a commemorative medal was coined, showing Louis seated in a chariot with the goddess of victory fluttering above. "To the king returning victorious from the Orient the citizens give joyful welcome," read the inscription. Since this legend, so blatantly inaccurate, may have given rise to derisive mirth in some quarters, a second medal was struck to prove that an actual victory had occurred. The only confrontation with the enemy

that might possibly have been interpreted as a victory was the minor incident at the Maeander River in Asia Minor, and therefore the medal
read, "Turks killed and in flight on the shore of the Maeander," a
pathetic enough summation of Louis's deeds and one better forgotten.

For Eleanor, the homecoming was made all the more desolating by
the confirmation of a suspicion that she may have felt even while crossing the Alps. To her consternation, she realized that she was pregnant.
Nothing could have sealed her future more decisively, for now there
would be no divorce, no possibility of going back to Poitiers, nothing to
look forward to but gray years stretching into the interminable future
with a man she despised, her priest disguised as a king. Louis, elated,
behaved as though he had forgotten the marital trauma of the past two
years. At last he could present an heir to his people. Even those Franks
who had been busy blackening Eleanor's name with gossip about her
alleged depravity in Antioch were obliged to regard the queen with new
respect. In hardly anyone's mind, and certainly not in the king's, did
there arise the possibility that the child might be a girl. Surely a conception so meticulously choreographed by the pope himself could result in
nothing but a healthy son.

To those who later recalled that winter, it seemed to be the coldest
they had ever known. The Seine froze over, the wine criers disappeared
from the streets, and in the bone-bitingly cold chambers of the Cité Palace, where Eleanor extracted what warmth she could from fires and
braziers, there was ample time for reflection. Peering out through the
slitted apertures that passed for windows, gazing at the winter mists rising from the Seine, there was nothing to remind her of the sun-sluiced
gardens of Antioch. Except for her daughter, Marie, an infant when she
left and now five years old, nothing had changed. The short, stout figure
of the indispensable Suger still padded through the halls of the palace;
Abbot Bernard still issued proclamations from the swamps of Clairvaux; the omnipresent Thierry Galeran still shadowed the king's every
move; Louis, prayerful as ever, visited Vitry-le-Brûlé, where he planted
some cedars that he had carried home from the Holy Land. The fabric
of the royal couple's relationship patched together with the flimsiest of
thread, they kept to their separate beds, and despite Louis's solicitude
when they met, they had nothing to say to each other. In those winter
days when her hands and feet were half-paralyzed with cold and her
body swelled under her robes, Eleanor experienced a special kind of
anguish. Never before had life seemed so worthless, so devoid of
warmth and joy. Even in her darkest moments in Jerusalem, she had de-
luded herself into believing that Pope Eugenius would confirm the con-

sanguinity, but instead he had prepared a terrible trap into which she had permitted herself to be flung. Now, like a butterfly frozen in a cake of ice, she was thoroughly immobilized. She was twenty-eight, and nothing about life pleased her anymore.

In the early summer of 1150—the exact date has not survived—Eleanor gave birth to a girl, who would be christened Alix. That day a few church bells chimed softly, but there were no public demonstrations to honor the new princess, no bonfires in the squares of the Île-de-France. The queen, that exasperating Poitevin, had failed again. The only demonstrations of joy were those made by Eleanor herself, in the privacy of her chamber with the bed curtains drawn, for she knew that, in failing, she had won.

It is interesting to speculate what might have ensued had Eleanor borne a son. Certainly the history of Europe would have been vastly different, because a male child would have been an heir not only to the Frankish throne but to Eleanor's dower land of Aquitaine as well, thereby creating a unified realm larger than any that had existed for the Franks since the time of Charlemagne. That had been the picture in Louis the Fat's mind on the day he learned of Duke William IX's death, that had been the vision that had sustained Abbot Suger these many years. As both of them understood, however, William's generous bequest would only be a first step; technically, Eleanor's dower lands could only be officially incorporated into the Frankish kingdom when she had borne a son and, moreover, when the son succeeded Louis on the throne.

Just as Eleanor's pregnancy had been a state affair, so now her incompetence in childbed became a national concern, and after she had proved her perversity a second time, the more uneasy members of Louis's council began to voice fears that the queen might continue to produce princesses, that is, if she ever conceived again. Until this point Eleanor's struggle for release from the bonds of marriage had been a private one, but after the birth of Alix she saw the emergence of barons who began urging Louis to divorce her. Of course these unwitting allies were utterly unconcerned with the queen's personal wishes and, in point of fact, regarded her as no better than a cart that had failed to function properly.

Louis, now thirty, looked older than his years. Certainly he no longer resembled the willowy blond youth who had appeared on the banks of the Garonne to claim his bride, and although by medieval standards he could be called neither young nor old, still he had been married fifteen years with nothing to show for it. Until now, fortune had always smiled upon the Capetians; every king since 987 had left a male heir to succeed him, and continuity of the dynasty never lay far from any Capetian's mind. If luck failed, they were not averse to taking other measures, and it was recalled, as a matter of precedent, that in the late tenth century, Robert the Pious had been forced to set aside two wives in order to assure the succession.

The one person in the kingdom who seemed least troubled by the unexpected appearance of Princess Alix was Abbot Suger. Optimistic, he pointed out that Eleanor and Louis, still young, might anticipate more offspring, hopefully one of them male. More importantly, it was unthinkable to speak of giving up Aquitaine, that rich dower that Louis the Fat had clutched with so much satisfaction on his deathbed. Those who pressed for annulment argued that Eleanor's duchy, the most turbulent in Europe, had never added any substantial revenue to the crown. In truth, even had Louis been a stronger personality, he lacked the resources to subdue Aquitaine—even future masters with greater assets would be unable to do so—and in the mid twelfth century the Frankish monarchy was not psychologically ready to assimilate such a huge piece of property. Nevertheless, Suger's will quietly prevailed, and the knotty problem of the succession was shelved for the time being. During the coming months it would be he who held the marriage together, for he alone in the kingdom had the foresight to understand that the real consequences of a divorce would be, not France's loss of Aquitaine, but in the case of Eleanor's remarriage the addition of her lands to some other lord, thereby lifting this unknown someone to a position of greater power than that of Louis. Precisely who this someone might be Suger had no way of knowing.

By the end of the summer the Crusade, while not forgotten, had nonetheless begun to fade from people's minds. What had happened could not be changed and even for Louis, architect of its failure, life had to go on. Upon his return the previous autumn, he had been carefully briefed by Suger on the various shifts in political alignment among his vassals during his absence. The name that arose most frequently in these conversations was Plantagenet, not a real surname but a nickname for the count of Anjou, whose habit was to wear in his helmet a yellow blossom from the broom plant, the planta genesta. Geoffrey Anjou might have been a prototype for the chivalrous medieval prince. Dashing, incredibly good looking, highly educated, he impressed his contemporaries with his charm, courage, and above all, cleverness. Like all the Angevins, Geoffrey was a great believer in self-help, a fact that had no doubt been responsible for the mammoth strides he and his family had made in recent years.

Looking back to the eleventh century, there had been four important feudal empires in France, the most formidable being the house of Blois because of their family ties with the counts of Champagne, who controlled the commercial city of Troyes. Normandy, poor and badly situated, could not have been called a major power, while the house of Anjou, with its command of the rich Loire valley, showed potential, but the Angevins were undisciplined and its counts known to be unstable. Each of these houses, however, presented obstacles to the ascendancy of the Capets, the only ones who could boast of being anointed kings. Then in 1066 the whole power structure suddenly blew to pieces when William, duke of Normandy, successfully conquered England. All at once the Normans, those poor cousins, possessed newfound wealth, and worse in the eyes of the Capetians, they had wangled themselves a crown. In the shuffle, the balance of power shifted drastically, with the already insignificant Angevins shoved farther down the ladder. Certainly by the time Geoffrey was born in 1113, his family counted for relatively little. In fact, Geoffrey's father, Fulk V, thought so little of his inherited fief that, at the age of forty, he abandoned it to marry Melisende, the heiress of Jerusalem, the title king of Jerusalem holding an infinitely greater appeal for Fulk than that of count of Anjou. From small beginnings, then, he was able to increase his heritage by marrying an heiress, a strategy of proven success that would not be overlooked by his descendants.

The event most critical to the rise in Geoffrey Anjou's fortunes took place in 1120, when he was only seven years old. At twilight on November 25, Henry I, youngest son of William the Conqueror, king of England and duke of Normandy, prepared to make a routine crossing of the English Channel. With him at Barfleur on the Norman coast were his entire household, including his seventeen-year-old son and heir, William, "a prince so pampered," wrote Henry of Huntingdon, that he seemed "destined to be food for the fire." The king embarked before dark, but the younger members of the royal entourage, "those rash youths who were flown with wine," lingered to carouse on the shore. In any event, they felt no pressing need for haste, since they were sailing on the *White*

Ship, the swiftest and most modern vessel in the royal fleet, and would easily be able to overtake the king. Loath to break up the party, they did not launch their vessel until after nightfall. It was a perfect evening for a crossing, with a gentle breeze and a sea as calm and flat as a pond, and they soon might have caught up with the king had not a drunken helmsman rammed the ship into a rock in the bay. Panic broke out. Attempts to push free with oars and boathooks failed, and the ship rapidly began to fill with water. Throwing a dinghy overboard, Prince William and a few companions abandoned ship, but at the last moment he went back to rescue his illegitimate sister, the countess of Perche. The small boat, "overcharged by the multitude that leapt into her, capsized and sank and buried all indiscriminately in the deep. One rustic alone, floating all night upon a mast, survived until morning to describe the dismal catastrophe."

The wreck of the *White Ship* was as enormous a calamity in the twelfth century as the loss of the *Titanic* in the twentieth, even more so perhaps because it would shake the fortunes of England for the next thirty years. Prince William was Henry's only legitimate son, but "instead of wearing embroidered robes, he floated naked in the waves, and instead of ascending a lofty throne he found his grave in the bellies of fishes at the bottom of the sea." Henry had fathered at least twenty bastards, but despite a hasty second marriage, he was never able to produce the needed male heir. Aside from the prince, he had one other legitimate child, his daughter, Matilda, the widow of the German emperor. Determined to pass on the crown to a member of his immediate family, the king recalled Matilda from Germany, and in January 1127 publicly recognized her as his successor and required his barons to swear fealty to her. It was an extraordinary decision, one that drew immediate criticism from all sides, but a few months later, before the shock waves had even begun to subside, he jolted the sensibilities of his barons anew by marrying his daughter to young Geoffrey of Anjou.

These unusual arrangements satisfied no one but the king himself. Most appalled was Matilda, "a young woman of clear understanding and masculine firmness," who had been dragged home from Germany much against her own inclinations. She was twenty-five, the daughter of a king and the widow of an emperor; Geoffrey was fourteen and the son of a count. But Henry would hear of no objections; he wished her wed to Geoffrey, an alliance of political importance, he said, and he would have his way. From every angle, Henry's barons found his schemes repugnant. Matilda was a stranger to them, and from what little they knew of her they had formed a patently unfavorable impression. Strikingly handsome but haughty and domineering, she had been sent to Germany at the age of eight, where she had been groomed in a rigid court etiquette alien to Norman tradition, though of course her greatest handicap was her sex. The Normans knew of no precedent for the rule of a woman. As for Matilda's marriage to Geoffrey, the idea was totally distasteful. The Normans believed the Angevins to be barbarians who desecrated churches and ate like beasts. According to a widely accepted tale, their ruling family had descended from demons and were shameless enough to tell this story on themselves. Worse, they laughed about it. In no way did Geoffrey, a beautiful adolescent boy, resemble a demon, but blood would tell, and the Normans feared that Geoffrey would rule for Matilda. The idea of an Angevin on the throne of England was intolerable.

Predictably, the unlikely liaison of Matilda and Geoffrey turned out to be miserable for both of them. There was no denying Geoffrey's learning and charm, but as Matilda soon discovered, the charm was shallow and his cleverness devoted to the promotion of Geoffrey. He made no secret of the fact that he had married Matilda only to gain control of Normandy—evidently he realized that he would never be accepted as king of England—or that he impatiently awaited the death of her father. Or that he disliked her. She was, he complained, rude, arrogant, and unfeminine, and once, in a temper, he sent her back to England. For these reasons, it took the couple seven years to have their first child, a son who would be known as Henry FitzEmpress, after his mother.

Two years after the birth of his grandson and namesake, King Henry returned from a day of hunting in Normandy and, ravenous, wolfed down a dish of lampreys, "a fish which he was very fond of, though they always disagreed with him and the physicians had often cautioned him against eating them, but he would not listen to their advice." A few hours later he was dead. Now that the moment had arrived for Matilda to claim her throne, it became clear that Henry had grossly misjudged his people. When his nephew Stephen of Blois heard of the death, he raced across the Channel from France and claimed the throne for himself. That he had been one of those who had pledged allegiance to Matilda was irrelevant, although Stephen did have the grace to excuse his defection by saying that he had vowed homage to the empress under coercion. No excuses were really necessary. "All the bishops, earls, and barons who had sworn fealty to the king's daughter and her heirs gave their adherence to King Stephen, saying that it would be a shame for so many nobles to submit themselves to a woman." Such a turn of events, as Henry should have known, was inevitable.

Stephen of Blois, like Louis Capet, lacked the necessary qualities for kingship. "He was," wrote Walter Map, "a man of great renown in the practice of arms, but for the rest almost an incompetent, except that he was rather inclined to evil." A weak man, soft and indecisive, he began many things but never finished them, and though he reigned for "nineteen long winters," he left little behind except a chapel at Westminster and the memory of anarchy. Not until 1139 did Matilda invade England, and for the next eight years the country reeled with civil war. Stephen's claim to the throne was, some thought, as good as Matilda's, but what rankled the empress most strongly were those Norman barons who had blithely disregarded their oaths of fealty. Not completely devoid of insight into the realities of her situation, she made it clear that she did not want the throne for herself but for her son, Henry; even so, she managed to immediately justify the worst fears of those reluctant to accept her claims. Headstrong, intolerant, unbelievably tactless, she was "always breathing a spirit of unbending haughtiness." In 1141 her battle almost appeared to be won when she succeeded in taking King Stephen a prisoner, but then she ruined it—and lost any goodwill she might have gained from the English—by keeping Stephen in chains at Bristol Castle. In her efforts to claim her crown, she had no help from her husband, who seemed to regard her actions as none of his business. When once she begged him for help in 1142, he ignored her request for reinforcements and instead sent to England their nine-year-old son as a morale booster for her partisans. It was neither callousness nor political naiveté but his intense dislike for his wife that directed Geoffrey's attitude. Never happier than when parted from Matilda, he took every opportunity to erase her from his mind. Moreover, during these years he was involved in a conflict of his own; in Matilda's name, he had the satisfaction of waging war against his family's traditional enemy, Normandy, and by 1144 he would win for himself the title of duke of Normandy. What happened to Matilda, or for that matter England, did not concern him.

In England, the barons were torn between two sovereigns claiming their allegiance, with the result that some threw in their lot with Stephen, then switched to Matilda, and finally went back to Stephen. After seventy years of strong monarchical rule and royal justice, they were now forced to live with the chaos of private wars so familiar on the Continent but almost forgotten in England. "Men said," the *Anglo-Saxon Chronicle* mournfully relates, "that Christ and his angels slept." In the north country, hordes from Scotland and Wales, "that execrable army more atrocious than the whole race of pagans," marched into the Yorkshire valleys, massacring the villagers and taking away the women, roped together naked, as slaves. In the Isle of Ely, foreign mercenaries held men for ransom, hanging them over bonfires by their feet, casting them in dungeons crawling with snakes. The best description of the universal turmoil during Stephen's reign is offered by Henry of Huntingdon:

> Food being scarce, for there was a dreadful famine throughout England, some of the people disgustingly devoured the flesh of dogs and horses, others appeased their insatiable hunger with the garbage of uncooked herbs and roots. There were seen famous cities deserted and depopulated by the death of the inhabitants of every age and sex, and fields white with the harvest but none to gather it, all having been struck down by the famines. Thus the whole aspect of England presented a scene of calamity and sorrow, misery and oppression.

Out of the disorder eventually grew a great longing for peace, and despite Matilda, eyes slowly began to turn toward the young Henry Plantagenet. The demons from which he had supposedly descended could not have been any worse than those presently ravaging England.

The Plantagenets were certainly not strangers to Eleanor. Nor to Louis, for Geoffrey, a familiar figure at court, had once held the post of seneschal of France. Although the two men had been on fairly good terms, Geoffrey had declined to accompany Louis on the Crusade, despite the fact that his half brother was the boy-king Baldwin of Jerusalem. Geoffrey, always looking to his own interests first, had recently overpowered Normandy and wished to keep a watchful eye on his newly acquired property. In contrast, any possible glory to be won on the battlefields of Palestine paled into insignificance.

Neither was Henry Plantagent a totally unknown quantity to the king and queen. In those hurried days before the departure of the Crusade there had been talk of a betrothal between Henry and the Capet's infant daughter, Marie. Judging from a letter that Abbot Bernard wrote to Louis about that time, it was Geoffrey who had proposed the marriage, possibly anticipating a day when Aquitaine, or some substantial portion of it, would fall into Plantagenet hands as Marie's dowry. "I have heard," wrote Bernard, "that the Count of Anjou is pressing to bind you under oath respecting the proposed marriage between his son and your daughter. This is something not merely inadvisable but also unlawful because, apart from other reasons, it is barred by the impediment of consanguinity. I have learned on trustworthy evidence that the mother of the queen and this boy, the son of the Count of Anjou, are related in the third degree." Accordingly Bernard warned Louis "to have nothing whatever to do with the matter," and the idea had been dropped. For whatever reasons, Bernard distrusted both Geoffrey and his son. Once, he had met Henry as a boy and, after studying his face closely, predicted that he would come to a bad end. If Henry had come to Paris with his father during the betrothal negotiations, Eleanor surely would have met him, but even so it is unlikely that much converse passed between the queen and a thirteen-year-old youth who was being inspected as a potential son-in-law. At that particular period she was much too engrossed in preparations for the Crusade to be interested in a barely pubescent boy.

When Louis left France in 1147, Geoffrey's son had been little more than a child; by the time he returned, the younger Plantagenet had become a person to be reckoned with. Suddenly the king was faced with the startling and dismaying prospect of Normandy, Anjou, and England being united under one ruler, for after 1149 nobody in England cared what King Stephen did; they were concerned with Henry Plantagenet. Never, apparently, had Louis seriously considered the possibility of Geoffrey Anjou's son becoming king of England. It was unthinkable. In the struggle between Matilda and King Stephen, Louis's sympathies leaned firmly toward Stephen, who happened to be the younger brother of Count Theobald of Champagne. Despite Louis's former conflicts with Champagne, the friction had been dissolved some time ago, and Theobald's son, Henry, who had accompanied him on the Crusade, would eventually marry his daughter, Marie. However, Capetian family ties with Stephen were closer yet because recently Louis's sister, Constance, had married Stephen's son, Eustace, who was to someday succeed his father on the throne. These growing interconnections between the Capets and the house of Blois/Champagne automatically ranged Louis against the Plantagenets. Ever since January 1150, when Geoffrey had turned over the duchy of Normandy to his son, it being tradition among the Angevins to invest their heirs with responsibility before their own deaths, Louis had begun to show signs of concern, especially since Henry disdained to pay him customary homage for his fief. This impolite young man, he decided, needed to be taught a lesson.

In the summer of 1150 Louis, joining forces with King Stephen's son, Eustace, began to position his troops along the Seine near the Norman border. Before hostilities could begin, however, Suger stepped in. The abbot may have been old and ill, but what little energy remained to him he used to thwart another of Louis's futile wars. On the grounds that the king could not declare war without his barons' approval, a consent that he knew would never be obtained as long as he had a voice in the matter, the abbot managed to arrange a truce. Louis and his army returned to Paris without encountering Henry Plantagenet, but it was a confrontation postponed rather than canceled. Of all the humiliations that Louis would have to face in his lifetime none would be more personally painful than those dealt to him by the son of Geoffrey Anjou.

Stalking the
Planta Genesta

By the summer of 1151, Eleanor had psychologically poised herself for flight. Developments in recent months had helped set the stage in her own mind for an escape from the hated Île-de-France, and she was busy dreaming of her return to the Maubergeonne Tower in Poitiers. At this moment, no definite date had been established, but she knew that her release was now only a matter of months.

In January, Abbot Suger had died and with his passing had crumbled the last remaining barrier between Eleanor and her liberation. Renewing her demands with greater urgency, she found Louis in a more receptive frame of mind, and while he still professed to love her, his protestations had grown considerably weaker. Perhaps he himself acknowledged that loving her had become a luxury he could ill afford. By this time his ardor had been greatly corroded by the nervous fear that he might die without an heir, and even had he and Eleanor been compatible, he might have entertained thoughts of divorce by now. As for those who reiterated Suger's arguments in protesting the loss of Aquitaine, Louis might well have retorted, "What good is Aquitaine to a king without a son?" After more than a century and a half of Capetian rule, was he to be the last of his dynasty? Eleanor, after all, had failed him. He had never been able to satisfy her, and as beautiful and exciting as she undeniably was to him, as magnificent her heritage, it was almost with a sense of relief that he agreed to relinquish the most highly prized heiress in Christendom. But with Louis, maddeningly hesitant and slow moving, a decision was rarely implemented with speed. Doubtless he must have pointed out to Eleanor that they were not persons of ordinary circumstance who could go their separate ways without careful preparation. There were Frankish garrisons in the major towns of Aquitaine, and now, in this delicate situation, they must be withdrawn in peaceful, orderly fashion before a divorce could take place. Then the

138

queen could return to her lands without anxiety about possible conflict between the king's men and her own vassals. This was an argument certain to sway Eleanor, who gave Aquitaine precedence in everything; indeed, as time passed, she would give the impression of being willing to level Europe if she thought it would benefit her homeland.

Even the lapse of centuries is unable to blur her impetuosity, but in this case, she stilled her impatience. That summer, standing on the brink of a new life, her mood was one of sheer radiant happiness. Just outside Paris, girls and boys were dancing the traditional *caroles* on the sloping grassy hillsides, clapping and chanting in the warm sunshine. In the cool green garden of the Cité Palace, under the pear and lemon trees and the wooden trellises, the queen's head buzzed with ecstatic plans for her homecoming. Now, surely, nothing could go wrong.

Unfortunately, we do not know the details of how Eleanor viewed her future. For years she had spent her time waiting—for pregnancy, for the departure of the great Crusade, and then for the leave-taking from the Holy Land, but most agonizing, the wait to be free of Louis Capet. Now that her wait had nearly ended, she must have formed in her imagination a thousand plans and visions, foremost among these the creation of a magnificent court in Poitiers, a mecca for troubadours and poets in the cultured tradition of her grandfather or of Raymond of Antioch, but one still uniquely her own. After her journeys to the East, she knew better than anyone the exquisite possibilities open to a person of determination and imagination, two qualities that she possessed in large amounts. Her nature had never been the compliant female so idealized in medieval times by the ruling class but yet, in reality, so rarely found. From her childhood in William IX's court, indulged, rarely disciplined, admired by parents and poets, she had developed a strong sense of her own worth, a healthy ego we would term it today, and she had never stopped rebelling against the secondary role foisted upon her as queen of France. After years of being caged, or at least thwarted in her desires, her need for independence converged with an overwhelming passion to rule. Pleasure in life, for the mature Eleanor, meant sovereignty, personal as well as political.

At the same time, with her keen intelligence, she must have been aware of the difficulties facing an unmarried female ruler of a land as violent as Aquitaine. Uneasily she would have recalled the incident of her father's betrothed being kidnapped by the count of Angoulême—and Emma of Limoges had only been a minor heiress. What was to prevent an ambitious knight, some younger son with no prospects, from boldly snatching her as she rode along a deserted road in Poitou?

To discourage such notions she would need an exceptionally strong bodyguard at all times. Or a husband. Unlike her childhood heroine, Saint Radegonde, who had fled her husband only to embrace the monastic life, Eleanor hungered for a man. Bearing in mind her robust sexual drive, unsatisfied for her entire adult life, there is no doubt that she must have given serious consideration to the question of remarriage. How eagerly she must have looked forward to romantic love and physical enjoyment. At that time, however, had she mentally run down the list of available lords of sufficiently high position, she would have regretfully concluded that not one was simultaneously unmarried, of a suitable age, and appealing. She had no intention of being pushed into another marriage of purely political convenience. When she married, it would be to a man of her own choice, a gallant *chevalier* on the order of her Uncle Raymond or even Geoffrey Anjou.

Since, at last, Eleanor would be taking her position as sovereign of her own fief, she had an exceptionally strong interest in the activities of Aquitaine's neighbors, especially its northern neighbors, the Plantagenets. During that summer, people in the Île-de-France spoke of no one but Geoffrey and Henry, against whom Louis was shortly to launch a campaign. The earlier confrontation had been aborted by Suger's truce, although scattered attacks on Norman castles had continued. But without the abbot's sagacious counseling, a real war now seemed inevitable. In early summer, Louis mustered his forces on one side of the Norman border, while Geoffrey and Henry assembled their army on the other. To Eleanor, observing these preparations, the dispute may have seemed petty and senseless. Apart from Louis's natural interest in seeing the Plantagenets ousted from Normandy, an objective that fell into the category of closing the barn door after the horse has bolted, because he had already confirmed Geoffrey as duke in 1144, the immediate pretext for hostilities concerned Louis's seneschal for Poitou. At Montreuil, on the frontier between Poitou and Anjou, Gerald Berlai had erected a well-fortified castle, from which stronghold he had, apparently, harassed the surrounding countryside. This troublesome Berlai so annoyed Geoffrey that he had spent nearly a year besieging Gerald's supposedly impregnable fortress and finally had managed to capture it, along with Gerald and his family. Gerald's importance as representative of Capetian royal interests in Poitou failed to deter Geoffrey, who suspected Louis of encouraging his seneschal's forays into Angevin territory. The count's summary treatment of his prisoners, incarceration in a maximum-security dungeon, seemed unnecessarily harsh to his contemporaries, and Louis, with nothing better to do at the moment, vowed that he would fight on Berlai's behalf. Behind this, of course, lay his marked sensitivity to Henry's neglect in rendering homage for Normandy. This act, by which an overlord formally confirmed a vassal in his possessions, in no way implied that Louis had any authority over Normandy. Nevertheless, feudal custom demanded that the fiction be observed. That the insolent youngster would blithely disregard his obligation implied, to Louis at least, a distinct lack of respect.

If Eleanor believed that fighting the Plantagenets was a waste of time, she needn't have concerned herself unduly, because the war collapsed in a farce typical of Louis's military ventures. At the last moment he suddenly developed a fever and, pleading illness, rushed back to the Cité Palace, where he took to his bed for the remainder of the summer. During his convalescence, royal advisers persuaded him that a king who had lately worn the Crusader's cross should hesitate to shed Christian blood, no doubt a polite way of suggesting that the Plantagenet grasp on Normandy was now too strong to be easily broken. In the end, Louis agreed to call upon Abbot Bernard to mediate a settlement.

In the last week of August, Geoffrey Anjou and his son arrived in Paris. Louis, still confined to bed, managed to rouse himself and greet the visitors, but from the outset, the atmosphere seemed highly unconducive to reasonable discussion. For one thing, the weather had turned oppressively warm and humid. The Great Hall of the palace felt like an oven, the courtiers sweated, and irritability made everyone's temper short. Moreover, the spectacle caused by the Plantagenets' insolent entry into the hall quickly dispelled any hopes of an easy reconciliation. Not only did they bear themselves in a manner shockingly defiant of their overlord—from another point of view their entrance might be considered wonderfully bizarre—but Geoffrey had dragged with him Gerald Berlai, swaddled in chains, to answer charges. This method of displaying a noble prisoner horrified the Franks, especially Abbot Bernard, who intensely disliked Geoffrey and who had already been instrumental in arranging for his excommunication over this matter. Nevertheless, the sight of Berlai in chains moved him to offer a lifting of the ban in exchange for the seneschal's freedom. Geoffrey's audacious response favorably impressed Eleanor, who herself was feeling little respect for the Franks or Abbot Bernard at that particular time: He would not release Berlai, Geoffrey stoutly announced to the old man, and for that matter he would have hung him long ago if not for the

Truce of God in effect while Louis had been absent in the Holy Land. Furthermore, he did not care whether or not Bernard absolved him. With that, he launched into a public prayer, declaring that if holding Berlai a prisoner were a sin, then he refused to be absolved. This appalling blasphemy catapulted Bernard directly into one of his prophetic trances in which he threatened that Geoffrey would surely meet an early and sudden death and, nothing if not explicit, added that the count would be dead within a month. Geoffrey did not appear to be in the least concerned.

This sort of tempestuous drama, at once stunning and titillating, had not been witnessed in the Capetian court for many years. If Louis needed further proof of the Plantagenet menace, Geoffrey's performance offered conclusive evidence. Cranky and feverish, the king did nothing to dissipate the tension, and the opening session broke up shortly thereafter when Geoffrey stalked from the hall in a fit of the black bile that the Franks commonly associated with the Angevins. To Eleanor, the scene must have brought back memories of her father and grandfather, neither of whom had been intimidated by the clergy and who, in fact, derived a singular pleasure from tweaking their noses. Clearly Geoffrey, no puppet to be danced on Bernard's strings, was a man cast from the same mold as her forebears, and she could not have helped but secretly applaud him.

During the parley, Eleanor had an opportunity to study both men. At thirty-nine, Geoffrey still retained the striking physical attributes that had won him the nickname *le Bel*. But it was Henry who drew her attention. While not as good looking as his father, he had a face and figure that riveted all eyes to him. He gave the impression of having superabundant physical energy, a magnetism that in theatrical parlance would be termed stage presence, and he exuded a rugged maleness. Eleanor's eyes must have traveled almost greedily over his broad chest and square shoulders, over his arms as muscular as those of a gladiator. His close-cropped reddish hair and the high ruddy color in his freckled face made everyone around him, especially the pale Louis, look frail and sickly in comparison. He had prominent gray eyes, clear and mild when in a peaceable mood but that day bloodshot and flashing like balls of fire, and a gravelly voice, like that of a man who spends most of his time out of doors. There was nothing monkish about him.

It was obvious to Eleanor that here was no mirror of courtly chivalry. On the contrary, from his appearance alone it was almost impossible to distinguish him from a servant. His hands looked rough and coarse, his clothing of good quality but carelessly worn; flung over his shoulders was an absurdly short cape, contrary to all the current styles for men. Apparently he did not care what he looked like, nor what others might think of him. Throughout the meeting, he never once sat down, but stalked about impatiently, as if he begrudged wasting his time on boring trivialities. This was not a man who indulged in coquetry or wooing. One might expect the elegant Eleanor to have dismissed the rough-hewn youth as one of many persons with whom she might have to deal when she resumed control of her duchy. Significantly, she did not.

Despite the angry manner in which the Plantagenets had left the meeting, they did not depart from the court. Their visit lasted several days, perhaps as long as a week, and at the end of it, with no further threats from Bernard, they agreed to release Louis's seneschal and, far more importantly, surrender a portion of the Vexin and the city of Gisors in exchange for Louis's recognition of Henry as duke of Normandy. The Vexin, a tract of land on the northeast frontier between Normandy and France, had been a bone of contention between the two powers since the tenth century, when it had been partitioned, the northern portion becoming part of the duchy of Normandy, the southern half part of the demesne lands of the Capetians. Although Henry and his father considered occupation of the Vexin vital to the security of Normandy, they had nevertheless already relinquished half of this buffer zone to Louis in 1144 as the price of Geoffrey's recognition as duke. Now, much to the amazement of the Franks, they volunteered to part with the remainder. Such totally baffling behavior was attributed to Bernard's dire warnings; on the face of it, the only possible conclusion to be drawn was that Bernard had worked another miracle. As Eleanor knew, this was not the case at all.

That something of significance happened during those few days in August would in time become clear. That Eleanor decided to marry Henry, and that he eagerly fell in with the idea, would also become clear. But why and how this decision came about remained a mystery to twelfth-century historians. William of Newburgh tried to explain it this way: "For it is said that while she was still married to the king of the Franks she had aspired to marriage with the Norman duke whose manner of life suited better with her own, and for this reason she had desired and procured the divorce." Apparently discontent with such a superficial analysis, William goes on to add that Eleanor "was greatly offended with the king's conduct, even pleading that she had married a monk, not a king." Newburgh, who wrote his history some forty years later while canon of an Augustinian priory, was a chronicler of sound judgment, but as a churchman, he could only hint at the underlying reason for a liaison between two such unlikely individuals as Eleanor and Henry. On the other hand, Walter Map, a courtier and clerk in Henry's household some years later, did not hesitate to repeat salacious gossip, but even so, his analysis probably came closer to the truth when he wrote that Eleanor "cast glances of unholy love" upon Henry. The whys and wherefores of sexual attraction, often discounted by historians, proved to be of overriding significance in the case of Eleanor and Henry.

We know nothing about the precise circumstances of their first tryst in the Cité Palace beyond the fact that it was initiated by Eleanor and must have been intense and conclusive. Perhaps taking advantage of Louis's incapacitation, Eleanor might have sent a trusted servingwoman through the dark, silent passageways with a message that brought Henry to her chamber after the palace had fallen asleep. Perhaps it did not happen that way. But in whatever manner they managed to meet, it was accomplished so skillfully, so secretly, that no one in the Cité Palace knew of it, an extraordinary feat considering that privacy in medieval castles was virtually nonexistent. Later, it would be said by their contemporaries that Henry debauched and filched his overlord's wife from beneath the king's own nose. If any seduction took place at this time, and it may well have, it would have been Eleanor who did the seducing, for the eighteen-year-old boy awakened an overwhelming feeling in her. Neither the eleven-year difference in their ages nor the obvious fact that he was no chivalrous knight with pretty speeches for the ladies could quench her longing. She was ready and ripe to be undone by a truly lascivious man. That the physical attraction was mutual is strikingly evident from the eagerness with which Henry responded to her advances, and perhaps it was to him that Eleanor remarked that she had married a monk.

And yet powerful sexual attraction can be easily assuaged—and was certainly done so in Eleanor's era—without resorting to marriage. Both Eleanor and Henry were far too practical to be swept away by physical passion alone, and their conversations in those secret meetings touched on more important subjects than the carnal. Their alliance had to be predicated on two developments that had not yet, and might never, occur: first, Eleanor's ability to secure a divorce and the restoration, free and clear, of her duchy; and second, Henry's rise to the throne of England. Doubtless Henry pointed out to her that his mother's, and his own, efforts to win over the English barons were finally beginning to bear fruit. During the past year, he had assumed a commanding lead in his struggle against King Stephen in that the English had grown heartily sick of civil war and now spoke of an arrangement whereby Stephen would rule until his death and Henry reign as his successor. While the risks for Eleanor and Henry were great, so were the stakes. For Eleanor, there was always the hazard of Louis's learning of her intentions and preventing a divorce but, on the other hand, a crown. The nature of the gamble was also clear to Henry: By marrying the queen he would incur Louis's hostility, but this seemed a small price to pay for a young man entertaining visions of an empire. Created duke of Normandy, he would inherit the counties of Anjou and Maine on his father's death, and now England too seemed within his grasp. By marrying Eleanor, he could take on Aquitaine as well. The prospects fired his imagination, for, if successful, he would someday rule an area from Scotland to the Pyrenees, an empire larger than any other feudal monarch. And another thought may have entered his mind. Henry was too realistic to overlook the fact that many believed the duchy of Aquitaine to be ungovernable, but this seemed a minor consideration compared to the dangers that Eleanor's remarriage to anyone else would have created for him. Her divorce would remove Capetian influence from Anjou's borders, but real security for Henry could only be found in marrying Eleanor himself.

In light of these considerations, the difference in their ages counted for nothing. In the future, Henry expected to have need of a queen, and one as beautiful and rich as Eleanor, regardless of her tarnished reputation as an adulteress, could certainly not be bypassed. Dominated as he was by his mother, he had no objections to an older woman, indeed the age difference in his own parents' marriage must have made it seem natural. From all contemporary accounts, Henry neither looked nor acted his age, and at eighteen he had already matured into a self-assured adult with a will of iron, a determination to achieve his ends no matter the cost, and a capacity for work that would never fail to astonish his subjects. All in all, he was the most formidable man that Eleanor had ever met, as well as the most businesslike. If it occurred to her that Henry desired her for her lands, that exploiting heiresses ran as a tradition in his family, she could afford to overlook the cynicism of such behavior. In actual fact she had as much to gain by the marriage as he. As immense as her physical needs might have been, it was not in Eleanor's character to settle for just any young stud. Whether she would have wanted Henry Plantagenet if she had not been convinced that he would be the next king of England is highly doubtful.

By the first week of September the hot weather still had not broken. The Plantagenets, grateful to be leaving the stinking, stifling alleys of the Île-de-France, made their amends to their Capetian overlord: Gerald Berlai and his family were released, the Vexin and Gisors formally relinquished, all the loose ends harmoniously tidied up. The count and duke, so recently testy, now appeared as mild as lambs, equably agreeing to anything, for the loss of the Vexin seemed a trifling cost to pay for the promise of Aquitaine. Louis marveled at his good fortune, and if any trace of a satisfied smile appeared on Henry's face as he solemnly placed his hands in the king's to swear fealty and then receive the kiss of peace, Louis failed to notice.

Years later, chroniclers would claim that Geoffrey strongly disapproved of his son's intrigue with Eleanor. According to Gerald of Wales, "When Geoffrey was seneschal of France, he had carnally known Queen Eleanor of whom he frequently forewarned his son Henry, cautioning him and forbidding him in any wise to touch her, both because she was the wife of his lord, and because she had been known by his own father." Gerald, who claimed that he had heard the story from Bishop Hugh of Lincoln who, in turn, had been told by Henry himself, cannot be regarded as an objective commentator because of his strong personal antipathy to Henry. Nor is Henry particularly reliable, because by that time he was not averse to spreading calumnies about Eleanor. Had she been Geoffrey's mistress, it would not have been in keeping with the count's character to have objected to the marriage on that ground, not in view of the lands that such a union would bring into the Plantagenet holdings. Moreover, it is difficult to explain his public conduct at Paris without assuming that he knew of Henry's pact with Eleanor—and approved it.

When the two men left Paris in the early days of September, they must have felt exhilarated by their success. They had, unfortunately, been compelled to barter the Vexin, but neither of them regarded this as anything but a temporary loss. Now that Henry had been recognized as duke of Normandy, he was in a far better position to further his ambition to invade England, and on September 14, he planned to meet with a council of his Norman barons to discuss that very project. His most immediate concern was raising money to pay an army of mercenaries, and now, in full control of his duchy, such funds could be more easily obtained. As they galloped along the road to Angers on September 4, evaluating their gains and losses, no doubt chortling treasonously over their ease in duping Louis, the heat and dust grew almost unbearable. At the river Loire, twenty-five miles southeast of the capital city of Le Mans, where Henry had been born, they stopped to swim in the refreshing water. That night, Geoffrey was seized with chills and fever, and three days later, as if to prove the uncanny accuracy of Bernard's prophecy, he died, all remedies having failed to save him.

Meanwhile, even before the news of Geoffrey's death had drifted back to Paris, Eleanor had already pressed Louis into taking the first steps toward a divorce. In late September they set out on what would be their last progress through Aquitaine. That this was no casual holiday was evidenced by the size and importance of their escort. Accompanying Louis were his secretaries, Thierry Galeran and Adam Brulart; his chancellor, Hugues de Champfleuri; and an imposing number of prelates and barons. Eleanor, however, seems to have had a separate retinue of southerners, including Geoffrey du Lauroux, the same archbishop of Bordeaux who had officiated at her marriage; her old friend Geoffrey de Rancon; the bishops of Poitiers and Saintes; and prominent vassals, such as the viscount of Châtellerault and the count of Angoulême. Most of these men were either close family friends or relatives. The royal retinue celebrated Christmas at Limoges and from there traveled south to Bordeaux. On February 2, 1152, they were at Saint Jean d'Angély, where they observed Candlemas in the local abbey. During this circuit, Aquitaine was stripped of its Frankish garrisons and administrators and the domain set in order for Eleanor's return. Later that month, Eleanor and Louis took leave of each other for the time being, she returning to Poitiers while he traveled on to Paris. Now all that remained was the formality of convening a special assembly to pronounce the decree.

In Eleanor's lifetime and for long afterward there was a widespread impression that Louis had sufficient cause to repudiate her on the grounds of adultery but, out of the goodness of his heart, settled for an annulment based on the legal subterfuge of consanguinity. The Minstrel of Reims embroidered a colorful scene that has no foundation in fact but nevertheless reflected popular perception of the divorce. "And he [Louis] took counsel of all his barons what he should do with the queen and he told them how she had demeaned herself.

"I' faith," said the barons, "the best counsel that we can give you is that ye let her go; for she is a very devil, and if ye keep her long we fear that she will cause you to be murdered. Furthermore, and above all else, ye have no child by her."

In the minstrel's opinion, Louis "therein did he act as a fool. Far better had it served him to have immured her; then had her vast lands remained to him during her lifetime, nor had those evils come to pass that did befall."

This excerpt underscores the agonizing dilemma facing Louis. If he divorced Eleanor for adultery, she would not be able to marry again during his lifetime and thus her fief would eventually be inherited by their daughters. But if he did that, he himself would not be able to remarry either. If he imprisoned her, Aquitaine would remain his, but again there could be no possibility of his remarriage. Foolish as his decision may have appeared to some of his contemporaries, in the end he had no choice. By 1152, not only were his barons eager for a new queen, but Abbot Bernard also sanctioned the divorce. Aside from Bernard's personal hostility toward the queen, there was the certainty of her consanguinity to the king; from every angle, he could not regret her loss to the kingdom of France.

On March 21, 1152, the Friday before Palm Sunday, Eleanor arrived at the royal castle of Beaugency near Orleans for the annulment proceedings. A great assembly had gathered for this important occasion, which, although dignified, turned out to be more or less routine, confirming the clauses already agreed upon. Witnesses came forth with recitals attesting that the king and queen were related by blood within the prohibited degree. The princesses Marie and Alix were declared legitimate and their custody awarded to the king. The archbishop of Bordeaux, acting on Eleanor's behalf, asked for reassurances that the queen's domains would be restored intact and, equally important to Eleanor, that she might marry again so long as she gave Louis the allegiance a vassal owed her overlord. Without further delay, the annulment was formally pronounced by the archbishop of Sens.

A chronicler of a later century would paint a fanciful picture of a distraught, weeping queen, fainting, protesting her innocence, carrying on in such hysterical fashion that the prelates and barons feared for her sanity. What more likely happened is that Eleanor and her escort of vassals mounted and rode away from Beaugency with the greatest possible speed. There is no reason to believe that she and Louis parted on anything but cordial terms, although the cordiality on the king's part would be short-lived. He had never truly desired the divorce, and the parting must have been unpleasant. On that final day of their marriage at Beaugency, the last time they would ever meet, there were surely moments when he regretted his decision. Perhaps he had been wrong to repudiate her, perhaps he should have allowed Marie and Alix to accompany her. Having no talent for prophecy, he wished her well.

If the day had seemed a sorrowful ending for Louis, it meant a bright new beginning for Eleanor. On that warm spring Saturday as she took the road south toward Poitiers, the countryside glistened, and every tree unfurled its green banners. It was a day when the towns bustled with activity, when people were stripping trees to make palms for the processions the following day or decorating the fronts of their houses. But part of the excitement was created by Eleanor herself, in that not every day did a divorced queen ride by. She had been preceded by news of her release, and people lined up to wave and stare. Near the city of Blois, however, she received her first real indication that life as the ex-queen of France might prove to be, not only difficult, but perilous as well. Stopping for the night, probably at one of the local abbeys, she learned that Theobald of Blois, second son of Louis's vassal the count of Champagne, was plotting to kidnap her. While Eleanor may have been prepared for such an attack at some distant time in the future, she must have been startled to find it happening the day after her divorce. Protected by her escort, she quickly left Blois and hurried south toward the county of Touraine, which belonged to Henry and might offer greater safety. Nevertheless, on her guard now, she took the precaution of sending scouts ahead to make certain that no other ambitious knights lay in wait. As she neared the river Creuse, where she planned to make a fording, she was warned "by her good angel" that Henry Plantagenet's seventeen-year-old brother, Geoffrey, had arranged a full-scale ambush at Port-de-Piles. Changing her route, she managed to detour around Geoffrey and finally crossed into Poitou "by another way." Although she had outwitted both would-be seducers, Eleanor would not have found these two escapades flattering; indeed, she must have felt highly incensed to know that she had become fair game for every unemployed knight. Used goods she might have been, a rich, no-longer-young woman who, gossip said, had been repudiated by her husband for unseemly conduct, but she was not yet reduced to marrying second sons.

By Easter, safely home in the Maubergeonne Tower, she began life anew. A household had to be assembled, clerks hired to write letters and charters, notices sent to her chief vassals informing them of her divorce and asking them to render homage and swear fealty to the countess of Poitou and duchess of Aquitaine, grants and privileges renewed for various abbots and abbesses. In the midst of the chaos, Eleanor's first preoccupation seems to have been her determination to rid Aquitaine of Frankish influence. While Louis's staff had been evacuated, she did not, evidently, believe this sufficient, for immediately she declared null and void every act she had made together with her ex-husband, as well as those he had made alone. During these first weeks after her homecoming, we have documents attesting to her industriousness as an administrator but not to the arrangements she was making in her private life. How she prepared for her marriage to Henry, what letters were sent and received, what last-minute reservations she may have experienced, have long been a subject of speculation. Although it is generally accepted that she summoned Henry to Poitiers, so shrouded in secrecy were their communications that no document remains to betray them.

Eleanor's position was extremely delicate on two levels. In her capacity as duchess of Aquitaine, she was a vassal of Louis's, and as in the case of any vassal, protocol demanded that she secure his approval before marrying, though obviously this was one formality she could not afford to render. As Louis's former wife, she knew intimately his feelings of dislike for Henry; aside from flouting his authority as her overlord, she was about to deliver a stinging personal blow by marrying his chief enemy, a factor that may well have been part of her initial attraction to Henry. In a sense, she was about to take a deadly revenge, both personal and political, for fifteen years of boredom and entrapment, but one false step now, and to her peril, she would find the king's army pouring over her borders.

In mid-May, Henry and a few companions arrived in Poitiers, and on Sunday, May 18, barely eight weeks after Eleanor's divorce, the marriage ceremony took place. No trumpets signaled their union. It was a subdued, almost surreptitious celebration, witnessed only by close friends, family, and household members. Although the occasion lacked the ostentation normally associated with the wedding of two distinguished persons, nevertheless precautions had to be taken in order to assure the validity of the marriage contract. Ironically, Eleanor was more closely related to Henry than she had been to Louis, their common ancestor being Robert II, duke of Normandy, and it was necessary to locate canonists who would issue the proper dispensations. The alliance so skillfully nurtured to fruition during the past seven months would have mighty and far-reaching consequences, but in May 1152, Eleanor was only concerned about the immediate ones, and the days following the wedding offered a temporary respite from the storm that she expected to break over her head.

Sexual attraction, her intuition that Henry would someday be the most formidable sovereign of his generation, a need for an efficient protector of Aquitaine, perhaps also her deep need to hurt Louis: These had been the main factors in her hasty selection of a husband. But she did not know Henry as a person. Now, during this honeymoon of sorts, she had an opportunity to scrutinize more closely the volatile man she had chosen. Basically she found that, though her judgment had been sound, he was a complex man with a host of contradictory qualities. Like herself, he had been given a first-class education, both at his father's court and in the English household of his uncle Robert, earl of Gloucester. Both Matilda and Geoffrey, despite their personal animosity for one another, had apparently been in agreement that Henry should be educated in a manner befitting a future king. Under the direction of his tutor, Master Matthew, archdeacon of Gloucester, Henry learned a smattering "of all the languages which are spoken from the Bay of Biscay to the Jordan but making use only of Latin and French." From his father he received the usual training in riding, jousting, falconry, and hunting, and as an adult, these arts were to be a consuming obsession with him; neither was his military education neglected, for Geoffrey was known to have owned a fourth-century Roman handbook on war. For a layman, Henry was well read, sometimes taking books to bed, and he sought out the company of intellectuals, with the result that he constantly squirreled away information. "Anything he had once heard worthy of remembrance he could never obliterate from his mind. So he had at his fingers' ends both a ready knowledge of nearly the whole of history and also practical experiences of almost everything in daily affairs."

From the earliest age, his head had been crammed full of tales about his illustrious ancestors: his great-great-great grandfather the legendary Fulk the Black, who had defeated an army of Bretons before the age of fourteen; his great-grandfather William the Conqueror, who had seized the throne of England after the battle of Hastings; his mother, who had escaped from beleaguered Oxford Castle by walking through Stephen's lines in the dead of a snowy night. Inspired by these daring exploits, Henry himself had made an expedition to England when he was fourteen to snatch Stephen's crown but, once there, realized that he had no money to pay his soldiers. In the end, Stephen had lent the young fighting cock the funds to return to Normandy.

Although Henry thought troubadours and games of chivalry a waste of time, he was not, Eleanor discovered, without refined tastes. His mother had taught him how to behave like a gentleman, and he was capable of great gentleness, courtesy, and at times even delicacy. In later years, on a windy day, he was out riding with a distinguished clergyman Dom Reric, when a Cistercian monk stumbled and fell in front of his horse. The wind blew the Cistercian's habit over his neck, exposing his backside. "Curse that religion that reveals the arse," muttered Dom Reric. Henry, however, looked away in silence and pretended to see nothing. Matilda also passed along a brand of cynical wisdom peculiarly her own, and in Walter Map's opinion, "to her teaching we may confidently impute all those traits which rendered him unpleasant." In one of her parables, she impressed upon her son that "an untamed hawk, when raw flesh is often offered to it, and then withdraw or hidden, becometh more greedy and is more ready to obey and remain," a policy of tantalization that Henry would put to good use in his relationships with family, friends, and enemies. Another piece of advice that Henry liked to repeat was Matilda's admonition to be "free in bed, infrequent in business." His freedom in bed Eleanor no doubt counted as a blessing, at least in the early stage of their marriage, and in this respect he must have provided a startling and delightful contrast to Louis Capet.

In personal appearance, however, Henry was anything but heroic, and as Eleanor now had a chance to observe, he was slightly bowlegged, a characteristic that would become more pronounced as he aged, and he complained incessantly about ingrown toenails and blisters on his legs. Although fairly slender for a stocky person, he had a phobia about growing fat, saying, whether true or not, that he possessed a natural tendency to corpulence. As a result he was forever dieting, fasting, or wearing himself out physically through violent exercise.

But his most remarkable characteristic, the one that amazed his contemporaries and must even have startled Eleanor, who herself possessed an abundance of vitality, was his demonic energy. In the twentieth century, he surely would have been diagnosed as a classic case of hyperactivity. Constantly in motion, he rose before cockcrow; seldom sat down except on horseback or at meals, which he ate quickly; and to the dismay of his subjects, he transacted all business standing up. While talking or listening, his eyes and hands were incessantly moving, touching birds, dogs, armor, hunting spears. Even during Mass, which he attended every day more out of duty than piety, he paid no attention to the service but could be seen talking business to his clerks, doodling, or looking at books. Never wasting a minute, he sometimes worked through the night and, wrote Ralph Niger, "shunned regular hours like poison."

To Eleanor, hearing him shout in his hoarse voice his favorite oath "By the eyes of God!" it must have seemed as though a tornado had descended on the Maubergeonne Tower. Had she ever been inclined to think of him as a raw, inexperienced youth whom she could dominate and advise, she would have realized her mistake during this period. Moreover, as distressing as it may have been to acknowledge, his behavior plainly indicated that he was not helplessly in love with her, or perhaps in fairness to Henry, he had bigger things on his mind at the moment. What need had he to tarry with a bride when there was an island to conquer, a throne to win? Eleanor, a realist, was also a romantic, and this realization must have hurt. Nevertheless, she understood that unforeseen circumstances had forced him to postpone his invasion of England several times. His father's death had obliged him to visit Anjou in order to take possession of his heritage and assure the fidelity of his vassals. Growing impatient, his supporters in England had sent Earl Reginald of Cornwall to implore haste, and on April 6, after a meeting of Henry's barons at Lisieux, preparations had moved forward, only to be canceled due to his wedding trip. Now he was in a fever to be off. Since we know that he was at Barfleur on the Normandy coast about the middle of June, he could not have stayed longer than two weeks with Eleanor, perhaps less, because nine days after the wedding, attending to business again, she granted a charter to the Abbey of Saint-Maixent.

Meanwhile, the tidings of Eleanor's marriage had exploded like a series of strategically placed bombshells in various cities of Europe. Among the disgruntled was Henry's brother, Geoffrey, so lately thwarted in his own ambition to marry Eleanor and still smarting at the disappointingly small inheritance—three castles—he had received from his father. Henry of Champagne, betrothed to Eleanor's seven-year-old daughter, Marie, and dreaming of acquiring Aquitaine in her name, saw his prospects melt away. And King Stephen's son, Eustace, clinging to the hope of being crowned king of England someday, could only gnash his teeth when he learned that his rival pretender now owned half of France.

The man most stunned, however, was Louis Capet. If he had considered the possibility of Eleanor's remarriage, it would have been to some inconsequential baron of his own choosing, not to Henry Plantagenet. The conspiracy perpetrated by his former wife and her new husband, the scope of their perfidy, their contempt for every tenet of feudal custom and law, overwhelmed him. The bitter sting of humiliation lay, however, in the realization that Eleanor, his vassal, had married without his permission, that Henry only last year had sworn fealty and received the kiss of peace. But other aspects of the disaster simply confused him: Had Eleanor forgotten that a marriage between Henry and the Princess Marie had been declared unlawful? How could the woman who had nagged him with her scruples about consanguinity from Antioch to Beaugency have now married a man to whom she was even more closely related? Burning with hatred of the crafty Plantagenet who had "basely stolen" his wife and, for the first time, with an equally intense hatred of Eleanor, Louis huddled with his advisers in an effort to surmount these calamitous developments. Solutions— revocation of the annulment, excommunication—were suggested and discarded. When a letter ordering the appearance of the duke and duchess in the French court to answer charges of treason failed to bring a response, Louis settled on more practical means of dealing with the situation. Provoked beyond endurance, he acted quickly for once and formed a coalition of all those who had a grievance against Henry. Backed by his brother Robert, Theobald of Blois, Henry of Champagne, Eustace, and Geoffrey Plantagenet, Louis decided against attacking Aquitaine, which the coalition had resolved to divide among themselves, but instead charged into Normandy to confront Henry directly. Immediately it became apparent that he had chosen the wrong tactic.

At a furious rate, Henry bore down from Barfleur to the Norman-French frontier, and so rapidly did he move his forces that, it was said, several horses fell dead on the road. He ignored Louis's troops and, like a whirlwind, began to ravage the Vexin and the lands belonging to Robert of Dreux before turning west to Touraine, where he deftly relieved his brother of those three castles that had comprised his miserly inheritance. Attacking here, counterattacking there, within six weeks he had routed each of his opponents. To Louis, it must have seemed that he could do nothing right. Bereft of hope, bewildered, he came down with another fever and retired to the Île-de-France to brood upon the irretrievable loss of Aquitaine, which, in his opinion, should have been the lawful inheritance of Marie and Alix.

These were anxious weeks for Eleanor as she waited for the attack that never came, but as news of Henry's successes filtered back to Poitiers, she must have been relieved at this confirmation of his abilities as a soldier. At the same time, however, she had reason for continued apprehension. By the end of June she had been forced to accept the disheartening fact that she had not conceived. Even though Henry desired sons with no less passion than Louis, he had married her despite her poor record as a breeder. Somehow she must have convinced him that those two lone pregnancies in fifteen years had been due to Louis's lack of libido, but now, desperately anxious to prove her fertility and give him an heir, she realized that conception might be equally difficult with Henry, for entirely different reasons. If Louis had rarely made use of his conjugal privileges, Henry simply was not present to share her bed. Under the circumstances, it was unclear when she might see him next, for once he reached England there was no way of telling how long he would remain. For the moment, all she could reasonably do, however, was live her own life as duchess.

About this time she had a seal made, which gives us a fairly good impression of her majestic beauty. On one side is the full-length figure of an extremely slender woman, bare-headed, arms outstretched, holding in one hand a falcon and in the other a fleur-de-lis; the inscription reads, "Eleanor, duchess of Aquitaine." On the seal's obverse side, inscribed with her newly acquired titles—duchess of Normandy, countess of Anjou—she wears a form-fitting gown with tight sleeves and, over her head, a veil that falls to the ground. Her charters and official proclamations in the early days of June 1152 convey a sense of her authority as well as pride in her new marital status: "I, Eleanor, by the grace of God, duchess of Aquitaine and Normandy, united with the duke of Normandy, Henry, count of Anjou . . . " Unlike most charters, these are strongly colored by emotions, positive as well as negative. To the Abbey of Montierneuf, for example, she reextended all the privileges granted by her great-grandfather, grandfather, and father, but she made no mention of her ex-husband, who had also accorded benefits to the monks. At the Abbey of Saint-Maixent, however, acknowledging the fact that she had taken back the woods that Louis had donated to the abbey, she renewed their rights to the lands "with a glad heart" now that she was joined in wedlock to the duke of Normandy. It was at Fontevrault, though, that her exhilaration shines through most clearly. To this abbey, which had meant so much to her grandmother Philippa and which would have enormous significance in her own life, she confirmed "with heartfelt emotion" all their existing privileges and added a personal donation of five hundred sous. In this particular charter, in which she mentioned her divorce and recent marriage to "my very noble lord Henry," she expressed her feeling that she had come to Fontevrault "guided by God," and certainly the deep impression made upon her that day would be confirmed by her continuing preference for Fontevrault above all other religious establishments.

While Eleanor had always been popular in Aquitaine, her vassals had never taken kindly to her first marriage. Whatever threats Louis had posed to their independence were nothing, however, compared to the ominous prospects of being ruled by Henry Plantagenet. When Eleanor had presented her new husband to her barons at the time of the marriage, they had given him a cool reception, and over the summer she had been forced to acknowledge a disquieting truth: If rumor could be believed, many of her vassals were saying that Henry had no claim on their loyalty, other than as the husband of their duchess, of course. Understandable was the deep misgiving with which they contemplated the possibility of Henry's ascension to the throne of England, since it presented to them the distasteful prospect of a ruler whose authority would be backed by massive resources. For a people intolerant of any authority but their own, Eleanor's new marriage came as an unwelcome surprise, which they did not intend to accept with good grace. At this time, however, Eleanor, perhaps sensibly, perhaps stupidly, seems to have given little thought to this problem, feeling no doubt that her vassals' hostility to Henry would dissolve in time, and in any case, they had no choice but to eventually accept him.

In late August, Louis Capet's threat to Plantagenet security over, Henry unexpectedly returned to Poitiers. Eager to take advantage of this opportunity to introduce a wider range of her vassals to their new duke, as well as to acquaint Henry with her ancestral possessions, Eleanor quickly arranged an extensive tour that would take them to every corner of the duchy. That autumn was, in retrospect, a joyous period, probably the most idyllic she would ever spend with Henry, because, for one thing, she had him to herself for four unbroken months. If, as far as Henry was concerned, the progress represented more or less a tour of newly acquired property, it was for Eleanor both a holiday and a homecoming, the first extended period she had spent among her own people since the divorce. Followed by mule trains and cartloads of baggage, they leisurely pursued the trails southward through Poitou, into the Limousin, down past the salt marshes of Saintonge, as far south as the rugged country of Gascony, all the while meeting old friends, sipping the hearty Bordeaux wines, loosing their falcons against the deep blue autumn skies. And everywhere that Eleanor traveled, she was followed by song and loud laughter, by boisterous crowds of knights, ladies, poets, and hangers-on. Every night there were banquets in great halls blazing with candles and the best plate; musicians to sing war songs, crusading songs, love songs, and, most assuredly, the bawdy songs of William the Troubadour; gossip of the latest seductions, marriages, and political feuds. There was talk of Byzantium and the Holy Land, with audiences eager for Eleanor's tales of her travels. Henry, affable and relaxed most of the time, seemed to find her duchy to his taste, particularly when he could indulge his love of hunting and falconry. At other times, sensing the hostility of Eleanor's vassals, he just barely managed to curb his temper, and on one occasion, he was unable to do so.

Henry and Eleanor had pitched their tents outside Limoges; despite the royal welcome extended by the townspeople, at mealtime Eleanor's cook complained that the town had failed to send the customary provisions to the ducal kitchen tent. When Henry demanded explanations for this oversight, the abbot of Saint Martial's informed him that the town was only obliged to provide victuals when Henry lodged within the city walls. This was putting altogether too fine a point on feudal obligations to suit Henry, and indeed the Limousins could not have made their low opinion of the duke more obvious.

There at Limoges, Eleanor had first witnessed one of Henry's temper tantrums. The Angevin reputation for "black bile," even her own fire-breathing father's outbursts, had not prepared her for the sight of Henry in the grip of rage. Losing every vestige of self-control, he rolled on the ground, shrieking, writhing, and kicking. With spittle leaking from his mouth, he bit blankets, gnawed on straw, smashed furniture, and lashed out with hand or sword at anyone foolish enough to remain in the vicinity.

In the midst of just such a fit, Eleanor had stood by while Henry ordered the newly built walls of Limoges to be razed and their bridge destroyed so that, in future, no abbot could use them as an excuse to withhold from their duke his just and reasonable dues. If she received a rude shock from both her husband's behavior as well as his order to tear down the town walls, she did not interfere because, as distressing as the command may have been, the insult reflected on herself as well and could not be tolerated.

Nevertheless, the southerners adored their duchess and delighted in making much of her, but if the limelight fell continually on Eleanor and rarely on Henry, he made no complaint. Even though the days seemed to pass in almost aimless fashion, appearances were deceptive. Like a businessman whose uppermost thoughts are always occupied by self-interest, Henry's seemingly lackadaisical behavior covered a shrewd analysis of his wife's resources. Taking advantage of all and any opportunities to further his invasion plans, he was quick to reconnoiter the harbor towns, where he made arrangements to hire ships; in Gascony he was able to recruit additions to his infantry. All in all, it was a productive trip.

By December the ducal *chevauchée* disbanded; Eleanor returned to Poitiers, while Henry went on to Normandy, where he visited his mother in Rouen and, perhaps more important, availed himself of the services of a moneylender. A man who "detested delay above all things," he set sail in a severe winter gale with a fleet of 36 ships, 140 knights, and

3,000 men-at-arms. On January 6, 1153, he landed at Bristol, but desire not always being destiny, his future was by no means a certainty.

Never the type of woman to depend upon the presence of a man to keep her occupied, Eleanor saw no point in playing the abandoned wife. Another woman, even now, might have retired to her quarters and resigned herself to sitting out the war, killing time as best she could until her spouse's return. Such meek behavior, however, required a less ambitious temperament than Eleanor possessed, and moreover, it did not, evidently, jibe with what Henry seemed to expect of her. He was not a man who scorned female intelligence, his mother having been the equal of any man and indeed, some said cuttingly, masculine enough in her thinking as to suggest that she might be the superior of most men. Growing up in the company of a mother such as Matilda, Henry emerged with a healthy admiration for high-spirited, assertive women, a factor that no doubt played an important part in his attraction to Eleanor. While by no means liberated from the masculine prejudices against women that were rife in his age, he nonetheless recognized administrative competence when he encountered it. If it occurred within his own family, so much the better, since he tended to distrust outsiders. If the capable person happened to be female, he was not so foolish as to reject her for that minor disability. Therefore, when he departed for England, he left Normandy in the care of his mother, while delegating Eleanor to rule over Anjou as well as her own estates. From a practical standpoint, it suited his purposes admirably to use Eleanor, now and in years to come, as a sort of stand-in for himself. Superficially it would appear, and may initially have seemed to Eleanor herself, that he was offering a position of corulership, an equal partnership in his government, but his magnanamity would turn out to be highly deceptive. Henry did not think of her as an equal nor could he bear to see power slip from his own hands, but it would be a number of years before Eleanor could acknowledge this fact. If she misjudged her husband, he was equally blind in reading her desires, for, like Chaucer's Wife of Bath, she was one of those "women desiren to have soverainetee."

It has been suggested that she now took up residence in Angers, the ancestral capital of the Angevin counts, although probably at least part of her time was spent in Poitiers. As her deputy in Aquitaine she appointed her uncle Ralph de Faye, who was her mother's brother and whom she trusted. If after her years of struggle to return to Aquitaine, she felt reluctant to pull up stakes once more, she made no objections. This was not the first time that she had been obliged to place a husband's priorities above her own, nor would it be the last. Her confidence high, she surveyed her present as well as her future and found it full of promise. Not the least of her satisfactions was the discovery, shortly before Henry's departure, that she was expecting his child. Exultant and no doubt enormously relieved, she had been able to bid him farewell with a full and optimistic heart.

The castle of Angers, still standing today, was completely rebuilt in the thirteenth century, but a hundred years earlier it still must have been a comfortable, imposing residence. The city of Angers itself, no provincial hinterland, had its full share of schools, churches, and convents; philosophy and poetry were not unknown there, and the Loire valley produced an exquisite *vin rosé*. In short, it offered possibilities for Eleanor who, instead of relaxing and slipping into a contented, idle pregnancy, embarked on a more strenuous program than she had undertaken in years, both as an administrator and as a woman intent upon enjoying herself. During 1153 she was free to live a life of her own design, and regardless of Henry's less than enthusiastic attitude toward troubadours, she had collected a number of them during her autumn travels. To Angers, then, she transported her household of Poitevins, her assorted vassals and relatives, including, no doubt, her sister, Petronilla, and her two illegitimate brothers, William and Joscelin, and the enthralled music makers who asked nothing better than to sing her praises. Released from all restrictions at last, she was able to push from her mind any lingering memories of Louis's puritanical court, even to some extent able to dismiss her young husband, who also had no use for the trilling of troubadours, and create for herself the milieu she loved best.

The glimpses we catch of Eleanor during this interlude come from poetry rather than from chronicles or charters, and they reveal a woman young, vibrant, and eager to be adored. Her pregnancy notwithstanding, there was no dearth of men ready to fall in love with her and, an equally important consideration, to receive the rewards she distributed with a generosity reminiscent of her grandfather. By right of inheritance and by her own intelligence, she was amply equipped for the role of literary critic and patroness and, quick to recognize artistic talent, she extended her patronage to Bernard of Ventadour, a gifted poet who had been banished from his last place of employment for making improper advances to the lady of the castle. The son of an archer and a kitchen servant, Bernard may have emerged from humble beginnings, but he had been taught the art of poetry by his master, Eble II of Ventadour. Just as Henry Plantagenet, the man of action, appealed to one side of Eleanor's nature, Bernard appealed to another: her love of romance; her fantasy of being worshiped; her belief that despite the teachings of the Church, women were not inferior to men, not their equals, but their superiors. The sensitivity of a man like Bernard, whom Henry would have dismissed as effeminate, was a magical quality that drew her just as strongly as Henry's quest for political power; she would never be satisfied with a man who combined anything less than both of these traits.

For Bernard's part, he could no more resist Eleanor than a bee the blossom. In 1153, times were hard in Europe; there had been famine in some places, and people were occupied by more serious matters than hiring poets. The duchess of Aquitaine, however, "was young and of great worth, and she had understanding in matters of value and honor, and cared for a song of praise." In the next century it would be claimed that Bernard became Eleanor's lover, but at the time there was no insinuation of overfamiliarity. On the contrary, Bernard's lyrical passion was entirely suitable in a troubadour addressing a beautiful young duchess. It was the sort of admiration—chivalrous, wildly romantic, essentially meaningless—that Eleanor had always enjoyed, something to which she had been accustomed at the court of William the Troubadour. In Bernard's panegyrics, we see Eleanor through the gallant eyes of the poet but perhaps as other contemporaries saw her as well: "gracious, lovely, the embodiment of charm," "lovely eyes and noble countenance," "one meet to crown the state of any king." When Bernard thinks of her, he feels "a wind from paradise," when he looks at her, his heart is so full of joy that everything in nature seems changed, and "I see in the winter only white, red and yellow flowers."

> I am not one to scorn
> The boon God granted me;
> She said in accents clear
> Before I did depart,
> "Your songs they please me well."
> I would each Christian soul
> Could know my rapture then,
> For all I write and sing
> Is meant for her delight.

In England, however, no troubadours composed songs, no ladies played games of love with their *preux chevaliers.* "The kingdom," said a chronicler, "was suddenly agitated by the mutterings of rumors, like a quivering bed of reeds swept by the blasts of the wind." England waited to see if Matilda's nineteen-year-old son, whom some called "intrepid" and others called "rash," would bring King Stephen to heel, or vice versa. Actually, from the moment of Henry's landing at Bristol, everything, the weather included, seemed to conspire in his favor. Undeniably, his own shrewdness was a factor, for instead of attacking Stephen at Wallingford, which had been under siege for a year, he made a surprise attack on Malmesbury Castle, a strategy that had the effect of obliging the king to come to him. When the rival armies finally faced each other across the Avon River, "the floodgates of heaven were opened and heavy rain drove in the faces of Stephen's men, with violent gusts of wind and severe cold, so that God himself appeared to fight for the duke." Henry, the storm at his back, calmly accepted the king's surrender of Malmesbury. After this bloodless victory, he ceased to be regarded as a brash young adventurer, and some of England's most powerful nobles began coming to his support with money and troops. Thus, by the beginning of summer, Henry felt secure enough to go to the aid of his besieged followers at the castle of Wallingford. Once again, circumstances—some said divine will—prevailed to clear the way for his success. When King Stephen was thrown from his horse three times prior to the battle, his advisers interpreted these incidents as ill omens. "It was," the chronicles tell us, "terrible and very dreadful to see so many thousands of armed men eager to join battle with drawn swords, determined, to the general prejudice of the kingdom, to kill their own relatives and kin." Standing on opposite banks of the Thames at a narrow place in the river, Henry and Stephen spoke together out of earshot of their armies. Shortly afterward, each man returned to his troops, announcing that the battle had been called off but offering no explanation.

King Stephen's son, Eustace, disgusted at what seemed to him spineless conduct on the part of his father, left Wallingford reeling with rage. However much detested throughout England for his obnoxious qualities, Eustace considered himself the rightful heir to the throne. Plowing through the Suffolk countryside, he rode up to the Abbey of

Bury Saint Edmunds, where he audaciously demanded money to pay his men. The monks, while welcoming him graciously, refused to part with their silver. On August 17, "he ordered all the country round about, and especially St. Edmunds' harvests, to be plundered and all the loot to be brought to a nearby castle of his." That evening, sitting down to a dinner of eels, he was said to have strangled on the first bite and to have died almost immediately.

Eustace's sudden death can most likely be attributed to tainted fish, but to the twelfth-century mind it seemed a punishment direct from the hand of God, who seemed to be laboring in the cause of Henry Plantagenet. On November 6, 1153, his support tottering, his spirit collapsed, Stephen met with Henry at Winchester to discuss terms of peace. The two men traveled together to London, where, in the presence of the leading nobles of the land, a treaty was hammered out: "Be it known to you that I, the King of England, Stephen, have made Henry, Duke of Normandy, the successor to the kingdom of England after me, and my heir by hereditary right, and thus I have given and confirmed to him and his heirs the kingdom of England." By the terms of the Treaty of Winchester, Stephen was to rule for the remainder of his life, with Henry, his "son and heir," to succeed him. After a generation of civil war, the vows of fealty that the English nobles had made to Matilda had finally come to pass, and the way was paved for the first of the Plantagenet dynasty.

Stephen, however, was fifty-eight years old, in fairly good health, and although he had agreed that "in all the business of the kingdom I will act with the advice of the duke," Henry knew that he had no real authority. He understood, too, that Stephen might live possibly another ten or fifteen years and that certain malcontents "whose teeth were spears and arrows" were already trying to sow discord between them. Having accomplished his objective and at a loss as to what to do next, Henry lingered anticlimatically in England until the spring of 1154. Around Easter, he decided to return to Normandy, where he "was joyfully received by his mother, his brothers and all the peoples of Normandy, Anjou, Maine and Poitou."

During Henry's sixteen-month absence Eleanor had produced a special triumph of her own. On August 17, the same day that Eustace had died, she had given birth to a son, whom she had taken upon herself to christen William, after the dukes of Aquitaine, and designate as heir to her duchy. If, as has been suggested, the name also honored Henry's great-grandfather William the Conqueror, this surely must have been a secondary consideration in her mind. Although the chroniclers neglect to mention Henry's wife in the list of those who joyfully welcomed his return, Eleanor had more reason than most for rejoicing. At thirty, she had killed off her past as certainly as if it had never existed, and it must have seemed as though the birth of her son represented a final ironic salvo to Louis Capet. One of the prices of divorce had been the loss of her daughters, with what anguish it is impossible to say, and any visiting privileges she may have been guaranteed had been immediately forfeit when she married Henry.

At last the self-contempt she had experienced through her inability to bear an heir for the Franks had vanished; at last the son for whom Louis had hungered had been born, but he would sit upon another throne. And as if to prove that her child were no fluke, no lucky accident from a woman almost past her prime as a childbearer, she became pregnant again just two months after Henry's return. Looking ahead, she could see only days of honor and glory in which regret would play no part. Henry's success in England had painted on her horizon the prospect of someday being the wealthiest, most prestigious queen in Christendom, and yet Eleanor was realist enough to understand that she never could have enjoyed that future had she not provided her young husband with a son. Henry seemed delighted with the eight-month-old infant, as he would be with all his children when they were young, spoiling them, making grandiose plans for their futures, lavishing paternal passion on them far in excess of what could be expected of the ordinary medieval father. Unknown to Eleanor at this time, William was not Henry's only son. In the previous year, probably a month or two after William's birth, a child had been born to an English woman of the streets, Ykenai, who, according to Walter Map, was "a common harlot who stooped to all uncleanness" and who had gulled Henry into believing the child his. "Without reason and with too little discernment," chides Map, Henry had received the child as his own and named him Geoffrey.

Eleanor's life underwent minor changes during the six months that followed Henry's return. Throwing himself tumultuously into the business of ordering his affairs, he relieved her of the reins of government, an authority Eleanor may have relinquished with some relief at that time. Some of her vassals in Aquitaine, taking advantage of both duke and duchess's absence, had begun to cautiously test their power, and Henry, after stopping at Rouen to see his mother, made a flying trip to the south in an effort to put down the smoldering fires of rebellion. Watching him in action, Eleanor was more aware than ever of the overwhelming force of Henry's personality and his thunderous roars when thwarted. By the end of June, he was back at his mother's court in

Rouen, where Eleanor joined him and met her mother-in-law. In her relations with Louis's mother she had been notably unsuccessful, mutual antagonism driving Adelaide from the court, but with Matilda it would be another story. There was much for Eleanor to admire in this remarkable, hard-headed dowager who had spent two decades fighting for her son's inheritance. Fascinated by Matilda from a distance, she found, however, that it would not be easy to like her at close quarters. Aside from the empress's cool, formal manner, she had a type of relationship with her son that immediately aroused Eleanor's natural jealousy. From the outset, it was made plain to her that Henry truly valued only his mother's opinion, and to a woman like Eleanor, with strong opinions of her own, this must have been exasperating indeed. The bond between Matilda and Henry, more akin to two generals than mother and son, stirred her antagonism. She soon discovered that if Henry wanted advice—and at this period he did, apparently, seek the opinions of others—it was to Matilda that he went for guidance; it was Matilda's judgment on political affairs that he valued above all others. This must have been a disturbing revelation to Eleanor, who considered herself, by virtue of age, experience, and her capacity as his wife, to be a more fitting confidante.

Eleanor's court was not able to survive the move from Angers to Rouen, since Matilda, though highly literate, preferred philosophers to poets; reluctantly, the troubadours made their way back to the more congenial southland. It promised to be an uneventful summer, although Eleanor would find the time passing quickly, and certainly she could never complain of boredom. Messengers, bringing news from London, Paris, and Rome, came and went continually. Henry, rarely home, had no sooner returned to Rouen than he began to think of leaving, once to besiege a troublesome vassal at Torigni, once in August to meet briefly with Louis Capet. In September, an illness sent him to bed, but he recovered rapidly, and by early October he was in the Vexin, campaigning again. During that summer reports about Louis's private affairs drifted into the Rouen command post. Rousing himself from post-divorce lethargy, Louis set off on a pilgrimage to Saint James of Compostela. Ostensibly a religious expedition, it was also for the purpose of inspecting the daughter of the king of Castile as a possible bride. Evidently Constance, a sober maiden who bore no resemblance in personality or looks to Eleanor, passed his scrutiny, for Louis returned to Paris betrothed. No doubt to Eleanor's amusement, her former husband traveled all the way to Spain and back by way of Toulouse and Mont-

pellier so that he would not have to ask Eleanor for a safe conduct nor
step foot on her territory.

Toward the end of October, with Henry still away in the Vexin, only
Eleanor and Matilda were in Rouen to receive a travel-stained courier
from England, the bearer of an important message from Archbishop
Theobald of Canterbury: On October 25, King Stephen had died at
Dover from "a flux of hemorrhoids"—Henry must "come without delay
and take possession of the kingdom." The call, which no one had anticipated for a decade or more, had arrived like a thief in the night.
Henry, who had a reputation for traveling faster than any other man in
Europe, rushed back from the Vexin, and within two weeks he had
collected a properly imposing retinue of soldiers, barons, and prelates,
men who had long ago tied their destiny to his, as well as old crusading
companions of Eleanor's, and hurried them all to the windy harbor town
of Barfleur to help him claim his first crown and Eleanor her second.
Matilda, oddly enough, would not be among those present at Henry's
anointing, for she either volunteered or was requested to remain in
Normandy to keep the peace, but among the party were Henry's two
younger brothers, Eleanor's sister and brothers, and the infant Prince
William.

In England, the throne remained vacant. Stephen was dead and with
him had died a generation of misery and civil war. He was not regretted,
but the new king, a mere lad, folk said, remained an unknown quantity.
Still, people hoped great things of Henry, peace if nothing else, and the
versifiers composed hopeful odes in his honor: "Then shall beam forth,
in England's happier hour/ Justice with mercy, and well-balanced
power."

Out to sea the thunder growled, and at Barfleur Henry, immobilized,
stared at the Channel churning with sleet, rain, and violent winds. Each
day he consulted his mariners and swore noisily; each day, restless as a
caged lion, he scanned the leaden November sky for a break in the
weather, but the storms perversely continued. Monotonously, the days
wore on until they had tarried in the inns and taverns of Barfleur a
whole month. Eleanor had time to watch the seabirds shrieking and to
converse endlessly with Petronilla and her brothers, time to ponder the
bizarre twists and turns that had brought her to this sleet-swept port.
Whether directed by her own sagacity or by God or even by some happy
conjunction of the planets, she had fastened her future to the Plantagenet star, which now seemed destined to dominate the heavens. The
weatherbeaten youth she had scrutinized so carefully in Paris only

three years earlier "seemed to have obtained divine favor in almost everything, not only from the beginning of his reign but even from his first year and his very birth." At the same time, she could not have helped but reflect how the rise in his fortunes had been connected to deaths, most of them untimely: Prince William drowning in the *White Ship*, Geoffrey Anjou's sudden passing, Eustace strangling on eels, Stephen's death only a year after Winchester. Each man's removal from the scene had brought Henry a step closer to the empire for which he hungered. She knew that his blood raced for yet more land, more power, because he had been known to say "that the whole world was too small a prize for a single courageous and powerful ruler." With this man she could not predict where the future might take her. For the moment there was England to think of, and from everything she knew of the country—its cold, damp climate; civilization's last frontier, inhabited by rude barbarians—it seemed the opposite of Aquitaine and far, far worse than Paris. But there would be no returning to Aquitaine, perhaps not for many years. Aquitaine must wait, as it had always waited for her, a fair and gracious sanctuary.

By December 6, after four long weeks of waiting, the wind slackened somewhat, but fog still shrouded the shore, and the sea looked as menacing as ever. Henry, however, had reached the limit of his patience, and "by God's eyes" he would delay no longer; the next day, he announced, was the feast of Saint Nicholas, protector of sailors and travelers, and they would sail, regardless of the weather. Before dawn, the voyagers heard Mass and then filed into the galleys. The sea was so hidden in silvery fog that the world might have ended just beyond the harbor. Eleanor, seven months pregnant and carrying her fifteen-month-old son, boarded one of the heaving vessels, which cautiously proceeded into the wrinkled face of the Channel. With her across that stretch of choppy sea she took more than her children, born and unborn; she also transferred Aquitaine to the dominion of the English crown, thus planting the seeds of that century-long conflict that would only be resolved, ironically, by another woman, Jeanne d'Arc.

On December 8, after a day and a night of rolling in the fog, the convoy finally dropped anchor on the southern coast of England, although the ships were scattered for miles along the coastline. The royal vessel landed in a harbor near the New Forest, but Henry, feverishly impatient as usual, could not be bothered to wait for his escort. Immediately, he and Eleanor set out for Winchester, which housed part of the royal treasury. The others were left to catch up as best they could. The English, incredulous at the rumor that Henry had ridden the waves of the storm, emerged from their hearths, sat down by the frozen road, and waited for a glimpse of their twenty-one-year-old king with his ruddy, leonine face and the famous queen who had divorced a dull king for a bold young warrior and who would ever be known to the English as the Eagle. By the time the royal procession neared London, its ranks were swollen by local barons and prelates and by crowds of villagers with snow-damp feet trudging in the wake of history.

Eleanor's first glimpse of London in that chill December must have given her a moment's pause. There is no exact way to fix the population of the city in 1154, although from various accounts an estimate of forty thousand seems reasonable. The chronicler William Fitz Stephen chauvinistically called London "among the noble and celebrated cities of the world," renowned for its healthy air, its honest Christian burghers and "the modesty of its matrons." The women, he added, "are very Sabines." Eleanor saw no Sabine women; rather it was a man's city to which "every nation under heaven delighted in bringing their trade by sea." By the docks along the Thames, she could see wine shops and painted women and ships being repaired with pegs and nails, ropes being hauled, and crews loading. "The Arabian sends gold . . . the Nile sends precious stones; the men of Norway and Russia, furs and sables; nor is China absent with purple silk. The Gauls come with their wines." London was a rich city, where trade was god and men thought mainly about making money, where one of the biggest attractions was the Friday horse fair at Smooth Field (Smithfield), where earls, barons, and knights came to buy the high-stepping palfreys with their gleaming coats, colts stepping with jaunty tread, war-horses with tremulous ears and enormous haunches, and where, in another part of the field, coun-tryfolk perused cows with full udders, woolly sheep, and mares fit for the plow. London, like Paris, teemed with people. The streets were lined with rows of wooden houses, firetraps smeared with red, blue, and black paint, and many of the residents were tradesmen who manufac-tured goods on their premises. In Chepeside, the busiest street in the city, the shops of the drapers and goldsmiths displayed silk mantles from Damascus and enameled trinket boxes from Limoges. Londoners were inordinately proud of their city. "The only plagues of London," conceded William Fitz Stephen, "are the immoderate drinking of fools and the frequency of fires."

The city's most wonderful attraction, the one its citizens boasted of most often, was not a cathedral or the Tower of London or even West-

minster Palace, but a public cookshop along the Thames that remained
open twenty-four hours a day.

> There daily you may find food according to the season, dishes of
> meat, roast, fried and boiled, large and small fish, coarser meats for
> the poor and more delicate for the rich, such as venison and big and
> small birds. If any of the citizens should unexpectedly receive
> visitors, weary from their journey, who would fain not wait until
> fresh food is bought and cooked, or until the servants have brought
> bread or water for washing, they hasten to the river bank and there
> find all they need.

When Eleanor rode into London, she may have wished herself, for
once, one of the common folk who could stop at the Thames-side
cookshop, because even though she and Henry were not exactly unexpected visitors, no proper preparations had been made for their arrival.
Westminster Palace, the official residence of royalty, had been so
despoiled by King Stephen's men that it now was far beyond human
habitation. While Henry might have happily bivouacked at Westminster had he been alone, Eleanor was accustomed to more comfortable surroundings. The royal family took up temporary quarters across
the river from the Tower of London, in the village of Bermondsey,
where there was an ancient Saxon palace and an abbey, newly built.

Eleven days after their arrival, on Sunday, December 19, 1154, Henry
and Eleanor were crowned king and queen of England in the abbey
church of Westminster, which was in scarcely better shape than the
palace. To Eleanor, the dinginess of London's great halls and the
dilapidated condition of its churches were telling evidence of the strife
that had rocked England during Stephen's rule. Nevertheless, no expense was spared to make the coronation as magnificent a ceremony as
possible. Into the abbey in solemn procession came the pages, knights,
and barons, followed by the bishops, abbots, and priests, their vestments gleaming with gold and precious stones, and finally Henry and
Eleanor, accompanied by Theobald, archbishop of Canterbury. The abbey shone with countless candles, the choir of monks sang lustily, and
the great bells in the tower crashed thunderously. During Mass, the
Archbishop anointed Henry and Eleanor with holy oils and placed the
crowns upon their heads. Immediately afterward, Henry issued the
customary coronation charter, a sort of printed inaugural address, in
which he ignored the twenty years of Stephen's reign as surely as if they
had not existed. In practically every other sentence he referred to his

grandfather, whose ruling precepts he vowed to follow: "I am granting and giving by this charter, confirmed to God and the Holy Church and to all my counts, barons and subjects, all the concessions and grants, liberties and free customs which King Henry, my grandfather, gave and granted them. Likewise I outlaw and abolish for myself and my heirs all the evil customs which he abolished and outlawed." Denying what displeased him, saying what people wanted to hear, harking back to the past, Henry freed himself to initiate whatever innovations he pleased. In reality, he had no intention of copying his grandfather's policies, and for that matter, the next thirty-five years would prove to be the most radical in the realm's history—for they were years in which the foundations of English common law were laid. No ruler of England, before or after, would so strongly influence the development of its institutions as Henry Plantagenet, and so thoroughly would he do his work that, after his passing, the royal government would be able to function, if need be, without a king.

Once Henry and Eleanor had been "crowned and consecrated with becoming pomp and splendor," they rode along the Strand among their subjects, the Londoners running up and down to stare at the lion and the eagle, booming out their approval with shouts of *"Waes hael"* and *"Vivat rex."* Henry, proverbially careless of his clothing, knew the value of putting on a good show, and that day he looked every inch a king, a worthy successor to William the Conqueror. As for Eleanor, a Victorian biographer would dress her in "a wimple or close coif with a circlet of gems over it; her kirtle or close gown has tight sleeves and fastens with full gathers just below the throat, confined with a rich collar of gems" and over this was added "an elegant pelisson, bordered with fur." Unfortunately, no contemporary description of Eleanor's coronation gown has survived, if indeed any of the sober church chroniclers thought to include a fashion commentary, but it is reasonable to surmise that she wore the best of her finery. The only fact of which we can be certain was that she was pregnant.

Queen of the English

Snow had blotted the roof of the Tower of London and spread a ghostly white sheet over Billingsgate and Castle Baynard. Along the embankment by the Thames, the choking aroma of woodsmoke from bonfires drifted over the frozen river. From the manor house at Bermondsey, Eleanor could watch girls and boys skating on the river, shrieking their pleasure at the sun. Some made sleds from blocks of ice and were pulled along by their friends; others tied to their feet the shinbones of animals, and with poles that they struck against the ice for momentum, they were "propelled swift as a bird in flight or a bolt shot from an engine of war." Around the entrance to Bermondsey hung the *ribauz*, those good-for-nothings who were always begging and plundering at the slightest provocation, and the king's bailiffs periodically shouted them away in "English," that queer Teutonic jargon spoken by the lower classes. Ever since Christmas, a constant stream of barons had been pouring into Bermondsey to discuss "the state of the realm and the restoration of peace" with their king, bringing with them their dogs, pet monkeys, parrots, and hawks. The Great Hall more nearly resembled a menagerie than a royal dwelling.

From the beginning, Eleanor felt ambivalent about her new land. England stirred in her a feeling of protectiveness, and in its hardworking people, level-headed and eager to reconcile liberty with order, she must have sensed a spirit akin to her own. Nevertheless, she who loved music and beauty, the gracious easy living that she knew so well, found none of it here. The civil war had ended, but its scars remained, and the memories of privations still cast their shadows over everyday life. Frivolity was not an attitude that came naturally to the English, nor did it appear to be one that might be induced in these sober tradesmen with their unpolished wives. Poetry they had little taste for, the etiquette of courtly love they would have greeted with open-mouthed gapes. Here was nothing of the silken charm of Aquitaine, of wit and romance, of troubadours wracked by containable passion for unattainable loves. While Henry had come to the throne with an abiding love and a practical working knowledge of the land he was to rule, Eleanor was too much a child of the south, too much a grandchild of William IX, ever to be completely at home in such a backwater of civilization, and in those early months of 1155 she must have felt alien indeed.

Perhaps the most striking fact about the first year of Henry's reign was Eleanor's utter lack of significance. Eagle though she may have appeared to her subjects, to the chroniclers she remained a cipher to be commented upon only for the standard female achievement—on February 28, 1155, she gave birth to her second son, who was christened Henry after his father and grandfather. Otherwise, the chronicles have nothing to say, and the reason, of course, may have been that Eleanor was content to spend her time tending her two infants, gossiping with her sister and Henry's half sister, Emma, an illegitimate daughter of Geoffrey of Anjou. It is difficult, however, to imagine Eleanor voluntarily insulating herself in the women's quarter at Bermondsey and bouncing babies on her lap, not because she lacked maternal instinct but because it was customary for upper-class women, and royalty especially, to hand over their infants to the care of a nurse almost immediately after birth. A more likely explanation for Eleanor's seeming inactivity was that her husband, having located capable men to assist him, had no particular use for her administrative talents at this time.

Once the formality of the coronation was out of the way, Henry immediately set himself to the task of resuscitating the kingdom from a state of total decay. Not only were the national resources exhausted, but also the legal and administrative machinery of government had rusted to a standstill. Working in his favor was one factor: For the first time since the Conquest, a new king had succeeded to the throne without a competitor and with the good will of his subjects. Still, the work cut out for him was nothing less than the creation of order out of chaos, and it is understandable if he approached it with some anxiety. The most important post he had to fill was that of the chief justiciar, the person who would head the judicial system, supervise the routine matters of government, and act in the king's place when he was out of the country. With a desire to show his subjects that he held no resentment toward those who had supported Stephen, that the past was past, he divided responsibility for this job between Richard of Luci, a man who had served King Stephen faithfully but who was also thoroughly familiar with the workings of governmental machinery, and Robert, earl of Leicester, who had been one of those barons to change his allegiance and come over to Henry during the campaign of 1153. As treasurer of the exchequer, Henry selected Nigel, bishop of Ely, and for his chancellor, accepting the recommendation of the archbishop of Canterbury, he agreed to take on Theobald's archdeacon and protégé, Thomas Becket. Theobald had assured him that Becket was an able person, and although Henry had brought to England his mother's chancellor, William de Vere, with whom he was well satisfied, he felt that it would be politic to accept Theobald's suggestion. It certainly would not hurt to put himself in the Church's good graces. The office of chancellor, important but lacking prestige, was mainly a secretarial position; it consisted of supervising the royal chapel, the collective name for the household clerks; heading the secretariat where the royal will was translated into charters, letters, and writs; and acting as custodian of the Great Seal. The appointment of a civil servant to handle his paperwork was not a decision that Henry pondered for long.

Thomas Becket had accompanied Archbishop Theobald to the coronation, and afterward he stuck close to his master's side during the trip from Westminster Abbey to Bermondsey. If Eleanor failed to notice him at the coronation, she could not have avoided him during the Christmas court at Bermondsey, where the cleric was first brought to Henry's attention as a prospective chancellor. Thomas was a slender, unusually tall man with dark hair, aquiline features, and hands so long and tapered that they would have looked well on a woman. Although he had a slight tendency to stutter, he spoke well, being one of those people with the facility for making complicated subjects seem plain to his listeners. Also notable were his intelligence, charm, and a gaiety of temperament, whether natural or assumed it was hard to tell. Whatever sparks of interest flew between Thomas and the Plantagenets at Bermondsey were solely on the part of Henry, who, always affable, seemed to take an immediate liking to the archdeacon and his cheerful badinage.

If the meeting at Bermondsey made little impression on Eleanor, it was the most momentous day in Thomas Becket's experience. Born in London, the son of a prosperous Norman merchant, Thomas was brought up in middle-class respectability, educated at Merton Priory in Surrey, and had also studied in Paris while Eleanor had been queen of France. As his father, Gilbert Becket, prospered, he managed to acquire some property and also served a term as sheriff of London. Into his spacious house came rich young noblemen, one of whom taught the boy

Thomas the aristocratic pleasures of hawking and hunting. His father's affluence did not, evidently, endure, for by the time Thomas had grown to adulthood, his father was poor, his mother had died, and entertaining was no longer done in his home. With no career prospects on the horizon, he was obliged to work for three years as a clerk and accountant in the business of a kinsman, a dreary existence for an ambitious young man with a taste for elegance. Finally, two of his father's friends recommended him to Archbishop Theobald, and Gilbert himself pulled strings by reminding the archbishop that long ago they had been neighbors in Normandy. As a result, Thomas was taken into Theobald's household and given a place on his staff. During the ten years that followed, and despite the fact that he was twice dismissed and then reinstated, Thomas rose to a high place at Canterbury, where he became Theobald's adviser, diplomatic courier, and general dogsbody. It was not until the autumn of 1154 that the archdeaconry of Canterbury fell vacant and Thomas had been appointed. Now, barely two months later, came the dazzling promotion to king's chancellor.

That winter Eleanor saw little of her husband, who, she knew by now, hated to remain in one place longer than a week and sometimes grew restless within a matter of days. Before the end of January, he was off to clean up unfinished business from Stephen's reign; first on his agenda was the demolition of unlicensed castles built illegally during Stephen's lax rule and the ejection from the country of the hated Flemish mercenaries, whom Stephen had used to buttress his position. There still were, in fact, a few rebellious barons who remained loyal to the dead king, and now Henry showed them that he would tolerate no opposition. Marching on Suffolk and then York, he besieged one castle after another until he had brought the troublemakers to submission. He was away when his son was born in February but returned to London several weeks later. Wasting no time in celebration or relaxation, he immediately called a council of all those bishops and abbots who wished to have their charters renewed. That Eleanor did attempt to involve herself in affairs of state at this time is evident from the fact that her name appears as a witness, along with Richard of Luci and Thomas Becket, on charters granted to the canons of Holy Trinity and Christ Church. Two weeks later, she traveled with Henry to Wallingford, where the king had called together the barons and bishops of the realm to swear allegiance to his eldest son and, in case of William's death, to Henry as his second heir. This must have been a jubilant occasion for the queen. Secure in the love of her powerful husband, the matriarch of a now solidly established dynasty, her position assured after her uncertainties in France, Eleanor, at thirty-three, was entering her prime. The attacks of melancholia that had oppressed her in the Île-de-France had evaporated in the April greenery of England; boredom had no chance of surfacing in this atmosphere, frenzied and vigorous, created by her youthful husband's zealousness and his passionate addiction to movement and power.

As pleased with herself at this point as she undoubtedly was, she had no intention of remaining at Bermondsey, in her opinion a less than appropriate residence for the royal family. In the spring, she prevailed upon Henry to begin renovations on the dilapidated palace at Westminster. The assignment was turned over to Thomas Becket, who threw himself into the work of supervision with such zeal that between Easter and Whitsuntide the restoration was completed. In fifty days he accomplished a job that normally would have taken several years. So many workers were hired that they could barely hear one another speak, and, the chronicles tell us, the scene resembled the Tower of Babel.

In early June, then, Eleanor and her household traveled up the broad strand of the Thames to the hamlet of Charing, past the gardens and suburban villas of wealthy Londoners, to Westminster Palace. The plan of the great block of buildings was, in fact, two palaces joined into one. The new palace, the home of the royal family, was adjoined on the east by orchards, gardens, and thick woods, which extended down to the edge of the Thames; the old palace, lying within a separate enclosure to the south, was chiefly used for business offices of state officials and as living quarters for the resident courtiers. There was a spacious courtyard, which, whenever Henry happened to be in residence, would be forever thronged with valets polishing his hunting spears, falconers sunning their hooded birds on stone benches along the walls, the king's shaggy wolfhounds, and an endless procession of clerks, sergeants, and men-at-arms, intent upon the king's business. Everything considered, the palace lacked the elegance of others Eleanor had observed during her travels—there were no mirrors of polished steel, no carpets, no mother-of-pearl inlaid chairs—but it was large, functional, and a great deal more comfortable and regal than Bermondsey. Some of her lack of enthusiasm for Westminster may have had more to do with the man who restored it than with the buildings themselves.

Thomas's efficiency notwithstanding, Eleanor soon found that there was more to Becket than had first met the eye, for the chancellor, so lately trodding the halls of Canterbury in his drab cleric's gown, had been transformed within the space of a few months from a sparrow into a peacock. And this metamorphosis, fostered by the king himself, had been accomplished so swiftly that Eleanor had no choice but to deal with it as an established fact.

Roger of Hovedon, a royal clerk, wrote sourly of the intimate relationship between Henry and his chancellor, commenting that the king "bestowed upon him many revenues, both ecclesiastical and of a secular nature, and received him so much into his esteem and familiarity that throughout the kingdom, there was none his equal, save the king alone." In Eleanor's mind, the king had only one equal, and as his consort, it should have been herself. With reasons that ran closer to the bone than mere jealousy, she was both angry and resentful at the unusual turn in the relationship between the king and his chancellor. Henry had embraced him with such affection, one could even say passion, that they might have been taken for soul mates. They became inseparable: "The King and Becket played together like little boys of the same age, at the court, in church, in assemblies, in riding." They were together when Henry resided in London and when he traveled through the country; they hawked and hunted, ate together, even caroused together, although the chaste and sober Thomas did not participate in Henry's wenching. This curious behavior, which would be highly suspect today, surprised Henry's contemporaries, but at the same time they read into it no deeper meanings. Outwardly, Thomas appeared more regal than the king. In contrast to his master, a man who "wears leggings without any cross-wrappings," whose "caps have no elegance," and who "wears the first clothes that come to hand," Thomas had so many silk cloaks that he was rarely seen in the same outfit twice. Displaying a self-made man's eagerness for the trappings of status and rank, he preened like a grand vizier, a fact that neither escaped nor distressed Henry. He found it a source of pleasure and sometimes enormous amusement. Various anecdotes were later collected by Becket's friends to demonstrate his intimacy with the king, such as this one by William Fitz Stephen. One cold day the two men were riding through the streets of London, when Henry noticed an old man in a ragged coat coming toward them.

"Do you see that man?" asked the king.

"Yes," replied Thomas. "I see him."

"How poor he is, how frail, and how scantily clad. Would it not be an act of charity to give him a thick warm cloak?"

Becket, not yet following Henry's train of thought, readily agreed. "It would indeed; and right that you should attend to it, my king."

Whereupon Henry lunged over and playfully tried to pull the

chancellor's cloak of scarlet cloth and gray fur from his shoulders. When the startled Becket resisted, the two of them played tug-of-war with the cape until their horseplay threatened to tumble both of them from their horses. "At last the chancellor reluctantly allowed the king to overcome him, and suffered him to pull the cape from his shoulder and give it to the poor man."

What Fitz Stephen neglects to mention is that Becket had dozens of capes just as fine.

Like a man with a new, adored mistress, Henry could not do enough for Becket. The riches that passed through the chancellor's hands were enormous, and almost daily Henry seemed to heap new honors upon him. He kept a residence of his own, paid for by the king, where there was open house every day, his table welcoming men of every rank, from visiting foreign dignitaries to ordinary knights. There was no stinting.

> He ordered his hall to be strewn every day with fresh straw or hay in winter, and with green rushes or leaves in summer, so that the host of knights who could not find room on the benches might sit on a clean and wholesome floor without soiling their precious clothes and fine underwear. His board was resplendent with gold and silver vessels and abounded in dainty dishes and precious wines, so that whenever food or drink was commended by its rarity, no price was too high to deter his agents from purchasing it.

The chancellor's personal brand of hospitality was as gracious as his menu was lavish. If we can believe the chroniclers, there was grace in his every gesture, refinement in his every word and action. He played the perfect host, supervising the smallest detail of domestic service, noting the position of each guest, inquiring for the absent, and if a man modestly took a lower place than his rank demanded, Thomas would have him reseated properly. So sumptuous was his establishment, so much the center of all that was going on in London, that Henry himself was known to ride his horse into Thomas's hall as he sat at dinner. Leaping over the table, he would sit down amid the courtiers in their finery and demand to be fed. But Henry was no fool, and above and beyond his love for Becket, there was another reason why he permitted his secretary to play king. Certain aspects of kingship bored him: Keeping a splendid court, extending hospitality to visitors, impressing foreign rulers, in fact all the pomp and ceremony associated with monarchy were chores on which he disdained to waste his time and which he willingly shifted to Becket.

To Eleanor's great chagrin, the court over which she should have presided and which no woman in Europe knew better how to conduct, had somehow slipped through her fingers and drifted down the Thames to Thomas Becket's splendid mansion. Visiting dignitaries who should have come to pay their respects to the queen were instead taking their meals and exchanging elegant chitchat with the chancellor, and even the king himself seemed to prefer Becket's company to her own. Whether or not she admitted it, Becket, so amusing and sociable, was better able to handle the king's moods than she. Like the doting mother of a temperamental child, Thomas could sense a storm coming before it arrived; he knew how to ward off Henry's unaccountable—and accountable—rages, gentle him along until he'd soothed his master into good humor once more. Standing on the sidelines at Westminster, Eleanor watched it all with detachment and made no attempt to compete. She was too experienced a woman to make an issue of her husband's infatuation with Becket, no matter how much she may have personally loathed the man, and she affected to notice nothing in the hope that their attachment would wear itself out in time.

In general, Eleanor was not overly fond of clerics, and the virginal Thomas, whose celibacy was unnecessary, since he had never taken priestly orders, impressed her as the worst kind of prude and hypocrite. Contemporaries, noting that in youth Becket had taken a vow of chastity from which he had never deviated, did not seem to find it unusual that he feared intimate relations with women, nor did any of them, friend or enemy, ever impute to him homosexual leanings, which of course does not mean that he did not have them. He did not seem to dislike women, although the evidence we have eight hundred years later to prove that he *did* is scant. It was said that he adored his mother, "taking her as his guide in all his ways, as his patroness in life, and placing all his trust in her, after Christ." And in a letter he wrote later in life to a nun named Idonea, he encouraged her to rely on female strength, citing Scriptural references to "the courage of a woman when men failed, leaders were terrified and the priests had fled." Despite his almost feminist rhetoric, he did not like the queen any more than she did him, but any open show of hostility would have been unthinkable. As a cleric, he probably inclined toward the Church's view of her, that she was a "loose" woman, who had divorced and remarried under highly suspicious circumstances. He had heard the tattle about her frivolous behavior in Paris and her reputed infidelity at Antioch and undoubtedly received an earful of gossip from his friend John of Salisbury, who had observed her firsthand while she was seeking Pope Eugenius's approval for a divorce.

If Eleanor resented the honors Henry bestowed so prodigiously upon his chancellor, she seemed to have adopted a mask of indifference to his growing wealth and power. By virtue of the fact that he was constantly at Henry's side, she had ample opportunities to observe the man, and her resentment toward the manner in which he had usurped her place would not totally have clouded her objectivity nor prevented her from making a sharp analysis of his motives. Like everyone else, she could see how much Henry adored Thomas, but what would have interested her far more were Thomas's feelings for her husband. Behind the chancellor's open, easy friendliness, did she detect hints of insincerity? In off moments, when Thomas let down his guard, did she catch some message in his eyes that spelled out less worthy emotions—that the chancellorship was a highly lucrative job and nothing more, that befriending Henry was a necessary, if tedious, requirement for keeping that powerful position? It is tempting to imagine that she sensed there would be no need of her interference, that Becket himself would be the architect of his own ruin.

For that matter, Thomas was not her only rival for the king's time and attention. As she had discovered by now, Henry was a notoriously unfaithful husband. As king, infidelity was his privilege and prerogative, one which he would make use of all his life. He took his pleasure among the trollops along the Thames; he scouted amusing taverns, where he picked up women; in his travels around the country, his retinue swarmed with "court prostitutes" and waferers, the makers of thin sweet cakes, who had a reputation for being pimps. Sometime after he and Eleanor arrived in England, she became aware of the existence of his illegitimate son, Geoffrey, the son of the prostitute Ykenai, and also another infant William, whose surname is recorded as Longspee or Longsword, and whose mother was probably also of low birth. The circumstances under which Geoffrey came to her attention have not been recorded—perhaps the child's mother died—but early in the reign, Henry recognized the boy as his son and brought him to live at Westminster, where he was placed under Eleanor's care. Why she tolerated the presence of Geoffrey in the royal household is anybody's guess. Perhaps she felt that Geoffrey, despite his unwholesome lineage, had done her no harm and, as Henry's son, deserved to be well treated; perhaps she wanted to impress Henry with his good fortune at having a wife who would treat his bastard like her own legitimate children. Most likely, however, the decision was Henry's, and she had no choice in the matter. In addition to Geoffrey, he had many other bastards, she knew not how many. Passing through a village, he would sleep with a girl once, get her with child, and then forget all about her. If this facet of her lusty husband's nature caused her any pain, it would have been beneath her royal dignity to express it.

In September, Eleanor moved her household to Winchester, joining Henry, who, in the company of Becket, had been away nearly the entire summer, chasing fox and deer in the New Forest and other royal preserves. "He delighted beyond measure in birds of prey," wrote Gerald of Wales, "especially when in flight, and in hounds pursuing wild beasts by their keen scent, both for their resonant and harmonious voices and for their swift running. Would he had given himself as much to his devotions as he did to the chase!" Now, after several months of relaxation, the king was ready to return to business. On September 29, which was Michaelmas and the traditional time of year for receiving reports from the exchequer, Henry was anxious to review the crown's revenues for the first nine months of his reign. On this occasion, however, he called together a council of his barons in order to introduce a plan he had been mulling over during the summer. This was not the first time Eleanor had heard him talk about conquering Ireland, and considering Henry's insatiable appetite for land, an appetite she saw no reason to curb, she may have encouraged him. If so, any influence she may have had was immediately dispelled by the presence of her mother-in-law. Living in semiretirement in Rouen, devoting herself to pious works and the management of Henry's Continental provinces, Matilda had maintained a strictly hands-off policy in regard to the English, and although no one could accuse her of meddling, she did surreptitiously counsel her son from time to time. On this, her first and last visit to England after Henry became king, Matilda firmly shoved Eleanor still further into the background. At Winchester, she dominated the council, immediately opposing Henry's plan to invade Ireland and give it to his youngest brother, William. In her opinion, Ireland, poor and barbaric, was not worth the trouble of conquering, but a more overriding objection lay behind her advice. She brought to Henry's attention the alarming information that his brother, Geoffrey, discontent with his inheritance, was claiming (and probably correctly) that his father had meant Henry to relinquish Anjou once he had succeeded to the throne of England. Since it was clear to him that Henry had no intention of abiding by their father's wishes, he was stocking his castles for war, and Matilda, whose shrewd old eyes were rarely fooled, saw that Henry stood in danger of losing one of his mainland estates.

While Henry and Matilda put their heads together over the embarrassing problem of Geoffrey, Eleanor was far from supine. If she could not establish her authority as a sovereign in England, at least she might reap some of the benefits of queenship by having an income of her own. To this end, she used this meeting of the exchequer to declare her financial independence from her husband and introduce an innovation, the payment of queen's gold. No consort before Eleanor, or after her for that matter, had access to her own financial resources. Although Eleanor received an allowance for her expenses from the treasury, and the pipe rolls are full of entries documenting such payments, she now instituted a method by which all payments to the king must be accompanied by a further payment to the queen. "Whoever promises a hundred or two hundred marks to the King is thereby indebted to the Queen in one mark of gold for 100 marks of silver, and so on." It is obvious that Eleanor carefully thought out her ingenious idea before proposing it. For instance, she had no intention of leaving her income to chance, nor would she rely on her husband or Richard of Luci to collect her queen's gold; at future meetings of the exchequer she would send her own specially appointed officers to handle her collections. "Observe too," commented the chronicler, "that though the King may refund part or all of a debt owed the crown, it will be for the Queen to decide about her share, and without her consent nothing owing to her can be refunded."

With Matilda's departure, Henry and Eleanor lingered at Winchester throughout the autumn and remained there to celebrate Christmas. These months were a period of inactivity. Eleanor had become pregnant again, and Henry, lacking battles to fight in England, brooded about his menacing brother. In the end, he decided that after the holiday he would cross the Channel to deal personally with Geoffrey. This would have been an ideal opportunity for Eleanor to visit Aquitaine, but such a trip did not, evidently, accord with Henry's plans. During his absence, England would be officially governed by Richard of Luci, but at the same time he promised Eleanor an active part in the government, even though he was unwilling to appoint her regent. These dollops of executive responsibility that Henry would dole out on occasion were not so much done to assuage Eleanor's desire for authority but rather for reasons of his own self-interest. His empire, too large to supervise personally, could not have been ruled without some delegation of authority. Never fully trusting his hired assistants during the early part of his reign, Henry much preferred to leave a member of his family on the scene. Eleanor he trusted, Eleanor was industrious, and he must have been aware that she knew how to rule as well as any man he had appointed to office.

The second year of the reign opened with the queen in full command.

In retrospect, it would prove to be a tranquil year, one without history, because the chroniclers do not record a single event of any consequence. For the first time, Eleanor had an opportunity to travel about on her own, and she began to develop a grudging kind of affection for the land, so different from her beloved Aquitaine. In the twelfth century, England was still covered with mile upon mile of dense forest, where wolves and wild boars could be hunted, but there were also huge open spaces of moor and fenland, unpunctuated save for the muddy tracks that passed for roads. The queen's retinue could be seen toiling over the green hills, through valleys where sheep and cattle grazed and where rye, barley, and wheat were cultivated in strips, through roofed and spired cities surrounded by their thick walls, past slumbering villages with thatched huts and, in the distance, a monastery or grim castle frowning down on the countryside. During the winter and spring Eleanor traveled extensively and lived on a more than comfortable scale, running up expenditures of more than £350, a considerable sum for the age. Normally, only Richard of Luci had authority to order payments from the exchequer in Henry's absence, but many of the writs authorizing payment during this period were signed by the queen herself, an indication of Henry's trust in her.

Although the English tended to be suspicious of foreigners, especially a foreigner with a reputation like Eleanor's, they discovered that the Eagle was more than a glamorous personality. Actually, the sight of the queen dispensing justice and conducting the affairs of the realm surprised no one, for England was full of competent women who spent their time running estates, fighting lawsuits, even standing sieges when their husbands were absent. There was a constantly recurring need for wives to take their husbands' places, and when a man was called away on business or on a military expedition, it was the wife who managed the manor or fief. A goodly share of the business Eleanor did during her travels was no doubt with members of her own sex. Working with Richard of Luci and her own chancellor, Matthew, she dispensed justice through a stream of writs, some of which still survive:

Eleanor, queen of the English, etc. to John fitz Ralf, sheriff of London, greeting. The monks of Reading have complained to me that they have been unjustly disseised of certain lands in London. . . . I therefore order that you enquire without delay whether this is so and if you find out that it is true, reseise the monks. Unless you do this, the king's justice shall do it for we will in no way suffer that the monks lose unjustly anything that belongs to them. Farewell.

With Henry and Becket away, Eleanor found herself in a position where she could do much as she liked. Significantly, we hear no reports of her court resembling any that she had presided over in the past; there were no poets, no troubadours, no sumptuous feasts à la Becket, in fact no gaiety to speak of, only sobriety and hard work. The pipe rolls show, however, that her personal standard of living remained high, her elegant tastes unchanged, and her family well cared for. There are expenditures for candles and incense, allowances for her two children, even an entry for the purchase of a baby carriage. With her she had Petronilla and her two brothers, all of whom she supported in generous style. During her first four years in England, the rolls show thirty-six entries indicating exchequer payments to her half brother William alone, as well as liberal allowances for Petronilla's wine. Neither did Eleanor care for the forebears of Courage, Watney's, and Whitbread; she disdained ale as an uncivilized beverage, much preferring the full-bodied wines of her homeland, and thus began the ever increasing importation of the wines of Bordeaux. Perhaps at this time she had built along Thames Street her own dock, Queenhithe, where the ships of Aquitaine tied up. Queenhithe, adjoining Vintners' quay, was a curved basin that cut deeply into the riverbank. Guarding the entrance to this prominent wharfing space was a gate that could be closed when necessary and a gatehouse tower. Years later, visitors would still consider it one of the most interesting sights in London.

While Eleanor was proving herself a highly efficient sovereign, Henry was having more difficulty than he had anticipated in handling his brother. Geoffrey's claims to Anjou and Maine were excellent, but what he failed to consider was that Henry never gave up any land he once acquired, and the loss of this territory, lying between Normandy and Aquitaine, would cut the two duchies off from each other. After a stormy meeting at which they failed to come to terms, Geoffrey sped back to his castle of Chinon with Henry and his army in hot pursuit. In the end, "now humbled and penitent," he was stripped of his castles and forced to forfeit all claims to Anjou and Maine and content himself intead with a promise of an annuity amounting to one thousand pounds sterling and two thousand pounds Angevin (one Angevin pound was worth about one-fourth of an English pound). At the time, this settlement may have sounded generous to Geoffrey, but he had no way of knowing the worthlessness of Henry's promises. In the two following years he received a total of only eighty pounds.

While Henry was fighting his brother in Anjou, Eleanor was fighting for the life of their two-year-old son, William, in England. Whether the child had been in poor health for some time or whether he succumbed to a passing fever is unknown. Poor sanitary conditions, combined with a primitive state of medicine, were sufficient cause for sudden death, and the lives of children, especially vulnerable, were often ended by smallpox, scarlet fever, diphtheria, and dysentery. The death of the young was part of the natural order of life, and even in the case of a prince, no cause of death was given, none requested. Although people of the twelfth century felt an immense resignation in the face of death, they were by no means indifferent to the loss of their children. The pain of losing their firstborn son would have deeply hurt both Eleanor and Henry. The little prince was buried in Reading Abbey, at the feet of his great-grandfather Henry I.

In June, still mourning for her son, Eleanor gave birth to her third child by Henry, a girl whom she named Matilda in honor of her mother-in-law. That summer she lost all interest in remaining in England; the reins of power had grown burdensome, and she wanted nothing better than to return to her homeland. In July, within weeks of Matilda's birth, Eleanor packed up her children and household, withdrew funds from the exchequer and, whether or not Henry approved, crossed the Channel to Normandy. By August 29 she was reunited with her husband at Saumur, in Anjou, and in October the entire family traveled back to Aquitaine. Henry agreed to this southern progress more to please Eleanor and mitigate her bereavement than from any inclination of his own. Moreover, it was becoming increasingly clear to the queen that, far from sharing her love of the south, he regarded it as a source of irritation and wished to spend as little time there as possible. In England, "swords were beaten into ploughshares and spears into pruning-hooks, and none now girded himself to battle" but none of his policies, none of his carefully devised instruments of government, worked with Eleanor's vassals. The region's natural anarchy, comparable to the disorders that had beset France 150 years earlier under Hugh Capet, offended Henry's every instinct for law and order. Louis Capet had been unable to rule it—his officials could not keep even a modicum of order—and if Henry had wondered whether he could do better, he was not long left in doubt. The ducal authority of Eleanor's forebears, that long line of Williams, had been acceptable to the southern counts and viscounts only so long as it remained ineffective, as fortunately or unfortunately it nearly always was. In Poitiers and Bordeaux, the Williams had maintained estates and fortresses, but in the rest of the vast region, authority rested in the hands of the local lords, whose word stood for law in their respective neighborhoods. The various subdivisions of the duchy professed to have nothing in common, save a long tradition of mutual enmity—the Gascons mistrusted the Poitevins, the Poitevins despised the people of Limoges. For that matter, in 1156 about the one thing Eleanor's vassals could agree upon was their dislike of Henry Plantagenet and his annoying attempts to introduce centralized government.

While Eleanor's liege men joyously received their duchess with troubadours and pretty speeches, they treated Henry, at best, as if he were merely a titular consort, at worst an object of contempt. As he had demonstrated at Limoges only a few months after their marriage, nothing could work him into a rage faster than the Aquitainian nobles, whose insolence and intractability he believed proverbial.

Henry's legendary tantrums were generally attributed to his demon ancestors, that is, they were excused as falling beyond the range of his control. But people do not get into rages in which they scream and bite the furniture because they can't help it. Under certain conditions, such as delirium due to illness or extreme intoxication, a person may lose all control, but these are exceptional instances. In a normal state, people are responsible for their behavior, and Henry, normally, was a responsible person. His fits of anger were nearly always a form of blackmail in that he performed in the presence of an audience for the purpose of gaining some goal. In early childhood he had perfected his act in hate-filled castles, where his mother and father had quarreled and screamed. His outbursts, done for effect, relieved him, but they also allowed him to get his way. It had worked in the nursery, and it continued to work when he grew up.

Even in the first months of her marriage, then, Eleanor had been aware of the spectacularly poor beginning her husband had made with her subjects, and she knew her people well enough to predict that Henry could look forward to a difficult task in introducing Anglo-Norman concepts of government.

In her assessment of the situation, Eleanor had been right. Even minor barons refused their feudal duties to Henry, and the oaths of homage he forced from them were of little practical value. That fall, however, as they made their progress through Poitou, Henry seemed determined to show them that he would tolerate no further defiance. In Limoges, he exercised his feudal rights by making the young heir to the viscountship his ward and then turning over the government to two Normans. In Poitou he unceremoniously ejected the viscount of Thouars from his lands and destroyed his castle, ostensibly for having aided Geoffrey Plantagenet in his recent rebellion but in truth because he found the viscount a troublesome vassal. He wished to leave no doubts in the minds of the southern nobles that he would assert his ducal rights, no matter how many castles he must raze, and in this he appeared to be successful. As the royal family traveled south to hold their Christmas court in Bordeaux, Eleanor's vassals came forth to offer homage to Henry as well as the two children, but an indication of how little he trusted their word is evident from the fact that he took hostages to ensure their fidelity.

In this depressing and unstable atmosphere, it may have seemed to Eleanor that she had lost Aquitaine forever. In some ways, her marriage to Henry and her ever-growing family (she had become pregnant again in December) had been made at a great price; the political realities of the situation were now coming home to her as she acknowledged Aquitaine as a place where she might never live again, at least not with Henry Plantagenet. Beyond that, her domains were a source of friction between them, for she did not completely agree with Henry's policies. In theory, she heartily approved of the concepts of centralized government, which she had seen operate successfully in England, Normandy, and Anjou, but in practice, she had little hope of their acceptance in her own land, where the autonomy of the barons was traditional. Moreover, Henry's policy of appointing foreigners to key government posts only exacerbated opposition. Eleanor had complete trust in her uncle, Ralph de Faye, and felt content for him to remain her deputy, but Henry viewed Ralph's supervision as ineffective, and by Henry's standards, it undoubtedly was. Eleanor must have suspected that the only way in which Henry could maintain his policies was by incessant war with her vassals or the constant presence of either Henry or herself. Henry had no intention of relocating in Aquitaine, nor would he permit Eleanor to return on a permanent basis. And by December he was already agitating for her return to England, where he had more urgent need of her services.

However reluctant to leave the south, Eleanor was back in London by February 1157. Henry had not accompanied her and the children, partly because he remained unsatisfied as to the security of his Continental possessions, partly because he still did not trust Geoffrey. When he finally joined her after Easter, it was not for long, because immediately he began planning an expedition against the Welsh.

Owain Gwynedd, prince of North Wales and a perennial trouble-maker, had taken advantage of King Stephen's laxity to push his way steadily eastward into England until, by 1157, he was threatening to capture the city of Chester. As far as Henry was concerned, the Welsh were a minor nuisance whom he had been able to place at the bottom of his priorities list; now, with both England and the mainland at peace, he was no longer content to leave the Welsh situation in this unsatisfactory state. While Eleanor supervised the routine business of government, Henry assembled an army and a fleet, hired archers from Shropshire, and ordered supplies of grain, cheese, and sixty casks of wine from Poitou.

Toward the end of July, he started out from Chester, working his way along the river Dee toward Rhuddlan, where he intended to join forces with his fleet. Before he had proceeded many miles, however, he realized that the Welsh might be more than he had bargained for. Despite his considerable experience in warfare, he had never before en-countered fighters like the men of North Wales, who, evidently, had not heard of chivalry or rules of war. Essentially guerrillas, they never fought on level ground if there were forests or mountains about; they disdained niceties such as armor and the etiquette of capturing and ran-soming knights. Instead, they cut off their enemies' heads. Owain's for-ces fell upon the English with such ferocity that the royal standard top-pled to the ground, and Henry himself was believed dead. In the end, af-ter sustaining heavy losses, Henry only just escaped with his life and managed to reach Rhuddlan and his navy. At that point, the king had had enough of the Welsh. Even though North Wales was by no means subdued, he established a truce with Owain and, Welsh encroachment into his kingdom checked for the moment, hurried back to Chester.

Immediately, Henry embarked on the next project on his agenda—a tour of England that would take him into every corner of his kingdom. Without returning to London, he summoned his entire court to join him at Chester. Becket, Richard of Luci, Robert of Leicester, and a host of minor officials hurried north, but Eleanor, eight months pregnant, re-mained behind at Westminster. In the last week of August, Henry began moving south through Warwickshire to Malmesbury, Windsor, Woodstock, and Oxford. Eleanor may have been feeling neglected, and no doubt she had been thoroughly frightened by Henry's near death, for suddenly, with the birth of her child imminent, she left the palace and hastened to Oxford, where she joined the court caravan. Her husband's conscientiousness in visiting every hamlet in England was all very well, but there must have been times when she was not content to languish, alone and pregnant. On September 8, at Beaumont Palace, just within the city gates of Oxford, she gave birth to another son, and the pipe rolls recorded an expenditure of twenty shillings for the lying-in. The child was christened Richard, although why this particular name was selected is not clear, since there had been no Richards in either the queen's or the king's immediate families. Perhaps the boy was named for Richard of Luci, whom both of them respected. A woman of Saint Albans, Hodierna, was chosen as nurse, and she cared for him together with her own son, who had been born on the same day. Hodierna and the infants may possibly have joined the royal progress, but it is more likely that Eleanor, so fearfully conscious of the high risks of infancy after William's death, may have felt reluctant to expose Richard to the ardors of travel at so tender an age.

There is no question that she had a special feeling about this son from the outset, making it quite clear to Henry that Richard would be her heir and designating him as the future duke of Aquitaine and count of Poitou as she had done with her dead son. A prophecy attributed to Merlin the Magician, whose anonymous predictions were generally regarded as a foreshadowing of the destinies of Henry II and his family, focused pointedly on this powerfully close relationship between Eleanor and her third-born son: "The eagle of the broken covenant shall rejoice in her third nesting." Those who made it their business to interpret prophecies declared that the eagle could only be divorced Eleanor "because she spread out her wings over two realms, France and England" and that her third nesting must be Richard, who "strove in all things to bring glory to his mother's name." Bending the facts to fit, the chroniclers conveniently overlooked one thing: While Richard was indeed Eleanor's third son, he was her *sixth* child. Daughters, evidently, did not count, either with the wizards or their interpreters.

During the next year, Eleanor and Henry would travel, at a conservative estimate, over 3,500 miles, and even though the medieval nobility took for granted a peripatetic mode of life, with frequent moves from castle to castle, this distance was beyond the ordinary. On the orderly, well-disciplined *chevauchées* of Eleanor's father and ex-husband, everything proceeded according to rule. The itinerary was planned in advance, its stages duly announced and strictly adhered to so that every subject who had business with the king knew exactly when and where to find him. Every member of the royal party, from the chancellor and chaplain to the porters and laundresses, knew when the retinue would arrive and depart. Eleanor's own *chevauchées* through England and Aquitaine hewed to a precise schedule, with the early part of the day devoted to business meetings and audiences, the later to socializing. A progress, no matter the country, had always been an exciting experience for Eleanor, and some of her happiest memories were her childhood travels. Touring with Henry, however, proved to be an entirely different matter and one that her contemporaries likened to a passage through the underworld.

When Henry promised to spend the day in a certain place, even if he had ordered his herald to publicly proclaim his intention, Eleanor could be quite sure that he would suddenly change his mind and decide to leave the town at daybreak. Then pandemonium would break out, with people rushing about as if they were insane, beating their packhorses and driving mulecarts into one another. Those who had been bled the previous night or who had taken a laxative were compelled to join the exodus regardless of their physical distress or be left behind. In vain did the courtiers protest their discomfort, for the word *consideration* did not exist in Henry's vocabulary, at least not on business trips. If, on the other hand, he announced that he would set out early the next morning, Eleanor took it for granted that he would sleep until noon, while the loaded sumpter horses stood waiting with their burdens and the court prostitutes and the vintners took advantage of the delay to do a bit of business. Finally, the enormous royal train, numbering over 250 persons, would straggle down the highroad, but where it might stop next, no one ever knew. "When our courtiers had gone ahead almost the whole day's ride," wrote the royal clerk Peter of Blois,

> the king would turn aside to some other place which had perhaps one single dwelling with accommodation for himself and no one else. I hardly dare say it, but I believe that in truth he took a delight in seeing what a fix he put us in. After wandering some three or four miles in an unknown wood, and often in the dark, we thought ourselves lucky if we stumbled upon some filthy hovel. There were often a sharp and bitter argument about a mere hut, and swords were drawn for possession of lodgings which pigs would have shunned.

Henry's way of conducting the government by fits and starts bewildered his courtiers and vexed his queen, even though she must have understood that his unpredictable movements did not always spring from mere caprice or perversity. He always had a reason, usually known only to himself, but nonetheless there was method to his disorganization. When he dragged them in one day over a distance that should have taken three or four, Eleanor saw that it was to forestall some bureaucratic disaster; when he made unscheduled stops, it was to catch his officials unawares and check if they were attending properly to their duties. Still, his management of everyday business was not terribly efficient. "He was slow in settling the business of subjects, whence it happened that many, before their affairs were settled, died or departed from him dejected and empty-handed."

Physical comforts were unimportant to Henry. But even though "the discomforts of dust and mud he suffered patiently," others cursed and complained about "the miseries of court life" throughout the entire tour. For Eleanor, the racket and disorder, the weariness of constant travel, were bad enough, but the meals were the worst trial of all. The bread was half-baked, the fish four days old, the wine sour or thick or greasy and always reeking of pitch from the cask. There were nights when she was served wine so muddy that she had to close her eyes and filter the liquid through clenched teeth. The meat, half-cooked, was tainted and foul, and, as Peter of Blois vividly remarks, they had to "fill our bellies with carrion and become graves for sundry corpses." There was nothing, evidently, that Eleanor could do to improve the court's incredibly low standard of living. Despite her capacity for roughing it, she was very particular in her domestic habits. Nevertheless, everyone, the fastidious queen included, resigned himself sooner or later.

By December, the royal progress was back in the north of England, and Christmas court was held in Lincoln. The new year of 1158 opened in the far northern reaches of the country, where Henry insisted on inspecting the garrisons of castles he had taken from the Scots. In mid-January, they began to perambulate down through the center of the island, through Yorkshire, then into Nottinghamshire, where Eleanor and Henry stopped at their royal residences of Blyth and Nottingham, and finally into Oxfordshire and Wiltshire. By Easter they were in Worcester, where Henry devised a novel idea: He decided that he and the queen would renounce their crowns. The trappings of royalty had always meant a great deal to Eleanor; the elaborate pageants at Christmas and Easter, the solemn placing of the crown upon her head, the formal processions into church, and the ceremonies surrounding the king and queen's offering and communion were highly gratifying. Nevertheless, at the offertory after Easter Mass, she and Henry laid their crowns upon the altar, vowing never to wear them again. Henry was pleased by the gesture, Eleanor no doubt less so. That year of touring with her husband must have been a disheartening, although enlightening, experience. Nothing had turned out as she expected. Long accustomed to luxury, she who had doted on gracious living, fine wines, and exquisite victuals had now spent eight months under conditions so vile that a peasant would have balked, and now she no longer had even a crown to show for it. Her feelings of discomfort were no doubt maximized during this period, because after Christmas she found herself pregnant again, for the fifth time in six years.

In the following months the court toured through Shropshire, Gloucestershire, Somerset, and Carlisle. Toward the end of July, they reached Winchester, where, fatigued and nervous after their long months of the road, they disbanded. When Henry departed for the Continent in the second week of August, Eleanor could not have been terribly sorry to see him go. She was eight months pregnant, and if she had planned on a rest, it was not forthcoming. Back at Westminster, which now must have appeared the most magnificent palace in the world, she immersed herself in work again. A writ issued in favor of Malmesbury Abbey and dated at this period reveals her as having viceregal powers, meaning that she was serving as coregent with Richard of Luci. On September 23, 1158, without fuss or fanfare and almost seeming to be an afterthought, she gave birth to another son, Geoffrey, and immediately went back to work. According to the pipe rolls, a considerable amount of business was conducted in the queen's court that autumn, some of it, evidently, requiring her to leave London. She traveled through Hampshire, Kent, Bedfordshire, Berkshire, Wiltshire, and Devonshire, and we know that on November 29 she was in the south of England, at Salisbury, because she issued a judgment on behalf of Matilda, countess dowager of Chester, as well as a certificate confirming a quit-claim. There was no time to think of troubadours or poetry, only trials to be concluded and orders to be dispatched "by writ of the king from Overseas." By this time she had proved herself capable of replacing her husband in every way, and she had accomplished more than he was capable of; she had peopled Westminster with three male heirs.

In later years it would be suggested that every unpleasant trait exhibited by her sons must have been due to the manner in which she raised them. To establish the unfairness in such a charge, one only has to look at Eleanor's activities during her childrens' infancies to understand that she had small role in their upbringing. There were nurses to feed her children, comfort them when they cried, teach them how to speak, dose them with medicines when necessary, even chew their meat before they had teeth. If Eleanor was a remote figure, Henry was even worse in this respect, for he was rarely at home, and when he was, he had little time or inclination for romping with toddlers. The discipline, which was a medieval father's primary duty, the scoldings, beatings, and admonitions to show "no glad cheer lest the child wax proud," he largely ignored. At the same time, however, his children were never far from his thoughts, which may have been what Gerald of Wales meant when he wrote that "on his legitimate children he lavished in their childhood more than a father's affection but in their more advanced years he looked askance at them after the manner of a stepfather." It is true that he and Eleanor spoiled their children in their formative years, but not necessarily with physical affection or attention. Henry, especially, dreamed immense dreams on behalf of his offspring, planning for them glorious futures that would reflect on the family and, not so incidentally, extend the power of the Angevin empire. Family, empire, children—these three were all that mattered to Henry and, as time passed, to Eleanor as well. Between them, they had created an empire as well as a dynasty to accompany it; their children would be the most fortunate youngsters in the world. Even as early as 1158, politics for Eleanor and Henry had come to mean a family affair and the children a means of extending their political influence.

Sometime during the early portion of their royal progress in 1157, Henry had concocted a scheme of such audacity that probably only his mind could have conceived it. There had been talk of Louis Capet and probably more than a little mirth over the fact that Louis's second wife had proved as inept as Eleanor in producing an heir for the French throne. In the four years since Constance of Castile had wed Louis, she had given birth to only one child, a girl named Marguerite, and Louis had been heard to grumble about his alarming superfluity of daughters. Aside from the obvious irony of Eleanor now having two sons and her former husband none, it occurred to Henry that perhaps Louis would never be able to sire an heir. Therefore, he boldly proposed to marry his eldest son to Louis's new daughter, a stroke of diplomacy that, he hoped, would bring France into the Angevin empire and one day give young Henry the crowns of both England and France.

In view of Louis's feelings about the parents of Prince Henry, broaching this outrageous idea to him required a considerable amount of tact and delicacy, not to mention nerve. Certainly no mention could be made of the possibility that he might never have a son; the negotiations must be conducted on a more impersonal level, such as Henry's desire for harmonious relations between the two states. Nor could the mission be undertaken by Henry and certainly not by Eleanor. There remained only Henry's alter ego, Thomas Becket, a man who possessed the style and diplomatic talent to carry it off.

In the spring of 1157, the chancellor had been reprieved from the barbarities of touring with Henry and dispatched to Paris with an entourage designed and choreographed to overwhelm both Louis and his court. Becket's trip may have been Henry's idea, but its details and execution could have been invented by no one but the queen and performed by none other than Thomas Becket. In one respect, Eleanor and Thomas were not so different; they were both adept at staging splendid shows. Collaborators for once, they created a pageant that would leave the Franks gaping in wonder, and it is almost comic to imagine the two of them, sitting in a hovel "pigs would have shunned," dreaming up a farce that would convince Louis of England's wealth and persuade him to give up his daughter to a man and woman he hated. When Becket's embassy rattled across the cobbles of Paris in June 1158, people streamed from their houses to watch him go by. Two hundred and fifty footmen singing Welsh and English songs led the procession, and behind them followed the chancellor's hounds and greyhounds, led on leashes by their keepers. There were "dogs and birds of every sort that kings and rich men use," not only falcons but goshawks and sparrow hawks. Eight great wagons, each of them drawn by five horses, were laden with the chancellor's belongings, and two carried English beer "made from a decoction of grain in water, in iron-bound kegs, to give to the French who marveled at that kind of a liquid, a healthful drink indeed, clear, of the colour of wine, and more pleasant to the taste." Each wagon was guarded by chained mastiffs and by "a stout lad in a new tunic," each horse carried a monkey on its back. Behind the wagons came twenty-eight packhorses carrying money, books, chests of gold and silver plate, and the chancellor's chapel. Finally, as if all this might not be sufficient to stupefy the Parisians, there marched the chancellor's personal retinue—two hundred squires, knights, clerks, stewards and lesser servants, and the sons of nobles. "All these men and all their followers shone in new holiday attire, each according to his station." And last of all, surrounded by a few of his intimates, rode the king's chancellor himself. To the Franks, he looked like a king; certainly, he was dressed like one, and in his chests he had brought twenty-four changes of clothing "whose texture mocks the purple dyes of Tyre," apparel that he planned to distribute among various influential men in Paris.

Never in their lives could the Franks recall an embassy of such magnificence, and they asked each other who this man Becket could be.

When they learned that he was only a servant of the English king, they said, "Wonderful indeed is this King of the English, whose chancellor comes in such great fashion." Eleanor could not have hoped for a more satisfactory response if she herself had put the words in their mouths.

In view of this ostentatious display of English wealth, it would have taken powerful extrasensory perception on Louis Capet's part to guess that his former wife was not living like a Byzantine empress. Becket's mission to France may have been a state affair, but Eleanor meant it to convey a personal message to Louis; she wanted to show him how far and how high she had come without him. He was a loser, she a winner, a perhaps cruel but common enough emotion among the divorced of any era.

One might think that Louis would have seen through this nonsense or have felt offended by such obvious showing off. But precisely the opposite seems to have happened. Perhaps he was just as bedazzled as his subjects, because he outdid himself as a host. He arranged for the embassy to be lodged in a new hall built by the Templars, the only one in the city spacious enough to accommodate so large a crowd of visitors. He also ordered the markets of Paris closed so that his guests would not be tempted to spend a penny in his capital, but Becket, who had instructions to give instead of take, sent his stewards into the suburbs to buy provisions just the same. The one-upsmanship mushroomed to absurd heights: Louis and his nobles entertained the chancellor's party at a magnificent feast, but the chancellor, not to be outdone, entertained Louis at an even more sumptuous banquet. Years afterward, the Franks were still talking about how Becket had paid 100s. sterling for a single dish of eels. Spending with the abandon of a man on an unlimited expense account, which is precisely what he had, Becket distributed gifts all over Paris—clothing, dogs, falcons, silver plate, and, of course, those barrels of English beer. In the student quarter, where he had once lived in obscurity during the time of Peter Abélard, he fêted the scholars and their teachers and paid the debts of English students. When it came time for departure, his chests and carts stood empty, but he triumphantly carried back to England the answer for which he had come—Louis's consent to the betrothal.

For this reason, after the tour had disbanded in the late summer of 1158, Henry had sent Eleanor back to Westminster to tend the kingdom while he rushed to the Continent to arrange the details of the royal alliance. He met with Louis near Gisors, in the Vexin, an appropriate conference site because of the schemes percolating in his fertile mind. In the fateful summer during which he had met Eleanor, it will be recalled, his father gave up the Norman Vexin to Louis as the price of Henry's recognition as duke of Normandy. There was no region Henry coveted more than this buffer zone between Normandy and the Île-de-France, and he had never regarded its loss as anything but temporary. Now he proposed that Louis dower his daughter with the Vexin and its castles. Since young Henry was only three and Marguerite less than a year, there could be no marriage for at least a decade, and in the meantime, France was to retain control of the Vexin. Louis had no objections, and the meeting ended on a friendly note. Just one detail remained: the transference of the infant Marguerite to Henry's possession so that she might be brought up, as was customary, with his family until old enough to be married. In September, Henry visited Paris for the first time in seven years, and considering the interim hostility between the two kings, he received a royal welcome from Louis and Constance. Henry's entrance into the city was in marked contrast to Becket's. He came as himself, simply dressed with only a few servingmen, playing the role of humble vassal to his liege lord. If there was a touch of hypocrisy here, it went unnoticed, for Louis, responding in kind, played the role dearest to him—the monk—and escorted Henry on a tour of Parisian churches, standing happily to one side as Henry distributed large sums of money to the monks.

It was, apparently, a time of remarkable harmony between the two kings, even though the occasion was overcast by the invisible, but palpable, presence of Eleanor. She had not been invited to Paris, of course, nor had Henry ever suggested bringing her. Such a three-way confrontation between the two kings and the woman who had had them both would have been in the height of bad taste, although one suspects that Eleanor might have enjoyed it. Certainly, the men avoided any open discussion of the queen, but finally, although indirectly, she entered the negotiations. Louis, surprisingly agreeable to every term Henry presented, balked at the thought of his daughter being reared by his ex-wife. Indeed, he flatly refused to hear of it. He did not regret retaining custody of her two daughters—how unfeminine and headstrong, how like their mother they might have turned out—nor did he regret their being raised by his pious second queen, who knew the value of docility in a female. Now he had no intention of turning over his third daughter to, in his opinion, an unfit guardian like Eleanor. Slightly annoyed but unwilling to see the alliance collapse over a minor detail, Henry suggested as an alternative that Marguerite be placed in the household of his chief justice for Normandy, Robert of Newburgh, whose castle was located near the French border. Since Newburgh was

known to be a man of unimpeachable character and exceptional piety,
Louis seemed mollified, and Henry was able to leave Paris with the
baby. Throughout the autumn, the mood of conciliation between the
Capets and the Plantagenets continued. In November, Louis decided to
make a pilgrimage to Mont-Saint-Michel in Normandy and requested
permission to pass through Henry's domains. Not only was it granted,
but Henry himself escorted Louis to the abbey high above the sea, hearing Mass with him and dining spartanly in the refectory with the monks.
Together in that silent abbey, with only the rush of the tide as
background music, they would never be closer, and afterward, Louis
was overheard to remark, to the astonishment of his retinue, that he
knew of no man so thoroughly lovable as the king of England. After
visiting his daughter and approving arrangements for her care, he
returned to Paris laden with gifts and the distinct impression that the
difficulties between France and England had been mended. It was an
impression that would not last for long.

In London, Eleanor had followed developments on the Continent between her present and former husbands with interest and possibly a
touch of amusement. Whatever other emotions she may have had at this
time, she had good reason to feel gratified. There was peace at home
and abroad. The quarrel sparked by her remarriage had been patched,
and now her eldest son stood an excellent chance of someday wearing
Louis's crown. In England the year 1158, marked by nothing more important than a new issue of coinage, was closing amid general tranquility. Well satisfied with her administration of the country, assured
that every situation remained under control, Eleanor left England in the
steady hands of Robert of Leicester and crossed the Channel to
celebrate Christmas with Henry at Cherbourg.

Domestically as well as politically, the Christmas court was a happy
one. With another son added to their family, with their domains in
peace and perfect order and the future so promising that it took one's
breath away, the Plantagenets had much cause for thanksgiving.
Possibly one dark cloud dimmed their euphoria, but even that turned
out to bear a silver lining. On July 26, Henry's twenty-four-year-old
brother, Geoffrey, had died. Shortly after Henry had bought him off
with an annuity in 1156, Geoffrey had stumbled across a piece of good
luck that undoubtedly saved him from the temptation of future strife
with his brother. Brittany, in a state of anarchy ever since its duke had
died twenty years earlier, was beset by rival claimants to the title, and

the citizens of its key city, Nantes, tired of lawlessness, had offered the dukedom to Geoffrey. Eager for standing in the world, he accepted with delight. Now, upon his death, Henry had no intention of allowing the duchy to escape from the Plantagenet circumference, even though his claim to Brittany rested on the shakiest of foundations. During his honeymoon with the Franks that fall, he persuaded Louis to recognize him as overlord of Brittany, and he then took an army to Nantes to make certain of the city's loyalty. When the citizens received him as Geoffrey's rightful heir, he placed the city under the supervision of a few trusted men. Certainly, Nantes was not the whole of Brittany, but Henry felt positive that the rest of the duchy would follow in time.

With Brittany more or less added to the empire, one might think that the Plantagenets would have been content. On the contrary, their mania for land and more land continued unabated. In this respect, Eleanor was no different from, or better than, her husband. Still laboring under the impression that she and Henry were partners in all enterprises—a justifiable impression at that stage, it must be admitted—she was eager to make a contribution to the Plantagenet holdings. She had, of course, already given him Aquitaine, a gift of dubious value, but now she presented another possibility. Even though Toulouse had not belonged to her family for nearly fifty years, she had never stopped considering the county part of her rightful inheritance. That her grandmother Philippa had ruled there and her father was born there overshadowed the fact that Toulouse had most assuredly passed into the hands of the house of Saint-Gilles. A realist in most ways, Eleanor must have known that Toulouse was irrecoverable by this time, especially after Louis's botched effort to conquer it eighteen years earlier, but that seemed to make no difference. During the Christmas festivities, when acquisition and expansion were on everyone's mind, it is easy to see how the subject of Toulouse came up quite naturally and how Henry must have needed little prompting.

At this point there was something curiously self-defeating about the Plantagenets' decision to gain control of Toulouse, however good their reasons for believing it a rightful portion of Eleanor's inheritance. Henry already had more territory than he could comfortably supervise, and the last thing he needed was another rebellious province like Aquitaine. Although the Toulousains gave nominal allegiance to the Capetians, their political interests were directed southward to the Mediterranean, to Provence and Barcelona, the far south comprising a distinct region of its own. And what is equally curious at this point is why Henry and Eleanor selected this particular moment to offend Louis Capet, whose sister, Constance, widowed upon the death of King Stephen's son, Eustace, had married Count Raymond V of Toulouse. In the past four years, Louis's sister had borne three sons, the only male children of the Capetian royal line as of that time. To press Eleanor's claim to the county by right of inheritance implied dispossession of Count Raymond and his family, something Louis was unlikely to regard favorably. With peace established between England and France, Henry and Eleanor could have selected no more inauspicious moment to bring up Toulouse. Perhaps Walter Map was correct when he wrote of Henry: "He was impatient of peace and felt no qualm in harassing almost the half of Christendom." But in this case, it was not merely a matter of impatience; plain and simple, his motive was greed. Toulouse was a rich county, and Henry could not resist. As for Louis, everyone knew that he could be easily duped.

Fortunately for the Plantagenets, the strained situation in southern France at that time lent itself to the kind of venture they had in mind. Count Raymond of Toulouse was already at war with Count Raymond-Berengar of Barcelona, in addition to other dissatisfied vassals. Henry was not so crass or unskillful as to announce his designs on Toulouse openly; instead, sometime in April 1159, he and Eleanor casually drifted south through Aquitaine, winding up at Blaye in Gascony, where he formed an alliance with the count of Barcelona. To sweeten the pot and to make certain that Toulouse, once taken, did not stick to Raymond-Berengar's fingers, Henry proposed a betrothal between his son, Richard, and Raymond's daughter. Their partnership sealed, he sent a formal summons to the count of Toulouse, demanding surrender of the county in Eleanor's name, which, of course, Count Raymond refused to do. For that matter, he responded by setting off an alarm and notifying his overlord and brother-in-law, Louis Capet, of the danger threatening.

If Louis received a rude shock from the man whom, just months earlier, he had called lovable, he did not allow it to affect his determinedly friendly policy toward the king of England. In 1159, he met with Henry in February and again in June, and although they could reach no agreement, they parted on warm terms. Louis was not the complete dupe he appeared. His hostility toward Henry had been, to a large extent, an expression of his resentment against Eleanor's remarriage, and it had run contrary to the policy laid down by Abbot Suger, namely that the military inferiority of the French made cooperation with more powerful vassals the only sensible course. Although Louis had reached a stage of life where he preferred sensibility, nevertheless this new development created a dilemma. He could not very well contest Henry's claim to Toulouse, because he himself had pressed it when he had been Eleanor's husband. But neither could he accommodate Henry in his aspirations. For the moment, then, Louis stood tactfully aloof.

The early months of 1159 passed in a flurry of war fever. It is probable that Eleanor resided first at Rouen and later at Poitiers, which seems to have been headquarters for the mobilization. To be at home again must have filled her with pleasure; to be preparing for a war that would certainly be won was doubly exciting. For there was no doubt in her mind that her masterful husband, his military record unblemished save for that better-forgotten clash with the barbaric Welsh, would emerge victorious. On March 22, Henry had issued a summons to his vassals in England, Normandy, and Aquitaine to assemble at Poitiers on June 24. Not wishing to inconvenience England, so long a journey from Toulouse, he demanded only the services of his barons. Any English knight who did not wish to make the trip was assessed the sum of two marks, which would pay for a mercenary to fight in his place. In addition to the levy of this scutage, he exacted contributions from towns, sheriffs, Jewish moneylenders, and, much to their consternation and indignation, the clergy. Since the tax on the Church was collected by Becket, many concluded that it was his idea, which was probably untrue. Nevertheless, some years later bitter churchmen would remember and charge that Thomas had plunged a sword "into the vitals of Holy Mother Church with your own hand when you despoiled her of so many thousand marks for the expedition against Toulouse." From laymen as well as churchmen, over eleven thousand pounds flowed into Henry's treasury during the first half of 1159, enough to support a siege for at least five or six months.

On the appointed day, banners flouncing, the army left Poitiers in splendor. Altogether it was a brilliant and impressive parade of Henry's vassals: the barons of England, Normandy, Anjou, Brittany, and Aquitaine; King Malcolm of Scotland, with an army that had required forty-five vessels to transport across the Channel; a showy contingent led by Thomas Becket, who, his ecclesiastical career rapidly fading into dim memory, headed not less than seven hundred knights of his own household, a tremendous force for that time and an indication of his extremely comfortable financial position. In addition, there was the count of Barcelona with some of the unhappy vassals of the count of Toulouse—William of Montpellier and Raymond Trencavel, viscount of Béziers and Carcassonne. The last time such a stupendous army had been seen in those parts was for a major Crusade.

By July 6, Henry's army had encamped outside the high red walls of

Toulouse and, siege engines and catapults in place, settled down for a lengthy stay. Medieval sieges were painfully boring for both besiegers and besieged. Those inside the walls of Toulouse grew claustrophobic and, to relieve their restlessness, would periodically sally forth to provoke Henry's men into a clash of arrows and swords; then they would retreat inside the walls once more. There was little for Henry to do beyond preventing food or military help from reaching the Toulousains. July and August passed to the monotonous thumps of the engineers working their stone throwers. Henry, who hated inactivity, lacked the temperament to conduct a long siege, although he had brought with him his clerks and he kept busy with administrative chores, issuing writs, hearing judicial cases, and listening to subjects who had followed him to the gates of Toulouse to seek favors or appeal law cases. Toward the middle of September, the general ennui was enlivened by a strange sight. Louis Capet appeared before the city gates and requested permission to enter. Since he had brought no army—indeed he meekly declared that he had come only to safeguard his sister—he was permitted entry. But Louis's unexpected arrival seemed to present Henry with a dilemma, or so he claimed. Within a week, he called off the siege, declaring that he had too great a reverence for the king of the Franks to attack a city in which his overlord resided. This, of course, was nonsense, for Henry had no reverence or even respect for Louis. Probably his real reasons for abandoning the siege were practical ones: The cost of feeding thousands was turning out to be an expensive business; the unsanitary conditions had caused an epidemic among his troops; and, of course, he was bored.

Henry's decision to abandon the war sparked the first recorded disagreement between the king and his chancellor. Thirsty for military victory, horribly disappointed that he had lost the chance to lead his troops into a real battle, Thomas angrily argued against giving up. "Foolish superstition" was what he accused Henry of, declaring that Louis himself had forfeit any consideration by siding with Henry's enemies. Not only that, but if Henry were to assault now, he could take Toulouse and make Louis a prisoner as well. Henry, barely controlling his temper, must have reiterated that he had, after all, done homage to Louis as his feudal overlord, and to attack his person would set a poor example for his own vassals. Without being explicit, the chroniclers hint that the disagreement between the two men grew heated. In any event, Henry left Toulouse on September 26, leaving behind his churlish chancellor, who then proceeded to assault several castles in the vicinity. By the time they next met, the clash would be seemingly forgotten.

It was a jubilant Raymond of Toulouse who watched the departure of that army whose vast stockpiles of arrows, siege machines, lances, and axes had rendered the chroniclers speechless. The duchess of Aquitaine had been foiled by his father, and now history had happily repeated itself. Someday Raymond would have revenge on Eleanor, but in the autumn of 1159, such events were still far in the future.

From a careful inspection of Henry's itinerary in the remaining months of 1159, it appears that he traveled directly north from Toulouse, by way of Limoges, to Beauvais in Normandy, where Louis's brother had been stirring up trouble along the border. One receives the distinct impression that he purposely avoided Poitiers, that after his argument with Becket he had small desire to face his wife. It is easy to guess Eleanor's surprise and chagrin; this had been the second time that she had sent a husband against Toulouse, and both expeditions had ended in failure. In Louis's case, defeat had been understandable, for he was hardly a warrior. But what excuse could she make for Henry? With his resources, in terms of both manpower and money, the capture of this single city, no matter how well defended, should have been an easy matter. It must have occurred to her that Henry was not the fighter that either his mother or father had been. He had spent half a year planning the war, raising a large army and vast sums of money, but when his opponent could not be intimidated, he had given up. Others might believe Henry's reluctance to attack his liege lord the height of scrupulousness, but Eleanor saw it as a dent in the image of a man she had regarded as invincible.

Above, the Palais de
Justice, Poitiers, formerly
Eleanor's ancestral
palace. On the *right* can
be seen the Tour
Maubergeonne, where
Eleanor's grandfather
William IX lodged his
mistress.

Right, Duke William
IX of Aquitaine, a por-
trait from a fourteenth-
century manuscript of
troubadour poetry in the
Bibliothèque Nationale

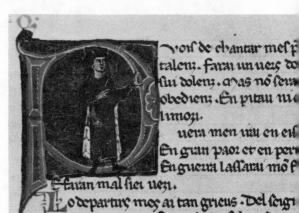

The figures representing a king and queen of Judah and believed to be likenesses of Eleanor and Louis were completed around 1150, shortly after the Second Crusade. From the west portal of Chartres Cathedral.

Rock crystal and pearl vase that Eleanor gave to Louis at the time of their marriage, now in the Louvre. The Latin inscription on the base reads that she gave it to her husband who presented it to Abbot Suger who in turn donated the vase to the Abbey of Saint-Denis. This is the only surviving object from Eleanor's life.

Photographie Giraudon

Entry of emperor Conrad III and Louis VII into Constantinople
during the Second Crusade, a fifteenth-century miniature from
"Grandes chroniques de France." The artist was mistaken because
the two armies entered the city at different times.

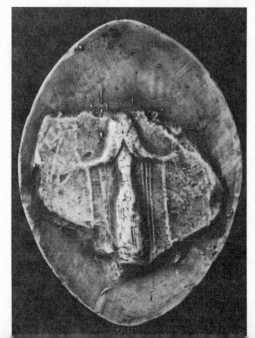

Archives de France

Crowned heads of Eleanor and Henry, an engaged capital from
the Church of Notre-Dame-du-Bourg near Bordeaux, which
now can be seen at the Cloisters in New York. Probably the carved
heads date from a progress they made through Aquitaine in 1152.

Left, the remains of Eleanor's seal, struck in 1152 shortly after
her marriage to Henry, from a charter in the Archives de France

Statue of Richard I by Marochetti, 1860, outside the House of Lords, London

Tomb effigy of King John at Worcester Cathedral. John was the first Plantagenet king to be buried in England.

King John signing the Magna Charta at Runnymede in 1215

The necropolis of the Plantagenets is in the abbey church at
Fontevrault. *Above*, the tomb effigy of Henry II; *right*, the tomb
effigies of Eleanor and Richard. Also buried at Fontevrault Abbey
are Joanna and Isabella of Angoulême.

Archives de France

The Abbey of Fontevrault near Tours, founded around 1099 by
Robert d'Arbrissel to house a foundation of monks and nuns under
the rule of an abbess. Here Eleanor spent the last years of her life.

Betrayals

Exactly how different the decade of the 1160s would be from the previous one the queen was soon to discover. Until the siege of Toulouse, the lucky years had shimmered and slid together, the future appeared so full of promise that the Plantagenets seemed touched by magic or the hand of a benign God. But Christmas of 1159 at Falaise cannot have been a happy one for Eleanor. For the past month, snow and biting winds had swept the Norman countryside, the December sky was colored like iron, and within the cheerless castle where William the Conqueror had been born, the atmosphere was overcast by failure. Henry was not a man to suffer patiently a wife's sarcasms or recriminations, but on the other hand, neither was Eleanor a person to dissemble her feelings about a war so closely bound up with her own personal ambitions. Like Becket, she could see that Louis, bumbler though he might be, had been successful in confounding the king. Accustomed as she had grown to thinking of Louis as a fool and Henry as the clever one, it must have been unsettling to discover that perhaps her images of both men had been distorted. Henry's failure at Toulouse seemed enormous to Eleanor, and although there was no open quarreling, the signs of coolness between them were apparent.

Usually, Christmas courts brought on a fierce lust in Henry, but this Christmas, unlike others, Eleanor did not conceive. Perhaps after six years of almost continuous pregnancy she was relieved to take a rest. Henry, a person who did not dwell for very long on either success or failure, had already appeared to have forgotten Toulouse, and now he grew adamant in pressing Eleanor to return to England. She had been absent from the kingdom for a year—he had been away for over two—and while his trust in Richard of Luci and Robert of Leicester remained intact, this was too long a period to leave England unattended by either himself or Eleanor. Perhaps more crucial, however, was his imperative need for money.

Before the Christmas holiday ended, Eleanor left Falaise, and on December 29, despite the bad weather, she boarded the royal yacht *Esnecca* with young Henry and Matilda and crossed the Channel. Her movements during the next few months are reminiscent of Henry's when the chroniclers declared that he appeared to fly from city to city throughout his domains. At Westminster and Winchester, Eleanor arranged for coin to be loaded on carts and packhorses. Whether following Henry's instructions or by her own authority, she escorted the treasury collection to Southampton, where it was loaded on the *Esnecca*, but instead of riding back to London, she accompanied the precious cargo to Barfleur, saw it safely unloaded, and then returned immediately to Southampton.

That unfortunate business at Toulouse began to recede from her thoughts as she plunged at once into her administrative duties. To judge from the pipe rolls, she led a peripatetic life, journeying from London to Middlesex to Southampton to Berkshire, from Surrey to Cambridge to Winchester to Dorsetshire, and everywhere she could see signs of growing prosperity. At the same time the records show that, no matter how slovenly a way of life Henry may have accepted, the Eagle believed in living well. During that winter of 1160, one of intense severity, she made numerous improvements in her quarters at Winchester; she ordered vast quantities of wine from Bordeaux, as well as incense, oil for her lamps, and toys for her three boys, now aged five, two and a half, and eighteen months. "For the repair of the Chapel and of the houses and of the walls and of the garden of the Queen . . . and for the transport of the Queen's robe and of her wine and of her Incense, and of the Chests of her Chapel, and for the boys' shields . . . and for the Queen's chamber and chimney and cellar. 22£. 13s. 2d." In Hampshire alone she signed thirteen writs authorizing payment to herself of £226, as well as £56 for the expenses of her eldest son, and in London she spent two silver marks on gold to gild the royal cups. By contemporary standards, she was living lavishly, even for a queen.

During this period, her life as regent of England was one in which her husband played little real part. Essentially a person of independent temperament, she functioned most happily when left to her own devices. Although couriers bearing instructions from the king constantly traversed the Channel, the responsibility for carrying out those orders devolved entirely upon herself. Perhaps it was her obsessive need for meaningful work that made her an ideal partner for Henry.

She was thirty-eight years old, no longer the rather frivolous girl who, in the Île-de-France, had been more concerned with banquets and clothes than attending meetings of the curia. By now, however, she had proved herself an efficient executive, a wife of unswerving loyalty who would dedicate herself to implementing policies that her brilliant young husband had devised. The day had not yet arrived when she would be less willing to play the role of workhorse who unquestioningly carried out policies in whose making she had had no voice.

In the meantime, Henry remained on the Continent for the third successive year. In the summer of 1160, a situation came to his attention that demanded some sort of action, although precisely what sort was not yet apparent. During the six years of Louis Capet's second marriage, Constance had conceived only once, the little princess Marguerite now under the care of the Plantagenets. Nobody knew quite so well as Eleanor how infrequently Louis made use of the marriage bed, and perhaps this accounts for the fact that both she and Henry had lulled themselves into believing that the Capetians would remain heirless. Now, however, came an unexpected and alarming piece of information: Queen Constance was expecting a child shortly. Not content to wait until the birth had taken place, Henry took steps to deal with all contingencies and in September he issued a frantic call to Eleanor, insisting that she drop everything and hurry to Rouen with young Henry and Princess Matilda. For a change, Henry's attention was focused, not on his son, but on his daughter, whom he intended to betroth to the house of Capet in case their latest issue should be male. If his son could not sit on the Frankish throne, then his daughter would. One way or another, he planned to emerge the victor. In the end, though, all his furious preparations and precautionary measures turned out to be useless.

On October 4, Louis Capet was struck by a double calamity, one that even the farsighted Henry could not have predicted. After a difficult confinement, Queen Constance was delivered of a second princess and then, as if determined to avoid facing the fresh catastrophe she had inflicted on the royal family, closed her eyes and "passed from this world." The effect on Louis was immediate and decisive. In this crisis, he was forced to face some painful truths: At the age of forty, he had four daughters, no son, and now, no queen. There was no time to waste. Within days of Constance's death, he arranged to marry Adele of Blois and Champagne, the youngest sister of his future sons-in-law, Henry of Champagne and Theobald of Blois, thereby renewing the possibility of his having a son and abruptly rearranging the chessboard of twelfth-century European politics. That Louis should form an intimate alliance with the house of Blois, from which King Stephen had come and from which a possible pretender to the throne of England might arise someday, provided a grave threat to Henry's security. Despite his rage at Constance, who had the effrontery to die in childbirth, and against Louis, who was behaving with uncharacteristic common sense, he never allowed himself to become the victim of circumstance if he could possibly help it. To retaliate, he countered with a move as ingenious as Louis's had been peremptory.

On November 2, while Louis was busy preparing for his wedding, due to take place the following week, the Plantagenets celebrated a marriage of their own; the Princess Marguerite, fetched from her guardian, Robert of Newburgh, was transported to Rouen, where she was quietly, one might even say sneakily, married to Henry's son, "although they were as yet but little children, crying in the cradles." Although they were hardly infants—Henry was five; Marguerite, two—the marriage of two such very young persons was, nevertheless, highly irregular, so much so that special dispensations were necessary. Fortunately for Henry, two cardinals seeking his support were residing at his court at that very time. After Pope Adrian IV died in 1159, schism rent the Church again as rival popes claimed the Chair of Saint Peter, and even though Henry had already assured one of the papal candidates, Alexander III, of his support, emissaries were still pleading his cause. Thus, when Henry needed a favor, they were only too eager to be of service. Henry did not invite the bride's father to the nuptials, although he was careful to conduct the affair strictly in accordance with the canons so that Louis would have no cause for complaint. A king who was to be married within the week had many important matters on his mind. He should not be distracted or inconvenienced by minor considerations. Since the bride was not yet of an age at which she might have demanded her father's presence, indeed it is doubtful whether she fully understood what was going on, Henry proceeded on fairly safe ground; immediately upon conclusion of the formalities, again without notifying Louis, he claimed Marguerite's dowry from the Order of the Templars, who had been holding it in trust for the princess. Having satisfactorily demonstrated that he had fulfilled the terms of this treaty with Louis, he received from the Templars the much-disputed buffer zone of the Vexin and immediately began to fortify Gisors and other principal castles.

In spite of Henry's precautions, it cannot have been long before Louis learned of what had happened. Coming so quickly on the heels of all the other racking upheavals he had recently suffered, he can be forgiven for overreacting to the indecent haste of a marriage that should not have taken place for at least another ten years and that neatly deprived him of Marguerite's dowry. Once again, Henry had made a fool of him. In reprisal, he expelled the untrustworthy Templars from Paris and, with the aid of young Theobald of Blois, fortified his future son-in-law's castle of Chaumont on the river Loire in an attempt to threaten Henry's territory of Touraine. Having anticipated such a counterattack, Henry immediately rushed to the scene of the action, where he dramatically relieved Theobald of his castle, a piece of real estate that he had been eyeing for some time. By this time, it was late November, and the season for fighting was at an end. Extraordinarily well pleased with themselves, the Plantagenets withdrew with their children and new daughter-in-law to Le Mans, where they celebrated an extremely exuberant Christmas. So clever had been Henry's moves to checkmate Louis that any lingering resentment Eleanor might still have harbored from the Toulouse war now largely evaporated. She could not be angry with a man of his genius, and that December she conceived again.

In April 1161, Archbishop Theobald of Canterbury died. If Eleanor and Henry owed their throne to any single person, it was to the old man who had faithfully supported Empress Matilda and arranged the Treaty of Winchester by which Henry was assured as Stephen's heir. It was he who had safeguarded the empty throne after Stephen's death, he who had brought about England's peaceful transition from the house of Blois to the new regime of the Plantagenets, and he who had bestowed upon the young king his much-beloved chancellor, Thomas Becket: Perhaps the aged archbishop was not expecting too much by feeling that Henry owed him, if not a huge debt of gratitude, then at the least a small amount of appreciation. During the illness preceding his death, he had sent a number of letters to Normandy, pleading and then ordering, with the king's permission of course, Becket's return to England before he died. Henry flatly refused. Thomas, he declared, was indispensable and could not be spared at that particular time. But behind these official protestations, Eleanor would have detected the symptoms of jealous paranoia that she now knew to be part of Henry's temperament: Those in his family and household could have no other affections, no matter how innocuous, and all interests must be subordinated to his needs. In a last pathetic letter to Henry, Theobald had written, "My flesh is worn, my limbs wearied by age and toil, and long and grave illness warns me that the end of my days will soon be upon me. I was hoping that I might once more look upon your face, so long desired, before I die." But Henry had other things on his mind that did not permit a visit to England.

At this time, a phenomenal building craze seems to have broken out all over Europe. In the Île-de-France, Louis madly built new churches, while Henry threw himself into a program of modernizing his castles, adding stonework to their facades and constructing more comfortable living quarters within. "He strengthened and repaired nearly all of his castles which were situated on the borders of Normandy and he made a royal park and a royal residence near Rouen. Near Caen, he built a house for lepers, an astonishing structure." Not only in Normandy but in England, Anjou, Maine, and Touraine he either repaired old castles or built new ones. Taking advantage of his new passion, Eleanor made certain that a goodly share of building funds went to Aquitaine, and it was probably at this time that she prevailed upon her husband to restore the city of Poitiers. New walls, bridges, churches, markets, and shops transformed her ancestral city into a showplace, a very model of the latest in urban development. In the refurbishing of the ducal palace can be seen the hand of the queen, who, if she did not supervise the construction, at least made sure that the rebuilding proceeded according to her own specifications. Unlike Henry's other castles, here was no drafty feudal fortress suitable for dogs and falcons and soldiers lolling on a straw-strewn floor, no milieu in which only a man would feel comfortable. Instead, the spacious hall was adorned with graceful arcaded walls and with windows opening out to an enchanting view of the valley and rivers below; small private chambers were added to the palace, intimate rooms where a lady might retire to be alone with her thoughts and desires, memories and fantasies. Although Henry's construction focused on the secular, two new churches were planned for Poitiers: the ornate Notre-Dame-la-Grande, whose sculptured facade resembles a gingerbread dollhouse, and the immense Cathedral of Saint-Pierre with its domed vault over a crossing of pointed arches, a style that would be known as Angevin, or Plantagenet, Gothic.

The summer passed pleasantly, and in September, Eleanor gave birth to her second daughter and sixth child by Henry at Domfront, in Normandy. The princess was given Eleanor's name and baptized in a showy ceremony by Cardinal Henry of Pisa, the same papal legate who had married young Henry to Marguerite. A few weeks later, Henry met with Louis at Fréteval, where they concluded once and for all their ten-year struggle over the Vexin. Louis, aware that Henry was too strong an adversary at this time and in any case having no alternative, agreed to his occupation of Marguerite's dower. The conference at Fréteval ushered in one of those rare interludes of peace for the Plantagenets. With no major crises threatening their security, they could turn their attention to more pleasant duties, such as their growing family, which, in many respects, suffered from periods of benign neglect. Young Henry, nearly seven years old and a married man, had reached the age when he should have begun his formal education. The fact that he had not and, furthermore, still lived with his mother, shocked some people, one of them being the archbishop of Rouen, who sent a polite reproach to Henry: "Although other kings are of a rude and uncultivated character, yours, which was formed by literature, is prudent in the administration of great affairs, subtle in judgments, and circumspect in counsel. Wherefore all your bishops unanimously agree that Henry, your son and heir, should apply himself to letters, so that he whom we regard as your heir may be the successor to your wisdom as well as to your kingdom."

There was no question in Henry's mind with whom the boy should be placed for his education in letters and knightly accomplishment. Becket, the most well-bred man in the empire, already had under his care a number of noblemen's sons, and now the prince was added to the group. While this move made sense to Eleanor, she could not have been completely enthusiastic, not when she heard Thomas referring to the prince as his adopted son. By this time, however, she had had ample opportunity to accustom herself to Becket and his relationship with her husband. Whatever resentment she had felt in earlier years had weathered into a sort of resignation by now, but even though the queen coexisted with the chancellor, she did not like him and never would. At any rate, ever since the Toulouse war she had noticed subtle changes both in Henry and in his affection for Thomas. In retrospect, their quarrel before the walls of Toulouse had marked a turning point; since then, there had been further differences, some of them fairly serious, and even though Henry won the arguments, the tenor of their relationship had gradually shifted from the social to the plane of pure business. The fact was, Henry had matured. At twenty-one, he had been a brash young man who needed a boon companion, someone with whom he could drink and hunt, a confidant for his youthful escapades. At twenty-eight, no longer so youthful or brash, his waistline thickened considerably, he had outgrown his boyish need of a buddy. Thomas's slightly tutorial manner, which he had accepted before, now chafed him. None of this was lost on Eleanor.

We may be sure, therefore, that it was with some astonishment that she heard Henry mention that he was thinking of appointing Becket as a successor to Archbishop Theobald of Canterbury. What first gave Henry the curious idea of transforming his worldly chancellor into the highest prelate in England is impossible to say. In an especially good humor after Christmas court at Bayeux, he had sent to England for falcons and falconers and spent most of his time engaged in his chief pleasure. Perhaps while hawking one amber afternoon along a stream in Normandy, the image came to him full-blown; more likely he was influenced by the fact that a similar arrangement was working well in the Holy Roman Empire, where the archbishop of Cologne also served as chancellor. However unaccountably the seed was sown, he seemed in no rush to do anything about the idea, one reason being that while the see of Canterbury lay vacant, its revenues accrued to the crown and thus enabled him to recoup some of his financial losses from the Toulouse campaign. Even though he tested the idea on Eleanor and other intimates, he deliberately refrained from speaking to Thomas, instead pondering the plan, weighing the advantages and, to a lesser degree, the disadvantages. As Eleanor knew, Henry never did anything without a good reason, and she could not argue with much of his logic. While he had not been seriously dissatisfied with the working relationship between State and Church during the first eight years of his reign, nevertheless he had experienced some opposition, particularly over taxes, and in the future he anticipated more problems over the question of ecclesiastical courts. Combining the offices of archbishop and chancellor seemed a perfect solution, and Becket the obvious choice; he had served the king loyally, and they had always been of one mind as to how the empire should be run. With an archbishop sympathetic to the crown, Henry could build an even more dominant monarchy without the threat of parallel leadership from the Church; not only that, he could also strengthen his courts at the expense of the increasingly independent Church courts. What better way to accomplish these aims than to install his alter ego at the head of the Church? But, of course, there were emotional factors, and to Eleanor it may have seemed, initially at least, that Henry's scheme was just a dying ember of a foolish infatuation. The great love affair had not, apparently, run its course.

There is no way of knowing whether Henry asked Eleanor for advice, although they surely discussed the subject on many occasions. She might have pointed out the obstacles to Thomas's election: He was neither priest nor monk and he had no reputation for holiness. Rather, apart from his efficiency as an administrator, he was best known for his excellent table, his lavish household, and his plumaged wardrobe. These objections Henry could not deny, but he did not anticipate difficulty on those scores. After years of maintaining stiff control over her every utterance in regard to Becket, Eleanor would not have said that she distrusted Becket. She had always believed him to be riddled with ambition, a man hungry for power. In the eight years she had known him, nothing had convinced her otherwise. Of course, he was most assiduously devoted to Henry, the perfect servant, correct, obedient, loyal. Small wonder that Henry counted on a pawn at Canterbury, but even pawns, she might have told him, sometimes assert their independence. In any case, Henry did not care what she thought, and as usually happened when he desired an opinion on important political matters, he consulted his mother. Probably to his annoyance, Matilda opposed the idea, but since she could give no concrete reasons beyond vague predictions of calamity, he was able to discount her forebodings. Perhaps he felt that Matilda, old by now, engrossed in pious works on behalf of the Church, had lost her normally keen judgment. In truth, he did not want anybody's opinion; he had already reached a decision, and now all he desired was reinforcement. In at least one respect, Eleanor may have endorsed his decision. Known to the queen and other intimates, Henry was possessed of an almost obsessive terror that his heirs would be prevented from succeeding peacefully to the throne of England. Haunted by his own struggles, he was given to periodic anxiety attacks over the possibility that Prince Henry would be deprived of his rights, a concern that Eleanor shared, since no regular principle of succession had ever been established. Even though Henry had already obliged his English barons to swear allegiance to his namesake, this failed to reassure him, and now he resolved to adopt the solution that had been devised by Charlemagne, who had crowned his sons as kings during his own lifetime. This practice had been used with no apparent ill effects in Germany and also in France, where Louis Capet had been anointed before the death of his father. It was, nevertheless, a radical departure for the English. Recalling that King Stephen's attempts to have Eustace crowned had been effectively scotched by both Archbishop Theobald and the pope, Henry anticipated the possibility of trouble. The point was—and this surely must have been a key factor in Henry's reasoning—that only the archbishop of Canterbury was authorized to consecrate an English king; with Thomas heading the Church of England, this delicate situation could be handled with the efficiency that Becket had always demonstrated in matters close to Henry's heart. On this basis alone, Eleanor may have suppressed any doubts about the chancellor's promotion.

In early May 1162, the royal family was residing at the castle of Falaise in Normandy. Over a year had elapsed since the death of Archbishop Theobald, months in which the court had murmured furiously with rumors, but Henry, blithely untroubled, had ignored the vacancy at Canterbury. If anything, he seemed titillated to play a prolonged game of cat and mouse with Thomas. "The chancellor, however, who from certain forebodings and conjectures already had an inkling of the king's purpose, kept silence about the matter, even as the king concealed his intentions." Nor did it appear that the game would be called in the near future, because Henry now seemed totally preoccupied with his eldest son. Anxious to exact from his English barons another oath of fealty, he ordered Becket to take the seven-year-old prince to England, where he would call together the Great Council in the king's name and require every bishop and baron in the realm to pay homage. Even though Eleanor and Henry would not be present, an appropriately majestic ceremony had been planned, and according to the pipe rolls, they paid the well-known financier William Cade the goodly sum of thirty-eight pounds six shillings "for gold for preparing a crown and regalia for the King's son."

On the eve of the departure, Thomas brought his young charge to Falaise so that Eleanor and Henry might say good-bye to their son. At the last minute, almost as an afterthought, Henry drew Thomas aside for a private conversation. "You do not yet fully comprehend your mission," said the king, as if he imagined that Thomas had been blind and deaf for the past year. When Thomas did not answer immediately, Henry added imperiously, "It is my intention that you should become Archbishop of Canterbury." Phrased in that manner, it was hardly an invitation. He did not ask Thomas for his opinion, nor did he leave room for discussion—it was his intention. There was an awkward silence, and when Thomas finally replied, it was in the bantering tone he often took with the king. With a deprecating smile he looked down and pointed to his expensive robe. "How religious, how saintly, is the man whom you would appoint to that holy see and over so famous and pious a congregation of monks." When Henry failed to return his smile, he rushed on in a desperately serious voice: "I know of a truth that, should God permit it, you would quickly turn against me and the love which is now so great between us would be changed into the most bitter hatred. I know that you would make demands that I could never meet with equanimity, because already you presume too much in Church affairs. And so the envious would find opportunities to stir up endless strife between us."

Henry dismissed his protestations almost as if he had expected them, and in fact, Thomas's speech almost sounds rehearsed. But it should not be supposed that Becket was insincere. No matter how tempting the offer—not every day did a merchant's son rise to the high place of Canterbury—he knew his master well, his jealousy, his sudden rages, his inability to tolerate opposition. According to Becket's close friend, John of Salisbury, "From these considerations he rightly drew the conclusion that, if he accepted the post offered to him, he would lose either the favor of God or that of the king." Whatever else may be said of Becket and his sincerity, there is no question that he warned Henry against the nomination. On the other hand, he does not seem to have protested at any appreciable length nor, in the end, did he refuse the offer. At any rate, it seems that Henry paid utterly no attention to the warning, because shortly afterward, perhaps the same day, he held a revealing conversation with Richard of Luci. "Richard," he demanded, "if I lay dead in my shroud, would you see to it that my firstborn son Henry were raised to the throne?" When Richard assured him that he would do so at the risk of his life and limbs, Henry instructed him to leave at once for England and, exerting whatever pressure necessary on the monks of Canterbury, see that Thomas was elected.

It was settled then. Thomas would become archbishop, young Henry crowned king in due time, the throne of England safeguarded for the golden boy whom Henry adored. The empire would endure. It was the king's privilege to have arranged these matters, but it would be a privilege for which he would pay heavily.

The salt wind swelled the silken sails of the *Esnecca*, skimming the royal barge closer and closer to the pale coastline of England. The Plantagenets had announced that they would celebrate Christmas in England, but impassable seas and contrary winds had delayed them many weeks in Normandy. They had been forced to spend a dismal, slapdash Christmas in Cherbourg, and it was not until the end of January 1163 that they had finally sailed for their island kingdom. On the dock at Southampton, an official delegation waited to hail a boisterous welcome to the king, who had been absent four years and the queen who had been away two. Those years in Normandy, while peaceful, had been dimmed for Eleanor by indefinable dissatisfactions, perhaps a sense of drifting more than anything else. She had lacked, of course, any challenge for her energies, and indolence never sat well with her. At the same time, the contours of her relationship with Henry were changing, and she must have noticed a certain restraint in his behavior since the birth of Eleanor fifteen months earlier. Close to forty, she had reached an age when women, no matter how beautiful, do not like to be reminded of their years, especially when their husbands are significantly younger, and she may have attributed Henry's indifference to the age factor. Not only did he take her for granted as a woman but, more distressing, he had shoved her into the background. No longer a working queen, she was expected to derive contentment from idleness. This was not easy for her to accept, and she would have expressed resentment, with grievances and misunderstandings accumulating on her side as well as on Henry's. The return to England and the prospect of seeing her son after a seven-month separation provided a welcome relief, more especially since his guardian's elevation to Canterbury had unloosed a torrent of highly diverting gossip.

Throughout the previous summer and autumn, word of Becket's activities had flown the Channel, with delighted talebearers repeating the latest news for the edification of the court. Ever since Becket's consecration on June 3, he had become, if gossip could be trusted, a totally changed man. "Putting off the secular man, he now put on Jesus Christ," throwing himself into the role of archbishop with a fervor equal to the enthusiasm he had exhibited as chancellor. It was said that he wore vestments of gold, but beneath was "a hairshirt of the roughest kind, which reached to his knees and swarmed with vermin." It was also claimed that "he mortified his flesh with the sparest diet and his accustomed drink was water used for the cooking of hay," that he exposed his naked back to the lash of discipline, slept on the bare floor next to a bed "covered with soft coverlets and cloths of silver," and washed the feet of thirteen poor folk every morning. "Contrary to the expectation of the king and all men, he so utterly abandoned the world and so suddenly experienced that conversion which is the finger of God that all men marveled thereat."

Eleanor, like Henry, tended to be cynical about such conspicuous miracles. For eight years she had seen the chancellor in many guises: as the oily-tongued courtier always ready with a quip; as the gourmet who decked his table with expensive wines and the best cuts of flesh; as a posturing soldier on his way to war; and as the resplendent diplomat, puffed up with self-importance and the ostentation of the nouveaux riches. Under the circumstances, his metamorphosis did not seem genuine. Within weeks of his consecration, however, there had come the first intimation that perhaps both Henry and Eleanor had misread Thomas Becket. They had been in Normandy when a Master Ernulf arrived, bringing with him a parcel and a message from Becket. When Henry saw that the package contained the Great Seal of England, he let loose with his favorite oath. "By the eyes of God!" he had shouted. "Doesn't he want to keep it anymore?"

"He feels," explained the messenger, "that the burdens of two offices are too much for him."

"*I* feel that he no longer cares to be in my service," snapped Henry, who, far from accepting Becket's excuse of overwork, interpreted his resignation as a slap in the face.

Becket's tactless haste in resigning the chancellorship provided an ominous clue that he planned to be his own master in the future, and other signs of trouble followed stealthily as he began to reassert Canterbury's claim to property the Church had lost during Stephen's reign. Wherever he found Church land, either farms or manors, in the hands of laymen, he dispatched his knights to seize it but, in his zealousness, very often neglected to bring the cases to court. Since Henry had granted him permission to reclaim alienated Church property, Thomas stood on fairly safe ground as long as he confined his recovery programs to small holdings; it was when he began laying claim to the castles of great lords that Eleanor noticed her husband's temper rising sharply. Before long, there were indignant protests, one of them from Earl Roger of Clare, who complained that Thomas was trying to deprive him of his castle at Tonbridge. As Eleanor could have predicted, Henry bristled noticeably at this particular complaint because Roger's sister "was more beautiful than any lady in the land and the king had at one time passionately loved her." This insult to the family of one of the king's mistresses was not taken lightly, but Henry, although worried now, pretended to overlook it. Soon afterward, however, had come Henry's resolve to return to England, and obviously Becket's new militancy was the cause.

Eleanor, too, was anxious to observe for herself the metamorphosis of the elegant chancellor into, as one chronicler described him, "an erect pillar in the Church of the Lord, a bright candle on God's candlestick." When they landed at Southampton, she caught sight of a gaunt Becket advancing toward them, her son Henry's hand clasped in his. After having listened to Henry's cautious fulminations against Thomas for some months, Eleanor must have watched their meeting with interest. Aside from a slight formality in Henry's manner, they greeted each other with kisses, embraces, and expressions of pleasure; that evening at supper and the next day traveling up to London the two men never left each other's side, chattering and laughing in a manner reminiscent of earlier days. If Eleanor had hoped for something different, she must have been disappointed; still, despite the show of cordiality and friendship, she knew Henry too well to believe that the breach had been fully mended.

At Westminster, Eleanor again found herself in the position of decorative queen, carefully restricted to the shadows. Judging from the pipe rolls, she must have arranged a festive party for young Henry's eighth birthday, but otherwise she seems to have been inactive. By this time, it must have been apparent that her vision of equal partnership with Henry had been a delusion, although during the periods of her regencies he had seemed pleased enough to benefit from her services. He had permitted her sovereignty under special conditions, namely during his absences, but when they both occupied the same territory, he would not countenance her interference. Only in separation, then, was she able to function with any semblance of autonomy or even productivity, but of this she was only imperfectly aware at this time. It has been suggested that she took small interest in the king's feud with Becket; on the contrary, feeling at loose ends and having little else to occupy her time during that restive year of 1163, she must have been a keen observer of the steady buildup of tension that resulted, in large part, from Becket's persistence in goading the king at every turn. Already, words had passed between them in public, and Eleanor, more than anyone else, would have been witness to Henry's private irritation, his charges of ingratitude, his rambling threats to cut the archbishop down to size—all embellished by cries of "By God's eyes!"

Eleanor's appraisal of the situation would have proceeded on a quite different level: Becket, a self-seeking hypocrite from the outset, a consummate actor, was merely showing his true colors at last. Rather quickly she must have perceived trouble ahead for Thomas, a prospect that did not at all displease her. Indeed, it would have been altogether less than natural if she had not felt much relieved to see her rival topple from the king's favor. In any case, she could hardly have held herself aloof from the controversy, since Westminster boiled with juicy reports of each encounter, the hostile courtiers baying triumphantly at the smallest black look the king gave Becket. A man who had accumulated as much power as Becket could not have helped making enemies, and now, explains one of Becket's biographers, they sowed their tares eagerly. "The king's courtiers, seeking to win his favor and itching to gain his ear, defamed the archbishop and hated him without cause." Eleanor would not have been among those who whispered malice into Henry's ear—not for nothing had she maintained a strict silence for the past eight years—because she understood to perfection that he would fall without her denigration, subtle or otherwise.

As spring drifted into summer, the drama between the two men grew more absorbing. In July, Henry held a council at Woodstock, and although the pipe rolls do not specifically mention Eleanor's presence, it seems likely that she and the children accompanied him to live in the splendid manor house set among the green woods of Oxfordshire. At this meeting Henry introduced the subject of sheriff's aid, a payment of two shillings per hide of land to the sheriff of each county as a token recompense for his administrative duties. Always alert to new sources of income, especially now that Canterbury was no longer vacant, he proposed that this customary gift to the sheriffs be paid instead directly into the treasury as a legal tax. The first person to voice an objection was Becket. Perhaps from force of habit, he momentarily forgot that he was no longer in a position to give the king advice, but more probably he believed it a grave tactical error to deprive the sheriffs of an important source of income, since it would encourage them to reimburse themselves by cheating the treasury. In any event, he took the king sharply to task.

"By God's eyes," Henry spat back, "it shall be given me as a tax and entered in the King's roll; nor is it fitting that you should oppose me when no one is trying to impose a burden on you or the Church." At this point Thomas would have been wise to have maintained a diplomatic silence. He, if anyone, knew how easily defiance could bring on an attack of Plantagenet fury, and as chancellor, he certainly would have known better than to answer. But he was no longer the king's creature; he was archbishop of Canterbury, and he vented his own temper, confidently matching oath for oath. "By the reverence of those eyes by which you have sworn, my lord King, not a penny shall be paid from any of the land under Church jurisdiction."

His face flushing crimson, Henry abruptly dropped the subject and moved on to the next item on his agenda. During this exchange, the barons had stirred nervously, waiting for the explosion that failed to come. But behind Henry's controlled, if untypical silence—the result of shock more than anything else—burned deep rage, because normally no one dared speak to him in so disrespectful a manner, especially before an assembly of his barons. Perhaps for the first time, he allowed himself to recognize that his long friendship with Thomas the chancellor was finished; thereafter, he would be forced to deal with Thomas the archbishop. Since Becket seemed to be spoiling for a fight, he would give him one, and before the Woodstock meeting adjourned, Henry hit upon a suitable means of retaliation. For some time now he had been concerned over what amounted to an unprecedented crime wave in England, and in fact, many of the offenses appeared to have been committed by clergy, either men in holy orders or those who had merely taken religious vows. These "criminous clerks," as they would henceforth be known, were in the habit of dressing up like monks, joining bands of travelers, and once they reached a forest or deserted stretch of road, robbing and murdering them. What especially enraged Henry was that anyone who enjoyed the status of clergy could not be tried in the civil court; they could plead clerical immunity and demand trial in the ecclesiastical courts, where, to the king's thinking, they received absurdly light sentences. At the worst, their punishment amounted to a severe penance, suspension from the exercise of their priestly functions, or confinement in a monastery for the remainder of the offender's life.

Since Henry had returned to England six months earlier, he had already clashed with Becket over several of these cases, Thomas having rescued the accused from the king's court by claiming jurisdiction. At Woodstock now, still smarting from his defeat over the sheriff's aids, Henry brought up the case of a Bedford canon, Philip Brois, who had been accused of murdering a knight. Tried in the court of the bishop of Lincoln, Brois had cleared himself by compurgation, an ancient practice in which the accused solemnly swears his innocence while twelve oath helpers also swear a similar belief on his behalf. This was enough for the Church, since the act of perjury jeopardized one's immortal soul; it was not enough for Henry, who felt convinced that justice had not been done and who, moreover, felt annoyed that Thomas had whisked Brois from the clutches of the common law. The meeting at Woodstock adjourned with Henry formally requesting a report on the number of capital crimes committed since 1154, paying particular attention to the crimes of the clergy. As of July 1, 1163, the fatal gauntlet had been thrown down to Thomas Becket.

What began at Woodstock as more or less a personal feud soon threatened to escalate into a full-fledged contest between Church and State. During the summer and into the fall, the nobility scrambled to take sides in preparation for the storm that now appeared certain. At the same time, Henry's ever-increasing fury at Becket reverberated through the royal household, and although he did not wholly neglect his other projects—later, in July, he arranged for Prince Henry to receive the homage of King Malcolm of Scotland—nevertheless, Eleanor and his family, indeed most concerns, faded into insignificance alongside his all-consuming anger. And yet he still oscillated between bouts of rage and periods of pure bewilderment, as if he were pinching himself in disbelief over what had happened. His treasured friend, the man he had been closest to during his entire life, had betrayed him. What galled him most perhaps was that he, the king who prided himself on judging men's characters, had made a colossal mistake in the case of Thomas.

On the first of October, after further clashes with Becket, Henry was ready to bring the warfare into the open. The royal family had moved back to Westminster, where Henry convened an assembly of his bishops and barons to settle—or so he announced—a dispute between the archbishops of Canterbury and York, who had been wrangling about the respective privileges of their two sees. However, his opening address to the convocation that morning had to do with a very different matter. As if four months had not elapsed since Woodstock, he again took up the question of criminous clerks. Before his listeners quite realized what was happening, Henry had briskly plunged into a peroration in which he demanded that "clerks seized or convicted of great crimes should be deprived of the protection of the Church and handed over to his officers." According to his records, in the nine years of his reign, over a hundred murders, in addition to uncountable rapes, thefts, and extortions, had been committed by clerics who, because of their immunity from civil trial, had gone virtually unpunished. The Church courts, he added, failed to impose severe enough penalties to deter lawbreakers from committing further crimes. Speaking with elaborate patience, Henry was careful to stress that he had consulted his legal advisers, and they too saw no reason why all subjects should not live under the same law. Thomas, invited to the council ostensibly for the purpose of discussing his quarrel with the see of York, quickly understood that he had been tricked and, furthermore, that the king intended to force the issue.

Now Henry directed his eyes squarely upon Becket. "My lord of Canterbury," he challenged, "I demand that with the consent of yourself and of your fellow bishops, clerks who are caught committing crimes, or have confessed them, be degraded, deprived of all protection of the Church and handed over to my court for corporal punishment." There was, he quickly added, no need for the Church to take alarm at his proposed remedy; it was nothing more than a return to the customs of the land when it had been ruled by his grandfather. It was, he implied, a tradition.

Even so, it was not a tradition that anyone remembered, and in fact, there is no evidence that Henry I had ever carried out any such procedure with lawless clerks. In the deathly silence that followed, Thomas and his bishops withdrew to consult among themselves. None of them had ever expected Henry to go quite so far, and some, frightened, argued that crimes of the clergy, more reprehensible by virtue of their order, should therefore be punished more harshly than the crimes of ordinary laymen. Thomas pointed out, however, that double punishment ran contrary to canon law: "God does not judge twice for the same offense." After further discussion, they agreed that the king had attacked the freedom of the Church and that they must not yield to his demand. Filing back into the hall, Thomas stepped before the king. He stood tall and proud in his costly archbishopric robes, his once handsome face now pale from fasting, and looked down his long nose at Henry. "The customs of Holy Church are fully set forth in the canons and decrees of the Fathers," his voice rang out. "It is not fitting for you, my lord king, to demand, nor for us to grant anything that goes beyond these, nor ought we to consent to any innovation. We ought to humbly obey the old laws, not establish new ones."

He was not demanding anything of the kind, Henry retorted with belligerence. He was only asking that the customs observed in the time of his grandfather be observed in his. And furthermore, he added cuttingly, there were holier and better archbishops than Becket in those days who never raised any controversy about them with the king.

Thomas answered without flinching. "What was done by former kings ought not to be called customs but abuses, and whatever practices were observed that ran against the laws laid down in the canons was done out of fear of kings." He continued to inveigh grimly against "such depraved practices," concluding that Henry would always find the clergy "obedient and ready to accord with your will and pleasure in everything that we can possibly consent to, saving our order."

Henry, his temper having grown progressively shorter as the day wore on, began to swear at Becket. "By the eyes of God!" he roared, "let me hear no word of your order! I demand absolute and express agreement to my customs." Rounding on the bishops, he asked each one in turn if he were willing to observe the customs of the realm, and all but one echoed Becket; they would obey the king in all things "saving our order." By shifting his ground from the abuses of criminal clerks to a general acceptance of what he called the ancient customs, Henry undoubtedly forced the bishops to make this reservation, "saving our order," to protect themselves, but his change of emphasis would prove to be a mistake. The behavior of some clerks was already a national scandal, and an impartial contemporary observer such as William of Newburgh, himself a cleric, deplored those bishops who were "more concerned with defending the liberties and dignities of the clergy than they were with correcting and restraining their vices, and they thought they were doing a service to God and the Church by protecting criminous clerks from public punishment." Henry's original desire to secure the peace and order of his realm, which is what he meant by "observing the ancient customs," soon became lost in semantics.

The whole day passed in argument, and now it was growing dark. Once again Henry turned to Becket. Puffing with anger, the king demanded that he and the other bishops take an oath to observe the customs "in good faith," without any reservation whatsoever. He wanted a clear answer. Thomas made a last effort to pacify him. "My lord king," he said soothingly, "we have already sworn fealty to you by our life and limbs and earthly honor, saving our order, and in that earthly honor were included all the customs of the kingdom." No oath they could take now would be more binding.

Suddenly Henry rose and bounded out of the hall without a parting word, without even waiting for the customary blessing of the bishops, leaving behind a confused hush. Before daybreak the next morning he sent a messenger to Becket dispossessing him of the manors of Berk-hampstead and Eye, which he had held since his chancellorship, and also removing Prince Henry from his tutelage. This done, he left Westminster without speaking to the prelates. What might have been a difficult but reasonable discussion on how best to deal with criminal clerks had now been blown out of all proportion, the issues forgotten in the clash of personalities. Even though Eleanor disliked Thomas, even though his recent problems had failed to call forth her sympathy, she still must have watched uneasily the extreme emotional reaction these encounters drew from her husband. For the first time since she had known him, he was allowing personal feelings to direct his actions. She had seen him rage and roll on the floor chewing straw, but this hostility, the result of emotions that ran even deeper than anyone had suspected, was something else. Betrayal was not, evidently, a situation that Henry could handle, although what in his background would have accounted for it is uncertain. Before her eyes, he was regressing from a clear-headed executive to a small boy wreaking vengeance on everything in sight. Nor was it easy to understand Thomas, his unyielding obstinacy, his determination to prove himself as powerful as the king. He knew that Henry did not restrain his anger, either in public or in private. What did he hope to gain by pushing the king?

Not long after that, Henry made his last peaceful overture toward his one-time friend. Meeting Thomas in a Northampton meadow on horseback, he spoke freely and plaintively: "Have I not raised you from poverty and lowliness to the pinnacle of honour and rank? And even that seemed little enough to me until I also made you father of the kingdom, placing you even above myself. How is it then that all these proofs of my love for you, which everyone knows, you have so soon blotted from your mind, so that you are not only ungrateful but oppose me in everything?" One feels, thinly disguised in those words, Henry's fantasy that something—a word, an embrace, a look—would restore their friendship. Whatever his hopes, he was not prepared for Thomas's rebuff.

The archbishop spoke very distinctly. "I have not forgotten your favors, my lord, favors which are not yours alone for God deigned to confer them on me through you." With that he went on at length to explain that when his duty to king conflicted with his duty to God, he had no choice but to obey the latter. His defense was turning into a lecture, and when he warned that "we must obey God rather than men," Henry would hear no more. "I don't want a sermon from you," he interrupted curtly. "Aren't you the son of a peasant of mine?"

"It is true that I am not descended from a long line of kings, but then neither was Blessed Peter, on whom the Lord bestowed the keys of the kingdom of heaven and dominion over the whole Church."

"That is true," Henry returned, "but he died for his Lord."

It was not meant as a threat, but Thomas, interestingly enough, seems to have interpreted it as one, for he answered gravely, "I too will die for my Lord when the time comes."

Again Thomas refused to omit those three exasperating words "saving my order" from his oath, and despite Henry's pleas and threats, they parted silently, neither having yielded an inch.

Eleanor and Henry celebrated Christmas of 1163 at the manor of Berkhampstead, one of the residences recently retrieved from Becket, and to indicate that it was to be particularly festive, the royal plate had been fetched from Winchester especially for the occasion. Ironically, Berkhampstead was more resplendent than most of the royal manors, because Thomas had spent large sums on its repair and redecoration. However, the Christmas festivities seemed oddly at variance with the real moods of the king and queen. The holiday, one of the most disturbing Eleanor had spent with Henry, was marked by cold rains, intrigue, negotiations, and ugliness. Henry's childish insistence on holding Christmas court at Berkhampstead, an obvious attempt to further humiliate Becket, indicated a pettiness of spirit, the more so because recent developments had given him every reason to believe that he had won his struggle with Becket. When the dispute had reached the ears of Pope Alexander, he had sent letters and messengers to Becket advising him to submit to the king and obey the laws of the land. Admittedly in a difficult position because he needed Henry's support in his battle against the antipope, Alexander nevertheless could not see that Henry had explicitly proposed anything directly contrary to the teachings of the Church. In fact, he had asked Henry for assurances on that point. To Alexander, the quarrel appeared simple: Thomas in open defiance had injured the king's royal dignity, and obviously Henry would lose face if he allowed himself to be beaten by the archbishop. To salve the king's pride, Thomas must omit the words "saving my order," and then there would be peace. In fact, Henry had assured the pope that he would drop any further mention of the customs. As a result, Thomas had given way and, in December, had met with Henry at Woodstock, where he humbly made his submission, swearing to observe the customs of the realm in good faith. But the killing game had not yet ended. Immediately upon hearing Thomas's recantation over the obnoxious *salve ordine meo,* he sprung his trap. Since Thomas had publicly defied him, an act of private submission would not suffice; the archbishop must repeat in public, in the presence of the Great Council, the oath he had just made privately. Under the circumstances, Becket could not refuse.

On January 25, 1164, the mighty of the realm assembled at the royal hunting lodge of Clarendon, near Salisbury. The benches of the hall were packed with archbishops and bishops, earls, barons, nobles, and elders, whose names the chroniclers meticulously recorded. Eleanor's is not among them, but it is fairly certain that she was with Henry at Clarendon, and it seems unlikely that she would have missed the opportunity to see Becket brought low. Moreover, her son Henry was presiding over the council along with his father for the first time. Exactly what took place at Clarendon is far from clear. We know, however, that Henry opened the proceedings by calling upon the archbishop to swear to the customs of the realm without any qualifications—and that Thomas, after some procrastinations and excuses, refused to take the oath. At which point, Henry flew into one of his famous rages, his outraged howls sounding to one witness "like the roaring of the lion." He swore that if Thomas did not promise to observe the customs and dignities of the kingdom, he would resort to the sword. Precisely what this last threat meant nobody was quite sure, but some remembered how Geoffrey Anjou, in a fit of Angevin rage, had ordered the bishop-elect of Seez to be castrated. Over the next three days, the heated debates continued, and Henry grew increasingly furious. At the point when the bishops had almost persuaded Thomas to submit—a purely formal act to satisfy the king's injured honor—Henry sprung another trap. He produced a written document, undoubtedly prepared in advance, listing the laws of the land as they were observed (he said) in the time of his grandfather. Hearing the Constitutions of Clarendon read aloud, Thomas immediately realized that he had been betrayed again;

in effect, the provisions placed the Church of England under the king's control, in that civil law was to take precedence over canon law. Churchmen were forbidden to leave the realm without Henry's permission nor were they permitted to appeal his decisions to Rome.

After the provisions had been read aloud, Henry said, "These customs have been conceded to me. Therefore, lest any question should arise concerning them in the future or lest any new disputes should perchance come up, we will that the Archbishop put his seal to them."

Becket's reaction was one of horror. "By Almighty God, never, as long as I live, will my seal be put to them!" Clutching the copy of the Constitutions that Henry had given him, he stalked from the hall without waiting for the king's dismissal.

The Constitutions of Clarendon stand out in the history of English common law for two reasons: It was the first time a king attempted to legislate in writing (until then the law consisted of general customs or tribal practices passed orally from one generation to the next); and, secondly, they contained the seeds of later legal innovations, such as the use of the jury of accusation for bringing to light offenses that individuals dared not denounce. Still, by putting the customs in writing and asking Thomas to sign them, Henry took their quarrel past the point of compromise. Taken in their entirety, the sixteen articles of the Constitutions would have destroyed the freedom of the Church of England, placing it subordinate to the king. Curiously, only one of the provisions dealt with clerical crime, the problem that had given rise to the whole controversy. So long as Henry had adhered to this issue he had remained on safe ground because Thomas's refusal to clean house within the Church had run contrary to common sense, and Thomas knew it. Henry had never claimed the right to judge clerks in his courts; he simply asked that a cleric accused of a serious crime be first brought to the king's court to answer for his breach of the peace. If he denied his offense and pleaded benefit of clergy, he would have the right to be tried in an ecclesiastical court. However, if convicted and degraded from his orders, then, as a layman, he would be handed back to the king's court for an appropriate sentence, either mutilation or death. But once Henry reduced the customs to writing, including among them practices that the Church had violently opposed in the past, he lost his advantage.

The terrifying scenes at Clarendon, the yelling and threatening, impressed one observer more than any other. Young Prince Henry, one month short of his ninth birthday, had adored Becket for his cheerful temper, his refinement and suave manners, for being everything that his rough, choleric father was not, and he had called him foster father. It is not known what type of explanations were made the previous autumn, when he had been abruptly removed from Becket's household. Instead of being returned to Eleanor, he had been given a house and servants of his own, and perhaps Henry had painted the best possible face on these sudden changes by designating them a special honor, something the heir deserved. At Clarendon, the boy would not have understood the issues to any appreciable degree, but he could not have helped but realize that his father wished Thomas harm. In the household of Henry Plantagenet, one could not remain neutral to his quarrel with Becket, and in those drab January days, young Henry chose his father's side. While it would have been unthinkable for the small boy to have indicated any overt support of Becket—he feared his father too much for that—he was left with an abiding hostility toward the king. In time, his affection for Becket would fade, but the dislike for his father generated at Clarendon would remain for the rest of his life.

A few days after Clarendon, Henry received news of his youngest brother's death, an event that only added further fuel to his hatred of Becket. Henry had always felt a special affection for William. Unlike his second brother, Geoffrey, whose ambition and jealousy created barriers between them, William seems to have demanded nothing. Earlier, the king had entertained thoughts of invading Ireland for the express purpose of providing William with a fief of his own, and only his mother's reservations had led Henry to abandon the project. Determined to provide for William, he tried to give him the hand and extensive estates of the widowed countess of Warenne, heiress to the earldom of Surrey. Due to Becket's intervention, however, the marriage had been forbidden on the grounds of consanguinity. This had been one of Becket's victories in the months shortly after his ascension, but it would be a victory he would come to regret. There was no denying William's very voluble disappointment, because he complained to his mother, to the monks at the Norman monastery at Bec, indeed to anyone who would listen. Thus, when he fell ill and died on January 30 at the age of twenty-seven, it was not surprising that people claimed he had died of a broken heart. Whatever the cause of death, Henry, inconsolable, held Thomas responsible.

To judge from the pipe rolls for 1164, Henry's melancholia found expression in a total incapacity for work. He and Eleanor spent the winter in the southern counties and then traveled up to London for Easter on April 12, but uncharacteristically, he accomplished nothing of note. For the months of May, June, and July the king and queen seemed to have dropped out of sight, because there is no record of their whereabouts, an extraordinary occurrence. Those months must have been fearful for Eleanor. It was a time of violent passions, a time of mourning, for Henry grieved the death of his friendship with Becket as strongly as he did his brother's passing, and a time of great hatred. The king had prematurely aged, in fact he suddenly seemed older than she, and the tyrant into which he had matured was not a person she could admire. One reason she had married him was her belief that he would develop into a great man, but whatever greatness he had once assumed in her eyes had dwindled during the quarrel with Becket. It had brought out the worst in him, and no one saw this more clearly than Eleanor. She saw, too, that Thomas, who had once preoccupied him by virtue of the pleasure he provided, continued to preoccupy him in hatred. It must have been a bitter and humiliating realization to know that Henry and Thomas hated as only those who have loved deeply can hate.

By the end of the summer it was apparent that matters were coming to a head. While Henry had exercised his right to influence Becket's appointment to Canterbury, and although he often ranted that he would bring him low and put him back where he had found him, still he could not remove the archbishop from office. It was necessary for Becket to resign, something Henry intended to humiliate him into doing. It was clear that the archbishop, for all his defiance, was a frightened man, because twice in early September he had made two abortive attempts to leave England, only to be turned back by the king's men at the Channel ports. Henry's taunts—"Has this island grown too narrow to contain us both?"—had the ring of a man who has backed his prey into a very tight corner. Now he pursued the archbishop as though he were a besieged castle that must be laid waste at all cost. As Eleanor well knew, there was no room in England for a queen let alone two kings, and Thomas had made himself a rival to Henry. During seven days in October, she received a telling lesson on how the king treated a rival whom he wished to destroy. After a complaint by one of his barons, John Marshal, that he had not received justice in the archbishop's court, Henry summoned Thomas to appear at Northampton on Tuesday, October 6, to answer charges of contempt. When Thomas arrived, he found that the lodgings reserved for his party had already been occupied by some of the king's men, who refused to move. He also discovered that the king had apparently forgotten his coming, because he had gone out to hawk along the river Nene. The king did not return until evening.

Early Wednesday morning, Thomas dutifully appeared at Northampton Castle, where the hearing was to take place. Informed that the king was attending Mass, Thomas sat down to wait in the corridor connecting the chapel with the main hall. When Henry entered, Thomas rose to greet him, but the king strode by as if the archbishop were invisible. The king, he was informed by servants, was going to have his breakfast. Later in the morning, when finally he was admitted to the royal presence, Thomas immediately referred to the complaint made by John Marshal. Why, he asked, was Marshal not present to press charges? The king replied that Marshal had been detained in London on business (Marshal, in fact, would never arrive). With that, he put over Thomas's case until the next day and sent him back to his lodgings.

Between Thursday, October 8, and Sunday, October 11, the king demanded that Thomas return all of the monies entrusted to him while he had been chancellor, the financial exactions including nine years' revenues from the manors of Eye and Berkhampstead as well as, curiously enough, five hundred marks that Henry insisted he had lent Thomas during the Toulouse war. In effect, what was being asked of Thomas was every penny he had been advanced for expenses during his eight years of service as the king's chancellor. One chronicler stated that Henry demanded a total of thirty thousand marks, a sum equivalent to the total revenues of the archbishopric of Canterbury for seventeen years or, in today's currency, almost $850,000. Few individuals in the world, kings included, could have paid such a colossal assessment.

After retiring for the night on Sunday, Thomas, who suffered from kidney stones, was stricken with acute renal colic so painful that he could not sit up in bed.

On Monday morning, he notified the king that he would not be able to appear that day due to illness. The king, suspicious, sent the earls of Leicester and Cornwall to Thomas's room to find out if he were malingering.

On Tuesday, October 13, a group of bishops begged Thomas to resign, because they had heard rumors that the king planned to condemn him as a traitor. Thomas refused. After celebrating Mass, he appeared at the king's castle carrying the great silver cross of Canterbury, a sight that caused onlookers in the courtyard to gape in amazement, for an archbishop's cross was customarily borne by his crossbearer. At the castle doorway stood Gilbert Foliot, bishop of London, and Hugh Nonant, one of Thomas's clerks. "My lord Bishop of London," said Nonant, "why do you allow him to carry the cross himself?"

Gilbert Foliot despised Thomas. "My good man," he snapped, "he always was a fool and he always will be."

Thomas entered the hall and sat down on a bench, holding the heavy cross before him. From a second floor chamber Henry sent down some of his barons to ask Thomas if he was prepared to account for his financial transactions while chancellor and to stand trial in the king's court. Thomas reminded them that he had been summoned to Northampton to answer John Marshal's complaint and for no other reason. For most of the day Thomas sat in the downstairs hall clutching his cross, while Henry, upstairs, badgered his council to pass sentence against the archbishop. When this information was relayed to Thomas, he pointed out that he had appeared before no court, had received no trial, and therefore could not be sentenced. After the barons retired to the second floor to report this latest development, Thomas picked up his cross and began to leave. Stumbling over a pile of fagots, he regained his balance and pushed his way through the crowd. "Where are you going!" someone called out menacingly; "traitor!" shouted the king's illegitimate brother, Hamelin. Some of the bystanders began to pelt him with handfuls of rushes and other refuse they scooped from the floor.

According to one chronicler, Thomas answered, "If I were a knight, I would prove thee a liar with my own hand." Others claimed that he made no answer at all, or that he replied violently, calling Hamelin "varlet and bastard."

That night, under cover of a storm, Becket left Northampton disguised as a monk named Dereman. For the next two weeks he traveled by night, moving from one monastery to another and finally reaching the coast at Sandwich, where he managed to hire a small boat. On the evening of November 2, 1164, he washed up safely on a beach in Flanders, accompanied by two canons and a servant, carrying with him only his pallium and his archiepiscopal seal.

When Henry learned of the archbishop's flight, he fell, it was said, into so spectacular a rage that he could not speak. Only when he had recovered his breath did he gasp, "We have not finished with him yet!"

The events at Northampton and Becket's escape had a subtle but dramatic effect on Eleanor's relationship with her husband; after five years of physical and emotional estrangement (how complete cannot be said) there now appears to have been a sort of reconciliation. With the object of Henry's persecution safely out of reach, he seems to have turned in his frustration to his queen, even though thoughts of Thomas constantly tormented him and he still thirsted for revenge. Immediately after learning of the archbishop's departure, he had sped an embassy to Louis Capet with a letter demanding Becket's extradition from France or Flanders or wherever he might have sought asylum. "Be it known to you that Thomas, who was Archbishop of Canterbury, has been pub-

licly judged in my court by a full council of the barons of my realm as a
wicked and perjured traitor against me. . . . Wherefore I earnestly beg
you not to permit a man guilty of such infamous crimes and treasons, or
his men, to remain in your realm. . . . Let not this great enemy of mine,
so it please you, have any council or aid from you and yours, even as I
would not give such help myself to your enemies in my realm."

It was a shocking letter, unstatesmanlike, whining, exaggerated, almost comical, and Eleanor no doubt suspected that if Louis had his wits
about him, he would use it to Henry's disadvantage. After all, of what
"infamous crimes and treasons" was Thomas guilty, except that he had
pitted his will against Henry? And while he had not exactly won,
neither had he lost. Common sense told her that Louis, always on the
lookout for ways to undermine Henry's authority on the Continent,
would be eager to take Thomas's part.

After Northampton, the court made a progress through southern and
southwestern England and then, as Christmas drew near, retired to
Marlborough for their court festivities. It was the time for feasting and
caroling, for festooning the Great Hall with boughs of holly and dragging in the Yule log to blaze on the hearth. If Eleanor had looked forward to a holiday without shadows, this hope was shattered on Christmas Eve, when the ambassadors whom Henry had sent to France finally
caught up with the traveling court. Louis, the envoys reported, had interrupted them before they had finished reading the first sentence of the
letter; a verb annoyed him. "Who *was* Archbishop of Canterbury?" he
had cried in agitation. "Who has deposed him? Tell me that, my lords,
who has deposed him? Who has deposed him?" When Henry's men
could think of no good reply to that embarrassing question, Louis rendered his opinion. "Certainly I am as much a king as the King of the
English, but I do not have the power to depose the most insignificant
clerk in my realm." This rebuke, which had been noted with satisfaction by the dignitaries attending Louis's court at Compiègne, caused
Henry to glare and breathe heavily. Did they remind the king of France
that Thomas, as chancellor of England, had seized some of his towns
during the Toulouse campaign? What did he say to that! What he had
said smacked of the tiresome sermonizing that invariably made Henry's
blood boil. As far as Louis could see, Thomas's conduct at Toulouse had
been in the service of his lord, and it ill became Henry to return evil for
good. Then the king of France had turned to a papal chamberlain standing nearby and said meaningfully, "Tell my lord Pope Alexander from
me that I hope he will receive the Archbishop of Canterbury with kindness, and not heed any unjust accusation against him."

By this time, Henry had worked himself into a seizure. Christmas

1164 was undoubtedly one of those occasions when "the King, burning with his customary fury, threw the cap from his head, undid his belt, threw far from him the cloak and robes in which he was dressed, with his own hands tore the silken coverlet off the bed and sitting down as though on a dung-heap began to chew the straw of the mattress." The next day he seethed impotently, his hands tied out of respect for the Lord's nativity, but on the day after that, "giving way to unbridled passion more than became a king, he took an unbecoming and pitiful kind of revenge by banishing all the archbishop's relatives out of England." In the dead of winter some four hundred persons of every age and sex were stripped of their possessions, herded into boats, and shipped to Flanders where they were forced to beg their bread on the highroads. It was a cruel and tyrannous act but one that seemed to surprise none of Henry's intimates and surely not the queen. What may have startled her, however, was that sometime during that violent Christmas court Henry returned to her bed. Early in the new year of 1165, at the age of forty-two, she found herself pregnant again.

With another child on the way, it was easy for Eleanor to entertain the illusion that her life with Henry had taken a permanent turn for the better. Becket, when she thought about him, may have seemed exactly what Henry had said—the son of a peasant—and as such, he had little significance compared to the Plantagenets' real business of governing their lands and establishing a solid empire for their heirs. During the past two years both Eleanor and Henry had lost sight of these goals, but now they turned their attention to the future of their eldest children. Ten-year-old Henry, the child of greatest importance, seemed nicely settled with Princess Marguerite in their own court, an honor that some thought unnecessary because the boy was already showing a tendency to nurse illusions of grandeur. It seemed virtually certain that someday he would preside over a greater territory than his father, since Louis Capet's marriage to Adele of Blois, now in its fourth year, remained childless. Of course, one undeniable inconvenience resulting from Becket's precipitate flight was the lack of an archbishop of Canterbury to crown the boy, but Henry vowed that this did not matter; he would find another archbishop to anoint his namesake. All in all, the prince's prospects seemed splendid.

Shortly after the beginning of the year, Henry began considering the future of his eight-year-old daughter; when he looked at Matilda, he did not see, as Louis Capet had once remarked about his girls, "a superfluity of daughters," but a channel through which he might extend Plantagenet power and also score another point against both Becket and the traitor's new patron in Paris. Sailing to Normandy in February, he entered into negotiations at Rouen with a delegation from the Holy Roman emperor, an action at once anti-Becket, anti-French, and antipapal. Pope Alexander, in exile at Sens, southeast of Paris, had received Thomas with tears and embraces, despite his reluctance to offend in any manner the king of England. The pope's greatest fear was that Henry would ally himself with the German emperor, Frederick Barbarossa, who had supported Alexander's rival for the papal throne. Even though the antipope, recognized in Germany as Victor IV, had died the previous year, the Germans had perpetuated the schism by recognizing a new rival, Paschal III. When Alexander learned that Henry had agreed upon a marriage between Matilda and the emperor's cousin, Henry the Lion, duke of Saxony and Bavaria, he grew alarmed, which was precisely Henry's intention.

Eleanor, who had remained in England, was not content to leave the matchmaking entirely to Henry, for in April the archbishop of Cologne visited England to speak with her and meet Matilda. Henry the Lion was thirty-six years old, Matilda only eight, an enormous age difference even for the twelfth century, but Eleanor does not seem to have regarded this an insuperable barrier. Henry the Lion was the most notable of the emperor's vassals; he had brought under subjection the eastern part of Germany, and by now had almost a free hand in the empire. Furthermore, he seemed to be the kind of man Eleanor admired: rich, powerful, a patron of the arts and of the Church, a man already famous throughout Europe for his courage and enlightenment; hence, she most likely believed it to be a prestigious match for her eldest daughter.

After Henry's departure, Eleanor remained at Winchester. She had been given no viceregal duties and seems to have spent the spring making short trips with the children to Sherbourne Castle in Dorset and what sounds like a seaside holiday at the Isle of Wight. In several respects, however, that spring of 1165 was a time of renewed hope. After five years of idleness, she was eager to reassume responsibility, and now circumstances combined in such a manner that Henry felt need of her assistance. Since the previous autumn, he had been planning another expedition against the Welsh, who had shown amazing persistence in pushing the English out of Wales. This time, however, determined to avoid the mistakes of 1157, he planned to campaign with footsoldiers instead of knights in cumbersome armor. Now that his energies would be devoted to war preparations, he decided to make Eleanor regent for Anjou and Maine. On May 1, she crossed the Channel with Matilda and Richard, her other three children remaining in England,

and joined Henry in Normandy. It was a brief reunion because two weeks later Henry returned to England, while she moved south to establish a headquarters at Angers. This was as close as she had come to her homeland in several years, and while there is no evidence that she visited Aquitaine, she does seem to have renewed contact with at least one member of her family, her uncle Ralph de Faye.

Shortly after she arrived in Angers, it appears that she was approached by supporters of Becket, who wished to solicit her aid. If the archbishop imagined that the queen might feel sympathetic toward his cause, he was either remarkably insensitive or perhaps merely desperate. If he had failed to recognize her hostility in previous years, this was due to the fact that she had covered her feelings well, but nevertheless he should have known better than to expect her support. While it is unclear precisely what sort of feelers may have been extended, we do have a letter indicating her reaction. In July, the bishop of Poitiers wrote to Becket, now living at the Abbey of Pontigny in Burgundy, that he should not expect the queen's intervention, since she was wholly under the influence of Ralph de Faye, one of the archbishop's enemies. The bishop, evidently a gossip, added gratuitously that the relationship between Eleanor and her uncle was subject to "conjectures which grow day by day and which seem to deserve credence." Although he fails to specify the nature of the conjectures, his implications are unmistakable. This was the first recorded scandal about Eleanor since she became queen of England, but it serves as a reminder that her past, those tales of adultery bruited about during the final years of her marriage to Louis, had not been forgotten. To the argument that Eleanor acted indiscreetly at Angers, it may be answered that she often behaved with excessive affection toward her relatives, and this was not the first time that outsiders attributed unwarranted significance to her actions. Even though accusations of illicit relations with uncles seem to have hounded her, there is no need to give any particular credence to the bishop's account. No doubt Eleanor felt relieved to be free of the morose English court, an atmosphere made all the more depressing by her husband's continual emotional outbursts. Twelve years earlier, during the first year of her marriage, she had been happy at Angers, and perhaps her renewed residence there brought back memories of carefree days when she had still been serenaded by poets. Angers was not Poitiers, but for the moment it was close enough to bring her a measure of happiness.

In August 1165, Gerald of Wales was still a student in Paris. The weather, he would recall years later in one of his chronicles, had been suffocating, and he had taken to studying his books in the evening when it grew cool. Shortly after midnight on Sunday the twenty-second, he suddenly heard a commotion that sent him running to the window. It sounded as though every bell in Paris were ringing, and at first he thought that there must be a very bad fire somewhere in the Île. When he leaned from his window, he saw the square below blazing with bonfires and Parisians racing about with torches, shouting and waving their arms. Calling down to a woman he knew, he asked what was going on.

"By the grace of heaven," she cried, "there is born in Paris tonight a king who shall be a hammer to the King of the English."

Louis Capet's prayers had been answered. At the age of forty-five, after twenty-eight years on the throne, he had given the Franks an heir. Small wonder that the boy would be called Philip Augustus and hailed by the Franks as Dieu-Donné, "the God-given."

The reaction of the Plantagenets to this depressing piece of news has not been recorded. Later it would be recalled, however, that two comets had been reported in the month of August, one in the west of England and another in the north. A comet, as everyone knew, appeared only at the death of a king or betokened the ruin of a nation. Hindsight notwithstanding, it did not take a wizard to understand that 1165 was a spectacularly poor year for the Plantagenets.

For the second time, Henry's expedition against the Welsh had ended in complete failure, and by September he was back in England with nothing to show for his months of planning and enormous expenditures, except a few hostages, whom he ordered savagely mutilated. In Angers, Eleanor was having troubles of her own because, despite the bishop of Poitiers's insinuations of sexual escapades, she had the difficult task of maintaining order in a region poised for rebellion. While Henry had been preoccupied in England with the Becket imbroglio, the border region where Brittany adjoined Anjou, Maine, Poitou, and Normandy had grown restless, and the border barons of Brittany and Maine had formed a league to resist his authority; in fact, during the previous summer, the constable of Normandy had been forced to muster an army against the confederates. As Eleanor must have known when she arrived to take up the regency, she had been assigned a tinderbox. She might ignore Thomas Becket, even dismiss him as a bit player on the great stage of kings and queens, but she soon discovered that his defiance of Henry and his widely publicized asylum on the Continent were having serious effects. Becket demonstrated to all with a mind for taking the law into their own hands that Henry Plantagenet was neither irresistible nor invulnerable. He could not only be defied but defied successfully. While Henry was fighting the Welsh, Eleanor found her orders treated with contempt. And it was not only in Brittany and Maine that discontented subjects opposed Henry's rule, but also in Aquitaine, where, she learned from her uncle that Earl Patrick, Henry's military governor there, was faring no better. After thirteen years of Plantagenet rule, Eleanor's vassals had had enough. "The Poitevins," reported Gervase of Canterbury, "withdrew from their allegiance to the king of the English because of his pruning of their liberties." If fact, some Poitevin nobles had appealed in desperation to the papacy, requesting that Eleanor's marriage be dissolved on the grounds of consanguinity, and they had laid before the papal legates a genealogical table to prove their case. Forboding reports of conspiracies came to Eleanor's ears, stories that the counts of Angoulême and La Marche had formed a confederation to break away from Henry and offer their allegiance to Louis Capet.

Unlike her previous tour of duty at Angers, this stay did not offer the leisure to create a court or invite troubadours. In October, Eleanor gave birth to another daughter, whom she named Joanna, but on the whole, there was little cause for rejoicing, and she must have waited anxiously for Henry's return. Even though the Welsh campaign had ended in late August, the king seemed in no hurry to leave England. He failed to return that year, not even to see her new baby or celebrate Christmas, the one time of the year they always spent together. Moreover, there seemed to be no good explanation for his absence. For a man who never stood still, who arrived at a place and then immediately ached to leave, Henry was behaving with strange lethargy. From September 1165 to the following March, except for brief trips to Winchester and Clarendon, Henry spent most of his time at Woodstock, near Oxford. In early March of 1166, he prepared to cross the Channel, but then at the last moment changed his mind and returned to Woodstock. Not until March 16 did he leave Southampton. Whatever suspicions Eleanor may have had, whatever tales of a new mistress may have found their way to Angers during those months, she seemed determined to ignore them. Or perhaps the rumors only heightened her desire to prove herself still desirable to Henry, because within weeks of his return to Normandy, she became pregnant. At this point she must have been nearing menopause, and one way of denying her age and maintaining at least the illusion of youth would have been maternity. On the other hand, this pregnancy, which would be her last, may simply have been an accident. She could hardly have failed to see that Henry had lost all interest in her—he wanted young women—but she struggled to keep him. Once back on the Continent, he reverted to his old habits, that is, he never stopped moving. According to the pipe rolls, he immediately set out for Maine to ravage the castles of those border barons who had been rebelling against Eleanor's orders. He spent Easter with her at Angers, but after that she could not have seen much of him. From Angers he went to Le Mans, in June he was detained at Chinon for several weeks due to illness, but by July 12 he was campaigning in Brittany, where he spent most of the summer, summoning eight-year-old Geoffrey from England and betrothing him to the heiress of Brittany, five-year-old Constance. If he behaved like a man on the run, it was from necessity, because every time he turned his back, his vassals eagerly took advantage. Even Louis Capet, puffed up with confidence since the birth of Dieu-Donné, had turned remarkably bold.

By October, Henry was back in Normandy, at Caen, where he began considering how best to deal with the rebels in Aquitaine, who, he had heard, were covertly intriguing with Louis. Apparently settling on a velvet-glove approach, he summoned the troublesome barons of Poitou to a conference at Chinon on November 20 and also announced that he would hold Christmas court at Eleanor's newly rebuilt palace in Poitiers, an honor that the Poitevins failed to appreciate. For some unknown reason, he decided against taking Eleanor to Poitiers, resolving instead to visit the south with Prince Henry so that he might present the queen's vassals with their future overlord. Surprisingly, Eleanor journeyed to England in the autumn. Certainly there were no pressing reasons for her presence there, and in her advanced state of pregnancy one would think that she might have preferred to travel south rather than to that foggy island on the rim of the world. Crossing the Channel with Matilda in October or November, she arranged for young Henry's trip to the Continent, receiving from the sheriff of Devonshire £100 for the prince's traveling expenses. In December, she traveled in Oxfordshire, and shortly before Christmas she retired to Beaumont Palace in Oxford, where Richard had been born. There, on Christmas Eve 1166, she gave birth to another son, whom she named John in honor of the saint of his natal day. It was a lonely, bitter, humiliating Christmas, spent in the company of a ten-year-old girl and a newborn infant, lonely because she longed to be in Poitiers, bitter because by now she had most likely discovered the existence of Rosamond Clifford. What she had learned by the day John was born filled her with raging hatred against her husband, and when she looked at the tiny, dark-haired infant, so different from her other golden children, she felt no joy. For the rest of her life, the sight of John would be sufficient to bring back memories of a man she despised, of that bitter Christmas she had spent in Oxford choked with shame and rage. Sometime during that Christmas season she resolved to return permanently to Aquitaine; she would no longer be a wife to Henry Plantagenet. From the devil he had come and to the devil he could go.

The Court of Love

Henry Plantagenet was in love. This time it was no comely damsel found in a Norman village where he had spent one night nor a sporting prostitute from the dockside taverns along the Thames nor a baron's daughter whose father sought to make his fortune by pimping for his overlord. Nor was it a queen whose lands and fame had aroused in him a greedy lust. This time it was a real love, perhaps the only one that Henry would ever feel for a woman.

> Her crisped locks like threads of golde
> Appeared to each man's sight;
> Her sparkling eyes, like Orient pearles,
> Did cast a heavenlye light.
>
> The blood within her crystal cheekes
> Did such a colour drive;
> As though the lillye and the rose
> For mastership did strive.

Rosamond Clifford is believed to have been the daughter of Walter de Clifford, a Norman knight living at Bredelais on the Welsh border. During Henry's campaign in Wales during the summer of 1165, de Clifford had been among those to join the king's forces. Afterward, Henry must have visited his castle, perhaps by invitation, but more likely on one of those unscheduled stops along the road that never ceased to irritate his traveling companions. In later centuries, it would be claimed that Rosamond was the mother of Henry's illegitimate sons, Geoffrey and William, an impossibility, since both of them were born in the 1150s and she was still a girl in 1166, when Henry first encountered her. There was something about Fair Rosamond and her idyll with the king that provided irresistible raw material for the weavers of fables and fairy-tales. That she was radiantly beautiful there is no doubt, and one can further guess that she must have had a pretty, compliant type of femininity that appealed to the king: "A sweeter creature in this world/ Could never prince embrace." Unlike Henry's other affairs, this was both serious and relatively stable, because it endured until Rosamond's death in 1176 or 1177. In the densely forested park at Woodstock, Henry built, or so the balladeers claim, "a bower the like was never seene," a secret love nest so cunningly concealed that it could only be approached through a maze. To shelter nature's work of art, his Rose of the World, from the rude eyes of men—and from his jealous queen— Henry contrived a labyrinth so intricate that "none but with a clue of thread could enter in or out." While he was away from England, however, the queen threaded the maze by following a silken string fallen from a marvelous needlework chest that the king had given Rosamond for her embroidery. Once inside the house, "the furious queene" offered her rival the choice between drinking a bowl of poison or death by dagger. In most versions of the fable, Rosamond, as brave as she was fair, chooses the poison.

In contemporary accounts, however, there is no hint of foul play in the death of Rosamond Clifford and certainly no evidence to support the story of Eleanor balancing a dagger and a cup of poison. The first association of Eleanor with Rosamond's death occurs in an anonymous fourteenth-century chronicle, *The French Chronicle of London,* but the jealous queen is not Eleanor of Aquitaine but Eleanor of Provence, the wife of Henry III. In this Grand Guignol account, the queen first strips Rosamond of her gown and roasts her naked between two fires, then finishes her off by placing two horrible toads on the fair lady's breasts while at the same time bleeding her to death in a bath. As the blood oozes and the toads suck, Eleanor cackles with pleasure. Except for this particular chronicle, no writer before the sixteenth century assigns Eleanor the role of murderess. Which is not to imply that her contemporaries ignored Henry and his new mistress. Gerald of Wales does not hesitate to state that the king, "who had long been a secret adulterer, now flaunted his paramour for all to see, not that Rose of the World as some vain and foolish people called her, but that Rose of Unchastity." For all her subsequent fame, Rosamond must be one of the most neglected concubines in history, because during the dozen years of their liaison Henry spent only a total of three and a half years in England. During those twelve years, she lived at Woodstock and then in retirement at the nearby nunnery of Godstow, where she died of natural causes and was buried by sympathetic nuns who had, apparently, found her a romantic figure.

A chronicler tells how Bishop Hugh of Lincoln was making his rounds in the Oxford countryside in 1191 and, entering the church at Godstow to pray, saw before the altar a tomb covered with silken clothes and surrounded by a considerable number of expensive candles. Making inquiries about this obviously well-tended shrine, "he was told that this was the tomb of Rosamond, who had formerly been the mistress of Henry, King of England, and that for love of her, he had shown many favors to that church." To this the horrified bishop made a predictably indignant reply. "Take her away from here, for she was a harlot; and bury her outside of the church with the rest, that the Christian religion may not grow into contempt and that other women, warned by her example, may abstain from illicit and adulterous intercourse." Rosamond was then interred in the nuns' chapter house, where, according to Ralph of Higden, her tomb was inscribed with a coarse punning couplet:

Hic jacet in tumba rosa mundi, non rosa munda;
Non redolet, sed olet, quae redolere solet.

Here lies the rose of the world, not a clean rose;
She no longer smells rosy, so hold your nose.

Long before Henry met Rosamond, the ancient manor of Woodstock had been a favorite royal palace. At the time of the Norman Conquest, a Saxon manor stood on the site, and later Henry's grandfather had built a hunting lodge in the middle of the great forest and surrounded it with a deer park that he then encircled with a stone wall seven miles long. Henry I had had a passion for rare animals, and behind his great wall he collected a menagerie of lions, leopards, lynxes, and even camels. His grandson used Woodstock as a meeting place for sessions of the Great Council, but mainly it was a hunting lodge. One can imagine that such an extraordinary place delighted the Plantagenet children, and perhaps Eleanor too had a special affection for Woodstock with its exotic animals and its treetops arching in vast shadowy caverns.

During those months in 1166 and 1167 when Eleanor struggled with the Breton and Poitevin insurgents at Angers, insistent tales must have drifted across the Channel to be repeated by the courtiers as the choice gossip of the moment. Judging from Gerald of Wales's remarks, "vain and foolish people" may already have dubbed the new mistress Rose of the World and described her as a fairy princess who had enchanted a king. Eleanor's extreme reaction to Rosamond Clifford is a continuing mystery to which there are few clues; nothing in her background easily accounts for it. From the outset, Henry's whoring had been an established part of her marriage, and by that time she would have taken it for granted that none of her household maids were safe with him and that his vassals locked up their wives and daughters when the king entered their neighborhoods. Neither should it be forgotten that Eleanor was a sophisticated woman who came from a region where adultery was not only tolerated but distilled into the wine of troubadour poetry and quaffed regularly to the tune of lute and drum. Her own grandmother, the viscountess of Châtellerault, had been one of the most notorious adulteresses of her generation, whose extramarital escapades had provided young Eleanor with romantic bedtime stories. At any event, no highborn lady of the twelfth century complained very strenuously about her lord's philandering, no matter how much she may have fumed in private. Lust, a man's nature, was accepted and ignored. For fifteen years Eleanor had looked the other way, indeed in the case of Henry's natural son, Geoffrey, she had done more than that, accepting him as a member of the family.

There is no proof at all that she suffered inordinate pangs of sexual jealousy. Granted, it could be true that she suddenly turned into a possessive termagant as she grew older and less desirable to Henry, but on the other hand, long practice had taught her to hide her inward feelings. And, if she had weathered his all-consuming passion for Thomas Becket, she certainly might have overlooked a provincial girl from the Welsh marches. There had been many, many women, too many to count, and luckily the affairs had always blown over quickly. Perhaps that was the trouble: Henry's feelings for Rosamond were special, like none he had felt before for any woman, Eleanor included, and somehow she became aware of this.

But that was less than half the story. What must have turned her against Henry so irrevocably was his public flaunting of Rosamond. Sometime during his stay in England after the Welsh campaign, he brought Rosamond to Woodstock and installed her with regal honors in Eleanor's apartments. Apprised of these developments by friends or informers, Eleanor lost no time in making her way toward the vicinity of Oxford once she reached England in 1166. There must have been a compelling reason why a woman whose pregnancy was nearly at term and who might have retired to her comfortable palaces at Westminster or Winchester would prefer to seek instead the spartan atmosphere of Beaumont. One can only guess that Eleanor, determined to investigate firsthand Henry's latest amour, found Rosamond living like a queen at Woodstock. Evidently reluctant to eject Henry's sweetheart from the palace, unwilling to remain under the same roof for her lying-in, exhausted and outraged, she must have withdrawn a few miles to the nearest royal sanctuary, which happened to be Beaumont Palace in Oxford.

There is no doubt that Rosamond Clifford touched a nerve in Eleanor, but it was a nerve already raw. Of late her relations with the king had grown steadily worse for reasons that had nothing to do with sexual jealousy. In large part her discontentment stemmed from the gradual waning of her influence. Whatever else Eleanor may have loved, she loved to rule best. To her, queenship meant sharing the regal power; queenship to Henry meant, when all was said and done, a woman who bore children and then had the sense to retire and take up pious work, a woman like his mother. Male and female had their assigned places, after all, and the throne of England was only big enough for one. Slowly, irrefutably, Henry had edged Eleanor further and further from the high place where he sat, and now, to add a gratuitous insult, he publicly honored a concubine, installing her in a palace where the queen had been undisputed mistress. Other queens might sit by helplessly and watch themselves relegated to a secondary role, but Eleanor had the resources to spare herself that humiliation. Before she had ever become queen of France or queen of England, she had been duchess of Aquitaine and countess of Poitou. Her vassals had never been happy under the rule of foreigners, and now a plan began coiling in her mind, a vision that suggested solutions to both her vassals' problems as well as her own. How she might put these visions into effect was quite another matter, however.

During the entire year of 1167, Eleanor chose to remain in England, ostensibly to prepare for her daughter's forthcoming wedding. Although the ceremony would take place in Germany, there was much to be done before Matilda's departure. Since the princess must arrive in her new land in a style that would reflect the power of England, she must be magnificently accoutered. To that end, Eleanor purchased sixty-three pounds worth of clothing, as well as "2 large silken cloths and 2 tapestries and 1 cloth of samite and 12 sable-skins." Other purchases recorded in the pipe rolls included twenty pairs of saddlebags and twenty chests, seven saddles gilded and covered with scarlet and thirty-four packhorses. To cover these expenses, Henry took advantage of his royal privileges. He had the right to exact a special aid from his barons on certain occasions: for ransom, in case he was captured in war; for the knighting of his eldest son; and for the marriage of his eldest daughter. Now his tenants were assessed accordingly, but he went further than previous kings by extracting a tax from cities, towns, even the tiniest villages. Altogether, the assessment for Matilda's trousseau brought in a sum of £4,500, almost one-quarter of the kingdom's total revenue that year. Obviously, the princess's bridal outfit did not cost anywhere near that figure, which meant that Henry was left with a handsome profit. In July, envoys arrived to escort Matilda to Germany, and in late September, Eleanor accompanied her daughter to Dover, where the enormous collection of chests, bags, and boxes was loaded onto German ships. One account claims that Eleanor embarked with Matilda, but this appears doubtful; if she did cross to Normandy, she must have returned immediately. At Winchester that fall, she behaved suspiciously like a woman who is about to leave her husband; she collected and packed every movable object that she could call her own in England, and when she finally set sail in December, it required seven ships to transport her accumulated belongings.

During Christmas court, celebrated that year at Argentan in Normandy, she informed Henry that she wished to return to her own estates. We do not know how she broke this news to him, only that she left for Poitiers immediately after Christmas. There was little likelihood that she displayed any open hostility, although Henry would not have been blind to her coolness, and she certainly did not mention divorce. What she seems to have had in mind was an unofficial separation in which she would go her way and the king go his. Whenever it came to disengaging herself from unwanted husbands, a situation into which she had now fallen a second time, she rejected personal or domestic arguments, always concentrating on practical reasons sure to carry political weight. Now, carefully avoiding any exhibition of defiance that might be interpreted as disloyalty and bring the sort of repercussions she had seen falling on Becket's head, she probably engineered her departure by suggesting that her presence in Aquitaine might help to ease the discord between her vassals and the crown. In setting up an administration of her own, she would attempt to restore the goodwill of her people and bring about a peace that had continued to elude Henry.

There is no doubt that Aquitaine stood on the brink of total rebellion by the time Eleanor returned to the Continent, and in fact, the south had occupied much of the king's time during the previous year. Forced to spend the first six months of 1167 in Eleanor's estates, Henry had taken an army of mercenaries into the Auvergne, where the local nobility had ideas of offering their allegiance to Louis Capet, a hope that Louis all too eagerly encouraged. Henry found himself in the position of a person trying to extinguish a roaring conflagration with buckets of water; each time he turned his back, a new blaze ignited. In the end, he agreed to Eleanor's plan simply because he had little choice. Perhaps those proverbially faithless southerners would respond best to their own duchess.

After Christmas court, Henry and his army personally escorted Eleanor to Poitiers so that on the face of it her return appeared to be part of Plantagenet policy for Aquitaine rather than any personal break between king and queen. By the time Eleanor arrived in her ancestral city, nearly all the land south of the Loire had broken into open rebellion under the leadership of the counts of Angoulême and La Marche, the Lusignan family, and Hugh and Robert of Silly. Girding himself for action, Henry wasted no time in mounting an attack on the fortress of Lusignan, and after capturing and garrisoning the castle, he razed its walls and ravaged the neighboring lands. Most of the ringleaders escaped, although Robert of Silly, who made the mistake of surrendering, was imprisoned and starved to death, Henry probably intending to make an example of him. By March 1168, some of the most noble families of Aquitaine were wandering the roads, homeless, hungry, and reduced to brigandage. Some found their way to the Île-de-France, where Louis's new foreign policy extended asylum to all Plantagenet enemies.

Aquitaine secure for the present, Henry left Poitiers before Easter and headed for the Norman frontier to attend a peace conference with the king of France. Ever since the birth of Philip Augustus, Louis had been sticking his fingers into Henry's affairs whenever the opportunity arose, an obvious means of keeping the Plantagenet uneasy. Now war between France and England appeared imminent, although at this point Henry was so beset by enemies that he barely knew in which direction to turn.

Although Eleanor had been left behind in the captured castle at Lusignan, she had not been abandoned to her own devices. Even though Aquitaine seemed quiet, sedition was the southerners' daily bread, and Henry, aware of Eleanor's trust in Ralph de Faye, took precautions lest she turn to the wrong person for advice. Rather than appoint her regent, he placed her under the protective custody of Earl Patrick, his military commander for the region, and in view of the unsettled conditions Eleanor may have been content with the arrangement. She soon discovered that Henry's security had been a mirage.

On March 27, just a few days after Henry's departure, Eleanor and Earl Patrick were riding near the castle with a small bodyguard. Since the men wore no armor, perhaps the party was hawking. Suddenly, there burst from an ambush a strong force led by two surly Lusignans, who, with the recklessness of those who have nothing more to lose, had decided to capture Eleanor and Earl Patrick and hold them for ransom. Accustomed to dealing with ruffians, Eleanor was off and riding toward the castle once she realized what Geoffrey and Guy de Lusignan had in mind. Earl Patrick called for his war-horse but before he could don his hauberk, he was slain from behind, the Lusignans not being sufficiently chivalrous to wait until their foes armed. As a result of this grievous incident, Eleanor's attention had been drawn to Earl Patrick's nephew, a young knight who fought "like a wild boar besieged by hounds" but who had, nevertheless, been captured. Twenty-two-year-old William Marshal was one of those landless younger sons, in fact the son of that same John Marshal whose complaints had brought Becket to Northampton. Knighted only a few months earlier, he had already distinguished himself in several tournaments, and Eleanor was not the first to remark upon his skill with sword and lance. Not only did she arrange for his ransom and release, she "bestowed upon him horses, gold and rich garments, and more than all opened her palace gates and fostered his ambition." Seeing something special in the young man, those virtues of courtesy, generosity, and perfect loyalty that always touched her, she brought him into her family as tutor, guardian, friend, and companion for Prince Henry, thus paving the way for Marshal's rise from knight-errant to, five decades later, regent of England.

With the death of Earl Patrick, Henry was too embroiled with other problems during the remainder of 1168 to pay much attention to Aquitaine. For the time being at least, Eleanor was on her own.

In Paris, in Rouen, and in London, there were whispers about the domestic affairs of the Plantagenets. It was noted that the king of England had kept Christmas court at Argentan in 1168, but the queen was nowhere to be seen. She had presided over her own Christmas court in Poitiers with her favorite son, Richard, and several of her younger children. Just as if she had no lord, she administered her duchy with a steady hand, no doubt putting to good use the lessons she had learned while serving her apprenticeship in the English law courts. She was, of course, closely supervised, for no one believed that Henry would cut adrift either his queen or her domains, no matter how troublesome Aquitaine had grown in recent years. There was more to this than met the eye, but exactly what lay behind these unusual arrangements within the English royal family no one could say for certain. Since no enlightenment was forthcoming from either of the principals, the nature of the breach between them—if there was one—remained a mystery to those who made it their business to keep abreast of international happenings.

Louis Capet, normally the last to traffic in domestic gossip, was not, nevertheless, so myopic that he could allow these odd rumors and reports to slide by without further investigation, especially since he counted the queen in her capacity as duchess of Aquitaine as one of his vassals and more especially since he had been engaged in a desultory war with Henry for the past year. Throughout 1168 Louis had sent raiding parties into the Vexin, and Henry had burnt villages along the French border; the skirmishes had been interspersed with cease-fires and feeble attempts on Louis's part to patch up their differences by diplomacy. If neither force nor diplomacy had proved effective in breaking up Henry's empire, perhaps yet another way remained. Louis was a slow man, and his ideas were never flashy nor executed with the electricity that marked some of Henry's programs. Louis chewed over imponderables until, sometimes, he was able to devise an inspired course of action. All things were possible if one had the patience to wait, and although Louis at forty-nine could obviously not wait forever, his strivings might not necessarily be in vain if Dieu-Donné could reap the harvest.

To break the diplomatic deadlock and secure peace in France and in Henry's mainland possessions, Louis proposed that Henry partition his empire among his three oldest sons; he should cede the counties of Anjou and Maine to Prince Henry, not quite fourteen, and then the boy might do homage to Louis for his lands. Likewise Richard should receive the duchy of Aquitaine and Geoffrey the duchy of Brittany on the same basis. To sweeten the pot, Louis offered to give Richard the hand of Alais, his daughter by Constance of Castile and the sister of Princess Marguerite. Although one might imagine that Henry would have seen through this thinly veiled attempt to divide and conquer, he did not. As we have seen, he was prey to intense anxiety that his sons might have to fight for their inheritances as he had. The surest way to provide for an orderly succession would be for them to do homage to the king of France while Henry was still alive. In fact, the more he thought about the idea, the more it appealed to him, and undeniably it fit perfectly into his cherished plan to have Prince Henry annointed king of England during his lifetime. Altogether, the arrangements suggested by Louis would provide him with some desperately needed peace of mind. If it occurred to him that Louis might be attempting to weaken his empire by driving a wedge between father and sons, he surely discounted the notion. He was not in the habit of crediting Louis with guile or even ordinary astuteness, and in any case, he had no intention of backing up these grants to his sons with any real authority. They were, after all, mere babes.

On the feast of Epiphany, January 6, 1169, Henry and Louis conferred at Montmirail, on the border of Maine near Chartres. Both potentates arrived with imposing retinues, especially Henry, who was accompanied by his three sons, each of them decked out in his finest clothes and surrounded with a household of knights and barons. Obviously glorying in this opportunity to show off his handsome offspring, Henry was in unusually high spirits that day. He opened the parley with a flowery speech of the variety that he rarely bothered to make. "My lord King," he said to Louis, "on this feast of Epiphany, commemorating the day on which the three kings offered gifts to the King of Kings, I commend my three sons and my lands to your safekeeping."

Louis swept his gaze over Eleanor's three sons and made the kind of holier-than-thou rejoinder that always succeeded in annoying Henry. "Since the King who received those gifts from the Magi seems to have inspired your words, may your sons, when they take possession of their lands, do so as in the presence of our Lord."

Allowing this lesson on the duties of a vassal to pass without comment, Henry proceeded to renew his homage to Louis for his Continental possessions and promised to return castles and lands he had taken from the Aquitainian rebels, many of whom were now refugees in France. Once these formalities had been taken care of, the conference shifted emphasis from the older generation to the younger. The next day, Henry brought forth his namesake, his pride and joy, Prince Henry, and watched proudly as the boy placed his hands in the palm of his father-in-law to render homage for his provinces of Anjou, Brittany, and Maine. (He had already done homage for Normandy in 1160.) To show his regard for the lad, Louis bestowed on him the post of seneschal of France. Then eleven-year-old Richard stepped forward to be confirmed in his inheritance of his mother's lands, that magnificent dower that had slipped through Louis's fingers seventeen years earlier, and to Richard he presented his future bride. Nine-year-old Alais Capet, orphaned at birth, was handed over to the Plantagenets to be reared in their court. And finally, Geoffrey, now ten, made his appearance to receive Louis's consent to his marriage with the heiress of Brittany. It was arranged that later in the year he would do homage to his brother Henry for his patrimony.

For the witnesses and spectators at Montmirail, it had been a confusing two days, and even afterward, they would have difficulty making sense out of these happenings. Most perplexing was why the acquisitive Henry had agreed to this division of his hard-earned lands to boys who had yet to be knighted. One theory held that he secretly planned to take the cross and depart for the Holy Land, others contended that he had been offered the Holy Roman Empire and therefore could well afford to dispose of his mainland holdings. And why did Eleanor remain sequestered in Poitiers? And why had Henry agreed to Richard's betrothal to Alais, making it possible for Aquitaine to one day be pulled back into Frankish domains? But there seemed to be no answers to these questions.

Among the spectators at Montmirail sat one man who watched the investitures with ill-concealed impatience. Thomas Becket had not seen Henry since their furious combat at Northampton four years earlier. For the archbishop, those had been years of prayer, study, and harsh, self-administered penances, a life of solitude far from the dazzling arena of kings and courts. As for Henry, time had accomplished what reason could not. Finally, he had succeeded in pushing Becket from the forefront of his concerns; or perhaps more accurately, he had faced more pressing problems in quelling various insurrections in his estates. By now, Becket had become a nuisance and a distraction—in fact, Becket had become an irritant for many people—because if Henry was willing to drop the quarrel, the aggrieved archbishop was not. Victory was his *raison d'être*, and he pursued Henry with all the indefatigable ardor of a rejected mistress. From the Abbey of Pontigny and later Saint Columba's Abbey near Sens, he pestered Henry with scolding letters urging penance and reflection upon wrongdoings and reminding him that he was the king's spiritual father. He collected works on canon law and spent his days working up an airtight case against the arrogant Plantagenet. He swamped Europe with a river of self-pitying correspondence in which he pressed for redress of his grievances. No suffering equaled his: There was, he wrote, no grief "like unto my grief." While Henry ignored the letters, other incidents moved him to fits of blind rage, which Thomas could inspire so successfully. On Whitsunday 1166, Thomas had celebrated Mass at Vézelay. At the conclusion of the service, he had excommunicated all of Henry's officers who had committed crimes, either against his person or against the see of Canterbury. Exempting Henry, who, he had heard, was ill, he had limited himself to a stiff denunciation and a warning that if the king continued to persecute the Church, he too would soon be bound by the chains of anathema. When reports of these holy thunderbolts had reached Henry at Chinon, he had turned his wrath upon his court, accusing everyone in sight of being a traitor who lacked the courage and enterprise to rid him of the pestilential archbishop. Thomas, he had cried, would not be happy until he had deprived him of body and soul.

Nevertheless, by 1169, the controversy had dragged on too long for the comfort of all parties, especially the papacy, and even Henry grew anxious for Thomas's return to England, if for no other reason than that he wished the archbishop to crown Prince Henry. Becket was the last item on the agenda at Montmirail. It was late in the afternoon of the second and final day when his tall, gaunt figure crossed the thronged field to where the two kings waited. Approaching Henry, he slumped to his knees and began to weep, but Henry quickly caught him by the hand and raised him to his feet. With burning eyes and a humility that he had not displayed in recent years, he began his capitulation by pleading for Henry's mercy, both for himself and the Church of England. Finally, he came to the words for which everyone was waiting. "On the whole matter which is in dispute between us, my lord king, in the presence of our lord the King of France and the archbishops, princes, and others who stand around us, I throw myself on your mercy and your pleasure." But then, to the consternation of all present, he added "saving the honor of God!" At these words, which nullified his capitulation, Henry unleashed a stream of abuse, most of it somewhat irrationally centered on the luxurious life that Becket had lived at his expense while chancellor. Finally, he turned to Louis and said:

> My lord, this man foolishly and vainly deserted his church, secretly fleeing by night, although neither I nor anyone else drove him out of the kingdom. . . . I have always been willing and am now to allow him to rule over his church with as much freedom as any of the saints who preceded him. But take note of this, my lord, that whenever he disapproves of something, he will say it is contrary to God's honor and so always get the better of me. Let me offer this, so that no one shall think me a despiser of God's honor. . . . Let him behave toward me as the most saintly of his predecessors behaved toward the least saintly of mine, and I will be satisfied.

The field rang with an approving chorus of "Hear! Hear! Fair offer! The king has humbled himself!" Even Louis seemed impressed. Turning to the archbishop, who had remained silent, he said: "My lord archbishop, the peace you desire has been offered. Why do you hesitate? Do you wish to be more than a saint?"

It was a question that only time would answer.

One hundred and twenty-five miles to the south, in her high tower above the rivers encircling Poitiers, the duchess of Aquitaine observed the feudal world of kings and archbishops with a skeptical eye, especially the pledges that her husband had made in the presence of that august assembly at Montmirail. Never having known Henry to willingly relinquish power, at least no more of it than was absolutely necessary, she, too, may have pondered the implications of his actions. He was thirty-five; obviously he did not mean to give up his titles or lands in favor of his sons until his death, an eventuality that still lay some distance in the future. And, yet, the acts of homage rendered by their sons were not merely prospective but immediate. They made Prince Henry and Richard the legal count of Anjou and duke of Aquitaine, respectively, not under the suzerainty of their father but under the direct overlordship of Louis Capet. In the case of Aquitaine, the practical result of Montmirail was that the duchy now had two dukes. At best, it was a complicated state of affairs, in which Henry's anxieties had triumphed over common sense and in which the only advantages could accrue to their sons—and to the French crown. If Henry did not see through Louis's scheming, Eleanor did, and for once she may have felt a grudging respect for her ex-husband. At that point, however, she was much too busy to allow herself to be drawn into any controversy with Henry over these matters.

When Eleanor had returned to Poitiers in 1168, she came with the intention of restoring peace to her domains. That she was not immediately permitted a free hand we know from the presence of Earl Patrick and the fact that Henry himself spent the spring and summer of 1169 in Poitou and Gascony, presumably for the purpose of restoring order. But after his departure in August 1169, he seems to have maintained a hands-off policy. Some historians give the impression that Eleanor kept continuous court at Poitiers for the next five-year period, never stirring from behind the city walls. The fact is, she traveled extensively in her own lands and from time to time in Henry's mainland provinces. During those years, her name crops up in the chronicles as being present at Falaise, Chinon, and other Plantagenet castles, nearly always on some occasion involving the children.

Just as her contemporaries were mystified by the private arrangements she had made with Henry, neither is it easy from the distance of eight hundred years to understand either her personal or her political relationship with the king of England. On the face of it there seems to have been, as we would say today, an amicable separation in which each observed a live-and-let-live policy. But this certainly fails to paint a complete picture. From everything we know of Henry, he was too much the autocrat to allow Eleanor total freedom in ruling a duchy he considered nominally his. On the other hand, curiously enough, he appears to have done precisely that. As long as Eleanor did nothing to jeopardize his interests, as long as she cooperated in matters concerning the children and pretended to be his loyal wife, then he did not interfere. Actually, in the short run, there were undeniable advantages; not only was he able to save face and avoid an open acknowledgment that he could not rule Aquitaine, but furthermore—and no doubt this was a consideration—he neatly rid himself of a wife he no longer desired.

By 1169, Eleanor could not have dodged an incontrovertible reality: She was no longer young. In fact, at forty-seven, she was at an age that the twelfth century considered rather past middle age and somewhat into the realm of the elderly. Life expectancy varied. If a man survived childhood, he could expect to live to his thirties; if he survived his thirties, then he had a good chance of living until the fifties. A woman's life was far more hazardous. If she survived her child-bearing years—and many women did not—she might live perhaps a few years longer than her husband. In the opinion of one chronicler, life beyond the age of fifty was undesirable, the afflictions of the elderly arousing more horror than pity. While still a stunning woman, Eleanor was no longer the young belle who had dazzled the world from Bordeaux to Antioch, not even the mature beauty whose perfect ripeness had lured young Henry Plantagenet and inspired sweet rhymes from Bernard of Ventadour. Called the flower of the world so often that she had come to believe it, she was now forced to acknowledge the deadly passage of time and the fact that a fresher blossom, the girl that people called Rosa Mundi, had taken her place. What remained to her at forty-seven were her children, especially her heir, Richard, and her heritage, and to these she gave herself wholesale. Their cause became hers.

For more than thirty years her subjects had patiently suffered occupation under her foreign consorts, but now, with the return of their duchess, a new regime had become possible. From 1169 on, Eleanor's twofold resolution stands out clearly: to cut off Aquitaine from the Plantagenet empire insofar as this seemed feasible, and to create for herself a realm that would reflect the splendors of the past and prefigure innovations of the future. To lance the fear and unease that roamed the duchy's cities and villages, Eleanor took to the highroads on royal progresses that carried her to the four corners of her land. Hers were no disorderly *chevauchées* such as those Henry had conducted through her dominions. She brought with her no army of mercenaries who forced vassals to huddle bitterly behind their barricaded keeps or sent them scurrying for the safety of the Île-de-France. With the pomp and majesty of which only she was capable, she came to her towns in peace, eager to make up for past abuses, asking for renewed oaths of homage, offering proudly for their approval and admiration her son and heir, Richard. With the soldiers and military governors gone, with Capetian and Plantagenet overlords occupied elsewhere, she began to undo the effects of oppression, using her considerable charm and influence to bring together feuding vassals and defuse their explosive jealousies.

Once more the ducal palace at Poitiers, darkened these many years, became the center of all that was civilized and refined. As in the time of her father and grandfather, troubadours, musicians, scholars, and literary types of all varieties were welcomed at court; traditional fairs and tournaments were revived; beguiling customs that had fallen into abeyance with the last of the male dukes were hauled from dusty recesses of memory and reinstated with full honors. Those who had sought refuge from the sword of Henry Plantagenet began to come home. Where Henry had razed walls and taken hostages, Eleanor salved raw emotions and attempted to exorcise bitter memories; where Henry had sneered at crowns and royal gewgaws, Eleanor gloried in peacock processions and pageants, deliberately seeking out occasions for ceremony. Wherever she went, she pushed Richard into the spotlight as the rightful heir of the Troubadour, providing the southerners with constant reminders that Henry had been replaced. In Poitiers, she arranged for the boy to be invested with the honorary title of abbot of Saint-Hilaire and called upon the venerable archbishop of Bordeaux to present him with the lance and standard that signified that distinguished office.

In Limoges, a city that had suffered Henry's wrath, she managed her son's investiture as duke of Aquitaine with a dexterity that suggested a shrewd eye for public relations. The monks at the Abbey of Saint Martial had recently discovered among their archives an ancient account of the life of Saint Valerie, the city's patron saint, a noble virgin who, according to legend, had been martyred for her faith at the dawn of the Christian era. In the days of Eleanor's forebears, the legend of Saint Valerie had played an important part in the coronation of the dukes of Aquitaine, and now Eleanor rekindled local chauvinism by reviving this ancient ritual. On the day of the coronation, a great procession escorted Richard to the Church of Saint-Étienne, where he contracted a symbolic marriage with Saint Valerie, her ring upon his finger signifying his indissoluble bond with the land of his forebears. Robed in a silk tunic and wearing a crown of gold, Richard led a procession of clergy to the altar, where he received his sword and spurs. Afterward, there was feasting and jousting the likes of which had not been seen in Limoges for many decades, and later, the delighted southerners declared that Richard's coronation outclassed any they had seen in Paris or Reims.

It should not be supposed that pageants and coronations suddenly transformed Aquitaine into a twelfth-century Camelot. Eleanor was swimming in a swift stream against the current, and the problems she faced in governing a traditionally ungovernable region had been found virtually insuperable by every man preceding her. While anarchy did not disappear, it did abate, and for a time, the land knew a precarious kind of peace or at least what passed for peace among the southerners. If it was not the government Henry had hoped to install, it was one that reflected Eleanor and her conceptions of the ideal state: music and poetry, love and laughter, freedom, justice, and a modicum of order. In the late sixties and early seventies, all roads in Aquitaine led to Poitiers and to the ducal palace, where events were taking place that intrigued the Aquitainians and amazed the rest of Europe. During these years, Eleanor's household sheltered much of the future royalty of Europe. The Plantagenet children, once dragged from castle to castle, country to country, often without one or both parents, had never known a proper home. Now she drew them together in the halls and gardens where she herself had grown up: Prince Henry and Richard, Eleanor and Joanna, Geoffrey and his future wife, Constance of Brittany. The only missing child seems to have been John, whose father, in a moment of levity, had nicknamed him Lackland because he had run out of lands to bequeath the boy. It is believed that John spent his childhood in the care of nuns at the Abbey of Fontevrault, possibly with his parents' intention that he devote his life to the Church, but more likely due to Eleanor's unmistakable aversion to the boy. In addition to Eleanor's own brood and their Poitevin cousins, circumstances had made her stepmother to the Capetian younger generation. Despite Louis's earlier objections to Eleanor as a mother, events had decreed otherwise, because now under her supervision were both daughters of his second marriage, Marguerite and Alais, and soon there would come to Poitiers, like a wraith from the past, Eleanor's firstborn daughter, the disappointing female she had borne to Louis before the Crusade.

The countess of Champagne, *née* Marie Capet, had never really known her mother. For part of her childhood, Eleanor had been absent in the Holy Land, and afterward had come the divorce. She had been reared in the strictly religious French court by two consecutive step-mothers, who provided her with the most conservative of upbringings and in an atmosphere where the name of Eleanor of Aquitaine must have been a byword for female irresponsibility, not to mention perfidy. The likelihood of her having any contact with Eleanor during those intervening years is extremely remote, and yet the young woman who journeyed down to Poitiers from Troyes about the year 1170 could not have been more attuned to her mother's thinking than if there had been no separation. More than any of Eleanor's children, including Richard, Marie was her mother's child. The manner in which this strange reconciliation came about is a detail that no chronicler saw fit to record; it is tempting to surmise that Louis, disturbed by the fact that two of his young daughters had fallen into undesirable hands, deliberately sent Marie to subtly keep an eye on the situation. At any event, she suddenly appeared as a leading figure at Eleanor's court, a woman in her late twenties who bore ideas that curiously paralleled her mother's.

Marie was already a person of some consequence in her own right. Even though she had been betrothed as a child, Louis had not seen fit to permit her marriage to Henry the Liberal of Champagne until she had reached the advanced age of nineteen. Unlike the Capetian court, her new home at Troyes was a center of culture and taste in northern France, and its sophisticated court a gathering place for poets such as Chrétien de Troyes. Marie gives the impression of being an aggressive woman who carved spheres of influence for herself, but, less politically minded than Eleanor, she took for her province of expertise the literary.

Something of the talent of William the Troubadour must have surfaced in the countess, a gift for inventing tales and creating worlds with words, but circumstances prevented a direct use of her talents. In her time, the idea of a female poet was not unknown—of the 450 troubadours known by name, 4 are women—but a daughter of Louis Capet did not take up the calling. Instead, she accepted outlets more appropriate to a woman and became a patroness of the arts, one of her protégés being Chrétien de Troyes, who composed, at her suggestion, the romance of the gallant Sir Lancelot and Queen Guinevere.

In the harsh authoritarian world of masculine kingship, the world from which Eleanor had so lately fled, the court at Poitiers stood as an oasis where a woman of independence and imagination might find the freedom to invent a milieu suitable to her own taste. It had, like all oases, a fantasy quality about it, although to Marie and Eleanor; to the countess of Flanders and the countess of Narbonne; to Henry Plantagenet's half sister, Emma of Anjou; to the dozens of highborn ladies in residence at one time or another, the court was reality, the rest of the world a distortion. They saw themselves as innovators of a rational new world, a prototype for the future perhaps, in which women might reign as goddesses or at the least mistresses of their own destinies. Eleanor and Marie and their friends may be forgiven their excessive optimism, because in some respects the twelfth century seemed the dawn of a new age for women. There is no question that the rigid feudal view of women had already begun to splinter. The Church's traditional misogynistic view of the female as an instrument of the devil, a thing at once evil and inferior, had given way to the cult of the Virgin, and all over western Christendom the gospel of Mary was slowly dispelling the image of Eve the temptress; Our Lady, the Queen of Heaven, was worshiped in the magnificent new Gothic cathedrals, in pilgrimages to various shrines throughout Europe, in festivals such as the Annunciation and Candlemas, which celebrated the main events of the Virgin's life. Along with the cult of the Virgin, there had appeared in more recent years the cult of chivalry, with the medieval lady as Mary's secular counterpart. While Mariolatry had swollen mysteriously among the general populace, the chivalrous cult of the lady was a deliberate invention of the aristocracy, encouraged if not specifically devised by women themselves. Even though God had seemed to change sex by the twelfth century, the position of women still oscillated between the depths and the unreal elevation of the pedestal. In this time of great confusion about the roles of male and female, some women—the nobly born, the educated—felt the need for a redefinition of the relationship between the sexes. The inferiority of the female they acknowledged to be a myth, and in the Middle Ages, as Henry Adams wrote, "the superiority of the woman was not a fancy, but a fact." It was not a fact that the average medieval man could readily accept, however, and women's ongoing struggle with men continued.

At Poitiers, the "man problem" was a matter of more than merely personal concern to Eleanor; it was, on the contrary, a political dilemma of disturbing proportions. Despite the professed ideals of chivalry and courtly love then current, the knights of Aquitaine were still, in her estimation, rude and barbarous beneath their veneer of courtesy. The young men who swarmed to her court, especially during the June "season" between Whitsunday and Saint John's Day, when there occurred the annual armistice in interbaronial fighting, were a restless, bellicose lot, many of them landless, penniless younger sons with no occupation except troublemaking. They came to joust and dice and find a woman, either on a permanent or on a temporary basis, and they brought to her court a disorder that she found potentially dangerous. In the past, this footloose segment of society had been siphoned off to Crusades or funneled into the Church, but Eleanor, wrestling with the perennial problem of anarchy in her estates, sought more long-range cures for this social ill. To her daughter she assigned the task of educating these high-spirited male subjects of hers so that the younger generation might be molded into civilized beings who, not so incidentally, would know how to respect women. Eleanor's ideas went far beyond what we today would call feminism, in the sense that equality of the sexes was not precisely her goal. Rather, she believed in the superiority of women. What was needed, in her opinion, was a code of civility to embody and publicize these ideas. Not for nothing had she labored in the service of the legal-minded Henry Plantagenet; if the king of England could write down laws for Church and State, as he had at Clarendon, then the duchess of Aquitaine could informally codify and commit to parchment a system of manners to regulate the social conduct of her male subjects.

From her court at Troyes, Marie had brought along a chaplain, Andreas Capellanus, who was called upon to assist in the work of writing a manual for the medieval male. Even though the chaplain set down in scholarly paragraphs the heretical doctrines dictated by the countess, the ideas were Marie's and, of course, Eleanor's; the cornerstone of their curriculum was love, their goal the guidance and education of the male to a higher level of consciousness. It is amusing that Marie should have been compelled to commission a male cleric as her ghostwriter in this attempt to dethrone masculine dominance, but even more amusing is Andreas's reaction. Obviously, he addressed himself to the task at hand with considerable reservations, because at some later date, he added a furious epilogue disavowing the work and calling down heaven's wrath on the female sex. Although *Tractus de Amore et de Amoris Remedia* (*Treatise on Love and the Remedies of Love*) bore Andreas's name, it was Marie's book, and the thirty-one articles of its Code of Love reflect the passions peculiar to women who have come into their own and feel confident enough to use their authority in unorthodox ways.

Modeled on Ovid's *Art of Loving*, the content owes little to the original, because in Ovid's textbook, man, the master, employs the art of love to seduce women for his own pleasure; in Andreas's treatise, the situation is reversed—the woman is the dominant figure, the man a pupil who must be carefully instructed until he becomes a fit partner for his lady. There is little that is poetic or ethereal about the principles set down in the code; rather it sets forth in practical terms the rules a man must remember when he deals with a woman: "Being obedient in all things to the commands of ladies, you must always try to ally yourself to the service of love"; "Thou shalt be in all things polite and courteous"; "Thou shalt keep thyself chaste for the sake of her whom thou lovest"; "Thou shalt not exceed the desires of thy lover." The themes of courtly love sung by the troubadour poets, those ungerminated seeds suggested by Eleanor's grandfather, now emerged full-blown, the raw materials reworked by the feminine sensibility until they almost seem a manifesto for some Amazon culture. The ladies of troubadour poetry were very often silent, passive goddesses who were adored whether they liked it or not. Since troubadour love was not always mutual, there was no reason to dwell on qualities that might make a lover acceptable. In contrast, the type of love defined in *De Amore* is certainly a great deal freer, in that the woman is no longer passive or silent. In finding her voice, however, she has made her views known: She is supreme, a goddess to be approached with reverence, and the man is her property. No chattel to be bought and sold and traded at man's whim, no sex object to be seduced or raped against her will, she holds the power to accept or reject a man and, however difficult the trials she sets for him, he must treat her with respect and humility.

To put it at its mildest, these precepts were so radical, so subversive to the whole divinely ordained plan, as to boggle the mind of the average man—and at the same time so novel that they quickly spread through the courts of Europe, where they were eagerly taken up as the latest fashion by both men and women of the aristocracy. These rather incredible notions emanating from Poitiers must have caused certain sovereigns to blink. Certainly, Henry Plantagenet did not subscribe to a single article of Andreas's Code of Love, nor did Louis Capet nor any self-respecting baron. No doubt Henry, who made it his business to keep abreast of developments in Poitiers, followed the new fads with amusement. Not only was his wife promulgating her sex as goddesses, but she sponsored courts of love in which confused men having problems with this new arrangement for the sexes might bring their questions before a tribunal of ladies for judgment. The women, sometimes sixty strong, sat on a raised dais in the Great Hall, while below them gathered the men, prepared to hear lengthy disputations on the nature of love, expositions on a man's duty toward his lady. One "case" that piqued more than ordinary interest was this one: Can real love exist between a husband and wife? In Countess Marie's opinion, it was doubtful whether love in the ideal sense could ever take place between spouses, but before giving a final judgment, she wished to refer the question to her mother. After due consideration, the queen allowed that it would be difficult to contradict her daughter, although she personally would find it admirable if a woman could find love in her marriage. One cannot help but sense the disillusionment behind her words. In fifty years she had not found romantic love with either of her husbands, and despite the tales of her adulteries, it is highly improbable that she found it outside of marriage either.

Andreas's description of formal tribunals of charming ladies, solemnly ruling on affairs of the heart and rendering verdicts to hapless males, is now generally dismissed as a twelfth-century conceit. While there is no historical evidence to prove the courts real in the sense that verdicts were taken seriously, nevertheless, that they did take place is well within the realm of probability. In an age when a woman was never her own mistress but always a minor in the tutelage of some male, when at the same time women like Eleanor were asserting their independence, the courts of love afforded a means of attacking male supremacy. Granted, the courts of love may have been an amusing game, but they still offered a direct challenge to the male establishment. And the fact is, the challenge was not totally unsuccessful either. Far from it. During the latter half of the twelfth century, the ideas made fashionable at Eleanor's palace were to insinuate themselves through the upper social circles of Europe and persistently reverberate down the corridors of history to the twentieth century. Our code of etiquette with its rules that women take precedence, our image of the courteous, housebroken male, must be considered the dying gasps of a bold new innovation that the noblewomen of Poitiers may have initially imagined would be a lever to raise the status of women. Unfortunately, their attempts to elevate women to a position of emotional and spiritual supremacy simply presented men with a convenient loophole by which they could pay lip service to the idea while at the same time continuing to withhold from women the smallest shred of real power. This irony would not have escaped a hardheaded politician such as Eleanor.

On Friday, December 25, 1170, the hunting lodge at Bures near Bayeux was decorated for Christmas. Logs burned on the hearth, jugglers and minstrels cavorted among the guests, and the hall shook with noise and boisterous laughter as it usually did when the Plantagenets came together. The remnants of the royal family, scattered these several years, had reassembled to celebrate their considerable blessings; Eleanor, stately *grande dame* who had forsaken a decorous Nativity at Poitiers for this murky castle where one stumbled over the hounds; Henry, his paunch more noticeable, his reddish hair flecked with salt; Richard, Geoffrey, Joanna, and, one chronicler claimed, even four-year-old John, making one of his rare public appearances. For a few days Eleanor and Henry had put aside past estrangement and gazed with the proud eyes of mother and father upon the dynasty they had created in happier days. It had been a consequential year for the family, one of those euphoric years when Eleanor and Henry could look back with a sense of satisfaction and accomplishment. The Plantagenet realm was at peace; thanks to Eleanor, Aquitaine was quiet for once, and Henry's reforms in England promised increased revenue. At last Prince Henry, now known as the Young King, had been crowned at Westminster, and this year he kept his own Christmas court in England. Princess Eleanor, nine, had been betrothed to the twelve-year-old king of Castile, Alphonse VIII, and crossed the Pyrenees to confront her destiny. In early August, Henry had fallen gravely ill of a tertian fever, and so close to death had he come that his departure from the world had been prematurely reported in France. Chastened, he had made a will confirming his division of lands at Montmirail and vowing that if God permitted him to recover, he would make a pilgrimage to the monastery of Rocamadour in Quercy.

And in that year, too, the king had made peace with "God's doughty champion," the archbishop of Canterbury. In July, Henry had held Thomas's stirrup at Fréteval and then had thrown his arms around him. "My lord archbishop," he had said, "let us go back to our old love for each other and let each of us do all the good he can to the other and forget utterly the hatred that has gone before." Admittedly, he had not given Thomas the customary kiss of peace but had sworn that "in my own land I will kiss his mouth and his hands and his feet a hundred times." In the end, he had not accompanied Thomas back to England as he had half promised, but he did write to the Young King in October to notify him of their reconciliation: "Henry, king of England, to his son, Henry the king, greeting: Know that Thomas, archbishop of Canterbury, has made peace with me according to my will. I therefore command that he and all his men shall have peace. You are to ensure that the archbishop and all his men who left England for his sake shall have all their possessions as they had them three months before the archbishop withdrew from England. . . . Written from Chinon." He had grown weary of the tradesman's son; he had done everything a king could possibly do to make amends, and now he preferred to forget the man. He would even ignore Thomas's parting words when they last met at Chaumont in mid-October.

"Go in peace," Henry had said. "I will follow you and I will see you in Rouen or in England as soon as I can." It was nothing more than conventional politeness, for he was in no hurry to see Thomas again.

"My lord," Thomas had replied, "my mind tells me that I will never see you again in this life."

His theatricality annoyed Henry, who said sharply, "Do you think I'm a traitor?"

"*Absit a te, domine,*" Thomas had answered. "God forbid, my lord."

While still on the Continent, Thomas had taken precautions to arm himself with a weapon in case Henry failed to keep his agreement. He had requested and received from Pope Alexander letters suspending the prelates who had participated in the illegal coronation of the Young King, letters to be used at his discretion in an emergency. However, on the day before he crossed the Channel, already doubtful of Henry's good intentions, he angrily sent ahead a messenger to deliver the letters excommunicating Archbishop Roger of York and the bishops of London and Salisbury.

On Tuesday, December 1, Thomas and his party of faithful followers landed at Sandwich, six miles from Canterbury, after an absence of six years. At the port, some of the king's men, surly and armed, attempted to seize the archbishop, but after being shown the king's letter of safe conduct, they permitted him to pass unmolested. "As he set out for the city he was welcomed by the poor of the land as a victim sent from heaven, yea, even as an angel of God, with joy and thanksgiving. . . . And though the road was short, yet amidst the thronging and pressing crowds he could scarce reach Canterbury that day, where he was welcomed with the sound of trumpets and organs, with psalms and hymns and spiritual songs."

A week later he set out for Winchester to visit his foster son, the Young King. "He had brought with him three costly chargers, of wondrous speed, beautiful in form, high-stepping, their delicate flanks rippling as they walked, their housing worked with flowers in various colours, which he intended to give as a gift to his new lord." When he had ridden only as far as London, however, he was halted by a messenger from the Young King, forbidding him to continue or for that matter to visit any town or city in England; he was ordered to return immediately to Canterbury and remain there. On the trip back to Canterbury, Thomas's knights, thoroughly frightened by the harsh tone of the message, rode with shield and lance to protect him.

Meanwhile, the excommunicated archbishop of York and the bishops of London and Salisbury had crossed the Channel and hurried to Henry with their complaints. "Their evil accusations were doubled by falsehood. It was reported to the king that the archbishop was careering about the kingdom at the head of an army. The king asked for their advice. 'Seek advice from your barons and your knights,' said the archbishop of York. 'It is not for us to say what should be done.' At length another of them said, 'My lord, while Thomas lives, you will not have peace or quiet, or see good days.' "

Exasperated, the king "waxed furious and indignant beyond measure, and keeping too little restraint upon his fiery and ungovernable temper, poured forth wild words from the abundance of a distracted mind."

In the crowded hall at Bures on Christmas Day his voice carried over the din. He raged impotently at Thomas and then began to scream at his barons and clerks in the hall. "I have nourished and promoted in my realm idle and wretched knaves, disloyal to their lord, whom they suffer to be mocked thus shamefully by a low-born priest." Since the king had expressed similar sentiments in almost identical words on previous occasions, undue attention was not paid to this outburst. Nor was it noticed when four of his barons, "men of noble birth and renowned in arms," disappeared from the noisy hall.

On Tuesday, December 29, Henry's four barons, accompanied by an attendant, pushed their way into the main hall at Canterbury. It was about three o'clock in the afternoon, the winter light beginning to fail, and the household was just finishing its meal, although the archbishop had already retired to his room with his clerks to discuss business. Invited to dine, the visitors refused, saying only that they had urgent business with the archbishop. Once admitted to his room, they examined him silently for a few moments and then at last one said, lying, "We have brought you a message from the King oversea." Shouting now, the knights accused Thomas of plotting to take away the Young King's crown, abusing him for excommunication of the bishops, and threatening him with dire punishments if he did not leave England. The voices grew louder; shouts and curses punctuated the air; fists clenched and unclenched. Becket's face was severe and decisive. "Stop your threats and still your brawling," he ordered. "I have not come back to flee again." At this, the knights "retired amidst tumult and insults," rushing into the courtyard, where they gathered under a mulberry tree to strap on their hauberks, helmets, and mailed gauntlets.

The archbishop calmly returned to his room. Soon afterward, the armored knights began to hack at the hall's barricaded door "with swords, axes and hatchets." Terrified, the monks urged Thomas to take refuge in the cathedral, but "he who had long since longed for martyrdom, now saw that the occasion to embrace it had seemingly arrived, and dreaded lest it should be deferred and even altogether lost if he took refuge in the church." He sat motionless on his bed, visions of eternal grandeur jostling in his mind, and "when he would not be persuaded by argument or entreaties . . . the monks seized hold of him, in spite of his resistance, and pulled, dragged and pushed him" into sanctuary. The monks who had been saying vespers in the cathedral broke off their chanting and ran to meet him; hearing heavy steps drawing closer and seeing unsheathed blades, they hurried to bolt the door, but Thomas wrenched them away. "God forbid that we should make His house into a fortress. Let everyone who wants to enter God's church come in. May God's will be done!"

It was nearly five o'clock now. The cathedral trembled in darkness, with only a few flickering candles splashing rings of light on the stone. Suddenly shrill voices tore through the shadows. "Where is Thomas Becket, traitor to the king and the realm? Where is the archbishop?"

The monks ran to hide, but Thomas did not move. "Lo, here I am," he answered fearlessly, "no traitor to the king, but a priest. What do you seek from me?"

"Absolve and restore to communion those whom you have excommunicated."

"I will not absolve them."

"Then you shall die this instant and receive your desert."

"I am ready to die for my Lord, that in my blood the Church may obtain peace and liberty. But in the name of Almighty God I forbid you to harm any of my men, whether clerk or lay."

The knights, "those satellites of Satan," rushed forward and tried to pull and drag him outside the church, but the archbishop clung to a pillar. Bowing his head as in prayer, he murmured the names of God and Saint Mary and the blessed martyr Saint Denis. A steel blade flashed through the air and sheared off the archbishop's cap and part of the crown of his head. "Next he received a second blow on the head, but still he stood firm and immovable. At the third blow he fell on his knees and elbows." The awful blade fell again and "by this stroke the sword was dashed against the pavement, and the crown of his head, which was large, was separated from the head in such a way that the blood white with the brain and the brain no less red from the blood, dyed the floor of the cathedral with the white of the lily and the red of the rose." The fifth murderer—no knight but a clerk—"placed his foot on the neck of the holy priest and martyr and, horrible to relate, scattered the brains and blood about the pavement, crying out to the others, 'Let us away, knights. This fellow will rise no more!' "

While the body still lay warm on the pavement, some of the townsfolk of Canterbury smeared their eyes with blood. "Others brought bottles and carried off secretly as much of it as they could. Others cut off shreds of clothing and dipped them in the blood. Later, no one would be satisfied if they had not carried off something from the precious treasure of the martyr's body. And indeed, with everything in such a state of confusion and tumult, each man could do as he pleased. . . . Thus the night passed in lamentation and mourning, groans and sighs."

By New Year's Day 1171, Henry had dismissed his Christmas court and moved on to Argentan, where he prepared to hold a meeting with his advisers. There he received news of the murder in the cathedral.

> At the messenger's first words, the king burst into loud cries of grief and changed his royal robes for sackcloth and ashes. Indeed he behaved as though he were the friend rather than the king of the dead man. At times he fell into a stupor but then he would begin groaning again and calling out more loudly and bitterly than before. For three whole days he remained shut up in his room and would take neither food nor admit any who wished to comfort him. It began to seem that his grief was so extreme that he had made up his mind to die himself. We began to despair of the king's life.

For forty days, Henry abstained from all business, exercise, and amusements, remaining alone within the walls of his palace, sighing and groaning and repeating, "What a disaster that this terrible thing should have happened."

At Winchester, the Young King lamented briefly for the man he had once called father. "What a pity!" he said, raising his eyes to heaven, "but thank God it was kept a secret from me and that no liege-man of mine was involved in it." One cannot help but read the insensitivity in his words.

To the queen, withdrawn behind her own borders, the assassination and its aftermath must have seemed a nightmare from which she too wished to disassociate herself. The murder of Thomas Becket pro-foundly shocked Europe. Many people said that it was the most terrible thing to have happened since the Crucifixion, and Archbishop William of Sens, a friend of Becket's, did not exaggerate public sentiment when he described the deed as surpassing the cruelty of Herod, the perfidy of Julian, and the treachery of Judas. "Almost everyone," wrote William of Newburgh, "laid the death of the blessed martyr at the king's door." Everyone included Eleanor and the children, for who knew better than they the anguish caused by Henry's insane, self-indulgent rages? The death of Thomas soon proved not an ending but a beginning: unceasing processions of pilgrims coming to Canterbury, the miracles people swore took place at the tomb, the prompt movement for the martyr's canonization. As if to prove that saints and martyrs rule from the tomb, Becket reached out to taunt Henry more effectively than he had ever done in life. The king became the most hated man in Europe, and even though he had written to the monks of Canterbury and to Pope Alexander declaring that he had never desired Thomas's death, he had, nevertheless, not seen fit to punish the murderers, and thus few believed in his innocence. His prestige at a record low, the storm of censure blowing without letup, he decided to undertake his long-postponed conquest of Ireland, a remote outpost of the world beyond the reach of papal legates who were threatening to excommunicate him.

At Poitiers, life slumbered along much as it had before. The carved saints adorning the Maubergeonne Tower caught the evening sun, the valley below undulated in waves of violet mist, and later the evenings throbbed with the strains of viol and lute and the aching beauty of the poets' songs. The night breezes swept into the Great Hall, where the ladies amused themselves with petitions to their court of love, and in the gardens and foyers the gilded youth talked of love and tournaments. They laughed and danced as if tomorrow would never dawn, and in fact, there seemed to be no good reason why their days would not drift on forever in this same joyous way. With so much evil afoot in the world, when an archbishop could be hacked to death before the altar of his own cathedral, how fortunate the children of Henry Plantagenet felt to be sheltered in their mother's domains, a silken cocoon of civility and sanity.

Life at the ducal palace moved slowly, and why not? There was no hurry. A high value was placed on amenities, especially on the art of conversation—intellectual, philosophical, and, of course, political. They spoke of Becket as a great man, a saint, and they discussed in clinical detail the aberrations of Henry Plantagenet. And they also talked of Louis Capet, whose defects now seemed delightful idiosyncrasies compared to the glaring irregularities in the character of the king of England. Time had done much to heal Eleanor's rancor toward her first husband; that desolate year in Jerusalem, the death of Raymond of Antioch, that dreadful, helpful smile of Pope Eugenius's at Tusculum—all these anguished memories had become mere silt in some far corner of her mind where they no longer had the power to hurt and humiliate. Louis, she was told, had grown mellow and wonderfully childlike. He played chess, dined frugally with the monks, and fell asleep in unlikely places. Once Marie's husband had found him dozing under a tree on a summer's day with only two servants nearby, and when the count had reproved him, Louis had only smiled serenely and replied, "Although I'm alone, I sleep free from danger for no one wishes to harm me." To those at Poitiers, the remark seemed pregnant with significance, especially when they tried to imagine Henry making such a statement. In fact, Louis had been known to compare himself with the English king. To Gerald of Wales he had remarked, "Thy master, the king of England, lacks nothing. To him belong men, horses, gold, silk, gems, fruits, wild beasts and all things else. As for us in France, all we have is bread, wine and joy." Bread, wine, joy and, for the moment at least, the psychological upper hand over Henry.

Slowly, Eleanor was edging out of the Plantagenet orbit and moving back toward the Capets. There was nothing definite about this, no meetings or letters that informers might report to Henry, perhaps nothing that even Eleanor herself could have recognized as a specific turning. If there was a conspiracy at that point, it was more a meeting of minds, at one in their contempt for Henry, a feeling shared by most of Europe. Not surprisingly, Eleanor's three older boys had been deeply affected by the events at Canterbury, but not in the way one might imagine. Only to young Henry had Becket meant anything personal; to Richard and Geoffrey, their father's great friendship was only a story people told. They themselves had been too young to remember. It was, rather, the universal condemnation heaped upon their father that helped to shatter their image of him. If he had once been a hero for them, this had not been true for several years, and by 1171, being the son of the king of England did not hold the prestige of former days. The chronicles give the impression that Henry's sons turned against him overnight and suddenly began to hate the father they had once adored. It is doubtful, in the first place, whether they had ever adored him. Feared and respected, undoubtedly, but loved, no. He was a remote figure, a larger-than-life apparition who would roar into their lives at Christmas or Easter after an absence of months or sometimes years to suddenly announce some honor he had arranged on their behalf; he would pluck them from their nurseries and tiltyards to receive the homage of a king or prince and then seemingly forget them again. But they could not forget him, his terrifying rages, his incomprehensible quarrels with the queen, his love for the woman at Woodstock.

As Eleanor moved about her court, hearing Richard recite a poem he had written or watching the pleasure on young Henry's face as he prepared for a tournament, she must have known that they spoke of their father with fierce disrespect, that soon after Montmirail they were quarreling among themselves over their prospective inheritances, bragging and sniping like little boys trying to divide a too-small sweet. Possibly she accepted their quarrels philosophically and laughed about them, as Geoffrey would do later when he said, "Don't you know that it is our nature to quarrel, our heritage that none of us should love the other?" Richard, too, was fond of joking about their demon Angevin ancestors, and he often repeated Abbot Bernard's famous words when he first met their father, "From the devil they came, to the devil they will go."

By 1172, the three oldest Plantagenet boys were no longer children who could be trotted out to perform on ceremonial occasions. Now seventeen, fifteen, and fourteen, they were young men of distinct but diverse personalities. The Young King was every twelfth-century woman's idea of a fairy-tale prince: "The most handsome prince in all the world, whether Saracen or Christian." Apparently, he had inherited the good looks of his grandfather, Geoffrey Anjou, and the chroniclers take great pains to describe his superficial attractions. "He was beautiful above all others in both form and face," declared Walter Map, "most blessed in breathing courtesy, most happy in the love of men and in their grace and favour . . . he was a man of unprecedented skill in arms." There is no doubt that his affability and his reputation for being a "fountain of largesse" helped him to attract a large following among his own generation. Like his mother, he had a taste for splendor, and he also prided himself on being the epitome of generosity and hospitality. Stories of his munificence flew about Europe, eventually finding their way into the contemporary histories. Once, he and his friends came to a spring after a tiring day of hunting. When he found that his servants had brought only one skin of wine, he emptied the skin into the water so that his companions might share what little he had. On another occasion, Christmas Day 1172, he invited all the knights in Normandy who bore the name William to share his dinner. One hundred and ten knights, we are told, sat down to a banquet of unprecedented extravagance. This was the public side of young Henry, and if that had been all of him, Eleanor might have had cause to rejoice. But there was more, and the rest of him she must have deplored. He may have been "noble, lovable, eloquent, beautiful, valiant, in every way charming, a little lower than the angels," but he was also weak, vain, shallow, empty-headed, and irresponsible—traits that his beauty made it easy to overlook, even by those who knew him well and especially by his father, who did not know him at all. He had a talent for saying the wrong thing, the exquisite manners he had learned in the households of Eleanor and Thomas Becket alternating with the most outrageous insensitivity and cruelty.

At the lavish banquet following his coronation in 1170, his father had insisted on serving the Young King himself, as a token of respect for his new exalted rank. Appearing before the boy with a mighty boar's head, he had smiled and joked, "It is surely unusual to see a king wait upon table."

"Ah," retorted the Young King, "but it is not unusual to find the son of a count waiting on the son of a king."

Henry's reply to his favorite son, if there was one, has not been recorded.

"Baseness of temper" is how Walter Map describes Eleanor's eldest son. "Foolishly liberal and spendthrift," adds Robert of Torigni. "He was a restless youth born for many men's undoing," sums up William of Newburgh.

Richard was Eleanor's favorite, which may have been one reason Henry disliked him. "He was tall in stature, graceful in figure; his hair between red and auburn, his limbs were straight and flexible; his arms rather long, and not to be matched for wielding the sword or for striking with it, and his long legs suited the rest of his frame." Physically, except for his height, Richard owed his looks to Henry: the reddish hair, ruddy complexion, his athletic prowess, and bold expression. In all other ways, he was Eleanor's son. Indeed, he was everything she had always sought in a man: a born warrior, a handsome chivalrous knight, a poet and musician, an intellectual. From his mother and his half sister Marie, he had learned to please a woman, and already he could compose delicate, sensuous verse and pay compliments in song to a lady. Blooming in the soil of Aquitaine as though he had been born there, he spoke the *langue d'oc* whenever possible, and despite his early years in England, cared nothing for the kingdom. He thought it no great honor that his brother would someday wear a king's crown; all Richard wanted was Aquitaine.

Neither Eleanor nor Henry seemed overly fond of Geoffrey. Considerably shorter than his two brothers, he also lacked their good looks and grace. Even though he possessed intelligence and accomplishments in knightly skills, probably more natural ability in tournaments than young Henry, he was a young man who inspired neither love nor confidence. Gerald of Wales described him as "overflowing with words, soft as oil, possessed, by his syrupy and persuasive eloquence, of the power of dissolving the seeming indissoluble, able to corrupt two kingdoms with his tongue; of tireless endeavour, a hypocrite in everything, a deceiver and a dissembler." Roger of Hovedon disposes of Geoffrey in a few words: "Geoffrey, that son of perdition."

By twelfth-century standards, Eleanor and Henry's sons were adults. Looking at a world full of exciting opportunities, they grew restless and ambitious, eager to be their own men and take their rightful places in society, but instead, Henry forced them to remain helpless dependents. He had seen fit to honor them with titles, but he still viewed them as children; the authority and revenues accompanying those titles he clutched tightly. One reason, of course, was his inability to relinquish anything that belonged to him, but at the same time, he could never quite accept the fact that his sons had grown up. This is difficult to understand, because at his eldest son's present age Henry himself was leading armies and planning invasions, and moreover, his own father had already turned over to him the duchy of Normandy. In his youth he had worked hard and played little; life was serious, and crowns had to be won. The younger generation baffled him because he could see no resemblance between himself as a youth and his frivolous sons, especially young Henry, whom he had raised to a station so lofty that no child would have cause to complain. Had he not turned his chancellor into an archbishop so that the boy might be anointed and had he not suffered from that decision as no king had ever suffered? He had given his beloved boy a title, and surely no son had a right to expect more. But now, to his astonishment, the boy actually expected Henry to step down from the throne of England, and others supported his incredible demand:

> Afterwards between you and your son a deadly hatred sprung up
> Whence many a gentle knight has since lost his life,
> Many a man has been unhorsed, many a saddle emptied,
> Many a good bucklet pierced, many a hauberk broken.
> After his coronation and after his investiture
> You filched from your son something of his lordship,
> You took away from him his will; he could not get possession.

Another reason that Henry had difficulty transferring authority to his sons was that he himself, carefully groomed for kingship since birth, was long accustomed to being the center of attention. As an adult, he continued to expect this kind of special consideration from everyone, his children included. Not having realized emotional maturity himself, he could not comprehend his sons' attitudes. Eleanor, on the other hand, recognized their immaturity, but she was also capable of understanding their impatience, and she must have strongly identified with them. There was no doubt that their ambitions outran their abilities at that point, but at the same time, deep resentments were building rapidly. She believed there would be no peace in the empire until Henry invested them with power and responsibility in some gradual recognition of their rightful claims. That he would agree to any such system she could never have seriously believed. She knew him too well. When had he ever allowed any member of his family to possess even a morsel of real authority? His voice must always reign supreme.

For those who kept track of prophecies and omens, the conflict between Henry Plantagenet and his sons had already been predicted by Merlin. "The cubs shall awake and shall roar aloud and, leaving the woods, shall seek their prey within the walls of the cities; among those who shall be in their way they shall make great carnage and shall tear out the tongues of bulls. The necks of them as they roar aloud they shall load with chains and shall thus renew the times of their forefathers." As dire prophecies go, this one would turn out to be fairly accurate, save in one detail: The awakened Plantagenet cubs would be led by their mother.

The Wheel of Fortune Turns

At Christmas 1172, Henry summoned Eleanor, along with Richard and Geoffrey, to keep the holiday with him at Chinon, but the occasion soon turned into a family brawl. Although the Young King and Queen Marguerite were in Normandy, the king and queen, the chroniclers tell us, quarreled furiously over their absent cub. Their son, nearly eighteen years old, was now demanding his heritage. He wanted someplace in the world that he could call his own—England, he suggested, and if not England then Normandy or Anjou. Had not Richard and Geoffrey nominal authority in their duchies? Why should he remain landless, a king without a kingdom, tied on a short leash by his father and forced to subsist on a meager allowance that he received at the king's pleasure? His coronation had been a farce, he whined, his crown only a plaything signifying nothing. How could he hold up his head before his friends when his father treated him like a babe? He wanted to become king of England while he was still young. The Young King burned with grievances, and when reproached by Henry, he had given a remarkable demonstration of Angevin black bile.

During the holiday, Eleanor must have pleaded vigorously on her son's behalf. She was convinced that his points were generally well taken, although at the same time she could not have truthfully denied that some of Henry's fears also seemed to be justified. It was clear that so far the boy had shown no desire for responsibility and had balked at Henry's attempts to teach him the real business of kingship. Anything that smacked of work brought on "a dreadful ennui"; he much preferred to spend his time with the knights and squires who had flocked to his side and followed him from one jousting field to the next all over western Europe. Nor could Eleanor deny that the young man spent money at an alarming rate. Still, she defended him. If he wanted to play at life, what was wrong with that? He was young. At his age she herself had felt much the same, and yet she had matured into a responsible administrator. In time he, too, would settle down.

But Henry would accept none of these arguments. Somehow, when his back had been turned for a moment, his darling boy had been transformed into an unrecognizable monster. Since the boy could do no wrong in his eyes, someone else must be responsible for the mysterious transformation, and he did not have far to look to understand whose handiwork he was seeing. The boy had been corrupted during his visits to Eleanor's court. His head had been stuffed full of Arthurian romances and Ovidian nonsense, unreal notions of knights-errant and women who fancied themselves goddesses. Did his son believe himself to be a hero out of the pages of a Chrétien de Troyes fantasy? He certainly behaved so. Real life was not only tournaments and courts of love; it was the sober conventions of councils and law courts. Henry did not care that the Young King had "revived chivalry, for she was dead or almost so." The tournaments that the boy adored fell into the same category as troubadours, both a waste of time. The king himself had no taste for such diversions. He had banned tournaments in England and now regretted that he had not extended the ban to his Continental divisions. If the Young King would attend to his duties as an apprentice monarch, he would have no time for mock wars; if he must pursue renown, let it be in the course of duty as Henry's assistant. The trouble was, the boy's mind had been warped by Eleanor and the *preux chevaliers* who clustered around the queen in Poitiers, her palace a trysting place for idlers who thought only of the next amusing adventure. For too many years he had closed his eyes to Eleanor's activities, but now he would make it his business to take more than a casual interest.

By the time that the rancorous Christmas court disbanded, there was no question that war had been declared and the battle lines drawn up, but what Henry failed to understand was that Eleanor had been arming for this conflict for some time now. God, as the Wife of Bath observed, has given women three weapons: deceit, weeping, and spinning. Since Eleanor by temperament lacked the taste for either of the latter, she had resorted to the former. While the troubadours were singing and her ladies passing judgments in the court of love, the queen had become involved in a serious development. With the aid of Ralph de Faye and other confidants among the Poitevin nobility and with the encouragement of her sons, she had somehow made contact with Louis Capet, and a conspiracy of sorts had been born. Unfortunately, the origins of the plot against Henry Plantagenet were never revealed, but it seems to have been a loose confederation of the king's disaffected vassals, a group that at that time included his wife, sons, and their champion the king of France. Although their united goal was Henry's removal and the elevation of the Young King, their individual motives varied widely. In Louis's case, his machinations aimed at breaking the power of the wily Plantagenet; the traitorous Aquitainian warlords would have jumped eagerly at any opportunity for revenge on what they considered an oppressive overlord; and Henry's sons were rebelling at an authoritarian parent who threw up barriers between them and their youthful desires. It is less easy to understand Eleanor's motives. She who had worked so hard in harness with Henry to forge an empire must have realized that Louis's long-range plans might destroy the very thing she had labored to build. Perhaps at that point her hatred of Henry had become so great that she was willing to see the empire fall along with its master. More likely she had convinced herself that it was time to pass along the holdings to the next generation. What she surely could not have believed was that Henry would voluntarily step down. While the chroniclers provide no insights into Eleanor's thinking, they are unanimous in crediting her as the ringleader, and they are equally unanimous in their condemnation. Gervase of Canterbury contended that the whole uprising had been devised and executed by the queen, "a very clever woman, born of noble stock, but flighty." The anonymous chronicler of the Gesta Henrici states emphatically that "the authors of this heinous treachery were Louis, King of France, and, as some say, Eleanor, Queen of England and Ralph de Faye." William of Newburgh is more discreet, only remarking dryly that after the Young King had reached manhood, "certain persons indeed whispered in his ear that he ought now by rights to reign alone, for at his coronation his father's reign had, as it were, ceased." Richard Fitzneale, a great admirer of Henry's, charges Eleanor with a calculated program of alienation of affections: "For while his sons were yet young and by reason of their age easily swayed by any emotion, certain 'little foxes' corrupted them with bad advice; so that at last his own bowels turned against him and told her sons to persecute their father."

It is difficult to unravel cause and effect. Did Eleanor, as the chroniclers claim, foster her sons' hatred of their father and incite them to rebellion, or did she merely support them in their own feelings about Henry? John, whom she did not raise and rarely saw, would later hold similar attitudes about his father. If Eleanor, as the custodial parent of Henry, Richard, and Geoffrey, did in truth turn them against Henry, she did a more thorough job than most separated wives, in that such attempts more often than not backfire. Her contemporaries, adamant in believing the worst about her, proceeded on the premise that a woman who had ostentatiously abandoned her husband and set up a court where women reigned supreme had to be wicked or, at the least, "flighty." Remembering her intrigue with Henry while she had still been queen of France, they viewed her as an unnatural woman, one who did not know her place and, as such, would be capable of anything, especially a strenuous campaign to poison her children against their father.

All efforts at changing Henry's attitude having failed, Eleanor took Richard and Geoffrey back to Poitiers, where plans for the uprising moved forward in a somewhat cautious manner. Mainly it was a period of waiting and watching for precisely the right moment to strike. Henry, however, took active steps to regain control of his heir so that he might undo the work of the "little foxes." Not only would he separate that young man from his mother and her obnoxious court, but he would also banish other undesirables who might be exerting a bad influence. Despite the Young King's howls of rage, Henry dismissed his favorite jousting companions and informed him that in future he would accompany his father and learn the profession of kingship. In early February, he more or less dragged young Henry to Montferrand in the Auvergne, where an important meeting had been scheduled with Count Humbert III of Maurienne, the lord of a spacious province extending southward and eastward from Lake Geneva to the frontiers of Italy and Provence. Two years earlier Henry and Humbert, who had no son, had tentatively agreed to a match between the count's daughter, Alice, and John Lackland, and now a formal betrothal was to take place. The contract drawn up, Henry promised to pay Count Humbert five thousand marks, while Humbert agreed to make John his heir to Maurienne. So far, young Henry had observed the negotiations without enthusiasm but with, perhaps, some jealousy. After Count Humbert had handed over the baby Alice to Henry, the entire party moved north to Limoges, where the king had summoned Eleanor and his two middle sons to confirm the settlement. During the week of February 21–28, he held court in Limoges, the first time he had stepped foot in Eleanor's provinces for several years, and he dominated the proceedings as though his wife did not exist. Calling together the barons of Aquitaine, he proudly announced his new alliance with Maurienne and then proceeded to take care of other business. With great ado, he acted as arbitrator between the feuding king of Aragon-Barcelona and Count Raymond of Toulouse, after which he received the homage of the count, who had recently severed his connections with the Capets.

Sometime during that week, Count Humbert, having disposed of both his daughter and the future of his fief, began to have annoying second thoughts. Perhaps he had made a poor bargain. Admittedly, his prospective son-in-law was the son of the king of England, but what did that mean exactly, since Henry had already divided his lands among his three eldest sons? What dower, he suddenly demanded of Henry, did he mean to set aside for young John? Placed on the spot, Henry replied that he would give the six-year-old boy the castles of Chinon, Loudon, and Mirebeau, a spur-of-the-moment decision that conveniently ignored the fact that those castles lay in Anjou, a county already assigned to his eldest son.

With no prompting from Eleanor, the Young King burst into loud protests, flatly refusing to give his castles to John, either then or at any time in the future. Indignant, he began to recite the whole chronicle of injuries his father had visited upon him, particularly the scorching insult of not being permitted to select his own friends. Although Eleanor, Richard, and Geoffrey supported him in refusing to ratify the marriage settlement, their refusals did not prevent Henry from assuring the count of Maurienne that his word remained law in the family. In the midst of this exceedingly public quarrel, the count of Toulouse saw an opportunity to settle an old score. Speaking privately to Henry, he suggested that the king might do well to open his ears and eyes a bit wider. Surely he could see that the queen had brainwashed their sons. Behind the floss and frill of her court of love, plots to depose him were being hatched, and for that matter, Raymond doubted if Henry had a loyal vassal left in the whole of Aquitaine. The king listened to this tale of sedition without revealing his emotions. Whatever else he might think of Eleanor, he could not readily believe that she would betray him, and he knew that Raymond, a past-master at treachery, certainly held enough of a grudge against the queen to concoct such a story. Henry, too, had his informers, and no reports of foul play had come to his ears. At the same time, he did not dismiss Raymond's warning; rather, he filed it as a subject worthy of further investigation.

When the conclave broke up at the end of February, Henry announced that he would continue to take charge of the Young King; to Eleanor's dismay, she was forced to return to Poitiers with only Richard and Geoffrey. As the king's entourage moved north, breaking their journey occasionally to hunt and hawk, there was no doubt that young Henry was being held under house arrest. His father did not allow him out of his sight, even insisting that they sleep in the same room. On the evening of March 5, after a hard day's ride, they reached Chinon, and that night Henry slept perhaps more soundly than usual, because the next morning he awoke to find his son gone. The drawbridge, he learned, had been lowered before dawn. Frantic, he dispatched messengers in every direction, and when he learned that the boy had forded the Loire and had been seen heading north, he sped after him. For the next two days Henry raced to overtake the renegade in a hopeless chase that took him from Le Mans to Alençon to Argentan. But on March 8, after an all-night ride, the Young King crossed the French border to rest safely in the domains of his father-in-law. Obviously, the escape had been carefully planned; fresh horses had been posted at intervals so that the Young King would have no trouble in maintaining a good lead over pursuers. Exactly who arranged these details is uncertain, although it would be reasonable to assume that Eleanor was responsible.

At the French frontier, shaking with frustration, Henry sent several eminent bishops to Louis asking for the return of his son and promising that if the boy had complaints, they would be rectified. In this matter he would, he vowed, even take Louis's advice.

Louis replied with a feyness that greatly amused his court.

"Who is it that sends this message to me?" he asked.

"The king of England," replied Henry's bishops.

"That is untrue," said Louis archly. "Look, the king of England is here with me and he sends me no message through you. But if you still call king his father who was formerly king of England, know that he is no longer king. Although he may still act as king, everyone knows that he resigned his kingdom to his son."

It was obvious to Henry that the time had come to put his house in order. If his heir mocked him, there still remained time to gather in the rest of the brood. Shortly, however, he discovered his mistake. "Soon after, the younger Henry, devising evil against his father from every side by the advice of the French king, went secretly into Aquitaine where his two youthful brothers, Richard and Geoffrey, were living with their mother, and with her connivance, so it is said, he incited them to join him and brought them back to France." With three sons now beyond his jurisdiction, Henry still did not take the runaways terribly seriously. Childish petulance was all that troubled them. Apparently undisturbed, he had his hawks and hounds shipped over from England and passed the time hunting. More or less impotent for the moment, he was reduced to threatening Eleanor. Through Archbishop Rotrou of Rouen he appealed to her to end the game, adding assurances that if she and the boys returned home, all would be forgiven.

"Pious queen, most illustrious queen," wrote the archbishop, "before matters come to a worse end, return with your sons to your husband, whom you are bound to obey and with whom you are forced to live; return lest he mistrust you or your sons. Most surely we know that he will in every way possible show you his love and grant you the assurance of perfect safety. Bid your sons, we beg you, to be obedient and devoted to their father, who for their sakes has undergone so many difficulties, run so many dangers, and undertaken so many labors."

The archbishop then lifted before the queen's eyes the specter of serious punishment. "Either go back to your husband, or by canon law we shall be compelled and forced to lay the censure of the Church on you. Although we say it unwillingly, unless you return to your senses we shall do this with grief and tears."

Eleanor did not deign to reply, indeed there was no reason at all to pay the slightest morsel of attention to either Henry's importunities or the archbishop's threats of excommunication. As for her husband's secondhand promises of "love" and "perfect safety," she was wary of the word *love* on his tongue. At any event, by Easter of 1173, the dagger was poised for the thrust, with the Young King's escape the signal for a widespread uprising against the king; in the half of western Christendom every baron with a grievance against his Plantagenet overlord saw that the hour had struck. The confederation, which months earlier had included mainly the queen, her sons, and her ex-husband, had now swollen to include a motley assortment of fresh recruits: the houses of Champagne and Flanders, liege men of the young princes, Poitevins burning for revenge, aggravated barons of Brittany, English lords eager to escape Henry's crippling taxes, roustabouts who had followed in the wake of the popular Young King; in the far north, even King William of Scotland threw his support to Eleanor's son. In England, Richard of Dover's investiture as archbishop of Canterbury was broken off in midceremony by a messenger from the Young King protesting an election held without his consent. In Aquitaine, all officials appointed by the king were promptly shown the door; in Anjou, Brittany, and Maine, the king's authority was stoutly repudiated. In that spring of 1173, only Normandy remained faithful to its overlord, and of all Henry's family, "John alone, who was a little boy, remained with his father." The Plantagenet edifice, constructed with such precision over the past two decades, seemed on the brink of folding like a house of cards.

Toward the end of June, the revolt began in earnest. On the twenty-ninth, Count Philip of Flanders invaded Normandy and captured Aumale north of Rouen, while Eleanor's sons, "laying waste their father's lands on every side with fire, sword and rapine," received their first taste of real warfare at the siege of Driencourt Castle at Neufchâtel. Louis Capet set up his stonethrowers and siege engines at Verneuil, one of Henry's strongest fortifications on the Norman-French border. By midsummer Eleanor must have felt confident that Henry Plantagenet's days on the throne were numbered. The king appeared to be stunned, not without good reason; Earl Robert of Leicester, the son of his former chief justiciar and one of his most loyal supporters, had deserted to the camp of the Young King, and the count of Flanders readied a fleet to invade England. Each day brought tidings of fresh disaster for the king and promises of a new regime for Eleanor. In August, however, the situation dramatically altered as the lion seemed to slowly shake himself awake and exhibit the speed he had shown in the early days of their marriage. With loyal vassals in short supply, certainly too few to form a decent army, Henry raided his treasury for funds to purchase mercenaries. Between August 12 and 19, he raced his army of ten thousand Brabantines from Normandy to Brittany at the rate of twenty miles a day. To Eleanor's consternation, he began to stamp out, one by one, the fires of sedition.

As autumn drew near, Louis Capet decided to go home. His vassals had committed their time to Young Henry's cause for only the traditional forty days of military service; if Louis remained in the field any longer, he would be obliged to pay them out of his own pocket, and even for his son-in-law, he would not go that far. From experience, Eleanor knew better than to trust Louis when it came to military ventures, but still she must have fumed to learn that he had requested a truce. On September 25, 1173, the two kings met under the spreading branches of a gigantic elm tree at Gisors in the Vexin, the traditional meeting place for the two rival powers. In the shade of the great tree, Henry's three sons faced their father and listened impatiently to his offers of allowances and castles. Quickly, they realized that their situations had not changed, for Henry made no mention of authority. Rejecting what they considered bribes with the supreme disdain of those who have not yet tasted defeat, they confidently turned their backs on him and rode back to Paris with Louis. The fighting season had ended for the year, but in the spring they would strike again, and next time the attack would be aimed at the heart of his power, England.

It was late September now, and Eleanor must have sat uneasily in her high tower at Poitiers. Her sons may have been safe at the Capetian court, but no such security was vouchsafed to Eleanor, whose future suddenly appeared perilous. Rattling their way over the highroads of Normandy and Anjou came dismaying reports that her husband, having nothing to fear from Louis for the moment, was methodically moving his Brabantines in a southerly direction, slowly but unmistakably bearing down on Poitiers and eager to lay hands on the taproot of all his afflictions. In Touraine and northern Poitou he was capturing castles and razing walls, burning vineyards, and uprooting crops; hardly a day passed without the sight of terrorized refugees seeking safety behind Poitiers's walls, their stomachs empty but their mouths full of horror stories about kin who had been captured and assigned to unknown Plantagenet dungeons. As the shadow of the king loomed closer, it was clearly time for Eleanor to leave her capital city, and yet she lingered. The reason for her delay can only be surmised: At that crucial moment when nearly the whole region north of Poitiers lay a smoking ruin, she must have disliked the idea of abandoning her province to the fury of her husband. Then, too, she must have experienced difficulty in coming to terms with the remaining alternative. If she fled, there was only one direction to go—the way of thousands of other refugees, including Becket and her sons. The wheel of fortune had made a cruel if complete revolution; at the age of fifty-one, was she reduced to abandoning her duchy and running to the Capets for protection? Undoubtedly, this was a step she wished to avoid at all costs, but in the end there was of course no choice. Even Ralph de Faye had deemed it prudent to winter along the Seine, and by the time Henry had set up his siege engines before the walls of Faye-la-Vineuse, he had already crossed into the Île-de-France. Only a few months earlier, one of Eleanor's vassals had written boldly, "Rejoice, O Aquitaine; be jubilant, O Poitou, for the scepter of the king of the North Wind is drawing away from you," but the rejoicing and jubilance had not survived the vintage.

When Eleanor finally decided to act, the last possible moment for flight had already passed. That she knew this is evident from the manner of her departure. She took with her no silken gowns or chests or maids. Disguised in a knight's attire, she set out astride her mount, accompanied only by a few knights of her household. Along some road in the north of Poitou the queen's little band was accosted, almost accidentally it seems, by a party of her own countrymen, unfortunately some of the few Poitevins still loyal to Henry Plantagenet and thus quick to assess the value of this prize that had dropped into their laps. Her capture was accomplished swiftly and silently. No chronicler had access to the facts, neither the date nor the place nor the names of her captors. The sole annalist to mention the episode was Gervase of Canterbury and then only to record his surprise that the most dignified queen in Europe should be found in men's clothes—"*mutata veste muliebri"*—with her legs vulgarly straddling a horse. A twentieth-century historian suggests that her betrayers were four Poitevin barons who later received valuable grants from Henry; if that were truly the case, the men would have been known to her, no doubt vassals who had sworn homage, who had lazed about the Great Hall of her palace listening to the troubadours and partaking of her hospitality, and on whom she had tried to graft an enlightened consciousness. Whatever the manner of the confrontation between these men and their liege lady—whether men and horses crashed to the ground as her escort attempted a defense, whether her party was led away in helpless silence—the betrayal took place with secrecy and murderous efficiency. Nor did the king advertise the capture of his royal prisoner of war. Her proverbially disloyal countrymen had neatly taken care of his problems, both marital and martial, and now he would deal with her privately as the poorest villein would punish a faithless wife. Swiftly, the unrepentant queen was stored in a convenient fortress, Chinon perhaps, but for many months her whereabouts must have remained a mystery to her sons and supporters. She had disappeared as if swallowed up by an extraterrestrial invasion party. At one point, however, Eleanor and Henry must have faced each other in bitter colloquy. Did Henry threaten to execute her for treason? Did he fly into one of his Angevin rages and roll on the floor? The answers to such questions lie hidden in the mists of history, if indeed they were ever publicly known. Perhaps Henry forewent the pleasure of a tantrum and informed her with a deadly calm worse than rage that her future lay solely at his disposal. Despite the propaganda emanating from her court of love, she was, after all, his property. The principles of feudalism rode triumphant.

On Whitsunday, May 12, 1174, Henry himself arrived in Poitiers to scoop up the remnants of Eleanor's court—Queen Marguerite and the Princess Alais; Henry's sister, Emma of Anjou, Constance of Brittany and Alice of Maurienne; his daughter, Joanna—and then he proceeded to clean house. The *chevaliers* and songsters were sent on their way, idlers and tourneyers banished, key rebels flushed from their burrows and assigned to chains. Trustworthy men were placed in charge of the duchy. Eleanor's famous court, the scene of brilliant fêtes and female fantasies of power, stood empty now. The Young King had gone, and Richard and Geoffrey—all moved on to challenge their destinies in the Île-de-France. Countess Marie, who had remained until shortly before Henry's purge, was now back in Champagne with her tales of Arthur and Guinevere. The countess of Flanders had returned to Arras, where her husband, refusing to tolerate Amazons or goddesses, hung a young

man who had dared to practice the principles of Andreas's *De Amore.*
The court of love was vacant now and the land in which it had
flourished left to the winds of anarchy.

All through that dreary winter and spring of 1174 we hear nothing of
Eleanor. The kings and knights, bishops and castles, even the pawns,
still moved about the political chessboard, but the queen had been
deftly removed and pocketed. It can be supposed, however, that her
hope of release remained high, and if communications from the outside
reached her, she would have been encouraged to learn that the Young
King and Philip of Flanders, their army and fleet assembled, now
waited only for a favorable wind to speed their flotilla across the Channel. The revolt by no means over, there always remained the chance of
rescue, either by her sons or by Louis or by some sympathetic jailer.

Suddenly in July, doors were unbarred and drawbridges lowered, but
not by friends. Eleanor was carried under close guard to the port of Barfleur "where a considerable number of ships had been assembled
against the king's arrival." In fact, forty vessels had been hired to transport across the Channel Henry's assortment of captive rebels and innocent bystanders; amid the crowd could be found the queen with her
jailers, the Plantagenet children and daughters-in-law anxiously
bewildered, and a number of well-known earls, countesses, and barons
dragging their chains. The Channel was rough and the Norman coast
lashed by summer storms. The first time Eleanor had watched the foam-
ing breakers and waited for weather in this port, she had been thirty-
two years old and held the world in the palm of her hand. In a storm,
she had crossed with her virile young husband to claim a crown, but
now, in another storm, she may have seen the Channel as a runway to
the tomb. She was an elderly woman whose moment had come and
gone.

Storms had not stopped Henry in 1154, and they surely did not deter
him now. To the terror of his sailors and captives, he ordered the fleet to
sail on the morning of Monday, July 8. Standing on the deck of his ship,
he lifted his eyes to the stormy skies and shouted above the gale a
message to God, his attitude toward the Almighty always being that of
one businessman to another, an equal from whom he expected fair
dealing. "Lord, if in my heart I nourish plans which will bring peace to
the clergy and the people, if the King of Heaven has decreed in His infinite mercy that my arrival shall mark the return of peace, then may He
grant that I come safely to harbour. If He is opposed to my purpose and
has decided to punish my kingdom, may I never be allowed to reach its
shores." The fleet rode into Southampton that same evening.

It was high summer in England, but the sun did not shine. Instead, rain and fog shrouded Southampton, and it was cold. Henry had no time to waste on his captives. Declining a proper meal, he wolfed down water and a chunk of bread before he disposed of his excess baggage with a promptness that suggests he had already allotted some thought to the matter. Marguerite and the other young ladies were sent to Devizes, his chained prisoners to Porchester, and the less dangerous to Winchester. But neither in Winchester nor in London nor in Oxford would he incarcerate Eleanor, nor in any site where a rising tide of sympathy and interest in the queen of England might lap at her walls. The queen was immured in the strong tower of Salisbury, not the Salisbury we know today but Old Sarum, where she would have ample time to examine her conscience and reflect upon the error of her perfidy. As for Henry, he felt the need to look into his own conscience. The next morning, he set out on a pilgrimage to Canterbury. Three miles from the town, he dismounted and walked the rest of the way barefoot. "His footsteps along the road seemed to be covered with blood and really were so; for his tender feet were being cut by the hard stones." It was a year since Thomas the martyr had been canonized, more than three years since the crime had taken place. Entering the crypt, Henry prostrated himself before the tomb and then stripped his pilgrim's smock for the lashes of the bishops, abbots, and monks. "There he remained in prayer before the holy Martyr all that day and night. He neither took food nor went out to relieve nature but, as he had come, so he remained and would not permit a rug or anything else to be laid under him." At daybreak on Sunday the thirteenth he heard Mass and received a phial of the martyr's blood. The following Wednesday evening the king, resting at Westminster after his exertions and fasting, was halfway between waking and sleeping when a messenger beat loudly on his chamber door. At that particular time he must have dreaded the approach of any courier, since nearly all reports turned out to be alarming; King William of Scotland was harrying his northern borders, mercenaries of the count of Flanders had already landed in East Anglia, and momentarily he expected to see the Young King himself at the head of an army. Under the circumstances, he braced himself for evil tidings: "Brien, what news do you bring?"

"The King of Scotland is taken and all his barons."
"Then," says King Henry, "God be thanked for it,
And St. Thomas Martyr and all God's saints!"
And the King is so merry that night and so joyful

That he went to the knights and woke them all up:
"Barons, wake up! This has been a good night for you!
Such a thing have I heard as will make you joyful:
Taken is the King of Scotland, so it has been told me for truth.
Just now the news came to me, when I should have been in bed."

The next morning, the bells rang in every church in London, and in the course of the next two months, Henry quenched the fires of rebellion in England and then on the Continent. On September 29, he met with his rebel sons at Montlouis, between Tours and Amboise, to dictate the terms of peace. Stripping them of independent authority, he gave the Young King two castles in Normandy and an income of £3,750 sterling a year. Richard was allotted two castles in Poitou and half the county's revenues, while Geoffrey was to have half the income from Constance of Brittany's marriage portion. His provisions for John, which had so provoked the Young King earlier in the year at Limoges, were now substantially increased, and instead of the three castles originally promised, he was to receive property in England, Normandy, Anjou, Touraine, and Maine, as well as considerable revenues. "Furthermore, King Henry, the son of the Lord King, and his brothers gave assurance that they would never demand anything more of the Lord King, their father, beyond the determined settlement" and that they would "withdraw neither themselves nor their service from their father." And so the cubs were pulled back into the fold so successfully that people said it must have been due to the intervention of the Blessed Saint Thomas. The king and his four sons, all very models of filial obedience, kept Christmas court at Argentan, where they feasted on "the meat of four score deer sent to the King beyond the sea." In victory, Henry had shown himself magnanimous, excusing his sons' treachery on the grounds of youth and blaming their excesses on troublemakers. His leniency did not, however, extend to his wife.

At Salisbury, the queen dined on disappointed hopes. There is no evidence she was confined to a cell or in any way physically mistreated, but at the same time there is no doubt that she remained very much a prisoner, always kept under strict surveillance by one of the king's watchdogs. Her pride shredded, her hopes and ambitions utterly destroyed, she who had been mistress of all she surveyed was now estranged from her children and cut off from the world's commerce, forced to rely on her keepers for news. With her she had a small household—her maid, Amaria, and perhaps a few other familiars—but she seems to have lived a comparatively mean existence. If the pipe rolls record the total extent of the allowances for her maintenance, her income would have permitted only the most spartan of lives. There had been method in Henry's disposition of her, a cruelty that comes of knowing a person intimately, for he understood that she had not the slightest passion for solitude. On the contrary, she gloried in the converse of people, and of course, she abhorred idleness. In clipping the Eagle's wings, he had deliberately condemned her to what he believed would be a living death.

Her state of mind at this time was as much a matter of conjecture to the twelfth century as it is now. In Aquitaine, her subjects cried out in vain against the imprisonment of their duchess, but whether their laments reached Salisbury cannot be determined.

> Tell me, Eagle with two heads, tell me: where were you when your eaglets, flying from their nest, dared to raise their talons against the king of the North Wind? It was you, we learn, who urged them to rise against their father. That is why you have been plucked from your own country and carried away to an alien land. Your barons have cheated you by their conciliatory words. In the old days, with your taste for luxury and refinement, you enjoyed a royal liberty. You lived richly on your own inheritance, you took pleasure in the pastimes of your women, you delighted in the melodies of the flute and drum. And now, Queen with two crowns, you consume yourself with sorrow, you ravage your heart with tears. Return, O captive, return to your own lands if you can. You may ask yourself: Where is my court? Where are the members of my family? Where are my handmaidens, my counselors? Some have been torn from their lands and condemned to a shameful death; some have been deprived of their sight, others wander exiled in far places. Eagle of the broken alliance, how much longer will you cry out unanswered? The king of the North Wind holds you in captivity. But do not despair; lift your voice like a bugle and it shall reach the ears of your sons. The day will come when they will set you free and you shall come again to dwell in your native land.

But Eleanor's voice trumpeted no farther than the moat at Salisbury. If she pleaded with Henry for her liberty, his ears were stopped against her words, and even her sons appeared deaf. She had played her dangerous game and lost, and now she must sustain herself with memories. One can imagine that her thoughts might have strayed back to the Île-de-France and the young man with whom she had intrigued on a few sultry August evenings twenty-five years earlier; she had loved him as passionately then as she now detested him. And she must have thought, too, of the children she had been so eager to bear. Her daughters, sensible girls bred for queenship, had never caused her grief: Matilda, prim, solid, always reliable; Eleanor and Joanna, spirited and beautiful. As for her sons, she could not have denied that they had become, in some curious way, thorns in her flesh. The Young King's enormous charm could not disguise a kind of stupidity in his nature, just as Geoffrey's sugared tongue could not overcome his craftiness and selfishness; John had the energy and nerve of his father, but in him Henry's vitality became nervous weakness, his bravado merely underhandedness. Of all her brood it was the thought of Richard that must have warmed her most isolated moments—Richard her love, the child with the greatest spirit, the most cultured, the most intelligent.

As Salisbury the days were long. She must have used every trick to nourish her hope of release before she died, but there was no trick. She could only wait, in apprehension and eagerness, watching the seasons unfurl and die, waiting for news of her children, turning over in her mind her yesterdays, when she had dreamed of an unreal love as sung by the troubadours. So many *cansos* only half-heard, so many lovely days wasted, so many roads ridden over without turning her head aside to watch the trees and fields, so many goblets of wine drunk hastily, so much of life consumed but never tasted.

In 1175, Eleanor was offered a possible chance of escape. She may have been removed from Henry's sight but not from his mind; indeed, one of his chief problems was her final disposition. Ironically, his dilemma was the same that had perplexed the king of the Franks some twenty-five years earlier; how to rid himself of the queen without also losing her duchy. Clearly, he had excellent grounds for divorce, because she was more closely related to him than to Louis, but he could also see that divorce might not be the answer. He had no intention of repeating Louis's mistake, for in setting Eleanor free, he would lose half of his Continental domains at one stroke to her and Richard. Surely it would be madness to place such weapons in the hands of a woman who hated him and a son who had already proved his intransigence. Still, other alternatives might remain that the spineless Louis had not dared to attempt. At the end of October 1175, Henry welcomed to England Cardinal Hugh Pierleoni, who had come on other matters but unexpectedly found himself the recipient of an astounding royal largesse. At Winchester, Henry loaded him with gifts and sweet words; indeed, the amount of silver that passed into the cardinal's hands suggested a barely concealed bribe. What Henry proposed was a divorce, after which the ex-queen of England should relinquish worldly pursuits and retreat into some honorable establishment for women where she could do no harm. Perhaps, he suggested, the queen might be prevailed upon to retire to Fontevrault, not as an ordinary nun but in the prestigious position of abbess. There in that famous and noble nunnery she might live out her few remaining years in the company of other rich old ladies, leaving him free to form a new alliance.

During that year, plague raged in England "so that on most days seven or eight bodies of the dead were carried out of every church for burial and immediately after this deadly mortality a dreadful famine ensued." The winter was so severe that snow and ice covered England from Christmas to Candlemas. How tempted Eleanor must have been by the prospect of returning to the southern abbey where she had always felt an unearthly serenity. And in the end, how vehemently she rejected the offer, even, it is said, appealing for aid to the archbishop of Rouen, who, despite his admonitions in 1173, apparently agreed that she had no vocation for the religious life. One can only surmise from this incident that she had not given up hope of eventual release, even though there seemed to be little foundation for such a hope. In truth, she was as much cloistered at Salisbury as she would have been in a cell at Fontevrault.

In the summer of 1176, her daughter Joanna came to Winchester prior to her departure for Sicily, where she was to marry King William. Entries in the pipe rolls suggest that Eleanor was temporarily released from Salisbury, probably at Joanna's intercession, to spend these last days in England with her daughter and that, moreover, she accompanied Joanna to Southampton. This was the first time that she had seen any of her children in two years. Perhaps due to Joanna's indignation about her mother's confinement, after Eleanor returned to Salisbury in the fall, her standard of living gradually began to improve. "For 2 cloaks of scarlet and 2 capes of scarlet and 2 grey furs and 1 embroidered coverlet for the use of the Queen and her servant girl, 28£, 13s. 7d., by the King's writ."

While time seemed to stand still for her, life surged on for those at liberty to order their existences as best they could. In 1177, the chroniclers duly reported the doings of Queen Marguerite, who, "being pregnant, went to Paris and was delivered of a stillborn son." And equally momentous events found their way into the records. "In this same year," noted Hovedon, "on the thirteenth day before the calends of July, it rained a shower of blood for two whole hours in the Isle of Wight, so much so that linen clothes which were hung out upon the hedges were stained just as though they had been dipped in blood." But of Queen Eleanor there is not so much as a single line. To her contemporaries, it was as if she were dead.

In the end, it was not Henry's queen who entered a nunnery but his mistress, Rosamond Clifford, with whom he had consoled himself in recent years. After Rosamond died at Godstow, about 1176, Henry took other women into his bed, one of whom must have filled Eleanor with more rage than she had ever felt for the Rose of the World. Alais Capet, the princess who had been promised to Richard at Montmirail and who had been reared in Eleanor's court, was sixteen in 1176. Although she was certainly of a marriageable age, Henry appeared to have forgotten her betrothal to his son, and after the court at Poitiers had been shuttered, she had been brought to England, where, rumor said, she had become the king's mistress. Gerald of Wales, an annalist who virtually made a career of chronicling Henry's vices, said that he consorted openly and shamelessly, first with Rosamond and then, after she had departed from the scene, with his son's betrothed, whom he intended to make queen of England. So uninhibited was Henry in his relations with Alais that rumors circulated thickly. It was said that Henry planned to disinherit his three eldest sons and name as his heir the only child whose mind had not been poisoned by his mother, and that Alais's hand would be conferred upon John Lackland. It was also said that, once he had divorced Eleanor, he would disinherit her ravenous eaglets and sire a new batch from his Capetian hostage. Despite the peace of Montlouis and his seeming affection for his sons, he was said to be disgusted with the lot of them. Had he not publicly declared to his bastard son, Geoffrey, "My other sons have proved themselves bastards but you alone are my true and legitimate son?" In any case, by 1177, the stories about the hapless Alais had become so rife that Louis Capet felt compelled to make inquiries, and receiving no satisfaction from Henry, appealed to Pope Alexander to enforce his daughter's marriage to Richard.

At fifty-nine, Louis was beginning to feel the weight of his years. Wishing to put his affairs in order, he determined to have his son, Philip, now fourteen, anointed and crowned king of France. For the date of the coronation, he chose the feast of Our Lady's Assumption, August 15, 1179, and summoned his vassals to assemble at Reims. Shortly before the appointed day, he and his son set out for Reims in a leisurely fashion, breaking their journey at Compiègne for rest and entertainment. Philip and his young friends eagerly went out to hunt in the forest, but the prince, chasing a boar, became separated and lost his way. Panicked, he spurred his horse this way and that, succeeding only in burying himself deeper in the woods. At dusk, after hours of shouting and weeping, he stumbled into a clearing where a charcoal burner made his home, a rude forest dweller who was no doubt more surprised to see a prince appear before his hovel door than Philip was to find him. Returned to his father, Dieu-Donné fell ill of a fever. Not only was it necessary to cancel the coronation, but the boy's life was despaired of.

Beside himself with anxiety, Louis slept fitfully, and on three successive nights dreamed of Thomas Becket. Said the martyr, "Our Lord Jesus Christ has sent me so that you may know that if you believe and with a contrite heart go to His servant Thomas of Canterbury, the Martyr, your son will recover from his illness." Although Louis's barons warned him of the perils he risked by undertaking a pilgrimage in Plantagenet lands, nothing would shake his resolve. On Wednesday, August 22, "assuming now the name and dress of a pilgrim, he most devoutly visited England, which neither he nor any of his predecessors had ever visited." Henry met him at Dover, and together the two kings traveled to the cathedral town, where Louis laid on the martyr's tomb a cup brimming with gold. Four days later, he returned to France to find that Prince Philip had completely recovered. The coronation was rescheduled for All Saint's Day, November 1, but "King Louis, laboring under old age and a paralytic malady, was unable to attend the coronation; for after he had returned from England and was staying at Saint-Denis, being struck by a sudden chill, he had an attack of paralysis and lost the use of the right side of his body." On September 18, 1180, in his city of Paris, the most pious and Christian king of the Franks "laid aside the burden of the flesh and his spirit fled to the skies to enter upon its eternal reward with the elected princes." In perhaps a more impartial obituary, William of Newburgh said, "He was a man of warm devotion to God and of great gentleness to his subjects and of notable reverence for the clergy, but he was rather more simple-minded than is becoming to a prince."

Eleanor's duplicity had affected Henry more than he cared to admit. He who could not tolerate having his will flouted or his trust abused had been forced to contend with two major betrayals, and as a result, he had developed an exaggerated suspicion of everyone's motives. There occurred an almost complete metamorphosis of personality, from the affable, forthright young man whom Eleanor had married to a suspicious, middle-aged tyrant replete with persecution complex, and still later to a dissembler whose promises and oaths were deemed worthless. His imprisonment of Eleanor may have solved one of his personal problems, but four even more agonizing ones remained—his sons who constantly harried him "until he could find no abiding state of happiness or enjoyment of security." When the rebellion had ended in 1174, Henry promptly resolved to straighten out the Young King, only to find that he had fled in terror to Paris lest he, too, suffer the same fate as his mother. It was not until the spring of 1175 that he came to his father at Bures and fell flat on the ground begging him with tears to receive his homage and allegiance. Finally, promised a larger allowance and assured repeatedly of his father's love, he agreed to return to England with the king. Ralph of Diceto described the remarkable amity between father and son at this period by saying that "every day at the stated hour for meals they ate at the same table" and at night slept in the same chamber. In his father's company, he made a progress around the island for the express purpose of learning to administer the kingdom that had the most ordered government in the world; he attended synods and council meetings, received foreign embassies, and destroyed illegal castles. But Henry's tutoring was lost on the youth, who found the routine of assizes and exchequers irksome. Indolent by temperament, he longed for tournaments and the company of those gallants whose freewheeling existence revolved about tourneying, drinking, and boasting. His father's insistence that he remain in England and the continual surveillance under which he lived suggest a state imprisonment little freer than his mother's imprisonment at Salisbury. Determined to escape at all cost, he requested permission to make a Lenten pilgrimage to Saint James of Compostela, a ruse that his father saw through immediately. Henry understood all too well that the boy fevered to join his profligate friends on the Continent, and it is a measure of his strong will that he succeeded in detaining the Young King for an entire year. Finally, able to hold him no longer, he gave permission for his son and Marguerite to visit Paris, with the stipulation that after they had paid their respects to Louis, the Young King should travel on to Aquitaine and give Richard a hand in his continuing struggles with the southern barons. In that way, Henry meant to give him useful work, and he further attempted to limit his carousing by allotting him only a modest allowance and assigning one of his trusted men, Adam of Churchdown, to travel with the youth as a "chancellor."

Upon the Young King's arrival in the Île-de-France in 1176, he immediately justified the king's worst fears. Seeking out young men with similar tastes, those very gallants whom Henry had dismissed as undesirables, he spent the summer traveling from tournament to tournament and even persuaded his cousin the count of Flanders to outfit him with arms and horses so that he might tourney in a style appropriate to a king. In the autumn, however, with the end of the tournament season, the Young King slumped again into depression. Having nothing better to do, he drifted into Aquitaine to give Richard the promised aid, but it is clear that he did so with the greatest reluctance. Why should he help Richard to settle the affairs of his duchy when he himself had nothing he could call his own? The most that can be said for him was that he put in a brief appearance at Angoulême, where Richard was conducting a campaign, and then almost immediately departed for Poitiers, where he rallied his old friends from his mother's court, many of them knights who had sided with him during the rebellion. In the southland, the kingdom of England seemed very far away indeed, and people talked candidly of subjects that were only mentioned in whispers elsewhere. The Young King's grievances against his father were sympathetically supported, and he found himself an object of great solicitude, if not an actual hero. To Adam of Churchdown, the conversations that he overheard among these *chevaliers* sounded suspiciously treasonous, perhaps the beginning of a second rebellion, and he dutifully wrote a warning to King Henry. His letters, however, were intercepted by the Young King, who ordered Adam's hands tied behind his back and the man to be whipped naked through the streets of Poitiers.

For some time the sporting life managed to absorb the Young King's energies. "Henry the young king," wrote a chronicler, "spent three years in tournaments and profuse expenditure. Laying aside his royal dignity and assuming the character of a knight, he devoted himself to equestrian exercises and carrying the victory in various encounters, spreading his fame on all side around him." But in the end, no amount of fame nor diversion could ease his cankerous discontent, nor was his temper improved when he thought of his brother Richard, whose constant warfare to keep his duchy in check left him no time for mock battles. At eighteen, Eleanor's heir proved a marked contrast to young Henry's frivolity. He had set about stamping out rebellion in Aquitaine with a grim earnestness that soon won him the hatred of his mother's vassals and, perhaps, the secret respect of his father. In 1176, he humbled the most persistent troublemakers, taking Limoges and Châteauneuf-sur-Charente in the process, and in the following year, with the northern sector of Aquitaine quiet, he marched his army into the south, where he forced the Basques and Navarrese to recognize his authority. In 1179, he captured Geoffrey de Rancon's supposedly impregnable fortress of Taillebourg and then, to the horror of the local citizenry, leveled it to the ground. Before he was twenty, Richard had already established a reputation as the most gifted military tactician in western Europe, a reputation which only fanned his older brother's jealousy.

The contrast between the mock king of England and the conquering hero of Aquitaine was not lost on either young Henry or on his contemporaries in the south. The troubadour Bertran de Born was probably reflecting popular opinion when, in a taunting *sirventès*, he termed the prince "lord of little land," and the Young King's position grew even more intolerable after 1177, when Henry crowned eleven-year-old John Lackland as king of Ireland.

By the end of 1182, Henry had grown desperate. His every attempt to appease his twenty-seven-year-old son had failed, including promises of a more generous allowance, and he was forced to admit that he had lost control of the situation. Frantically casting about for some means of humoring his heir, without, of course, giving him authority or land, he determined to hold a particularly sumptuous Christmas court of the sort that might appeal to a young man who doted on splendid banquets. Choosing the city of Caen as the gathering place, he forbid all local baronial courts in his provinces and invited noblemen and prelates to renew their homage at what the chroniclers would call the most splendid court ever held in Normandy. A crowd of over one thousand arrived to keep the cheer with their overlord that year: Geoffrey with his testy Breton barons; Richard trailing the vassals and troubadours of the absent queen; Matilda and Henry of Saxony, exiled from Germany by the Holy Roman emperor, along with their children and an enormous household; Queen Marguerite, haughty, beautiful, barely on speaking terms with her husband because of his unfounded jealousy of William Marshal, who, he believed, had dared to love his wife. The Young King arrived at Caen in a sullen humor and immediately made himself unpleasant to everyone. For all Henry's elaborate preparations, the young man ignored the tables groaning with good wines and game and fowl and, throwing venomous glances at Richard, began his usual plaints. Richard, he declared, had erected a castle along the frontier between Poitou and Anjou—but he had had the impudence to build his fortress on the wrong side of the border. His brother, young Henry demanded, must give up this stronghold, which clearly lay outside of his patrimony.

When Henry failed to show any particular concern over Richard's lone castle, the Young King flew into a temper, renewing his ceaseless pleas for power to match his titles. Beset by devouring jealousies, he was reduced to threats and ultimatums: Unless his father met his demands immediately, he would renounce those absurd empty titles; he would take the cross and go to Jerusalem, never to return; he would, he vowed in a burst of angry tears, take his own life.

Henry demonstrated a remarkable capacity for self-deception when it came to his eldest son. No matter how outrageous the youth's attempts at blackmail, he viewed him with a merciful eye, and on this occasion, to mollify his distraught son, he called together all three of his boys and asked Richard and Geoffrey to do homage to their older brother for their lands. While Geoffrey expressed willingness, Richard utterly refused even to consider the suggestion, saying that he held Aquitaine, not from his father, but as a gift from his mother. Not only had he been crowned duke with Eleanor's consent, but three years earlier, she had succumbed to Henry's pressure and ceded him the duchy; furthermore, he had already done homage for it to the king of France, the lawful overlord of the dukes of Aquitaine. Shaking with cold fury, he went on to bluntly inform his father what he thought of his mother's imprisonment. As for his older brother, if he wanted land, let him go out and fight for it. With that, Richard turned on his heel and strode out, "leaving nothing behind save threats and defiance." It is impossible to say which enraged Henry more, his son's defiance or his bringing up the subject of the queen, but in a passion, he turned to the Young King and gave him permission to "curb Richard's pride."

Young Henry, accompanied by Geoffrey, rode into Poitou in early 1183, where he ostentatiously joined those very discontented barons whom Richard had been fighting for the past eight years. Within a few weeks, it was plain to Henry that he had made a serious mistake; the rivalry between his sons had somehow escalated into a full-scale revolt, which now included Philip Augustus, the duke of Burgundy, and the count of Toulouse. Quick to perceive that unless he rescued Richard, Aquitaine would be lost, Henry himself went to Limoges in February to reason with his heir. Arriving before the walls of the city, he was greeted by a shower of arrows, one of them, to his horror, piercing his cloak. That evening young Henry paid a call on his father to explain that the arrow had been an accident, the random shot of a trigger-happy burgher. Nevertheless, nothing about the young man's manner inspired Henry's confidence. Dressed in his coat of mail, he refused either to lay aside his arms or to sit down and dine with his father. Eager to be off, he swore that he would persuade the rebel barons to submit to the king, and if he could not, he would leave them to their own devices and rejoin his father. Once back in Limoges, however, he urged the rebels to begin fortifying their city against the king's attack. When Henry saw them furiously digging moats and tearing down churches for stones to feed their catapults, he wearily rode up to the city walls a second time to plead with young Henry and Geoffrey. Once again he was greeted with arrows, this time very nearly taking his life; only the sudden rearing of his horse caught the arrow that would have pierced his chest. After this ominous incident, the Young King again came to Henry's tent with apologies and assurances of his fidelity, this time, as if to dispel suspicion, giving Henry his armor and remaining for several days. While he was keeping the old king occupied, however, Geoffrey was leading a band of mercenaries on a plundering expedition in the neighborhood, looting monasteries and stealing altar vessels.

The Young King's behavior at Limoges revolted his contemporaries. "War was in his heart," observed Walter Map, who went on to term him a parricide who lusted for his father's death. "Where is your filial affection?" demanded Peter of Blois. "Where is your reverence? Where is the law of nature? Where your fear of God?" It was said that the Young King, at twenty-eight, had fulfilled Merlin's prophecy of him: "The lynx, penetrating all places, will strive for destruction of his own race."

While Henry was occupied with the siege of Limoges, a mood of madness seemed to take possession of his son, who fitfully careened about the Limousin like an overgrown adolescent delinquent. Bored with the fighting, he looked for means to enhance his funds, since Henry had cut off his allowance. Toward the end of May 1183, he wandered south with William Marshal and a band of mercenaries, plundering and spreading terror throughout the countryside. In early June, they scaled the rocky heights of Rocamadour, that famous shrine in the Dordogne where pilgrims had long flocked to gaze upon the great iron sword of Roland. Young Henry grew reckless: If his father insisted upon keeping him a starveling, then he would find other means of succor. To the amazement of the pilgrims who had climbed up the steep and narrow steps to the shrine, the Young King and his rowdies looted the altar, stuffed their bags with treasure, and rode off in the burning June heat. Before they had traveled more than a few miles, however, the Young King complained of feeling ill, and they were forced to turn into the village of Martel, where they took lodgings in the house of a burgher, Étienne Fabri. There the Young King was seized by fever and dysentery, that "flux of the bowels" that accounted for so many deaths in the twelfth century. As his condition worsened, a messenger was sent to fetch the king.

Henry's advisers, remembering the arrows before the walls of Limoges, adamantly opposed any such trip. He should send a physician or money, but he should not expose himself to possible treachery. In the face of his son's bizarre behavior of late, Henry reluctantly agreed, and the messenger returned to Martel with a precious sapphire ring that the king had inherited from Henry I. On Saturday, June 11, the dying Young King ordered a bed of ashes spread on the floor. Naked, he prostrated himself on the ashes and had bare stones laid at his head and feet. It was late afternoon when he died. Since none of his companions felt eager to face the king, a monk from Grandmont was sent to tell him of the death. He found Henry near Limoges, taking refuge from the afternoon heat in a peasant's cottage.

"What news have you?" the king asked calmly.

"I am not a bearer of good news," said the monk.

Dismissing those who had crowded into the hut to hear the latest reports, the king interrogated the monk for every detail of his son's last days, and then when there was no more to learn, he "threw himself upon the ground and greatly bewailed his son."

Soon after, Henry sent Thomas Agnellus, the archdeacon of Wells, to inform the queen. Arriving at Salisbury, Agnellus was surprised to learn that Eleanor already knew of her son's death. Their interview provides one of the few clues to Eleanor's life in detention, and only now does it become obvious that prison walls did not prevent her from keeping abreast of the world's news. In all probability she received information from sympathetic jailers and informers, although obviously this was not a fact that she wished to advertise. In a speech that reads as if it had been well rehearsed, she explained to the archdeacon that she had been notified of young Henry's passing in a dream. He had appeared to her wearing two crowns, one the crown he had worn at his coronation, the other a band of pure light that shone with the incomparable brightness of the Holy Grail. She asked Agnellus, "What other meaning than eternal bliss can be ascribed to a crown with no beginning and no end? And what can such brightness signify if not the wonder of everlasting joy?" Solemnly, tactfully, she sent the archdeacon on his way praising her "great discernment," "strength and equanimity," and her clairvoyance.

The Young King's untimely death placed Eleanor's *preux chevalier*, her valorous Richard, as heir to the throne of England, at once upsetting twenty-five years of dynastic planning and causing enormous apprehension for all concerned. Obviously, the Plantagenet inheritance must now be redistributed, but exactly how the king intended to arrange matters was a question that Eleanor must have pondered with some anxiety. She had not long to wait for an answer. Three months after young

Henry's death, the king summoned his three remaining sons to Angers, where he ordered Richard to surrender Aquitaine to his youngest brother and, at the same time, said absolutely nothing about making him heir to young Henry's patrimony. This unexpected move staggered Eleanor no less than it did Richard. It was clear to her that Henry meant to disinherit her son. What other meaning could she read into his order, except that John, his darling now, was to have not only England, Normandy, Anjou, and Maine but Aquitaine as well? She could not have helped but look upon Henry's decision as another expression of his hatred for her; he had destroyed her, and now he would destroy the person she loved best. Clearly another bitter power struggle loomed ahead, only this time, Eleanor, a captive, was in no position to fight. At the same time, however, she realized that Richard was an adult capable of waging his own battles. He had left Angers without a word, and after riding back to Poitou, he had sent his father a message. Under no circumstances would he yield his land to anyone so long as he lived. For the time being, then, the matter rested there uneasily.

One of her dead son's last requests had been that Henry show mercy to the queen. Whether or not as a result of this, Eleanor suddenly found the restrictions upon her begin to slacken. In 1184, she received permission to leave Salisbury and travel through her dower lands, a strange order indeed, for as far as she knew, she no longer possessed any dower lands. Soon, however, she understood that Henry, who never did anything without a reason, was using her as a pawn in his own political games. Soon after young Henry's death, he had encountered trouble from Philip Augustus, who demanded that the widowed Marguerite's dower—the Vexin and certain manors in England—be returned to the Franks; Henry had countered by brazenly asserting that these lands had already been bestowed upon the queen, and now, to prove his point, he wished Eleanor to make a tour of "her dower."

After April 1184, her name begins to figure more frequently in the pipe rolls. Apparently, her household had been considerably enlarged, because there are payments for expenses to her clerk, Jordan. Between Easter and Saint John's Day—April 1 to June 24—thirty-four pounds fourteen shillings were paid for her allowance. We know that she spent Easter at Thomas Becket's former manor of Berkhampstead, and then, as if determined to revisit other sites of strong memories, she visited Woodstock; in June, she joined her daughter Matilda and the duke of Saxony at Winchester, where Matilda delivered another child, and in July, the party moved on to Berkhampstead for the remainder of the summer. Reveling in her freedom, Eleanor spent liberally on clothes and wine, and if she was forced to tolerate the presence of one of Henry's mistresses, one can safely assume that she was long past caring: "For clothes and hoods and cloaks and for the trimming for 2 capes of samite and for the clothes of the Queen and of Bellebelle, for the King's use, 55 pounds, 17s." It is possible that Bellebelle may have been Eleanor's maid, but if so, she hardly would have been styled "for the King's use." Although Henry had released the queen from solitary confinement, there was no question of his accepting her back into his affections or totally restoring her freedom of movement. The rules were made quite clear. She was permitted a limited degree of freedom at his pleasure, but, like Bellebelle and Alais Capet, whom he kept at Winchester, she existed solely for the king's use, and as his property, he would deploy her as he saw fit. Perhaps to Henry's surprise, old age had not warped her faculties, and if anything ten years at Salisbury seemed to have instilled in her those feminine traits that she had sorely lacked during her younger years—subservience and reasonability. As he soon discovered, however, there were limits.

On November 30, the court convened at Westminster. It was both a meeting of the king's council as well as a family reunion. Matilda and her family were there, and after a decade, Eleanor was able to see her sons again. The occasion was not, however, one of unalloyed rejoicing. Shortly, it became clear that both she and the boys had been assigned roles to play, and moreover, they were expected to perform according to Henry's directions. Ordered to attend a council meeting, she was led to a place of honor, thus signifying to the assembled barons that she had once again taken her legitimate place in the royal family. That made clear, John and Geoffrey, who had spent the autumn burning towns in Poitou, and Richard, who had retaliated by raiding Brittany, were called forward to forgive one another and make peace. These public gestures of reconciliation completed to Henry's satisfaction, the court moved on to Windsor for Christmas. No expense had been spared to make the holiday special, and the pipe rolls are full of entries recording purchases of wine, spices, wax, cattle, furs, and "entertaining trifles suitable for feasts." The fragile picture of the harmonious Plantagenets presented at Westminster did not withstand the journey to Windsor, for now Henry asked Eleanor to endorse his new disposition of the empire. She refused. Ten years of imprisonment had not stripped her of stubbornness, nor her dislike of John, a young man who had little to recommend him as far as she was concerned. The conclave broke up in a flurry of indecision and bitter feelings.

The year 1185 opened with Richard's return to Poitou and Geoffrey's dispatch to Normandy to assume control of the duchy, an astounding move on Henry's part and one that suggested to Eleanor that he contemplated making Geoffrey his heir. That winter, Eleanor stayed with Matilda and her family in England, where she watched developments with an anxious eye. The elevation of nineteen-year-old John continued when Henry knighted him in March and sent him off to assume the throne of Ireland. From the day of his landing, he demonstrated his total and utter irresponsibility. Greeted at Waterford by the Irish chieftains, John and his friends had burst into derisive laughter at the sight of the Irish in their long beards and native costumes. Not only had he pulled their beards and mocked them, he snatched lands and castles from English colonists and awarded them to his favorites, in one stroke alienating both natives and colonists before a week had passed. Even the Young King, with all his faults, would never have behaved so stupidly.

Meanwhile, on the Continent, Richard tried to make sense of his father's puzzling actions. It seemed certain that Henry's advancement of John and his appointment of Geoffrey as custos of Normandy foreboded his own downfall in one way or another. Actually, he did not really care if Henry passed over him in favor of Geoffrey or John, but the possible loss of Aquitaine, his home, was more than he could bear to consider. Arming his castles, he launched an attack on Geoffrey and, according to Hovedon, took his brother prisoner.

Those who cast their eyes to the future in search of auguries agreed that the world might gird itself for evil days. The previous year, the astrologers had unanimously forecast "slaughter by the sword, shipwrecks, scanty vintage, universal carnage, the fall of mankind and the sudden ruin of the world with mighty winds which shall destroy cities and towns." Like most visions of holocaust, little of this happened, but in April of 1185, "a mighty earthquake was heard throughout nearly the whole of England, such as had not been heard in that land since the beginning of the world." Whether Eleanor suffered hardship as a result we do not know, but it was recorded that Lincoln Cathedral was demolished and many houses destroyed. Undeterred by natural disasters, Henry crossed the Channel on the day after the quake to confront his warring sons. Apparently, his initial effort to reduce Richard to a state of obedience proved unsuccessful, because two weeks later, he was forced to devise some stronger means of persuasion. On his orders, Eleanor was brought to Normandy in late April, and shortly after her arrival at Bayeux, "the king immediately ordered his son Richard to give up Poitou, with its appurtenances, without delay to Queen Eleanor because it was her inheritance." Furthermore, if Richard failed to comply, then Eleanor would be placed at the head of an army to take Poitou away from him by force. Eleanor could only have blinked at this bizarre proposal. Obviously, Henry had no intention of sending her back to that proverbially faithless province with an army. At sixty-two, however, she had grown adept at playing Henry's games, especially when there was nothing to lose. On her advice, Richard surrendered the province to his mother's representatives and returned to his father's court in Normandy. "And then," says a chronicler, "he remained with his father like a tamed son."

Eleanor remained on the Continent until the spring of 1186. The restoration of her queenly dignity still extremely precarious, she appears to have emulated the obedience she advised Richard to follow. Docile, she traveled with the king, keeping her eyes and ears open but her lips closed. From her vantage point, she had ample opportunity to form her own conclusions about many subjects, and one of these would surely have been the new king of the Franks. It was apparent that the prince for whom Louis had waited nearly three decades owed nothing to his father; no one would ever call Dieu-Donné "more simple-minded than is becoming to a prince." Even at fifteen, when he had assumed the throne, he had worn his toughness like an ominous challenge to the Plantagenets. He had none of the charisma, none of the humor and grace, that marked even the least of Eleanor's sons. In adolescence he had been ill-kempt, nervous, and subject to sickly fears and hallucinations; his intellectual gifts were modest—he cared so little for books that he failed to learn Latin—but, nevertheless, he owned a kind of keen practical intelligence. At twenty, he was clever, humorless, dogmatic, and coldly calculating. Obsessed by the dream of destroying Plantagenet rule on the Continent, he had already discovered that his most powerful allies against Henry Plantagenet were Henry's own sons. "I wonder," he had once mused idly to a courtier, "if it might ever please God to grant that I, or some heir of mine, should restore the kingdom to what it was in Charlemagne's time?"

Such daydreams made Eleanor nervous. Although she could find little to like or trust about the bloodless Philip, it was apparent that her sons did not feel the same way. The Young King had preferred to spend his time in Paris, and now Geoffrey was following in his footsteps. During the year that Eleanor stayed on the Continent, Geoffrey lived with Philip Augustus at the Cité Palace, as close, some said, as a blood brother. Dissatisfied with his inheritance of Brittany, he stood now on this side of the Franco-Norman border, now on that, wavering between loyalty to his father and loyalty to Philip, who had made him seneschal of France. William of Newburgh claimed that "while engaged in active service with the King of France, he made great efforts to annoy his father." The conspiracy they were hatching—an invasion of Normandy—Eleanor could only guess at. Leaving Geoffrey to his scheming, she returned to England with Henry on April 27, 1186. Three months later, on August 19, Geoffrey and his horse were thrown to the ground in a tournament at Paris. When he refused to yield to the knights who had attacked him, "he was so trodden by the hoofs of the horses and so severely shaken by the blows that he shortly finished life." His body was laid on the high altar of Notre Dame, and "there he was buried with but few regrets from his father, to whom he had been an unfaithful son, but with sore grief to the French." Overcome, Philip Augustus had to be forcibly restrained from throwing himself into the tomb, and the Countess Marie of Champagne, who was present at the requiem, demonstrated her abiding affection for her half brother by establishing a Mass for the repose of his soul.

Of the five male children Eleanor had born to her second husband with such relief and pride, only two remained.

In the autumn of 1187 a wave of consternation rippled throughout Europe. Every appalling portent uttered by the astrologers suddenly seemed to be materializing, not in the local spots where most had expected them but far away, in Outremer: Saladin, the most terrible Saracen of all, had wrenched Jerusalem from Christian hands; the citizens had been massacred and the king of Jerusalem taken captive; and, worst of all, the True Cross and the tomb of Christ had fallen into the hands of "infidel dogs." The news had not been entirely unexpected by Eleanor, for in early 1185, Heraclius, the patriarch of Jerusalem, had visited England to warn of approaching disaster and to beg Henry to defend the Holy Land as king of Jerusalem. At the time, Henry had refused to even consider such a notion. Crusades were for the young and romantic, and instead, he had offered Heraclius fifty thousand marks, an offer that the patriarch had literally spat upon with contempt. Now the fever for crusading that had possessed Eleanor and Louis in the 1150s began to envelop the conscience of Christendom once more. The fall of Edessa, however, was as nothing compared to the idea of Jerusalem itself in the hands of Saladin. Young gallants in every castle and village square talked about taking the cross; King William of Sicily, Joanna Plantagenet's husband, put on sackcloth and retired to mourn; Pope Urban III died, from grief some said. And Richard Plantagenet, receiving the news late one afternoon in early November, took the cross the next morning near Tours.

When Henry heard of his son's action, he responded with a grief he had shown only upon the deaths of Becket and the Young King; he withdrew to his chamber and suspended all business for four days. At fifty-four, surely an age at which a man might expect peace, crises threatened him on every side. After siring a fine brood of boys, he was left with an eldest son whom he disliked, a boy as obstinate and head-strong as his wife; but even though he privately accepted Richard as his heir, he would not give him the pleasure of recognizing him as such publicly. For how much trouble had he not reaped by prematurely declaring his intention to the Young King? He had meant to discipline Richard by keeping him uncertain, but now the boy had foolishly run off and taken the cross. Not only was there Richard with whom he must contend but Philip Augustus with his embarrassing questions as well. How many times had he not met the Capetian boy under the elm at Gisors only to hear him complain of his half sisters Marguerite and Alais and their dowers? Why, the young Capetian asked repeatedly, was Alais still a maiden at the age of twenty-seven? When would her marriage to Richard take place? Can a man under suspicion of dis-honoring a woman tell her kin that they lie, especially when they are not lying? Loath to give up his mistress, he had promised that the girl would be married soon, without of course committing himself to a defi-nite date. Alais and the custody of the Vexin, these were needles with which Philip Augustus regularly prodded him.

On January 22, 1188, Henry and Philip drew up their retinues under the elm once more. They had scarcely settled down to business, those wearying topics of Alais and the Vexin, when the archbishop of Tyre arrived, having lately traveled across the Mediterranean and over the Alps for the express purpose of stirring Europe to action. By chance he found his way to the elm of Gisors, and so powerful were his exhorta-tions that within a day both Henry and Philip Augustus had taken the cross. It was, people said, a miracle. To others, Eleanor perhaps, Henry's sudden reversal suggested less lofty motives. A Crusade would, at the very least, distract Philip from his perennial harping about Alais; it would rid Henry of his two main irritants, his son and Louis Capet's son; and in the end, there might be a way of wriggling out of his Cru-sader's vow before the expedition set out, some fifteen months hence.

Back in England in 1188, Henry abruptly sent Eleanor into close con-finement again at either Winchester or Salisbury while he solaced him-self with Alais Capet and tried to forget Philip's persistent attempts to harass him. By July, however, it was clear that Philip could be restrained by no other means than force. Despite Henry's age, corpulence, and increasing ill health, he resolved to tolerate the impudent king of the Franks no longer, even blaspheming before his horrified prelates, "Why should I worship Christ? Why should I deign to honour Him who takes my earthly honour and allows me to be ignominiously confounded by a mere boy?" On August 16, he met with the "mere boy" under the Gisors elm, and for three days listened to Philip's demands for the retrocession of the Vexin and the marriage of his aging sister. Henry, sitting in the shade, hardly bothered to give his attention. In his opinion, the Norman Vexin rightfully belonged to him. To treat it as the dower of a Capetian bride was wholly beside the point. To Philip, however, the Vexin and Alais were merely proofs of Henry's bad faith. At some undetermined point in the negotiations, the Franks, who had been sweltering on the sunny side of the elm, suddenly rushed at Henry's entourage with drawn swords, sending the English to the shelter of the nearby castle. Infuriated, Philip ordered the elm cut down so that no parley might ever take place there again with the treacherous Plantagenets. Seeing the mutilated stump, Henry calmly declared war, but although subsequently he plunged into France to ravage a few castles near Mantes, in truth he had no appetite for fighting.

During the winter of 1188–89, Henry, ill and depressed, stayed at Le Mans in the castle where he had been born. He had developed an anal fistula, and by March it had grown badly abcessed. With him were his illegitimate son, Geoffrey, William Marshal, and perhaps, John. Richard he preferred not to think about. When he had last met with Philip in November, he had been shocked to see Richard among the retinue of the Capetian king. In the hearing of the courtiers, Richard had asked Henry to recognize him as his heir. Henry had refused. "Now," cried Richard, "at last I believe what heretofore has seemed incredible!" And throwing himself on his knees before Dieu-Donné, he had done homage for all the lands to which he claimed inheritance and had sworn fealty to him as his liege man. Henry's thirty-one-year-old son had ridden away with Philip, and soon curious reports were drifting back to Le Mans: The Capetian so honored his son that every day they ate from the same dish and at night they slept in the same bed. Such brotherhood was too remarkable not to be widely commented upon; gossip was rife, and people whispered of the sin of Sodom. Henry, ignoring the sexual innuendoes, mourned because he wanted his son back.

After a series of fruitless conferences with Philip in the spring of 1189, Henry returned to Le Mans, even though his bishops and barons warned him that Philip and Richard were leading an army through Maine, taking every castle in their path. It was not until Sunday, June 11, when Philip's army appeared before the walls of Le Mans, that he was forced to acknowledge the danger. To avoid a battle, Henry ordered one of the suburbs set afire in the hope that he could drive the French away. Suddenly, however, the wind changed, and flames began to suck the walls of the city. In the blaze that followed, the French poured through the gates, while Henry had no choice but to rally his seven hundred knights and flee. On a hill two miles north of the city, he drew rein and turned for a last look at the inferno raging in his birthplace. The bitterness poured out. "O God," he cried, "Thou hast vilely taken away the city I loved best on earth, the city where I was born and bred, the city where my father is buried. I will pay Thee back as best I can. I will rob Thee of the thing Thou lovest best in me, my soul!" According to Gerald of Wales, he said a great deal more, which the chronicler thought safer not to record.

With Philip and Richard hard on his heels, he pressed furiously north, while William Marshal covered his retreat. Out of a cloud of dust came the vanguard of the French army, with Richard in the lead. Marshal turned and leveled his lance.

"By God's legs, Marshal," shouted Richard in his only recorded instance of fear, "do not kill me. I wear no hauberk."

"May the Devil kill you," cried Marshal, "for I will not." With that, he plunged his lance into Richard's horse.

The day was extremely hot, the road narrow, the retreat confused, and many of Henry's knights died from heat and fatigue or fell prostrate along the roadside. His advisers counseled him to strike northward to the heart of Normandy, where he could find reinforcements for his army or send to England for help. Although he agreed to send his troops on to Alençon, he himself turned south into Anjou. For two weeks he traversed the backroads that he knew so well, twisting and turning over nearly two hundred miles of trails, somehow evading Philip's army, which had overrun the province. The killing ride combined with the heat opened his wound, and by the time he reached his great fortress of Chinon, the poison in his blood had virtually robbed him of the use of his legs, and he could neither sit nor stand comfortably. Aware that the roads were infested with Franks, that castle after castle had fallen to them, he clung feebly to Geoffrey and William Marshal. Somehow, in the melee, he had lost his youngest son. Where was John?

At dawn on the morning of Monday, July 3, Philip's soldiers set up their scaling ladders against the walls of Tours, and by midmorning, the city had fallen. The following day, he summoned Henry to a conference at Ballan, a few miles southwest of the captured city. Racked by intense pain, Henry nevertheless set out from Chinon with William Marshal and a small party of knights to meet his victorious enemy. When they reached the house of the Knights Templar in Ballan, he was so exhausted that he fell upon a cot. "Marshal, sweet gentle sir," Henry said, "a cruel pain has seized my toes and feet and is piercing my legs. My whole body is on fire." Some of his knights rode off to the conference site to inform Philip that the king was ill, but Richard warned that his father was feigning; no doubt he had another trick up his sleeve. Stung when he learned of his son's taunt, Henry made a supreme effort to rise and ordered his knights to seat him on his horse.

It was a clear sultry day, the sky cloudless and the air still. As Henry advanced toward Philip and Richard, a clap of thunder was heard and then another. At the sight of Henry's ashen face, Philip, moved to pity, hurriedly ordered a cloak to be folded and placed on the ground so that Henry might sit. He had not come to sit, Henry replied, but to learn the price he must pay for peace. Remaining on his horse, his men holding him upright, he listened as the humiliating terms were read. He was to do homage to the king of France for all his Continental possessions. He was to place himself wholly at Philip's will and pay an indemnity of twenty thousand marks. He must give up Alais Capet so that Richard might marry her on his return from Jerusalem. He must agree to Richard receiving the fealty of his father's subjects on both sides of the sea as lawful heir to the Plantagenet lands. As a pledge of his good faith, he must surrender three major castles in Anjou or the Vexin, and to prevent him from taking revenge on any of his barons who had deserted to the Frankish camp, it was stipulated that they would not return to the king's service until a month before the start of the Crusade.

Rolls of thunder rent the afternoon sky as Henry murmured his assent and motioned his knights for departure. Philip stopped him. He must give his son the kiss of peace. As Richard advanced for the embrace, Henry drew back and whispered fiercely, "God grant that I may not die until I have had a fitting revenge on you."

An ailing lion savaged by jackals, he was carried back to Chinon on a litter, cursing the day he was born and calling down Heaven's wrath on his son. In his fortress high above the Vienne, physicians were summoned, but the king, groaning on his couch, lay far beyond the reach of their potions. He had left behind one of his men, Roger Malchael, to secure from Philip a list of those who had deserted him and who were to be exempt from punishment. When Roger returned with the parchment and began to read, his voice suddenly failed. "Sire, may Jesus Christ help me!" he exclaimed. "The first name written here is Count John, your son."

The king gave an anguished cry. "Is it true that John, my heart, John whom I loved more than all my sons and for whose sake I have suffered all these evils, has forsaken me?" Turning his face to the wall, he motioned Roger away. "Say no more. Now let the rest go as it will. I care no more for myself nor for aught in this world."

The will to live had faded. He lapsed into delirium, sometimes appearing to sleep, occasionally breaking into wild moans of grief and pain. His son Geoffrey cradled his head and fanned away the flies. In the final hours, Henry was heard to cry over and over, "Shame, shame on a vanquished king." Crying shame, he died on Thursday, the sixth of July, 1189, in the thirty-fifth year of his reign.

Because servants had ransacked the corpse for clothes and jewels, his friends had difficulty laying out the king's body properly, and they collected makeshift trappings from wherever they could: a ring for his finger, an ersatz scepter for his hand, and for his crown a band of tattered gold embroidery donated by an obliging woman. The next morning, his body was borne on the shoulders of his few remaining faithful barons, down from the castle on the rock of Chinon, across a viaduct above the swampy meadows, and then northward along the left bank of the Vienne to the abbey church of Fontevrault, where the veiled sisters gathered to keep watch over the bier. William Marshal had sent word to Richard, but not until nightfall did he finally appear, slipping quietly into the church to stand and gaze down at his father. "One could not tell from his expression whether he felt joy or sorrow, grief, anger, or satisfaction." Then he knelt to pray, remaining on his knees "scarcely longer than the space of a Paternoster." At that moment, "blood began to flow from the dead king's nostrils and ceased not so long as his son remained there." It was, a chronicler said, "as if his spirit were moved with indignation," the fiery king still venting his famous Angevin temper from beyond God's other door.

In July of 1189, Eleanor of Aquitaine was sixty-seven years old. She had been her husband's prisoner for sixteen years.

Autumn and After

When William Marshal arrived at Winchester in mid-July with instructions to unlock Eleanor's prison gates, he found the lady already at
liberty, no one having dared detain her a single hour after news of the
king's death had reached England. To William's astonishment, the
sixty-seven-year-old woman advanced to greet him with all the grace
and civility he remembered from her court in Poitiers. Even though the
years that should have been filled with contentment and enjoyment of
the honors due great queens had been stolen from her, she had somehow managed to preserve herself, physically as well as mentally. If
Marshal had anticipated a frail, doddering relic warped with bitterness
and grief, he did not find it. It seemed as if she had used her enforced
tranquility to purge her spirit of imprudence and self-indulgence, to
broaden her understanding of politics and sharpen her instincts about
the affairs of humankind. For sixteen years she had looked deeply into
her soul to glean eternal truths, and now that her hour of liberation had
come, she was ready.

William carried with him letters from Richard giving his mother full
command of the realm until he had settled his affairs in Normandy and
would be able to join her. But Eleanor, perhaps using that clairvoyance
credited her by the archdeacon of Wells, had already taken the first
steps toward assumption of the regency, and to Winchester subjects
were flocking, eager to pay homage at the court of "Eleanor, by the
grace of God, Queen of England." After Marshal's arrival, she immediately gathered up her household and set off for London, where she convened her court at Westminster and summoned the barons and prelates
of the realm to make their oaths of allegiance to the new king. All the
while, she evidently felt that this act was not sufficient to secure for her
son the love of the English. Although born in Oxford, he had never considered his birthplace any more than an easily rectified accident. Since

childhood, he had made only brief visits to the island; he neither spoke English nor did he have more than a vague familiarity with the terrain of the kingdom. Aquitaine was his home, and from infancy Eleanor had been instrumental in directing her heir's eyes away from the island kingdom, the feudal prerogative of her eldest son, and toward her own provinces, where one day he would be master. Circumstances having overturned a lifetime of careful planning, she now saw that the situation must be remedied as quickly as possible. At this late date there was, obviously, little that she might do to instill in her son a belated affection for England, but she could do something to promote the island's enthusiasm for the foreigner whom they called "Richard the Poitevin."

With a sagacity that recalls her introduction of Richard to her southern vassals in the late sixties, she abandoned London after a few days in favor of a tour of England, "moving her royal court from city to city and from castle to castle, just as she thought proper." There is no doubt that the sight of the Eagle in her new incarnation helped to reassure the English and, to a great extent, dulled the memories of those who a few weeks earlier had been shaking their heads in alarm over the unnatural conduct of King Henry's disobedient son. As Eleanor well knew, it would take more than a royal *chevauchée* to blot out fifteen years of family brawling and implant in her subjects' minds the idea that a new reign was beginning. In a frank appeal for popularity, she sent messengers to every county in England ordering that all captives be liberated from prison because "she had learnt by experience that imprisonment is distasteful to mankind and that it is a most delightful refreshment to the spirits to be liberated therefrom." Opening the dungeons "for the good of King Henry's soul," surely a barely veiled sarcasm, she issued a general pardon to all those who had trespassed against Henry's forest laws, who had been imprisoned "by the will of the king or his justiciar," and to those who had been jailed for a half dozen other reasons, the principal condition of release being a promise to support the new government in preserving the peace. Within days, the smallest village in the realm teemed with liberated jailbirds singing the praises of the liberal Richard Plantagenet. Only William of Newburgh had an acid word to say about this: "At that time the gaols were crowded with criminals awaiting trial or punishment but through Richard's clemency these pests came forth from prison, perhaps to become bolder thieves in the future."

But Eleanor's largesse extended beyond the kingdom's malefactors. Henry had been in the habit of stabling his horses in abbeys, the better to undertake his lightning dashes around the country, but a practice that caused no little inconvenience and expense to the chapters; Eleanor promptly relieved the clergy of this burden. She also made plans to introduce a new standard coinage that would be valid anywhere in England, as well as a series of uniform weights and measures for corn, liquids, and lengths of cloth. Roger of Wendover records that "she arranged matters in the kingdom according to her own pleasure and nobles were instructed to obey her in every respect." In these summer days, the chronicler adds, was fulfilled the prophecy of Merlin, "The Eagle of the broken covenant shall rejoice in her third nesting."

In a few short weeks, so thoroughly did Eleanor prepare the ground that when Richard dropped anchor at Portsmouth on August 13, his previous image as a parricide was quite forgotten in a tide of popular goodwill. In the midst of her journeying, Eleanor had not neglected preparations for his coronation. No doubt remembering those hectic days of December 1154 before her own hasty coronation, she determined to make Richard's an occasion the English would never forget. It was significant that, on Eleanor's advice, he was not crowned immediately. There was no need for haste; unlike every other king of England since the Norman Conquest, he had neither enemies nor rivals, and thanks to his mother's proclamations, he had made a host of new friends. So complete was his security that the next two weeks were spent in a leisurely progress, marked at every stop by scenes of rejoicing and cheering. Briefly, Richard and Eleanor stopped at Salisbury; at Marlborough to witness the wedding of John to Isabelle of Gloucester; at Windsor, where they greeted Richard's half brother, Geoffrey. On September 1, the royal party made a splendid entry into London, where, in Richard's honor, the streets had been cleaned and spread with fresh rushes and the house fronts festooned with tapestries and blossoms. The crowning was set for Sunday, September 3, an unlucky day according to the calendar, but Eleanor could not be bothered with superstition. With her superb sense of pageantry, she had devised a ceremony not easily forgotten, and in fact, the coronation of Richard Plantagenet would establish the procedure, still in use today, for crowning a monarch of England. Through the nave of Westminster Abbey wound the royal procession: the taper bearers and censers, the abbots and bishops, the officials bearing Richard's spurs, scepters, sword, bonnet, and royal vestments. And then came the tall figure of Richard himself, walking under a canopy of silk and and looking like a young god. At the high altar he took three formal oaths, swearing that he would honor the

Church and its decrees, grant justice to his subjects, and keep the laws and customs of the kingdom. After he had removed his robes and was dressed in the royal vestments. Archbishop Baldwin of Canterbury anointed him with the sacred oils and then lifted the crown from the altar and placed it upon his head. With a golden scepter in each hand and the crown on his head, the new king was led to the throne, and the abbey was filled with the sound of the *Te Deum*. Richard, duke of Aquitaine, had become Richard I of England. Three days of festivities followed, each state banquet as decorous as it was lavish, and the guests "feasted so splendidly that the wine flowed along the pavement and walls of the palace."

Eleanor had done her best to personally inaugurate her son's reign with memorable splendor, but despite her exertions to ingratiate her son with his subjects, she could not disguise the fact that Richard regarded the island as little more than a milk cow for the sustenance of his most important concern, the Crusade to rescue Jerusalem. His dilemma was clear. He had committed himself to a military expedition that would require enormous sums of money; at the same time, the royal treasury at Winchester, which had been quickly canvassed the moment he had arrived, proved to be virtually empty, and after the Saladin tithe that Henry had levied before his death, the pockets of the new king's subjects were equally empty. Unfortunately, Henry's levy for the Crusade had already been handed over to the Templars. Now, perhaps to Eleanor's astonishment, her son demonstrated an ingenious talent for extracting money where none seemingly existed. Two days after the coronation feasts had ended, he put up for sale everything that he owned—castles, towns, manors, lordships, public offices, favors of all kinds. Every sheriff in England found himself removed from office until such time as he could redeem his position with hard cash. William Longchamp, one of Richard's favorite attendants, paid three thousand pounds for the office of chancellor. Cities discovered that they might obtain new and more liberal charters in return for sizable payments. Monasteries whose privileges were abruptly revoked were able to buy them back for a consideration. When Abbot Samson of Bury Saint Edmunds offered five hundred marks, the assessed value, for the royal manor of Mildenhall, Richard had the temerity to reply, "My Lord Abbot, the amount you offer is absurd. Either you shall give me a thousand marks or you shall not have the manor." The chronicler goes on to note that Samson also paid Eleanor her queen's gold in the form of a golden cup worth one hundred marks, but that she returned the cup "on behalf of the soul of her Lord King Henry." Eleanor's attempts to ameliorate the effects of the great national auction did not prevent the entire business from degenerating into a most undignified and jocular spectacle. Suddenly nearly everything in the kingdom could be had, if the price was right, and even those who had taken Crusader's vows were able to find release. The king, people said, was most obliging in relieving all those whose money had been a burden, and Richard himself joked, "I would sell London itself if I could find a buyer."

Once the money began flowing in at a reassuring rate, Richard departed for the Continent; Eleanor, however, remained behind in a state of uneasiness. The popularity she had so energetically drummed up for him was already wearing thin as many dismayed subjects, reviewing objectively the new king's actions during the first four months of his reign, declared that he must be unbalanced. Contrary to their expectation that he would be a more liberal sovereign than his father, he had multiplied their taxes until the kingdom had been squeezed dry, and he had recklessly overturned Henry's government by firing experienced officials and giving their jobs to the highest bidders. No amount of public relations on Eleanor's part could stifle these denunciations, nor could she scotch the persistent rumor that Richard never intended to return. How did it happen that a king would sell his income-producing property? It was said that he planned to turn over the kingdom to John and return to Aquitaine. It was said that he would mount the throne of Jerusalem. And it was said that he suffered from some secret malady and would never live through the Crusade. His arrangements for the administration of England during his absence struck many as dubious, and even Eleanor, who could find little fault with her son, would have recognized that he had inherited little of her political acumen and none of Henry's knack for judging people's characters. As regents, he had appointed two fairly sober and experienced men: William de Mandeville, a trusted friend of his father's; and Bishop Hugh of Durham, a kinsman of the royal house and a man long experienced in politics, who nevertheless had been compelled to buy his appointment for ten thousand pounds. Unfortunately, de Mandeville died that autumn, and in his place Richard had substituted his chancellor, William Longchamp, a Norman making his first visit to England. Although Gerald of Wales's description makes Longchamp seem like a repulsive, misshapen dwarf, no amount of tact could disguise his physical infirmities. He was short, lame, and unprepossessing; he spoke no English and, further, had an aversion to the country. On the positive side, he was unscrupulous in defending his master's interests. Between the two regents, Richard left his mother as a balance wheel. Although some chroniclers and even historians of later periods have claimed that Eleanor was regent, this does not seem to have been the case. The most that can be said is that even though Richard gave her no formal appointment, he did regard her as an unofficial super-regent with full power to step in whenever circumstances warranted. Totally preoccupied with preparations for the Crusade, he must have felt that his mother, the most experienced sovereign in Europe, would guard his realm if the appointed officials failed in their duties.

In December, Richard kept his Christmas court in reasonable state at Bures in Normandy, but the minstrels, in whom he normally reveled, were missing. The talk was of ships and arbalests and the latest in military gadgetry. Having cut his teeth on Eleanor's stories of the disastrous Second Crusade, he was determined to avoid the errors of Louis Capet, whom he had come to regard as an idiot. He would make no such stupid mistake as bringing his army overland through enemy territory, planning instead to travel to the Holy Land by sea. Already along the coast of England, the great fleet was being readied, one hundred ships and fourteen busses, "vessels of vast use, wonderful speed, and great strength. The lead ship had three rudders, thirteen anchors, thirty oars, two sails and triple ropes of every kind; moveover it had everything that a ship can want." On board would be loaded the wealth of England translated into gold and silver, arms of all sorts, supplies of bacon, cheese, wine, flour, pepper, biscuits, wax, spiced meats, and syrups. No pilgrims or Amazons, no camp followers or troubadours, found their way into the ranks of Richard's army. The Third Crusade, a purely military expedition, would be governed by strict rules of conduct. "Whoever shall kill a man on ship-board," the king wrote, "shall be bound to the dead man and thrown into the sea. . . . If anyone shall be convicted of having drawn a knife, he shall lose his hand. . . . If any man shall curse, swear, or revile his fellows, he shall pay an ounce of silver for each offence."

In February 1190, Eleanor left behind the fog and darkness of the English winter and crossed to the Continent as a free woman for the first time in seventeen years. Her memory, stretching back nearly seven decades, now enabled her to sort the chaff from the wheat. The crusading fervor that had enveloped Europe in a white heat of religious emotion lacked the power to rouse her, and with a cynicism reminiscent of her late husband's, she saw the rescue of the Holy Land as a distraction from the important business of the Plantagenets. Let those who had nothing better to do fritter away their energies in Outremer; the real concern, as she saw it, was not Saladin but the preservation of the house of Plantagenet and especially the rock on which it had been built, England. In those months of early 1190, she detected a host of dangers threatening her house, both within and without. Perhaps at her insistence, a family council was held at Nonancourt in March to clarify the king's arrangements for England and to weatherproof the kingdom during his absence. Present at the meeting were her youngest son and Henry's bastard, Geoffrey, now archbishop of York, both of whom Richard required to take an oath that they would stay out of England for three years. His objective was fairly clear: to prevent two potential troublemakers from encroaching upon his royal prerogatives and to leave the regents a free hand in conducting the affairs of the kingdom. Eleanor did not, evidently, wholly agree with this policy, because soon afterward, she prevailed upon Richard to allow John's return, no doubt believing this the lesser of two evils.

To judge from the charters she signed that spring and early summer, the queen resided in Anjou and Normandy. During this time, Richard made a trip to Aquitaine, but Eleanor, curiously, did not accompany him, nor did she visit her homeland on her own, the betrayals of 1173 possibly having left an unconscious residue of distaste for the land of her forebears. Despite her cynicism for the Crusade, she must have felt a pride in her warrior son that made up for all the years of imprisonment and struggle on his behalf. Already Richard Plantagenet was being extolled as the hero of the century, a prince to whom no amount of praise could do adequate justice. His contemporaries, unable to compare him to any great personage of their own time, looked to the pantheon of heroes from the past; he had, they vowed, the valor of Alexander and Roland, the eloquence of Nestor, the prudence of Ulysses. "But why need we expend labour extolling so great a man? He needs no superfluous commendation. He was superior to all others."

The Third Crusade was not, of course, a project of Richard alone—the leadership was to be shared with Philip Augustus—but even before it departed, the Capetian had been shoved into the background. When the crusading host convened at Vézelay in the first days of July, it was Richard to whom the knights flocked for information and counsel, it was Richard who looked like a god in his mantle spangled with silver crescents and his cap of scarlet and gold, his Spanish stallion equipped with a gorgeous inlaid saddle and a bridle set with precious stones. Already people called him a lion, and perhaps on that field in Burgundy many remembered Bertran de Born's waspish *sirventès*, "Tell Sir Richard from me that he is a lion and King Philip seems to me a lamb."

Under the circumstances, it was not surprising that by the time the

Crusade set off on July 4—Richard bound for Marseille to meet his fleet, Philip heading over the Alps to Genoa—the king of the Franks had fallen into a bad humor. In recent months, he had grown increasingly hostile to Richard, a phenomenon that so puzzled their contemporaries that some put it down to the work of the devil. Bedfellows only a year earlier, they now sniped and snarled, their great affection failing to survive Henry's death. To Richard's dismay, Philip had insisted upon renewing his tiresome harangues about his half sister Alais. Now that Henry was dead, there was, of course, no reason for delay, and yet Richard seemed no more eager for the wedding than his father had been. A few weeks before departure, Philip had issued an ultimatum: Either Richard must marry Alais immediately or return her to her kin, along with her dower. Richard, however, proved as slippery as Henry in the matter of A s. Since women were forbidden to join the Crusade, he stalled Philip by promising that the marriage would take place on his return from the Holy Land. And with this, Philip had to be content.

Not without cause did Eleanor despise Alais Capet. When Louis's nine-year-old orphaned daughter had arrived at Poitiers in 1169, Eleanor had treated her as one of her own children, even going out of her way to love the child and polish her as a fit partner for her special son. Alais had been thirteen when Henry brought her, along with Eleanor and his other captives, to England in the summer of 1174, and somehow, soon after, he had seduced the girl. Eleanor did not know how that unnatural relationship started, but it affected her more deeply than Rosamond Clifford or any of Henry's other women. Even though her husband had made his court a brothel after she had left him, Eleanor could excuse the other women who shared his bed. Lowborn, they could be charitably forgiven for responding to the overtures of a mighty king. But apparently she could not excuse a royal princess. In her eyes, Alais must have willed the affair, and for that, Eleanor could never forgive her. She knew, too, that Alais had borne Henry a child, although it did not survive. For years, Alais must have eaten at her like a cankerworm, because one of her first acts after Henry's death had been to order her imprisonment. That a woman who had opened the dungeons of England because she knew the miseries of confinement firsthand would have decreed that selfsame fate for Alais Capet is an excellent measure of the intensity of her feelings.

The cries of Philip Augustus for Richard's marriage to Alais affected the queen as little as the birds chirping in the trees. As she knew and as she had made Richard understand, the shopworn Alais Capet was no longer marriageable, at least not to the king of England. Eleanor was not above advising Richard to lie when it was necessary, and so Philip had been pacified with promises of Alais's marriage at the conclusion of the Crusade. In the meantime, Eleanor determined to take the matter into her own hands. Her greatest anxiety since Henry's death was the question of the succession. Of the five sons she had borne, only two remained, lion-hearted Richard and light-minded John, and the insecurity resulting from that unalterable fact must have been overwhelming. At the age of thirty-two, Richard still had not wed; he had no direct heirs, and if he should perish in the Holy Land, what would become of the Plantagenet empire?

There were three possible aspirants to the crown, none of them acceptable to Eleanor: her grandson Arthur, a child born posthumously to Geoffrey, was only three years old, but both the boy and his mother, Constance, were loathed by the Plantagenets. The second possibility was Henry's illegitimate son, Geoffrey. Eleanor distrusted him, for despite his bastardy, she saw him as a possible pretender, and perhaps she had taken undue alarm over a report that he had placed a golden bowl on his head and called out in jest: "Is not this skull fit to wear a crown?" In order to discourage Geoffrey from any further thoughts in this direction, Eleanor reluctantly considered Henry's deathbed wish that his son become archbishop of York. Geoffrey, hotheaded and quarrelsome, was noted for neither learning nor piety and, as far as Eleanor was concerned, totally unqualified for the position of archbishop. Nevertheless, she decided to support his cause, because the taking of holy orders would render him ineligible for further mischief. The third candidate for the throne was her youngest son, a strange and self-centered boy in whom she had no confidence whatsoever. In fact, the idea of John on the throne of England was a possibility not to be contemplated without crying aloud. In view of these distressing alternatives, Eleanor determined that Richard must marry quickly and produce heirs of his own. Quite apart from her wish to secure the succession, there was another special reason for her great concern over Richard's marriage. Although he had always been close to her and even though he had been reared in a feminine court where women were to be respected, he did not like the female sex. Not only was he averse to marrying Alais because she had been his father's mistress, he objected to marrying any woman. It would be interesting to know how this knowledge initially affected Eleanor, but surely it must have caused her some pain. For good or ill, she had molded him into a beautiful, glorious warrior, the Coeur de Lion, whose name would still be synonymous with valor eight centuries later. The only flaw in her planning was that her son was a homosexual.

Despite the delicate nature of the subject, the question of Richard's homosexuality seems to rest in the area of certainty rather than of probability. While contemporary historians were unwilling to discuss the matter at any length, they made repeated innuendoes about his unnatural appetites while at the same time making the nature of their charges abundantly clear. Not only was it backstairs gossip in every court in Europe, but Richard himself confessed to homosexual affairs on two occasions. Certainly, Philip Augustus, who may have been one of his partners, understood that Richard felt no inclination to marry Alais or any other woman. Whatever the dismay or grief Eleanor may have felt about this matter, in the end she came to view it as an irrelevancy. Richard's unconventional sexual habits did not negate his primary duty as king: to marry and sire a male heir. She knew that he slept with women occasionally, because he had an illegitimate child from a woman of Cognac, a son then about five years old who had been named Philip in honor of his closest friend.

In those months between Henry's death and the departure of the Crusade, Eleanor brought Richard to terms with the necessity of marrying and marrying quickly. Scanning the royal houses of Europe for a possible bride, one who would not be disqualified by consanguinity, Eleanor was careful to take Richard's preferences into consideration. It seemed that some years earlier he had briefly made the acquaintance of the daughter of King Sancho of Navarre. While attending a tournament at Pamplona in the company of the king's son, one of his favorite jousting companions, Richard had even addressed some passionate verse to the Princess Berengaria. This was enough for Eleanor. Barely had the Crusade left Vézelay than she stored Alais Capet, securely guarded, in Rouen and began a *chevauchée* into the deep south, traveling either to Bordeaux or, according to some accounts, as far as Navarre to fetch the princess. On meeting Berengaria, the queen must have realized that this was not a woman to reverse Richard's history of sexual deviation. There was no fault to be found with her; she was attractive enough, and even though the chroniclers called her "more learned than beautiful," they also described her as "a prudent maid, a gentle lady, virtuous and fair, neither false nor double-tongued." But Berengaria, for all her admirable virtues, lacked spirit. Unlike Eleanor, she was a passive female who would allow herself to be buffeted by the winds of circumstance and never raise a finger in her own behalf. No doubt overawed at the prospect of becoming Coeur de Lion's queen, she delivered herself into Eleanor's hands like a lamb being carried to slaughter.

The passage of time pressed heavily upon the queen's shoulders. She had no intention of waiting until the Crusade had returned for Richard to be married—the risks of death in the Holy Land were all too familiar to her—and before Christmas, with Berengaria in tow, she was already on the road, hastening to overtake the army. The prospect of a winter journey through the Alps would have daunted the hardiest knight, but Eleanor, like Henry, refused to wait for weather. Fortunately for her purposes, the combined armies of Richard and Philip were wintering at Messina in Sicily, and it was there that the queen hoped to present her son with a bride, although one receives the impression that she would have followed Richard to the gates of Jerusalem if necessary. For several months her exact whereabouts are unrecorded, but next she comes to light at Lodi, near Milan, and then it is possible to trace her steps down the western side of the Italian boot from Pisa to Naples and finally to Brindisi, where one of Richard's ships waited to bring her safely to Messina. The terrain was not unfamiliar; forty years earlier, a Crusader herself, she had come to Brindisi, sick in mind and body, to collect a shipwrecked husband. It was in these lands that she had learned of Raymond of Antioch's death and here that she had laid her hopes in the hands of a kindly pontiff, only to be outsmarted. Louis, Raymond, Eugenius, all of her generation and even some of the next already lay in the dust.

Her arrival at Messina on March 30, 1191, created a sensation among the Crusaders, and perhaps it was inevitable that her appearance would call forth those tangled legends that clung like barnacles to her reputation. "Many know what I wish none of us had known," wrote Richard of Devizes. "The same queen, in the time of her former husband, went to Jerusalem. Let none speak more thereof; I also know well. Be silent." Even half a lifetime was not enough, evidently, to completely wash away the gossip of her youth, although by this time her contemporaries were compelled, on the basis of her age if nothing else, to view her with a certain degree of awe. "Queen Eleanor, an incomparable woman, beautiful and chaste, powerful and modest, meek and eloquent, which is rarely to be met with in a woman; still indefatigable in every undertaking, whose power was the admiration of her age." Eleanor remained in Messina only four days, but this was sufficient to bring her up to date on events of consequence. Meeting in family council, the Plantagenets —Eleanor, Richard, and Joanna, whom the queen had not seen for fifteen years—traded information and reached decisions. Eleanor received the latest news on her son's continuing quarrel with Philip Augustus over the future of his sister. Declared Philip violently, "If he does put her aside and marries another woman, I will be the enemy of him and his so long as I live." To which Richard had replied that on no account would he marry Alais "since the King of England, his own father, had been intimate with her and had had a son by her." Before a convocation of the crusading barons and prelates, Philip had been compelled to release Richard from his oath, and Richard had promised to return Alais's dower. But despite the settlement of this old question, Philip's wrath for the Plantagenets had not abated, in fact so anxious was he to avoid his father's first wife that he set sail for the Holy Land on the morning of her arrival.

At Messina, problems confronted the queen on every side. Her daughter Joanna, widowed only four months earlier, twenty-five and childless, had lost her throne after King William's death and it was only with the greatest difficulty that Richard had been able to secure her property from William's illegitimate nephew, Tancred, who had seized the throne. Joanna's bed, her gilded table twelve feet long, her dinner service of twenty-four gold and silver plates and cups had been returned, but what to do now with a throneless daughter and with the Princess Berengaria were questions Eleanor pondered and then resolved quickly. Since it was Lent and Richard could not be married immediately, she remanded the maid of Navarre into the custody of her experienced daughter and, ignoring the crusading ban on women, directed that the two ladies accompany Richard to the Holy Land, where the marriage could be celebrated at the end of Lent. In Eleanor's view, the wedding could take place none too soon, for at Messina she doubtless heard the disturbing tale of how a few weeks before her arrival, Richard had presented himself, in only his breeches, at the door of a local church and had made a public confession of his homosexuality. Such an immoderate spectacle of penance would not have convinced her that her son would mend his pederastic ways, nor would she have been reassured by the news that he had recently referred to his nephew, Arthur of Brittany, as heir if he himself died without issue.

At this meeting, Eleanor reported the news from England: John's perambulations around the country as though he were king, his outrageous announcement that Richard would not return from the Crusade, his collusions with Geoffrey of York. And as if all this did not forebode enough trouble, Eleanor already had her suspicions about Richard's chancellor, William Longchamp, who, said a chronicler, "acted entirely in such a way that he seemed to strive to put himself on a level with God." Already the mistakes of both Eleanor and Richard were being brought home: Eleanor's error in convincing Richard that John would do less harm in England than on the Continent, Richard's foolish choice of

William Longchamp as a regent. At any rate, Eleanor took steps to deal with any and all eventualities, and before she left Messina on April 2, she had secured the necessary royal permissions to curb Longchamp or, for that matter, anyone who required curbing. Her homeward journey took her first to Rome, where she conferred with Pope Celestine III, whom she had known as an archdeacon twenty years earlier, and where she straightened out the matter of Henry's illegitimate son. Against the opposition of the suffragans of York, she secured the pope's approval of Geoffrey to the see of York and then, remaining in the Eternal City only long enough to borrow eight hundred marks from a moneylender, she struck off for the Alps. By the end of June, she was back in Rouen, where she settled down with one watchful eye trained on the Continent and the other on developments across the Channel.

In England, disorders soon began to mount. Geoffrey of York, banished from England during Richard's absence, now felt secure enough after Eleanor's negotiations on his behalf to ignore the prohibition. As soon as he stepped ashore at Dover, however, he was not only prevented from taking possession of his see but also arrested by Longchamp and thrown into a Dover dungeon, where he was treated in a manner most people believed grossly inappropriate for an archbishop. John, loath to pass up a profitable opportunity, now saw the chance to rid himself of the arrogant chancellor whom he regarded as his chief enemy. Calling together the bishops and justiciars at Reading, he convinced them that Longchamp, a man who "moved pompously along bearing a sneer in his nostrils," had overstepped his authority and should be called to account, but when this message reached the chancellor, he pleaded illness and retired to the security of the Tower of London. Soon after, however, an assembly convened at Saint Paul's Cathedral stripped Longchamp of his authority and banished him from England. Thrown into a panic and doubtless in fear of his life, Longchamp apparently believed it safest to leave the island in disguise. "Pretending to be a woman, a sex which he always despised, he changed his priest's robe into a harlot's dress" and made for Dover, where he hoped to find transport. Sitting on a rock near the shore, his green gown and cloak attracted the attention of a sailor "who wished for some sport with the women" and began to embrace him. In the course of their colloquy, the sailor discovered that Longchamp was a fake. "Come here, all of you," he shouted to his companions. "Come here and look at a man in a woman's dress!"

After this humiliating adventure, the deposed chancellor finally managed to reach the Continent and headed straight for Paris, where he made contact with two cardinals and managed to rouse their concern for his plight, even persuading them to plead his cause with Eleanor. That lady, however, only too happy at Longchamp's expulsion, had no intention of negotiating with the cardinals. When they attempted to cross the border at Gisors without first asking her for right of passage, they found the drawbridge hastily raised and the seneschal of Normandy on hand to explain the necessity of safe-conduct letters to two foreigners who perhaps were not familiar with local customs. A gale of excommunications resulted from this incident, but the queen stood firm. In December, she was holding her modest Christmas court at Bonneville-sur-Touques when she got word of an altogether more alarming piece of information: Philip Augustus had just arrived in Paris to be greeted as a hero by an overwhelmed citizenry, and he had repaired to Fontainebleau for his Christmas court. Philip's arrival brought the first eyewitness accounts of the war, although, to be sure, they were from the Capetian's point of view and totally unreliable in Eleanor's eyes. According to Philip, the capture of Acre on July 12 had been the doing of his heroic Franks, and as for his sudden abandonment of the Crusade, that was due to the treachery of Richard Plantagenet, his sworn ally, who had forced him to request release from his Crusader's vow and flee from the Holy Land lest he be murdered. It was true that Philip had suffered at Acre: the oppressive Syrian climate, the mosquitoes, the pestilential trenches where his soldiers had died like flies, the nightmarish mountains of unburied corpses—all had filled him with disgust. He had fallen ill, and although God had mercifully granted his recovery, he had, to his horror, lost his hair and the nails of his fingers and toes. Suspicious of plots against his life, he recklessly charged that his illness had resulted from a poisoned drink. In truth, Philip suffered from other maladies that, in the end, proved far more critical.

On Saturday, June 8, he had stood on the shore at Acre when Richard and his great-sailed ships, pennants streaming from the masts, had sailed into the harbor to be greeted by a fanfare that might have roused a greater man than Philip to the most intense jealousy. Even though Philip had been at Acre for six weeks and had enjoyed a certain prestige, he counted for nothing from the moment of Coeur de Lion's arrival. That day the crusading camp went delirious with jubilation. Those who were guarding the camp deserted their posts and rushed down to the strand; knights and squires jumped into the water and swam to Richard's ship; the frantic shouts of acclaim from the shore drowned out all other sounds; there was not a man in the Holy Army who that day was not in love with Richard, king of England, the deliverer of the Promised Land. Walking among the masses of soldiers, towering a head above Philip, Richard grasped the hands outstretched to him in love and adoration. That night, there was singing and the music of horns, drums, and lutes. Wine cups were filled over and over. So many candles were lit that the whole valley became a sea of lights, and Saladin, watching from his headquarters ten miles southeast of the besieged city, feared that the Christians had set the plain on fire.

Shortly after Richard's arrival, both he and Philip were stricken with a kind of malarial fever that raged in epidemic proportions throughout the Crusaders' camp. Although Richard's bout with the fever seems to have been more severe than Philip's, he was anxious to get on with the business of capturing Acre and had himself carried in a silken litter to the walls of the besieged city, where he supervised the crews operating the latest in war machinery: the great crossbows mounted on platforms; the spring-loaded espringals, which loosed spearlike missiles powerful enough to impale a horse; the wheeled mangonels, which catapulted rocks and bundles of tar-soaked straw over the walls; the massive trebuchets for hurling showers of flint; the assault towers sixty feet high; the ladders, grappling hooks, and battering rams. Day and night the army rained missiles on the beleaguered city, while its defenders retaliated with burning pitch and the explosive Greek fire. On Friday July 12, after a month of ceaseless fighting, the Moslem garrison had no choice but to raise the white flag, and then the Crusaders had poured into the city, their standards soon fluttering from buildings and walls. Richard, along with his sister and wife, took up residence in the royal palace. On the day of his entry into Acre he noticed another banner flying from the royal palace and, upon inquiry, was told that it belonged to Duke Leopold of Austria. Grossly offended that the duke should dare to infringe on his glory, Richard ordered his men to pull down the Austrian banner and fling it into the filth of the moat; Richard himself, apparently in the grip of an Angevin fury, personally addressed a number of insults to Leopold. That very night, the duke of Austria and his followers withdrew from the Crusade amid vows of vengeance on the arrogant Plantagenet.

Ten days after the fall of Acre, Philip Augustus sent a delegation of magnates to Richard's palace. The Franks, weeping, could barely deliver their message. Richard, however, had no trouble guessing the nature of the mission.

"Cease your weeping," he told them, "for I know what you have come to say. Your lord, the King of France, wishes to go home and you have come to secure my consent to this breach of our compact as brothers-in-arms."

"Sire," said Philip's spokesman, "you have divined what is in our minds. We are compelled to ask your consent for our lord king will surely die if he does not quickly leave this land."

There followed a rendition of Philip's physical symptoms, from most of which Richard also suffered. His reply barely concealed contempt: "If he leaves undone the work for which he came here, he will bring shame and everlasting contempt upon the Franks. I will not give my consent but of course if his life is in the balance, let him do as he sees fit."

Back in Paris, Philip did not wait long before he came banging on Eleanor's door. On January 20, 1192, he appeared below the walls at Gisors, and "producing the charter of the king of England which had been executed at Messina, he demanded of William Fitz-Ralph, the seneschal of Normandy, his sister Alais whom the king was to have taken to wife; the seneschal, however, refused to give her up." On Eleanor's instructions, Fitz-Ralph explained that he had no such orders from the king, at the same time reminding Philip that it was a clear breach of the Truce of God to lay hands on a Crusader's property. Having foiled the Capetian, Eleanor strengthened her border defenses, reinforced garrisons, and continued to uneasily scan the frontier for Philip's invasion forces. Within days, however, it became apparent that she had been facing the wrong direction: Trouble came from across the Channel with word that John was assembling a fleet and recruiting mercenaries at Southampton. "Fearing that the light-minded youth might be going to attempt something, by the counsels of the French, against his lord and brother, with an anxious mind she tried in every way to prevent her son's proposed journey. With all her strength she wanted to make sure that faith would be kept between her youngest sons at least, so that their mother might die more happily than had their father."

Even at the age of seventy, Eleanor was able to move faster than John. Unmindful of winter storms, she arrived at Portsmouth on February 11 and, ignoring her son, went straight to the kingdom's barons. "All the great men of the realm were called together, at Windsor, at Oxford, at London and at Winchester. Through her own tears and the prayers of the nobles she was with difficulty able to obtain a promise that John would not cross over for the time being." Without opposing her son directly, she shrewdly engineered the collapse of his foreign expedition, thus preventing him from offering his homage to Philip and handing over Gisors in exchange for Capetian recognition of his claims to the duchy of Normandy. Although John retreated sullenly to his manor at Wallingford, Eleanor was under no illusion that his retirement was anything but temporary. About this time, she began sending to the Holy Land messengers who described to the king the disorders in England as a result of John's seditious plotting with Philip Augustus. Richard must, she urged, abandon the Holy War and come home, lest he lose his kingdom.

During the spring and summer of 1192, the war continued, and tales of Richard's valorous exploits drifted back to Europe: glorious battles in which the desert sands had run red with the blood of Christian and Saracen; the king's negotiations with Saladin to marry Joanna Plantagenet to his brother, Saphidin, and Joanna's outraged refusal; his brilliant victory at Jaffa, where he had formed a wall of shields to repulse the Saracen horsemen; stories of Moslem women disciplining their children with threats that *"Malik Ric"* would get them. Twice the crusading army came within sight of Jerusalem but had been obliged to fall back, and in the end, Richard had been forced to conclude a truce with Saladin. For all the expense and the thousands of lives forfeited, the Christians were to retain only a strip of the coast between Tyre and Jaffa and the right to make pilgrimages to Jerusalem. After the truce, Saladin graciously invited small parties of Crusaders to visit the holy places. The bishop of Salisbury had toured the shrines, as had Richard's jongleur, Ambrose, but the king himself refused to accompany them. Exhausted and suffering from a recurrence of fever, he had turned away from the domes of Jerusalem in tears. "Sweet Lord," he had cried, "I entreat Thee. Do not suffer me to see Thy Holy City since I am unable to deliver it from the hands of Thine enemies." On September 29, 1192, he put Joanna and Berengaria on a vessel bound for Brindisi, and he himself took ship at Acre ten days later. The Third Crusade was over.

In England, Eleanor was expecting her son home for Christmas. All through November and early December companies of Crusaders had begun arriving in the kingdom; in the ports and marketplaces there were firsthand reports of the king's deeds in Palestine and plans for celebrations once he arrived. But the days passed without news, and newly arrived contingents of soldiers expressed astonishment that they had beaten the king home although they had left Acre after Richard. Along the coast, lookouts peered into the foggy Channel in hope of sighting the royal vessel, and messengers waited to race over the frozen roads toward London with the news of the king's landing. Eleanor learned that Berengaria and Joanna had safely reached Rome, but of her son, weeks overdue, there was an alarming lack of information. She held a cheerless Christmas court at Westminster, her apprehension mounting with each day, her silent fears being expressed openly in the ale houses along the Thames: The king had encountered some calamity, a storm along the Adriatic coast no doubt, and now he would never return.

Three days after Christmas, the whereabouts of the tardy Richard Plantagenet became known, not at Westminster but at the Cité Palace in Paris. On December 28, Philip Augustus received an astounding letter from his good friend Henry Hohenstaufen, the Holy Roman emperor:

> We have thought it proper to inform your nobleness that while the enemy of our empire and the disturber of your kingdom, Richard, King of England, was crossing the sea to his dominions, it chanced that the winds caused him to be shipwrecked in the region of Istria, at a place which lies between Aquila and Venice. . . . The roads being duly watched and the entire area well-guarded, our dearly beloved cousin Leopold, Duke of Austria, captured the king in a humble house in a village near Vienna. Inasmuch as he is now in our power, and has always done his utmost for your annoyance and disturbance, we have thought it proper to relay this information to your nobleness.

Shortly after the first of the new year, 1193, the archbishop of Rouen was able to send Eleanor a copy of the letter, accompanied by a covering note in which he cited whatever comforting quotations he could recall from Scripture to cover an outrage of this magnitude.

Eleanor's most imperative problem—finding the location where Richard was being held prisoner—she tackled with her usual energy and resourcefulness. From all points, emissaries were dispatched to find the king: Eleanor herself sent the abbots of Boxley and Pontrobert to roam the villages of Bavaria and Swabia, following every lead and rumor; Hubert Walter, bishop of Salisbury, stopping in Italy on his way home from the Crusade, changed course and hastened to Germany; even William Longchamp, the exiled chancellor, set out at once from Paris to trace his master. It was not until March, however, that Richard's chaplain, Anselm, who had shared many of the king's misadventures, arrived in England, and Eleanor was able to obtain authentic details.

According to Anselm's story, Richard had set sail in early October with Anselm himself, a clerk, the noblemen Baldwin of Béthune and William l'Etang, and a number of Templars, or men disguised as Templars. His original destination was Marseille, but three days out, perhaps while putting in at Pisa for news and supplies, he had learned on good authority that Count Raymond of Toulouse, still smarting over old wrongs, had ambushed the Mediterranean ports. Since stormy weather prevented him from traveling through the Pillars of Hercules and around Spain to his own provinces, he was forced to backtrack down the Italian peninsula and head for the island of Corfu off the Greek coast. There, approached by two Rumanian pirate ships, he came to terms with the brigands and arranged for them to take him up the eastern coast of the Adriatic, where he may have had some notion of crossing into his brother-in-law Henry's friendly territory of Saxony. But once again the weather turned rough, and the king's party, washed ashore at Ragusa in Rumania, had boarded another vessel only to be shipwrecked. About December 10, they landed in territories held by Count Mainard of Gortz, a vassal of Duke Leopold of Austria. Considering that he was on the worst possible terms with Leopold, Richard understood the potential danger of his situation. Adopting the disguise of a merchant, he sent a ruby ring to Count Mainard and asked permission for pilgrims to pass through his lands. The count, not unnaturally, asked for the names of these wealthy pilgrims. Baldwin of Béthune, he was told, and the merchant Hugo.

Mainard, as if he possessed some uncanny psychic powers, turned the ruby ring over between his fingers. "His name is not Hugo," he said, "but King Richard. I swore that I would arrest any pilgrims who set foot on my shores. However, in view of the value of this gift and the high condition of him who thus honors me, I shall return the gift and give your lord leave to continue his journey."

Distrusting such unusual magnanamity, Richard and his party hired horses and fled that very night. Several days later, still keeping his disguise as a merchant, Richard was recognized and very nearly taken, but his captor, a native of Normandy, burst into tears and sent him on his way. By this time, rumors of the king's presence had flown through the region. Leaving behind Baldwin of Béthune to draw attention to himself as a person of consequence and perhaps be mistaken for a king, Richard took with him only William l'Etang and the young clerk, who spoke German, and headed for Vienna. After three days of riding without rest, they came to the small town of Ginana, a suburb of Vienna, where Richard, worn out and shaking from a recurrence of malaria, found lodgings at a tavern and fell into a fevered sleep. Meanwhile, his German-speaking clerk went out to buy provisions, but since he had no Austrian currency and attempted to make purchases with a gold bezant of the type used in Syria, he was detained and sharply questioned by authorities. Insisting that he was merely the servant of a very wealthy merchant, he was able to secure his release and run back to the tavern, where he urged the king to flee. But Richard, in a stupor, could not be roused. By December 20, the clerk was again compelled to return to the marketplace for food. This time he made the mistake of appearing with the king's handsomely adorned gloves thrust into his belt, an accessory that immediately attracted attention. Arrested and tortured, he finally confessed the identity and whereabouts of his master.

In Vienna, Duke Leopold was holding his Christmas court when he received news that the insolent Coeur de Lion had miraculously fallen into his grasp, and he lost no time in ordering the tavern surrounded. Hearing the commotion, Richard improvised a new disguise. Running to the kitchen and pulling on a servant's smock, he sat by the hearth, where he busied himself with turning some birds on a spit. His disguise fooled nobody, of course. Outnumbered and cornered, he demanded that Duke Leopold himself be fetched to accept his surrender. Two days later, he was taken from Vienna to Durrenstein, a remote castle in the hills above the Danube, and placed in strict confinement, his guards having been ordered to watch him day and night with their swords drawn.

Treachery was rife not only in Germany but in Paris and Rouen; it even percolated rapidly in the queen's own family. Before Eleanor could take steps to secure Coeur de Lion's release, she was faced with more immediate catastrophes in the form of Philip Augustus and his newest ally, her son John. These two proceeded on the assumption that Richard, king of England, was dead. Or as good as dead. But before Eleanor could take her youngest son in hand, he fled to Normandy, where he declared himself the king's heir, an announcement the Norman barons greeted with disdain. John did not wait to convince them, proceeding instead to Paris, where he did homage to Philip for the Plantagenet Continental domains and furthermore agreeing to confirm Philip's right to the Vexin. Heartened by these developments, Philip apparently felt justified in abrogating the Truce of God; on April 12, a few days after Easter, he once again fronted the fortress at Gisors and this time the seneschal surrendered it without protest. From Gisors, Philip moved directly to Rouen, where he demanded the immediate release of his sister. The seneschal of Rouen, a man whose lands had recently been restored to him through Eleanor's intervention, knew on which side his security lay. He had no orders to release Alais, he said, but he would be happy to escort Philip, alone and unarmed, into the princess's quarters for a visit. In the course of some on-the-spot reflections, it did not fail to occur to Philip, who had as keen an imagination as Eleanor, that he had only to step unarmed across the drawbridge at Rouen and the queen would have a superb hostage with whom to barter for her son. Furious at the realization that the queen had thwarted him, he smashed his own siege engines and spilled casks of wine into the Seine. Rouen, he swore, had not seen the last of him. In the meantime, Eleanor, "who then ruled England," had taken the precaution of closing the Channel ports and ordering the defense of the eastern coast against a possible invasion, her hastily mustered home guard being instructed to wield any weapon that came to hand, including their plowing tools.

At this point, Eleanor's dilemma in regard to her sons would have taxed the most patient of mothers. John, returning to England, swaggered about the countryside proclaiming himself the next king of England—perhaps he sincerely believed that Richard would never be released alive—and, never known for his sensitivity, constantly regaled Eleanor with the latest rumors concerning the fate of her favorite son. Her actions during this period indicate clearly that she failed to take John seriously. Although he was twenty-seven, she thought of him as the baby of the family, always a child showing off and trying to attract attention. Her attitude was probably close to that of Richard's when, a few months later, he was informed of John's machinations: "My brother John is not the man to subjugate a country if there is a person able to make the slightest resistance to his attempts." With one hand, Eleanor deftly managed to anticipate John's plots and render him harmless; with the other, she worked for Richard's release. After Easter, the king had been removed from Durrenstein Castle and the hands of Duke Leopold and, after some haggling, had been taken into custody by Leopold's suzerain, the Holy Roman emperor. As the emperor's prisoner, Richard found himself the object of high-level decisions. His death, it was decided, would achieve no useful purpose; rather the arrogant Plantagenets, or what remained of them, should be made to redeem their kin, but at a price that would bring their provinces to their knees: 100,000 silver marks with two hundred hostages as surety for payment. The hostages, it was specified, were to be chosen from among the leading barons of England and Normandy or from their children.

Relieved as Eleanor must have felt to learn that her son could be purchased, she could only have been appalled at the size of the ransom. The prospect of collecting such an enormous sum, thirty-five tons of pure silver, seemed impossible after Henry's Saladin tithe and Richard's great sale before the Crusade. Where was the money to be found? Where were two hundred noble hostages to be located? At a council convened at Saint Albans on June 1, 1193, she appointed five officers to assist with the dreaded task. During the summer and fall, England became a marketplace to raise the greatest tax in its history. The kingdom was stripped of its wealth: "No subject, lay or clerk, rich or poor, was overlooked. No one could say, 'Behold I am only So-and-So or Such-and-Such, pray let me be excused.' " Barons were taxed one-quarter of a year's income. Churches and abbeys were relieved of their movable wealth, including the crosses on their altars. The Cistercians, who possessed no riches, sheared their flocks and donated a year's crop of wool. Before long, the bars of silver and gold began slowly to pile up in the crypt of Saint Paul's Cathedral under Eleanor's watchful eyes. But not quickly enough to comfort her. Even more painful was the job of recruiting hostages from the great families, their lamentations and pleadings rising like a sulphurous mist all over the kingdom and providing constant agony for the queen.

From Haguenau, where Richard was incarcerated, came a flood of letters to his subjects and most especially to his "much loved mother." He had been received with honor by the emperor and his court, he is well, he hopes to be home soon. He realizes that the ransom will be difficult to raise but he feels sure that his subjects will not shirk their duty; all sums collected should be entrusted to the queen.

Richard also addressed correspondence to his captor, Henry Hohen-staufen: As a king, he had no need to account for his actions to anyone but God, but nevertheless, he wished to set the emperor straight. What were his crimes that he should be held against his will like a common highroad robber? "It is said that I have not taken Jerusalem. I should have taken it, if time had been given me; this is the fault of my enemies, not mine, and I believe no just man could blame me for having deferred an enterprise (which can always be undertaken) in order to afford my people a succour which they could no longer wait for. There, sire, these are my crimes."

As for Philip Capet's calumnies upon the king's good name, "I know of nothing that ought to have brought on me his ill-humour, except for my having been more successful than he."

Like his mother during her imprisonment, Richard never allowed his spirit to be broken. He was "always cheery and full of jest in talk. . . . He would tease his warders with rough jokes and enjoy the sport of making them drunk and of trying his own strength against that of their big bodies." Deeper feelings were expressed, however, in a *sirventès*

that he composed for his half sister Marie of Champagne and that must
have sorrowed Eleanor to the quick.

> Feeble the words and faltering the tongue
>> Wherewith a prisoner moans his doleful plight;
> Yet for his comfort he may make a song.
>> Friends I have many, but their gifts are slight;
>> Shame to them if unransomed I, poor wight,
>>> Two winters languish here!
>
> And they, my knights of Anjou and Touraine—
>> Well know they, who now sit at home at ease,
> That I, their lord, in far-off Allemaine
>> Am captive. They should help to my release;
> But now their swords are sheathed, and rust in peace,
>> While I am prisoner here.

Eleanor, sixteen years in confinement, read the despair behind those
lines of verse. It is said that in her anguish she addressed three letters to
Pope Celestine III imploring his assistance in securing Richard's release
and in her salutation addressed the pontiff as "Eleanor, by the wrath of
God, Queen of England." One of the letters reads:

> I am defiled with grief, and my bones cleave to my skin, for my
> flesh it is wasted away. My years pass away in groanings, and I
> would they were altogether passed away. . . . I have lost the light of
> my eyes, the staff of my old age.
>
> My bowels are torn away, my very race is destroyed and passing
> away from me. The Young King and the earl of Brittany sleep in the
> dust, and their most unhappy mother is compelled to live that she
> may be ever tortured with the memory of the dead. Two sons yet
> survived to my solace, who now survive only to distress me, a mis-
> erable and condemned creature: King Richard is detained in bonds
> and John, his brother, depopulates the captive's kingdom with the
> sword and lays it waste with fire. In all things the Lord is become
> cruel towards me and opposes me with a heavy hand. . . . I long for
> death, I am weary of life; and though I thus die incessantly, I yet
> desire to die more fully; I am reluctantly compelled to live, that my
> life may be the food of death and a means of torture.

Why, she demands, does the sword of Saint Peter slumber in its scab-
bard when her son, a "most delicate youth," the anointed of the Lord,

lies in chains? Why does the pope, a "negligent," "cruel" prevaricator and sluggard, do nothing?

These letters, supposedly written for her by Peter of Blois, are so improbable that it is surprising that many modern historians have accepted them as authentic. While preserved among the letters of Peter of Blois, who is undoubtedly their author—they are characteristic of his style and use his favorite expressions—there is no evidence that they were written for Eleanor or that they were ever sent. Most likely they were rhetorical exercises. No contemporary of Eleanor's mentioned that she wrote to the pope, and not until the seventeenth century were the letters attributed to her. From a diplomatic point of view, they are too fanciful to be genuine; Eleanor, clearheaded and statesmanlike, was never a querulous old woman complaining of age, infirmities, and weariness of life. On the contrary, her contemporaries unanimously credit her with the utmost courage, industry, and political skill. A second point to notice is that the details of the letters misrepresent the facts of Richard's imprisonment. He was never "detained in bonds," and as both she and the pope knew, Celestine had instantly, upon receiving news of Richard's capture, excommunicated Duke Leopold for laying violent hands on a brother Crusader; he had threatened Philip Augustus with an interdict if he trespassed upon Plantagenet territories; and he had menaced the English with interdict should they fail to collect the ransom. Under the circumstances, Celestine had done all he could. In the last analysis, the letters must be viewed as Peter of Blois's perception of Eleanor's feelings, a view that may or may not be accurate.

In December 1193, Eleanor set sail with an imposing retinue of clerks, chaplains, earls, bishops, hostages, and chests containing the ransom. By January 17, 1194, the day scheduled for Richard's release, she had presented herself and the money at Speyer, but no sooner had they arrived than, to her amazement, Henry Hohenstaufen announced a further delay. He had received letters that placed an entirely new light on the matter of the king's liberation. As the gist of the problem emerged, it seemed Philip Augustus and John Plantagenet had offered the emperor an equivalent amount of silver if he could hold Coeur de Lion in custody another nine months, or deliver him up to them. These disclosures, and Henry's serious consideration of the counteroffer, provoked horror from the emperor's own vassals, and after two days of argument, Henry relented. He would liberate Richard as promised if the king of England would do homage to him for all his possessions, including the kingdom of England. This request, a calculated humiliation, would have made Richard a vassal of the Holy Roman emperor, a degradation that the Plantagenets were hard put to accept. Quick to realize the meaninglessness, as well as the illegality, of the required act, Eleanor made an on-the-spot decision. According to Roger of Hovedon, Richard, "by advice of his mother Eleanor, abdicated the throne of the kingdom of England and delivered it to the emperor as the lord of all." On February 4, the king was released "into the hands of his mother" after a captivity of one year six weeks and three days.

Seven weeks later, on March 12, the king's party landed at Sandwich and proceeded directly to Canterbury, where they gave thanks at the tomb of Saint Thomas. By the time they reached London, the city had been decorated, the bells were clanging furiously, and the Londoners ready to give a rapturous welcome to their hero and champion. Her eldest son "hailed with joy upon the Strand," Eleanor looked in vain for the remaining male member of her family, but the youngest Plantagenet was nowhere to be found. Once Richard's release had been confirmed, he had fled to Paris upon Philip Augustus's warning that "beware, the devil is loose." Despite a certain anxiety about her son's whereabouts, the next six weeks were to be ones of great happiness for Eleanor. It was spring in England, the air opaque and moist, the budding earth exhaling aromas of ineffable sweetness. With Richard, she made a relaxed progress to Nottingham, to the forests of Sherwood "which the king had never seen before and which pleased him greatly," to Northampton, where they celebrated Easter, and finally to Winchester, where Richard was crowned a second time. Despite the holiday atmosphere, Richard was impatient to sail for Normandy. On April 25, he and Eleanor went to Portsmouth, but their crossing was delayed by bad weather for more than three weeks. Not until May 12 were they able to reach Barfleur, where the Normans greeted Richard with the same enthusiasm as had the English. Their progress took them to Caen, Bayeux, and around mid-May, to the city of Lisieux, where they spent a few days in the home of John of Alençon, a trusted friend and the city's archdeacon. It was here that the junior Plantagenet, fearful and trembling, appeared one evening at dinnertime asking to see his mother. It is clear from the reception John received that Eleanor had already discussed him with the king. Neither of them took seriously the boy's antics; he was, after all, their kin. If he had played the fool, they would not reproach him; rather they would deal later with those who had led him astray. The important matter was to bring him back into the family and convince him that his future interests lay with them rather than with Philip Capet.

When John was brought into the king's room, he threw himself at Richard's feet and let loose with a flood of tears. But Richard pulled him up and kissed him. "Think no more of it, John," he said gently. "You are but a child and were left to evil counselors. Your advisers shall pay for this. Now come and have something to eat." He ordered that a fresh salmon, which had just been brought in as a gift, should be cooked for his brother.

According to the chronicles, "the king and John became reconciled through the mediation of Queen Eleanor, their mother." In the circumstances, it seemed the safest course as well as the wisest. There was no doubt in Eleanor's mind that the boy, now twenty-eight, could not be held responsible for his actions, that he was, as Richard of Devizes termed him, "light-minded." But at that moment, he was the last of the Plantagenets. With luck, Richard might reign another twenty-five years or more. Who was to say that he would not produce an heir of his own? Thus the queen must have reasoned in the spring of 1194 when her son, after so many adversities, had come home to her.

In her seventh decade, Eleanor grew impatient with wars and politics. It was as if Richard's capture and ransom had drained her emotionally, and now she sought surcease from the confusions of courts and councils. She had preserved his kingdom from wolves, she had expended her dwindling energies to rescue him from his enemies, she had served her people as peacemaker. If she did not go quite as far as Henry when he had said, "Now let the rest go as it will, I care no more," at least she was beginning to remember her age. In 1194, she put between herself and a demanding world the plain high walls of Fontevrault, not as the abbess that Henry had attempted to make of her twenty years earlier but as a royal guest accompanied by a modest household. There on the border of Poitou and Anjou, where the river Vienne wound its silvery path through valley and forest, she made herself comfortable among the devout and learned sisters. In addition to the convent, Fontevrault included a residence for penitent harlots, a monastery for monks and lay brothers, a hospital for lepers, and an old-age home for monks and nuns. There was a vast complex of halls and refectories connected by cloisters and an elaborate octagonal kitchen with five fireplaces and twenty chimneys. For a woman who had always believed in the superiority of her own sex, Fontevrault, where the monks and nuns were ruled by a woman, provided a refuge much to Eleanor's taste. Then, too, she must have felt as though she had come home to rest among familiar surroundings—her grandmother Philippa was buried there, and in the nun's choir of the domed abbey church slept Henry Plantagenet, his hands calmly folded upon his breast.

Protected against life's burdens and annoyances, Eleanor could pick and choose her activities just as she liked, and from now on her name figures rarely in the official records. We know that on one occasion she supported the archbishop of Rouen in requesting that the king remit part of a fine due from Reading Abbey and that on another she aided the abbot of Bourgueil, who was having difficulty paying a local wine tax. Also during these years, she was instrumental in arranging for the marriage of her widowed daughter, Joanna, to Raymond VI of Toulouse, a settlement that no doubt gave her wry satisfaction after two husbands had failed to reclaim her inheritance.

The years passed in comparative quiet, although those interminable struggles between the Plantagenets and the Capets continued. Alais Capet, finally returned to her kin at the age of thirty-five, had been promptly married to one of Philip's vassals, Guillaume de Ponthieu, and stepped forever from the glare of history. In 1196, Richard had been compelled to return the Vexin, a disaster that boded ill as far as Eleanor was concerned, for Normandy now lay open to possible incursions by Philip. But far more worrisome than the loss of the Vexin was Richard's lack of an heir. Although he had married to please her, he had done nothing more. He had ignored Berengaria at Messina, he had married her at Cyprus and ridden off within hours of the wedding, and during the war in Palestine, he had treated her like a leper who must keep its distance. Berengaria, queen of England, had not yet laid eyes on her kingdom, and the marriage that Eleanor had been so anxious to arrange remained a mockery, if in fact it had ever been consummated. Since Richard and Berengaria had parted in the Holy Land, she had lived in seclusion, virtually a widow, on her dower lands in Maine, while the king satisfied his sexual needs with men. In 1195, a hermit visiting the king took the occasion to warn of God's vengeance if he persisted in the sin of Sodom, a sermon that Richard did not accept kindly. Soon afterward, however, he fell seriously ill and suddenly recalled the hermit's warning. Calling his confessors, he spilled out the details of his misdeeds and received absolution; Berengaria was summoned to join him, but their reconciliation did not result in a pregnancy.

Despite the Treaty of Louviers, which had restored the Norman Vexin to Philip, neither he nor Richard regarded the agreement as definitive, and desultory warfare continued on their frontiers. In the summer of 1196, Richard began to construct a fortress that he hoped would act as a deterrent to any future moves that Philip might be considering in the direction of Normandy. At Les Andelys, on the right bank of the Seine, stood a mighty rock that offered a panoramic view of the entire river valley, and on this promontory Richard laid out an imposing stronghold that he christened Château Gaillard. His Saucy Castle, with its impregnable walls and powerful bastions, took three years to build, and when it had been completed, Richard, who had personally supervised its construction, could barely contain his pleasure. It was, he crowed, his daughter. From its lofty eminence he could look down in derision upon the king of the Franks and his schemes for the conquest of Normandy. When finally Philip got his first glimpse of the Saucy Castle, he could only bluster, "If its walls were made of solid iron, yet would I take them!"

When his defiant boast was relayed to Richard, he countered with his own oath. "By God's throat, if its walls were made of butter, yet would I hold them securely against Philip and all his forces!" And as if to prove his patience with the Franks exhausted, he proceeded to drive Philip out of the Vexin with such ferocity that Dieu-Donné was nearly drowned in the hasty retreat.

By the spring of 1199, Richard had turned his attention to other matters, one of them being the condition of his treasury. The construction of Château Gaillard had, unfortunately, helped to wipe out his resources. In March, his mind on the troublesome subject of money, he heard of an incident that immediately piqued his interest in that it seemed to offer the possibility of quick profit. A peasant plowing in a field on the outskirts of Châlus in the Limousin had accidentally unearthed what was claimed to be a treasure trove. The precious object was, the report said, a set of gold and silver figurines representing a king seated around a table with his family, perhaps some buried relic from Roman times. Viscount Aymar of Limoges, quick to claim the booty, failed to reckon with Richard's interest, and when the king claimed his right, as overlord, to all buried treasures in his domains, Aymar apparently sent only a portion of the find. Richard's response was to gather his mercenaries and hie himself to the Limousin. The castle of Châlus was but a puny fortress, virtually unarmed and surely no match for the great Coeur de Lion. Sappers were set to work on the walls.

After supper in the early evening of March 25, Richard went for a stroll around the walls to check on the sappers' progress. Arrows flew sporadically from the castle's garrison, but Richard, careless of his own safety, paid little attention. Perhaps he was amused when his men pointed out a fellow standing on the walls with a crossbow in one hand and a frying pan in the other. All day he had been fending off missiles by using his frying pan as a shield, and now, when he deliberately aimed an arrow at the king, Richard greeted the bowman with a shout of applause. Suddenly, however, another arrow whistled through the dusk and, unerring, came to rest in the king's left shoulder near the neck. Without uttering a cry, Richard mounted his horse and rode back to camp as if nothing had happened. In the privacy of his tent, he tried to pull out the arrow but only succeeded in breaking off the shaft. The iron barb remained imbedded in the rolls of fat on his shoulder. A surgeon of sorts was summoned—Hovedon called him a "butcher" who "carelessly mangled the king's arm"—and by lantern light finally managed to extract the arrow. Even though lotions and unguents were applied and the wound bandaged, it immediately became inflamed and began to swell. While Richard's army kept up its assault on Châlus, his wound grew steadily worse, and when gangrene set in and he was forced to acknowledge the fact that he would not survive, he sent for his mother.

With an old friend, Abbot Luke of Torpenay, and a small escort, Eleanor set out for Limoges, over a hundred miles from Fontevrault. Even though she traveled day and night, her son was beyond anyone's help by the time of her arrival. There remained only the disposition of his possessions. He bequeathed to John his lands on the Continent and his kingdom of England, the island for which he cared so little that in a reign of ten years he had spent only six months there, and to his nephew Otto, the son of his sister Matilda, he left his jewels. He further willed his heart to be buried at Rouen and his body at Fontevrault at the feet of his father. To Aquitaine, for their perfidy, he bequeathed his entrails, and to England, the land that would worship him as a national hero and fill their squares with statues, he left nothing. His affairs in order, he sent for the crossbowman who had wounded him. He proved to be little more than a lad.

"What evil have I done to you that you have slain me?" asked Richard.

"Because," replied the boy, "you slew my father and my two brothers and you would have killed me. Take on me any revenge that you think fit for I will readily endure the greatest torments you can devise now that you, who have brought such evils on the world, are about to die."

"I forgive you my death," Richard answered, but the boy continued to stand there in scowling disbelief. "Live on," Richard assured him, "and by my bounty behold the light of day." He ordered the youth, variously called Bertran de Gurdun, John Sabroz, and Peter Basili by the chroniclers, who did not know his real name, to be released and sent away with a gift of one hundred shillings.

On Tuesday, April 6, "as the day was closing, he ended his earthly day" in Eleanor's arms. Her son was forty-one and childless except for his bastard son, Philip. For his greed over a few gold figurines "the lion by the ant was slain," and even his last act of chivalry came to nothing, because Mercadier, his mercenary chief, seized the boy with the frying pan and, once the king was dead, had him flayed alive.

One son remained.

The Last Battle

On Palm Sunday, Eleanor laid to rest her dearest son in the abbey church of Fontevrault, but circumstances permitted few moments of solitude in which to embrace her inexpressible sorrow. In those dark, confused hours following Richard's death at Châlus, she had been torn not simply by grief but by a sense of impending doom, and yet, she refused to stand by helplessly. Messengers had been secretly dispatched to publish the tragic news to those who must know: John, who was, ironically, visiting her grandson Arthur in Brittany; Berengaria; William Marshal; the Abbess Matilda of Fontevrault; and a few others. To the rest of the world, she announced nothing, and it was not until the dead king's cortege began to make its long, slow journey through the Limousin that men and women came out of their halls and huts and markets to huddle in silent amazement by the side of the road. Coeur de Lion was dead, but who among them could hail long life to his successor? Indeed, it was a matter of uncertainty who would be the next king.

The fact that on his deathbed Richard had designated John as his heir was influential but, as Eleanor understood, not at all decisive. The confusion about the rules of hereditary succession that had so troubled Henry that he had made an archbishop of his chancellor and had crowned his eldest son with illusions of grandeur now came to rest resoundingly around the queen's head. She was all too familiar with the debate circulating among contemporary jurists as to whether John Plantagenet or Arthur of Brittany took precedence. Ranulph de Glanville, Henry's justiciar, had expressed doubt whether a king's younger brother or the son of a dead brother had a better claim to the inheritance and, after presenting arguments on both sides, he had ended by favoring the nephew; on the other hand, a Norman legist had decided that "the younger son is the nearer heir to the father's inheritance than the child of the elder brother who had died before the father." Although there is no way of knowing Eleanor's private views about this question, it is reasonable to assume that she felt much the same as William Marshal. On the evening of April 10, the news of Richard's death reached Marshal at his lodgings near Rouen just as he was going to bed. Dressing hurriedly, he hastened to the residence of Archbishop Hubert Walter of Canterbury, who was staying nearby. Apart from their grief and consternation, what most troubled the two men was the future.

"My lord," said Marshal, "we must lose no time in choosing someone to be king."

"In my opinion," declared the archbishop, "Arthur should rightfully be the king."

Marshal disagreed. "I think that would be bad. Arthur is counseled by traitors and he is haughty and proud. If we put him at our head, we shall suffer for it because he hates the English."

"Marshal," asked the archbishop quietly, "is this really your desire?"

"Yea, my lord, for unquestionably a son has a nearer claim to his father's land than a grandson. It is only just that John should have the crown."

"So be it then," said Hubert Walter, "but mark my words, Marshal, you will regret this more than any decision you have ever made."

Marshal had no illusions about John Lackland, whom he had known for thirty years. "Perhaps you are right," he answered, "but I still believe it best."

For Eleanor, as for William Marshal, the most important question was not which of Richard's possible heirs had the better legal claim to the throne—it was not even which of the two would make the most satisfactory sovereign—but which would make the least unsatisfactory king. In the end, it was a matter of choosing between evils, and of the two, she was obliged to select John, a choice she did not make on the basis of kinship nor of his character nor of any personal feelings of affection. She knew John—by this time everyone knew John—and contemporary historians had already rendered their evaluation. *"Hostis naturae Johannes,"* wrote William of Newburgh, "nature's enemy, John."

We do not know how well Eleanor knew Arthur of Brittany or, for that matter, whether she had ever met him. What the twelve-year-old boy might someday become was impossible to say, but still she knew enough about him to understand that he must not be permitted the throne. His very name was ominously significant. Arthur had been born to Constance of Brittany on March 29, 1187, eight months after Geoffrey's death in Paris. Henry had wanted the infant to be named after himself and his grandfather, but Constance had defiantly refused; instead, as a badge of Breton independence and hostility toward the Plantagenets, she had named the child Arthur after the legendary king who the Bretons claimed had once ruled their land and who, the prophets said, would return. From the time of Henry's death, Constance had more or less governed Brittany in her son's name and trained him to insubordination against Plantagenet rule, but more alarming to Eleanor, Arthur had been taken into custody by Philip Augustus in 1196 and raised in Paris with Philip's own son, Louis. To confer the Plantagenet throne on Arthur would be to lay the empire at the feet of the king of the Franks. It was the consciousness of this fact that had caused Richard to abandon any momentary thoughts of designating Arthur as his heir and that now made Eleanor, her eyes wide open to John's faults, fight for his succession to the throne.

On Richard's accession, Eleanor had been obliged to ingratiate him with the public, but Coeur de Lion had offered a splendid figure for this sort of exploitation; in John's case, her task can only be described as thankless. She understood that some people possess a talent for ruling, while others do not; John clearly fell into the latter category. A lack of intelligence was not the problem, since he had very real ability and had inherited much of his father's energy and genius for administration. When Henry twenty-five years earlier had dragged the bored Young King on a tour of England's law courts, these lessons in the profession of governing had been wasted on his eldest son, but young John, who often accompanied his father, developed a lifelong fascination for public business and in years to come would prove himself an indefatigable ruler. He also possessed whimsical charm, the reason that Eleanor and Richard were able to treat his lapses as the peccadilloes of a wayward boy, and he was something of a farceur who could not resist a joke, even a dangerous one. By temperament inclined toward indolence, he loved to saunter through life enjoying the best food and drink, jewels and rich garments, pretty women and amusing companions with whom he could while away hours in chatter and eternal games of backgammon. But, as no one knew better than Eleanor, John had always lacked balance and self-discipline, his moods shifting unpredictably from brilliance to the most inordinate stupidity and cruelty. Whether responsibility would teach him discretion, perhaps even wisdom, remained to be seen, but she intended to keep him under close watch in the hope of preventing any fatal misstep.

During Richard's last hours, Eleanor had sent messages to John instructing him to leave Arthur's court at once and take control of the great fortress of Chinon that held the Angevin treasure, and at the same time she persuaded the seneschal of Anjou to surrender the castle and swear fealty to John as Richard's successor. While these matters prevented John from attending Coeur de Lion's funeral on Palm Sunday, he finally arrived at Fontevrault on the Wednesday before Easter in the company of Bishop Hugh of Lincoln, whose low opinion of Eleanor's son could not have been more apparent. Wishing to view his brother's tomb, John pounded furiously on the choir door. He was told, however, that Abbess Matilda was away and no visitor, however eminent, might enter without her permission. Standing on the porch with the bishop, he withdrew an amulet from around his neck and said that it had been given to one of his forebears with the promise from Heaven that whoever of the Plantagenets owned it would never lose their dominions. Annoyed, Hugh advised him to trust in God instead of stones and, pulling him over to a sculpture depicting wicked kings being cast into eternal hellfires on the Last Judgment, delivered a solemn lecture on the perils and responsibilities facing a ruler during his brief time upon earth. John, unimpressed, dragged Hugh to another sculpture where angels were leading righteous kings to everlasting happiness. "You should have shown me these," he said, "for it is the example of these kings that I intend to follow."

During the next three days at Fontevrault, John assumed a posture of exaggerated piety so completely uncharacteristic that he only succeeded in arousing suspicion. Finally, on Easter Sunday, his mask of humility dropped suddenly to reveal that prospective kingship had not altered his behavior one whit. At High Mass, Bishop Hugh took the occasion to preach, for John's benefit, a lengthy sermon on the characters of good and bad kings and the future rewards of each. The congregation, which probably included Eleanor, listened patiently, but John, who had as little patience as his father for sitting still in church and receiving lectures from the clergy, began to grow fidgety. Three times during the sermon he interrupted the bishop with demands to cut short his sermon. He wanted, he declared loudly, his dinner. When Hugh ignored him, he horrified the congregation by jangling some gold coins that he had brought for the offering. Finally, Hugh could tolerate the disturbance no longer.

"What are you doing?" he called out to John.

"I am looking at these gold pieces and thinking that, if I had had them a few days ago, I would not have given them to you but put them into my own purse."

Blushing vehemently, the bishop said, "Throw them into the dish and begone."

On the very day that this appalling levity scandalized the Easter worshipers at Fontevrault, Eleanor's worst fears were rapidly materializing only thirty miles away. An army of Bretons led by Arthur and Constance had marched on Angers and won it without striking a blow, after which a gathering of barons from Anjou, Maine, and Touraine accepted Arthur as their rightful sovereign. On the Monday after Easter, John hurried to Le Mans, but its citizens received him coldly, and the garrison refused to admit him. Learning that the Breton army and a force under Philip were converging on the town, he only just escaped capture by slipping away before daybreak on Tuesday. That day, Philip and Arthur triumphantly entered Le Mans, where Arthur did homage to the Capetian king for the counties of Anjou, Maine, and Touraine. With the capitals of Anjou and Maine under enemy occupation, John had no choice but to flee for the safety of Normandy, where he was proclaimed duke at Rouen on Sunday, April 25. The ceremony, notable for its lack of dignity, tells us as much about John's unreliable character as it does about the causes of Eleanor's apprehension. While the ducal coronet of golden roses was being placed on his head by Archbishop Walter, a group of John's cronies began to chuckle audibly and make mocking remarks about the solemn rites, no doubt the idea of their boon companion as hero of the ceremony being too much for them. From time to time, John himself turned around to join in their revelry. At the moment when Archbishop Walter presented him with the ducal lance, he was paying attention to his snickering friends, and the lance slipped from his hands to the ground. In later years, this untoward incident would be interpreted as an omen, but the horseplay that had caused the mishap was ominous enough in itself.

Meanwhile, Eleanor was left to staunch the anarchy that her son's death had loosed. Even though Philip and Arthur had been quick to seize the moment, she determined that their triumph should be short-lived. With her at Fontevrault she had Richard's mercenary captain, and now she ordered Mercadier to bring up his *routiers* from Châlus, where they had been left at Richard's death. Unheeding of her age or the possibility of danger, she herself went to recover Angers with her hastily recruited army of cutthroats. Apparently Arthur and Constance did not expect such alacrity from John and certainly not from an aged queen, because at her approach they hastily retreated and fell back to Le Mans, while Mercadier ravaged Angers and took a throng of prisoners. Inspired perhaps by his mother's example, John collected an army of Normans and marched south to Le Mans, but by this time Arthur had moved on, and John was only able to wreak his vengeance by pulling down the city's walls, razing its castle, destroying houses, and seizing its leading citizens. But the danger was by no means over. Twice the Plantagenets had tried to capture Arthur, twice they had bungled. For John to remain now in the southern counties would have been to leave Normandy open to attack and very likely to risk capture himself. Leaving Anjou and Maine to the care of his mother and Mercadier, he retreated to Normandy, and at the end of May, sailed for England with a few close friends. On May 27, he was crowned at Westminster in a ceremony that the chroniclers disposed of briefly and matter-of-factly: seventeen prelates, ten earls, and "many barons" were present; twenty-one fat oxen were supplied for the banquet afterward. Other than this, they have little to say. Obviously, Eleanor's touch was missing.

Back at Fontevrault, Eleanor quickly took stock of the crumbling Plantagenet empire. It was hard to believe that decades of planning could be overthrown in a few weeks. Brittany was irretrievably lost, and despite her exertions, Anjou, Touraine, and Maine floated precariously within her grandson's grasp. For the time being, she remained fairly sure of Normandy, if only because the Normans had no wish to put themselves under the rule of a Breton, and as for the English, there was never a moment's question about their aversion to Arthur. Her own estates of Aquitaine remained a question. There was little that spoke of hope in the spring of 1199, but Eleanor, her iron determination never more in evidence, resolved to secure what provinces she could for John and check the aggressions of Louis Capet's son. Toward the end of April, she left Fontevrault with a small escort and set off on a political tour of the land of her birth. Avoiding only the Limousin, where Richard had been killed, she paid official visits from the border of Anjou to the frontier of Spain: On April 29, she was at Loudon; on May 4, at Poitiers; and then she sped southwest to Niort and La Rochelle. On July 1, she visited Bordeaux, and on July 4, Soulac. Aware that her people had grown heartily weary of Plantagenets, she did not come as a herald of any son but instead cut a wide swath through her lands as duchess of Aquitaine and demonstrated the largesse that had characterized the grandest of her forebears. As she explained in one of the many charters granted at this time, God having still left her in the world at the age of seventy-seven, she felt obliged to provide for the needs of her people and the welfare of her lands. Her political insight honed to a fine edge, she understood that the time had passed for buying support with gestures such as emptying jails and relaxing oppressive laws. In this crisis, she felt the necessity of securing loyalties with more durable coin. From her ducal inheritance she plucked castles, tithes, and privileges, dispensing them with an open hand to the abbots and castellans who flocked to her side. Justice was dispensed, old grievances redressed, manors and castles traded for fortresses, and one of the assets she bartered away in this manner was the ducal hunting grounds at Talmont, the seaside preserve that had been her father's favorite and where the newly wed Louis Capet had very nearly lost his life in an ambush.

On this last grand tour of Aquitaine, a castle wall, the dip of a hill, an abbey, a mill, the sudden glimpse of a river brought back a flood of bittersweet memories. Here she had been born when the century was still young, and now, in a few months' time, she would see the beginning of a new century. Around her that spring crowded unseen presences, ghosts from the far-off days of her youth: her quiet, sweet-faced mother and the baby William, who had deserted her so suddenly; William the Troubadour and his voluptuous viscountess of Châtellerault; her handsome father, who could eat enough for eight men and who had not returned from Compostela with the promised cockleshell; her uncle Raymond, the blond lion of a boy who could bend an iron bar and who had deliberately sought the blade of a Saracen sword in Outremer. Their bodies slept in crypts and churchyards all over Christendom, their souls had moved on to unknown planes, but the memory of their passages through these lands remained with her. Petronilla as a small, naughty girl who followed her like an adoring puppy; Petronilla, who could not live without her count of Vermandois; and later still, Petronilla with her only son, who had contracted leprosy. And there must have been others, too. The troubadours whose songs still eddied in her mind—Jaufre Rudel, Bernard of Ventadour, Marcabru with his cynical woman-hating verses. And the husbands that destiny and her own desires had brought to her—Louis Capet with his endless prayers and simple smile, and the man whose shouts of "By God's eyes!" would always reverberate dimly in her ears. Henry FitzEmpress, Henry Plantagenet, King Henry II of England.

Her mind had become a library cataloguing the history of her time, all of which she had observed and much of which she had helped to make, and yet, unlike many aging people, there is good evidence that she refused to dwell in the past. Keenly aware of the changes that had taken place in her domains, she concentrated on the present and future. Where there once had been only cities and deserted countryside, now new conglomerates of people had sprung up, and in fact, the phenomenal growth of cities and towns had been the predominant characteristic of her era. These burghers and artisans who were proving so troublesome to local lords she released from their feudal obligations and invested with the civic liberties for which they clamored. At La Rochelle, she granted to the citizens a corporation "which shall enable them to defend and preserve their own rights more effectively," and at Poitiers, where sixty years earlier Louis Capet had herded the burghers' children into the main square as hostages because they had dared proclaim themselves a commune, Eleanor now presented the city with its charter of freedom. By granting these conciliatory charters of independence to town after town and releasing them from their obligations to local lords, she made it compulsory for them to contribute to their own defense, a strategy of such shrewdness that it would shortly be adopted by Philip Augustus. Did Eleanor perhaps foresee that one day these communes would impose on anarchistic Aquitaine the law and order that Henry had never been able to accomplish with fire and sword? One cannot know.

Between April and mid-July, Eleanor covered over a thousand miles, but the most personally difficult part of her mission still lay ahead. In July, she swallowed her pride and sought out Philip Augustus at Tours, where she did homage for her patrimony. A declaration of her independence from the struggle between Plantagenet and Capetian, which now had dragged on for two generations, this legal act excluded John from any claim to her inheritance and at the same time robbed Philip as well as Arthur of Brittany of any excuse to launch an offensive against her part of the empire. The accounts of the chroniclers provide only the barest details of this meeting, which must have been an unpleasant ordeal for both Eleanor and Philip, neither of whom had any illusions about the other. Philip, giving her the traditional kiss of peace, could not dispute her right to that vast territory that so many men had eyed hungrily, but he must have suspected that she was playing her cards close to her chest. What he could not know was that two months later, she would prepare a legal document ceding the duchy to John "as her right heir," commanding her vassals to do him homage and receive him peaceably but retaining to herself sole sovereignty for the remainder of her own life.

In September, Eleanor joined her son in Rouen, where she brought up urgent business. Shortly before Richard's death, there had been talk of a family alliance between Plantagenet and Capet, a project that Eleanor believed might help to cement a lasting peace and that she now urged John to revive in the hope of stalling Philip's schemes. But before Eleanor could put these plans into effect, she was beset with further tragedy. Her daughter, Joanna, former queen of Sicily, present countess of Toulouse, had not found happiness as the wife of Raymond VI, the son of Eleanor's old betrayer. In the course of the queen's tour that summer, she had unexpectedly encountered Joanna, who had a story of woe to tell. Her husband, evidently, had proved to be as unchivalrous as his father, and he treated Joanna, his fourth wife, with as little kindness or fidelity as he had shown his previous spouses. She had borne him a son and that year was pregnant again when, her husband away fighting one of his vassals in Languedoc, she had been compelled to put down a revolt. While besieging the castle of Cassès, some of her husband's knights had betrayed her by sending supplies to the castle and, as the last affront, set fire to her camp. Somehow, Joanna had escaped, and unable to rely on her husband, she had been fleeing north to seek the help of Richard when she learned of his death. At Niort, Eleanor had taken charge of her grieving and ill daughter and had sent her to the nuns of Fontevrault to recuperate. In September, however, Joanna arrived in Rouen, where, to the astonishment of all, she demanded to be made a nun of Fontevrault. Despite the fact that such a proceeding would be highly irregular—she was married and pregnant—Joanna persisted, and no amount of reasoning would deter her. In the end, Eleanor had supported her aspirations, and canon law had been overridden. It must have been obvious that her daughter, sick and worn, had reached the end of her days. Unable to stand when she took her vows, she closed her eyes a few days later and, minutes after her death, was delivered of a son, who lived only long enough to be baptized. In Rouen that autumn, the queen mourned her many recent losses. Alix of Blois had gone, leaving a daughter who had become a nun at Fontevrault. The lovely Countess Marie of Champagne had died the previous year, some said of sorrow when she learned that her eldest son, Henry, the king of Jerusalem, had fallen to his death from the window of his palace in Acre. Then Richard, and now Joanna. Of the ten children Eleanor had borne, only two remained: her namesake in faraway Castile and John Lackland.

In the first days of January 1200, the kings of England and France met on their mutual border to formally conclude a five-year treaty of peace. John, finally accepted as Richard's heir for the Plantagenet lands on the Continent, did homage to Philip as his overlord; Philip, for his part, relinquished his claims to Maine and Anjou in Arthur's name and agreed that the boy should do homage to John for Brittany. He refused, however, to give up custody of the youth. The treaty was sensible and fairly simple. If John had to pay thirty thousand marks of silver for his overlord's recognition, something neither Henry nor Richard would have been asked to do, times had changed, and such a sum of money only reflected the growing domination by the French monarchy in the affairs of Europe. At any event, part of the succession duty was designated as a dower for a princess of Castile, who, according to the treaty, should marry Philip's heir, Louis. At the conclusion of the negotiations, Gervase of Canterbury reported, the two kings "rushed into each other's arms."

Eleanor's chests had already been packed, her escort mounted, and once the treaty had been formally concluded, she set off with all possible speed to her daughter's court in Spain to bring back a bride for the young Louis Capet. Her route took her south to Poitiers and then down the highroad toward Bordeaux. Just past Poitiers, she entered the territory of the Lusignans, that quarrelsome and very numerous tribe who, thirty years earlier, had tried to abduct her and against whom the youthful William Marshal had demonstrated his knightly prowess. That generation of Lusignans had passed away, but another, just as nasty, had risen to take its place; as if to prove that history repeats, Hugh le Brun waylaid the queen's party and insisted that she visit his castle, a polite invitation to a kidnaping. Hugh did not intend to detain her unduly, only long enough to adjudicate a grievance that, apparently, she had overlooked during her goodwill tour a few months earlier. For some years, he had been vying with the lord of Angoulême for control of the rich sprawling county of La Marche to the east. Decades earlier, Henry had acquired the county from the Lusignans, and Richard had taken care to keep La Marche in his hands, but now Hugh made it clear that Eleanor would be released only on the condition that she surrender the highly prized fief. Knowing the uselessness of argument with Hugh le Brun, thrown back on her own resources, the queen exchanged the county for her freedom so quickly that within hours she was back on the road again. And so swiftly did she urge her escort through Gascony and over the Pyrenees that she arrived in Castile before the end of January.

Lively and charming, polished at the court of Poitiers for her high calling, Eleanor Plantagenet had been only nine years old when she had bid farewell to her mother and departed for the Castilian court. During the three intervening decades, it is doubtful whether they had met, and now, in the winter of Eleanor's life, it must have been a shock to see that the little damsel of her memories had become a thirty-eight-year-old mother of eleven children. For all her hurry to fetch a bride for the Capets, Eleanor seemed entranced once she arrived. The court of Alphonse VIII wore a civility and gaiety reminiscent of her own famous court at Poitiers; it was a place where troubadours gathered and poets still composed verse for a queen-patroness, who, like her mother, knew the value of beautiful words. With the Pyrenees between her and the maelstrom of problems in Europe, Eleanor settled into the sunny southern haven to renew thirty years of events with her namesake and make the acquaintance of her grandchildren. For two months, she tarried in her daughter's company, and when finally the moment for departure could be delayed no longer, she did not leave with the grandchild for whom she had come. The queen of Castile had three daughters of marriageable age: The eldest, Berengaria, had already been betrothed to the heir of León (and would become the mother of Saint Ferdinand of Spain). The second girl, Urraca, had been set aside for Louis Capet, but Eleanor's attention kept turning to the youngest of the three, twelve-year-old Blanche. There was something about the child that reminded her of herself, a streak of energy and ambition, perhaps that same vein of female strength that had safely borne Eleanor through the violent ebb and wash of twelfth-century politics. To justify her choice and prevent hurt feelings, it was necessary, however, to make diplomatic excuses. Urraca's name, the official explanation went, was too Spanish for the French people, the very sound of it would seem harsh to them. Blanche, on the other hand, would roll easily in the *langue d'oil*. Thus, Urraca was promptly betrothed to the heir of Portugal, while Blanche set off with Eleanor shortly before Easter. The roads through the Pyrenees were crowded with Easter pilgrims making their way toward Compostela, and perhaps under other circumstances, Eleanor might have joined the procession and visited the shrine where her father lay buried. But she had no time to spare for personal business, and soon she and Blanche had arrived at Bordeaux, where they rested for a few days at the Ombrière Palace. Looking down at the Garonne River or out toward the hills of Larmont, she might have pointed out to Blanche the field where Louis Capet's knights had raised their colorful tents and their banners fluttering the fleur-de-lis. Between the aged queen and the young girl, who, like Eleanor herself, would someday take her place as the queen of a Capet named Louis, there must have been many words, the oral history that women pass from one generation to the next, as well as the whole chronology of hatred between Plantagenet and Capet.

Tutoring her granddaughter for life among the Capets, the queen strolled in the dappled shade of the Ombrière gardens, but her strength suddenly began to diminish. Weary past weariness, she nevertheless participated in the Easter festivities and dutifully received her vassals, one of whom was the man upon whom she had relied so heavily in recent months, the mercenary Mercadier. Now, however, another prop was abruptly removed. "While she was staying at the city of Bordeaux on account of the solemnity of Easter, Mercadier the chief of the Brabantines came to her and on the second day of Easter week he was slain in the city by a man-at-arms in the service of Brandin." Come to pay his respects and escort his liege lady through Poitou, he had been killed in a street brawl. "After this, Queen Eleanor being fatigued with old age and the labour of the length of her journey, betook herself to the abbey of Fontevrault and there remained; while the daughter of the king of Castile, with Archbishop Elias of Bordeaux attending her, proceeded to Normandy and there was delivered into the charge of King John, her uncle." On May 23, 1200, Blanche and Louis were married at Portmort in Normandy, just across the border from France. The bride could not be married in her new land because the kingdom lay under an interdict as a result of Philip's misdeeds with a mistress; indeed, the king himself was not permitted to attend the ceremony. Nevertheless, he provided handsomely for entertainment. The sun shone, the banners flew, and the fields rang with song and the clashing of arms from the jousting arena.

At Fontevrault, the black-cowled figures silently trod the cloisters; the queen of England remained in her chamber, attended by her women. The chroniclers do not specify the nature of her illness, and perhaps at her age no explanation was necessary. Her travels during the past year had taxed her strength beyond the breaking point, and whatever maladies she might have suffered, no doubt exhaustion could be counted among them. From deep within herself she had dredged up unsuspected reserves of energy, and perhaps only when the crisis had passed did she allow herself to give way to natural fatigue. She had, for the first time, illusions about the future: She had secured the succession for John, she had placated Philip to some degree by doing homage for Aquitaine, she had married her granddaughter to the Capets. Henry's empire—her empire—remained more or less intact. Although she did not underestimate Philip and his dream of Carolingian domination, there seemed to be nothing more that she could do for the moment.

In the first summer of the thirteenth century, there was peace. Secure in his relations with the Capets, John cautiously undertook a tour of Aquitaine, making sure, of course, to bring along a sizable army. He was in the merry mood of a man who has just become a bachelor after a decade of dull matrimony. For ten years, he and Isabelle of Gloucester had barely tolerated each other. She had not been crowned with him the previous May; indeed, she rarely saw him and had borne no children. Perhaps at Eleanor's instigation, John had begun to consider his own posterity, and finding canonists to declare some glaring flaw in the marriage bond, he had become a single man again at the age of thirty-five. Undoubtedly, he had discussed with his mother the necessity of a second marriage as well as possible candidates, and their eyes had turned south to Portugal, where the king had a marriageable daughter. Early in 1200 tentative negotiations had begun, and during that quiet summer, John had dispatched an embassy to Lisbon for further discussions. Within weeks of its departure, however, the king's eyes had settled elsewhere. In July, he was in Poitou visiting the ancestral castle of the Lusignans, who, now that they had unceremoniously wrested La Marche from Eleanor, were anxious to make peace with their overlord. Although John could not have been pleased with their *fait accompli*, he had no choice but to make the best of it. Arriving at Lusignan during one of those great fêtes for which the south was famous, he found that the gathering included Count Aymer of Angoulême, a traditional enemy of the Lusignans and until recently a rival contender for La Marche. Lately, however, the difficulties between these two unruly houses had been patched up, and Hugh le Brun of Lusignan had been betrothed to Aymer's daughter, Isabella.

John, unlike Coeur de Lion, appreciated women, especially attractive ones. The twelve-year-old Isabella of Angoulême, as lovely and fresh as a newly budded rose, attracted him with a violence that completely knocked out of his head any marriage with an unknown Portuguese princess. Here, truly, was a feast to set before a king. Undismayed by Isabella's youth, on the contrary probably aroused by it, he began to outline in his mind a bold plan. Under the roof of his unsuspecting hosts, he pulled aside Count Aymer and dangled before his astonished eyes the vision of his daughter on the throne of England, an offer that caused the count to immediately discard any idea of Hugh le Brun as a son-in-law. It was agreed, however, that in view of the well-known violent disposition of the Lusignans, their conversations should remain secret. "On seeing that the king of England had a fancy for her," Aymer unhesitatingly removed the damsel from the household of her betrothed and whisked her back to Angoulême, while John found a pretext for dispatching the Lusignan brothers on missions to remote regions. Then he too left the region and continued south as far as Bordeaux. Not until August 23 did he casually arrive at Angoulême, but by this time he had added to his entourage the archbishop of Bordeaux. On Sunday the twenty-fourth, the date originally set for Isabella's marriage to Hugh le Brun, Archbishop Elias married the king to his child bride. Before news of this event could reach the Lusignans, John took the precaution of leaving the neighborhood and hastily beat a path to the safety of Chinon.

Later, the chroniclers would date John's subsequent troubles from this unprecipitate marriage, charging that Isabella had bewitched him, that in the grip of passion he had forgotten questions of policy or the possibility of repercussions. Actually, this does not seem to have been completely the case, although as often happens in matters of political policy, personal factors certainly played a role. The idea of the two rival houses of Angoulême and Lusignan resolving their differences could only have distressed John, and further, the prospect of Hugh le Brun eventually becoming lord of Lusignan, La Marche, and Angoulême would have disturbed him even more deeply. With Hugh ruling an area as large as the whole duchy of Normandy, the balance of power in Aquitaine would have been threatened; one way to avert this danger was for John to marry Isabella himself. At the same time, however, the exploit appealed to his sense of humor; at one stroke he could curb the Lusignans, take revenge for their kidnaping his mother and stealing La Marche, and possess a nymphet for whom he lusted. These delights far outweighed any fear of Hugh le Brun's indignation over the loss of his fiancée.

It has been suggested that John consulted Eleanor before he took this important step and that she gave her approval if not her joyful consent. But Eleanor's attitude has not been recorded, and perhaps her illness prevented her from accurately gauging the risks that John was taking in alienating the Lusignans. In the hands of an adroit king, such an exploit could be conducted successfully, but with John one never knew. It is possible that she, too, felt overjoyed to see Hugh le Brun cut down to size after his presumption in accosting highway travelers. At any event, John and Isabella visited her at Fontevrault that autumn, and as evidence of her goodwill toward the couple, she dowered Isabella with the cities of Niort and Saintes. At the beginning of October, the newlyweds went to England, where they were crowned together in Westminster Abbey on the eighth. Across the Channel, it was easy to forget the Lusignans; the king and queen made a grand tour around the country, one of those sweeping trips Henry had so loved, with John poking his nose into the tiniest hamlets, accepting homage from his vassals, hearing law cases, visiting Bishop Hugh of Lincoln in his last illness and remaining to act as a pallbearer at his funeral. During these months, the English could not help but make comparisons, and after a decade of absentee kingship, no matter how glorious Coeur de Lion had been, they felt grateful for a king who liked them well enough to live in their midst. It was, some people said, almost like a return to the days of old Henry FitzEmpress. By the middle of March 1201, John and Isabella were still in England, and on Easter they made a pilgrimage to Canterbury, where they wore their crowns and attended a lavish banquet as the guests of Archbishop Hubert Walter.

With the royal couple thus occupied, Eleanor continued to watch for trouble in the Continental provinces. Weak and bedridden, she nevertheless retained her sensitivity to gathering storms, and one of the areas on which she trained her ears was the Lusignan fortress in Poitou; indeed, it would not have required a seeress to anticipate trouble. Curiously, however, the clan had nursed their injuries in silence since the previous summer, hoping perhaps that John would recompense them for their loss. But John had no such intention, and for that matter, success having bred overbearing confidence, he deliberately provoked them further by authorizing his officials to take back the county of La Marche from Hugh and to attack Ralph of Lusignan's county of Eu and "do him all the harm they could." Disturbed by rumors of imminent defections and conspiracies, Eleanor sent for Viscount Amaury of Thouars, a kinsman and one of the most powerful barons of Poitou. In the uncertain days after Richard's death, he had joined Eleanor in her attack on Angers, and John, no doubt at his mother's behest, had rewarded the viscount with the wardship of Chinon and also made him seneschal of Anjou and Touraine. Once the danger had passed, however, he had taken these offices away again. Now, fearful of war in Poitou, Eleanor hastened to remedy this blunder and to reattach the viscount to their side. Writing to John of her diplomatic triumph, she said:

> I want to tell you, my very dear son, that I summoned our cousin Amaury of Thouars to visit me during my illness and the pleasure of his visit did me good, for he alone of your Poitevin barons has wrought us no injury nor seized unjustly any of your lands. . . . I made him see how wrong and shameful it was for him to stand by and let other barons render your heritage asunder, and he has promised to do everything he can to bring back to your obedience the lands and castles that some of his friends have seized.

Both Eleanor and the viscount wrote to warn of impending trouble and urged John to return immediately to the Continent.

The king, for whatever reason, took his good time in answering their appeals and delayed his arrival until June, at which time he must have decided that his ailing mother's anxieties were completely groundless. It was true that Ralph and Hugh le Brun of Lusignan had renounced their allegiance and appealed to the king of France with complaints that John had unjustly attacked them. But even though Philip accepted the appeal, he handled the matter cautiously. When John arrived at Barfleur, Philip persuaded the Lusignans to suspend their attacks against the Poitevin government and went to meet John personally at Château Gaillard, where they talked the matter over. And a few days after that, John and Isabella paid a state visit to Paris, where they were entertained lavishly at the Cité Palace, Philip himself having vacated the palace in their honor and retired to Fontainebleau. In this atmosphere of conviviality, the two kings worked out a reasonable compromise on the question of the Lusignans: Philip would not press their appeal for redress if John would give them the chance to submit their grievances at a formal trial. Having reached a sensible solution and drunk vast quantities of champagne, the rivals parted with embraces and protestations of brotherly love.

In the summer of 1201 not a cloud marred John's horizons. His mother's fears had proved baseless: Philip Augustus had behaved like a lamb; Aquitaine had been secured by John's friendship with Amaury of Thouars and his new father-in-law Aymer of Angoulême; Constance of Brittany had died, and hopefully there would be no further trouble with Arthur. His future, at last, seemed secure. That summer, too, no more was heard from Eleanor, who seems to have vanished among the shadowy cloisters. Unfortunately, security had the effect of arousing John to further exhibitions of high-handedness, or perhaps it was only a manifestation of his bizarre sense of humor. Instead of giving the Lusignans their day in court, he charged them with treason and invited them to prove their innocence by fighting a duel. The ordeal of battle, while no longer fashionable, was nevertheless still recognized as legally proper. The Lusignans, however, scorned to fight the professional duelists whom John had recruited, insisting that they were answerable only to their peers. Once more, they protested to Philip Augustus that they were being denied justice. Throughout the autumn and winter, the diplomatic farce continued, with John fixing dates for trials and then inventing elaborate excuses why the trials could not take place. Again Philip intervened, and again John promised the Lusignans justice.

Normally an impatient man, Philip Augustus had personal reasons for staying his hand. For the past decade, he had been involved in a distressing scandal with women. In 1192, the widowed Capetian had married Princess Ingeborg, sister of the king of Denmark, and had her crowned queen of France. The day after the wedding, however, he changed his mind and attempted to send her back to Denmark, but the outraged queen retreated only as far as a convent at Soissons, where she sped an appeal to Pope Celestine. While the aged Celestine did little for her restoration, he was succeeded by the more forceful Innocent III, who supported Ingeborg's claims, and in 1200, lowered an interdict on Philip's lands, not only for having forsaken Ingeborg but also for contracting an illegal union with a German heiress, Agnes of Meran, who had borne the king a daughter. Overwhelmed by these marital and extramarital problems, Philip spent much of his time negotiating with Rome. In the previous year, he had been forced to take back Ingeborg as his lawful wife, but he imprisoned her and continued to live with Agnes, who had a second child, a son. It was not until July 19, 1201, that "his German adulteress" relieved him of his problems by conveniently dying. Now only one legal entanglement remained—Rome's recognition of Agnes's children as legitimate—and until he received a favorable response from Innocent, he dared not make a move against the Plantagenets lest he jeopardize his case.

In March 1202, just as Philip's patience with John neared its limit, he received word that the papal curia had legitimized his son and daughter as royal heirs of the house of Capet. On April 28, Philip was ready to realize the ambition of his life, the destruction of Plantagenet power. Using the Lusignans as his pretext, he ordered John to answer charges in Paris and to undergo sentence by a court of French barons. John airily replied that, as duke of Normandy and king of England, he could not be summoned to a Parisian court, to which Philip retorted with equal aplomb that he had addressed the summons to John as duke of Aquitaine, count of Poitou, and count of Anjou. It was not his fault that John happened to be duke of Normandy and king of England as well. John, quite understandably, did not appear in Paris on the appointed day, and therefore "the assembled barons of the King of France adjudged the King of England to be deprived of all his land which he and his forefathers had hitherto held of the King of France." Fifty years earlier, John's father had treated a similar summons with scorn when he had married without the permission of his overlord—but John was not Henry, and Philip Augustus bore little resemblance to Louis Capet. Philip could hardly be called a man of courage—he would mount only the most docile horses, and he saw assassins behind trees—nor was he a venturesome military tactician. But what he lacked in boldness he made up for in cunning and persistence.

The man born to be a hammer to the king of the English had pounded doggedly but, in the end, impotently upon the shields of Henry Plantagenet and Richard Coeur de Lion, but time had fought on Philip's side. Finally, there remained only the feckless John, and even though it was common knowledge that he followed his mother's advice, the eagle-eyed grandam, half dead at Fontevrault, had not been heard from in some time. When John failed to answer his summons, Philip first declared forfeit all John's lands except Normandy and England and then he fell upon eastern Normandy. Not for Philip Capet any bold conquistadorial sally down the valley of the Loire; instead, he attacked piecemeal, raiding border towns, snatching a county here, besieging a castle there. At Gournay, in July, he knighted Arthur in the presence of the French barons and received the boy's homage not only for Brittany but for all the Continental lands inherited by John save Normandy, which Philip intended to keep for himself. Furthermore, he betrothed Arthur to his five-year-old daughter by Agnes of Meran and then endowed his prospective son-in-law with two hundred Frankish knights and instructions to take possession of his inheritance. The first target: Poitou.

Hearing of these events, Eleanor took violent exception to Philip's disposition of her domains. At eighty, she could not deny that her end was drawing near, but duty, pride, and no doubt anger would not allow her to lie in her abbey bed while Louis Capet's hated son dismembered the Plantagenet empire. She must have acknowledged the likelihood that someday Philip and Arthur would seize Anjou and Maine, but one humiliation she would not tolerate: She would not permit them to have Aquitaine while she possessed life enough to stop them. Accompanied by a small escort, she left the safety of Fontevrault toward the end of July and set out for Poitiers, where perhaps she believed that her presence alone might stiffen her vassals' resistance to Arthur's onslaught. We do not know the precise state of her health that summer; it is conceivable that during her convalescence she had regained some of her strength, but even so, it is not hard to imagine her weakened condition. For this reason, she was compelled to travel slowly and break the fifty-mile journey now and then. In the last week of July, she was at the castle of Mirebeau on the border of Anjou and Poitou.

During that same week, John was in the vicinity of Le Mans. Ever since his peace treaty with Philip two years earlier, English barons had taunted him with a new nickname, John "Softsword," but at this stage of the crisis he was behaving with remarkable capability. In the hope of diverting those Bretons intending to join Arthur, he had sent part of his forces to harass eastern Brittany, and his Norman garrisons he left to fend off Philip's attacks. He himself rode south with a hastily recruited army of mercenaries to protect Maine and Anjou, the vulnerable heartland of the empire.

In the meantime, Arthur, flushed with confidence and "marching forth with a pompous noise," had arrived in Tours with his force of borrowed French knights. While waiting there for the arrival of his Breton barons and making preparations for the assault on Poitou, he was joined by three of the Lusignans. Impatient and full of strategies of their own, the brothers disdained to wait for the Bretons and instead urged an immediate attack on Poitou; indeed, they proposed an even bolder plan. Intelligence had come to their ears that the old queen was stopping at the castle of Mirebeau.

For fifty years, the Lusignan family seems to have been obsessed with the idea of kidnaping Eleanor. Twice before they had made attempts, the most recent of which had worked out with unexpected success. In this situation, her worth as a hostage would be considerable, for it would enable them to wrest from John any concession they liked. The loss of his mother would rob the king of his most sagacious counselor; furthermore, as duchess of Aquitaine in her own right, it was in Eleanor's power to make Philip's declaration of forfeiture null and void in Aquitaine so long as she lived to assert her claims. While Arthur had no feelings of loyalty or affection for his grandmother, he hesitated on the grounds that he wished to wait for reinforcements from Brittany. But in the end, the impetuous Lusignans prevailed. It would be an easy matter to take Mirebeau: The queen's escort was insignificant, the risks minimal, and her capture would bring the soft-sworded Plantagenet king to his knees. In the closing days of July, the boy duke of Brittany and his Frankish knights followed the Lusignans down the back roads toward Mirebeau.

Of all the places that Eleanor might have stopped to rest, Mirebeau was the least secure. A half century earlier it had been a formidable castle; Geoffrey Anjou had bequeathed it to his younger son, and when the young Geoffrey planned his uprising against Henry in 1155, he had added fortifications to make it impregnable. By the summer of 1202, however, the walled castle encircled by a walled town had become as invincible as a child's sand castle. Not only did it totter on the brink of collapse, but it was not stocked to resist a siege.

Arthur's arrival did not catch the queen unprepared. She, too, had her sources of information, and before the first thud of hoofbeats reached her ears, she had already sent a messenger riding hard toward Le Mans in search of her son. It is generally believed that this was an urgent plea for rescue, but since John was not known for speed or military prowess, it seems equally likely that she dispatched the messenger only as a means of informing the king of his enemies' movements. In any case, she knew that she could not hold out long. Few details of the siege have been preserved, but it seems that Arthur coolly opened negotiations with his grandmother by demanding her surrender and offering a promise of release if she would confirm Philip Augustus's arrangements for her inheritance. In no position to disdain parley, Eleanor pretended to bargain, but she took care to play for time by drawing out the negotiations as long as possible.

By Monday, July 31, Arthur's army had taken possession of the town as well as the castle, forcing Eleanor to withdraw into the keep with a few soldiers. Only the portcullis stood between her and capture. That evening she could stare down upon the comings and goings of her besiegers. Having barricaded all the town gates except one, which they left open to receive supplies, the soldiers began to settle themselves for the night. It was a warm evening with a sky full of magnificent stars. With their quarry at their mercy, the men seemed to be in a casual, almost festive mood. Putting aside their armor, they made their beds in the streets and in the inner enclosure of the castle under the open sky, and they fell asleep knowing that in the morning they could storm the keep without losing a man.

While Mirebeau slumbered, John and his forces were approaching the outskirts of the town. Traveling by day and night in an eighty-mile forced march from Le Mans, he had covered the distance in less than forty-eight hours with a suddenness reminiscent of Henry's astounding ability to pop up in unexpected places as if carried effortlessly by the wind. With John came William des Roches, the seneschal of Anjou, who offered to lead the attack on the understanding that John would not put to death Arthur or any of the rebels, that captives would not be removed from the county until a truce had been established, and that des Roches would have a chief say in Arthur's future. John agreed. Dawn was breaking on Tuesday, August 1, as des Roches and his men crept up to the one open gate. When they rushed in with drawn swords, Hugh le Brun and his brothers were having an early breakfast of roast pigeons, but most of the besiegers were still snoring or were slumped halfdressed. By the time that the sun broke through the clouds, the whole of Arthur's forces had been either slain or captured; not a man escaped. Exultant over his victory, John himself described the feat in a letter to his English barons:

Know that by the grace of God we are safe and well and God's grace has worked wonderfully with us, for on Tuesday before the feast of Saint Peter ad Vincula, when we were on the road to Chinon, we heard that our lady mother was closely besieged at Mirebeau and we hurried there as fast as we could. And there we captured our nephew Arthur, Geoffrey de Lusignan, Hugh le Brun, Andrew de Chauvigni, the viscount of Châtellerault, Raymond Thouars, Savary de Mauleon, Hugh Bauge, and all our other Poitevin enemies who were there, being upwards of two hundred knights, and not one escaped. Praise God for our victory.

Undoubtedly it was an astounding achievement for in a few hours, John had succeeded in capturing the most important of his rebel enemies. Some said that his demon ancestry had carried him to Mirebeau so swiftly, others called it a miracle, and Eleanor, continuing safely on her journey, may have felt for the first time in thirty-five years that her youngest son might be a great king after all. In Normandy, where the king of the Franks was occupied with the siege of Arques, the news of John's incredible exploit cast the Capetian into a fit of depression. Dismantling his siege engines, he hurried south to see if anything might be retrieved from the disaster, but he was too late. His dream of reviving Charlemagne's empire had been shattered by the stupidity of the Lusignans: Arthur captured, his best knights in chains, his Poitevin allies dispersed, the incompetent Lackland in control, and all for the sake of capturing an eighty-year-old woman whom the world would soon forget. Venting his frustration by setting fire to Tours, Philip Augustus could do nothing ultimately but smolder, and "at length he retreated to Paris and remained inactive there for the rest of the year."

Meanwhile, John was making a leisurely progress through Anjou and Normandy, parading his manacled prisoners as a warning to those considering sedition. The spectacle of the leading barons and knights of France, Brittany, and Poitou in chains was not witnessed by Eleanor, who had reached Poitiers, but the wretched sight would be remembered by others and detailed with sad astonishment by the chroniclers. "Having secured his prisoners in fetters and shackles and having placed them in cars, a new and unusual mode of conveyance, the king sent some of them to Normandy and some to England to be imprisoned in strong castles." Hugh le Brun, securely fettered, was consigned to a special tower at Caen, while less important prisoners were shipped to Corfe Castle and other strongholds in England, where some died of starvation and a very few managed to escape. As for the prize captive, the duke of Brittany was placed in a dungeon at Falaise on August 10.

That year, John kept Christmas court at Caen, "feasting with his queen and lying in bed till dinner-time," but the holiday was marked by a sense of uneasy triumph for Eleanor. In Poitiers, safe in her high tower above the Clain, she had genuine reason for optimism in that, for the moment at least, the Plantagenets held the trump cards in their struggle with Philip Augustus. If someone had told her that the triumph of Mirebeau would be the last great victory of an English king on French soil until the fourteenth century and that within the next two years even Normandy, the most loyal of the Plantagenet fiefs on the Continent, would virtually be lost, she might have laughed in derision. And then again she might not have. Even by Christmas of 1202 the ominous signs were there for those possessing the perception to read them. She was aware that John trod on extremely delicate ground with regard to the imprisonment of Arthur and the rebels, since these imprisonments had followed ruthlessly on John's oath to William des Roches at Mirebeau that he would not take vengeance. Perhaps Eleanor herself had genuinely, if naively, expected John to keep his promise. But after des Roches and Amaury of Thouars had seen their relatives and friends tied to oxcarts on the road to Normandy, these barons and others had turned away from John in disgust and transferred their allegiance to the French king. By midautumn they had captured Angers, the city Eleanor had personally retaken in the weeks after Richard's death, and soon the roads between Chinon and Poitiers became unsafe for travel. As Eleanor might have told John, victory in itself is meaningless if one lacks the intelligence to profit from it, but the closeness of her relations with her son at this period is unclear. With the rebels holding much of the territory between Poitiers and Chinon, communications were often poor. However, from rumor if nothing else she would have known of the pressure being brought to bear on the king for Arthur's release, some of his vassals even offering their homage to Philip for the duration of Arthur's imprisonment. In November, John had released the Lusignans, a foolish concession, because despite their pledges of loyalty, they immediately joined the rebel party.

Admittedly, the question of what to do with Arthur was a thorny one, and perhaps on Eleanor's advice, John tried to make peace with his nephew. According to Roger of Wendover, he visited Falaise in January 1203 and ordered the boy brought to him. "The king addressed him kindly and promised him many honors, asking him to separate himself from the French king and to adhere to the side of his lord and uncle." But the boy regarded John as he would a worm in a bowl of porridge.

Arthur ill-advisedly replied with indignation and threats, and demanded that the king give up to him his kingdom of England with all the territories which King Richard had possessed at his death. Since all these possessions belonged to him by hereditary right, he swore that unless King John quickly restored the aforesaid territory to him, he would never give him a moment's peace for the rest of his life. The king was much troubled at hearing his words.

More than "much troubled," John was infuriated at the youth's audacity. After six months in the dungeons of Falaise, an experience sufficient to humble the most stiff-necked, the boy's overweening pride remained intact, and his haughtiness seemed as strong as ever. But more than outraged, John grew panicky. Something about the interview frightened him and frightened him so badly that he at once began to consider drastic measures. Perhaps he was convinced that the boy seriously meant his threats and would truly remain a source of anxiety and potential uprising for the remainder of John's days. Afterward, a chronicler said, John took counsel with certain advisers (which ones are unspecified) who urged him to have Arthur castrated and blinded so as to eliminate him as a rival. Orders for the mutilations were given, but the two men sent to carry them out lost their stomach for the ghastly operation upon hearing Arthur's howls and finally his jailer, Hubert de Burgh, sent them away. After countermanding the king's orders, de Burgh took it upon himself to announce that Arthur had died of natural causes; bells were rung at Falaise, and the boy's clothing distributed to charity. This quickly proved to be a miscalculation on de Burgh's part, because instead of removing the wind from the Bretons' sails as he had hoped, the announcement only roused Arthur's partisans to new heights of hysteria, in which they swore undying vengeance on John. At this point, de Burgh hastily amended his report and swore that Arthur was still alive; no one, however, believed him.

In February or March, John "gave orders that Arthur should be sent to Rouen to be imprisoned in the new tower there and kept closely guarded." And then, the chronicler added abruptly, "the said Arthur disappeared."

The disappearance of Arthur of Brittany remained the great unsolved mystery of the thirteenth century. It is true that after the gates of Rouen clanged shut behind him, he was never seen again, but ugly rumors had circulated while he was still alive at Falaise. Sinister stories were told in Paris, in Brittany, even at the queen's own court in Poitiers, to the effect that the king of England had murdered his own nephew. The fact is that no one, probably not even Eleanor, knew for certain what had happened to Arthur. The chroniclers could only report rumors: "Opinion about the death of Arthur gained ground by which it seemed that John was suspected by all of having slain him with his own hand; for which reason many turned their affections from the king and entertained the deepest enmity against him." One of the few people in a position to know what actually happened was William de Braose, the man who had captured Arthur at Mirebeau and later the commander of the new fortress at Rouen, where Arthur was imprisoned after he left Falaise. One of John's cronies, de Braose remained high in the king's favor until about 1210, when he dropped so suddenly that he was forced to take refuge at the French court. Long after people had stopped guessing about Arthur's whereabouts, monks at the Cistercian abbey of Margam in Wales set down in their annals a detailed account of the duke's death. Since the de Braoses were patrons of the abbey, it has been concluded that the monks received their information from de Braose himself or some member of his family. The chronicler described the following events as taking place on April 3, 1203:

> After King John had captured Arthur and kept him alive in prison for some time in the castle of Rouen, after dinner on the Thursday before Easter, when he was drunk and possessed of the devil, he slew him with his own hand and, tying a heavy stone to the body, cast it into the Seine. It was brought up by the nets of a fisherman and, dragged to the bank, was identified and secretly buried, for fear of the tyrant, in Notre Dame des Pres, a priory of Bec.

Toward the end of April 1203, Eleanor and her barons received a messenger bearing a letter from John, written at Falaise on April 16 and witnessed by William de Braose. "We send to you brother John of Valerant, who has seen what is going forward with us and who will be able to appraise you of our situation. Put faith in him respecting those things whereof he will inform you. God be thanked, things are going better for us than this man is able to tell you." It has been suggested that this cryptic last line was John's way of informing his mother that the Plantagenets had nothing more to fear from the duke of Brittany. If this was truly so and Eleanor was able to read between the lines of her son's letter, she must have realized that Plantagenet rule in France had become no more substantial than a guttering candle.

It was spring again. The sap had begun to rise in the withered trees, the rivers gleamed like wax, plowmen turned over the good black earth, small birds swooped and dipped against the canopy of the sky. It was the season of renewal and also the season for going to war. The king of France roamed the Plantagenet provinces at will; sailing down the Loire by boat, he leisurely took possession of fortresses along his route, and in ensuing months, he would have those famous castles where Eleanor and Henry had kept their Christmas courts, brought children into the world, made love, and quarreled furiously: Domfront, Le Mans, Falaise, Bayeux, Lisieux, Caen, Avranches. "Messengers came to John with the news, saying that the King of the French has entered your territories as an enemy, has taken such and such castles, carries off their governors ignominiously bound to their horses' tails, and disposes of your property at will without anyone stopping him. In reply to this news, King John said, 'Let him alone! Someday I will recover all I have lost.' " By August 1203, Philip had reached the Rock of Andelys and cast his eyes up at Château Gaillard, the fortress that Richard had boasted he could defend if its walls were made of butter. The seat of Plantagenet power on the Continent, it was the one castle that by all logic the Capetian had no hope of winning and, by the same token, John had no fear of losing. Even so, Philip set up his siege engines and catapults.

"In the meantime," Roger of Wendover writes, "the king was staying inactive with his queen at Rouen, so that it was said that he was infatuated by sorcery or witchcraft, for in the midst of all his losses and disgrace, he showed a cheerful countenance to all, as though he had lost nothing." The chronicler omits a few important facts. At the end of August, John devised an imaginative plan for the relief of Château Gaillard, a night operation to bring supplies to the castle by land and water, but a miscalculation of the tides on the Seine turned the expedition into a disaster, and John's army was repulsed with heavy losses. The king's failure to relieve Château Gaillard provided the final blow to the confidence of his Norman barons. By the autumn of 1203, his military resources were exhausted, and even William Marshal bluntly advised him to abandon the struggle.

"Whoso is afraid, let him flee!" answered John. "I myself will not flee for a year."

"Sire," Marshal pointed out, "you have not enough friends. You who are wise and mighty and of high lineage and whose work it is to govern us all have not been careful to avoid irritating people."

By the first week of December, there remained on the Continent little that John could call his own except Rouen, the beleaguered Rock of Andelys, and the Norman shores of the Channel. On December 5, he sailed from Barfleur with Isabella, William Marshal, and a few others. He was leaving, he said, to seek the aid and counsel of his English barons; he would, he promised, return soon. Exactly three months later, on March 6, 1204, the Saucy Castle hung out a white flag. Those Norman barons who had remained loyal sent couriers to England notifying the king of their precarious position, "to which messages King John answered that they were to expect no assistance from him but that each was to do what seemed best to him."

Among those thus cast upon their own resources was Eleanor, but by this time she had, evidently, slipped into a coma, the annals of Fontevrault stating that she existed as one already dead to the world. She would not live to witness the loss of Normandy, to watch Louis Capet's son march into Poitiers, to hear of Runnymede or Magna Charta, and of course she would never know that only one king of England would be named John. Perhaps even the fall of Coeur de Lion's Château Gaillard failed to penetrate the private cocoon into which she had withdrawn.

The last months of her life are blank. The chroniclers were too busy documenting the smoking rubble of Henry's great dream to concern themselves with an octogenarian queen, and later, they would not even agree on the place where she had spent her last days. The chronicle of Saint Aubin of Angers claimed that she died in her native city of Poitiers, but others declared that prior to her coma, she had made her way to Fontevrault, where she took the veil. During those last fatal months, whether at the ducal palace of her forebears or among the veiled women at Fontevrault, she had been a queen for sixty-six years, but she did not count the time. Born with one foot on fortune's throne, crowned with garlands of rare intelligence and beauty, loving when she could and hating when she must, she had traveled a long weary road through the highest citadels of Christendom. On April 1, 1204, her turbulent pilgrimage ended.

Eight centuries later, the traveler driving along the Loire toward Tours may turn down N 147 at Montsoreau village and ride the few miles to Fontevrault Abbey. There in the cool south transept of the church can be seen Eleanor of Aquitaine lying between the second of her husbands and her beloved Coeur de Lion. The Gothic effigy on her tomb, ravaged by time and revolution, shows her lying full length, her ageless face framed by a wimple, her expression radiating dignity and the faintest suggestion of a smile. Her graceful fingers clasp a small open book—and who can tell from the stone image whether it is a missal or a volume of those *cansos* that meant so much to her? In the shadows, alone with her book, she reads on in peace and serenity.

Notes and Sources

Prologue

3 "Aquitaine, wrote Ralph": Ralph of Diceto, vol. 1, p. 293.

5 "When they set themselves": *Ibid.*

5 "Nowadays, scornfully wrote": Geoffrey of Vigeois, Delisle, vol. 12, p. 450.

6 "Unlike their counterparts": Barber, p. 79.

6 Arrival of the troubadours: Briffault, p. 85.

A Child in the Land of Love

7 "Duke William IX": In the following account of Eleanor's grandparents and parents I have relied mainly on Alfred Richard's *Histoire des comtes de Poitou, 778–1204,* unless otherwise indicated.

9 Pope Urban's speech at Clermont: Viorst, pp. 40–44.

11 "In the fall of 1096": During the First Crusade, Count Raymond of Toulouse was better known as Raymond of Saint-Gilles.

12 William IX's Crusade: Oldenbourg, pp. 175, 182; Runciman, vol. 2, pp. 28–29.

13 "At home again, his restlessness": Ordericus Vitalis, vol. 3, p. 300. Prior to William's stay in Antioch, he had had other opportunities to hear Moorish music. His father, William VIII (Guy-Geoffrey), is said to have brought back captured female singers from an expedition against the Moors in 1064, and William also must have heard this type of music while courting Philippa in Aragon.

13 William's love poems: Creekmore, p. 39; Flores, *Medieval Age,* p. 102; Marks, p. 73.

13 "Although Philippa's dream": Bertrand followed his father to Syria and died there in 1112. Since his heir, half brother Alphonse-Jourdain, was only nine, William was able to take back Toulouse for his wife in 1113.

14 "William of Malmesbury related": William of Malmesbury, vol. 2, pp. 510–511.

14 Founding of Fontevrault: Marks, p. 62; White, p. 60.

14 "Flinging himself": William of Malmesbury, vol. 2, pp. 510–511.

15 "But William replied jokingly": *Ibid.*

16 "Among the women": James, *Letters,* p. 181.

17 "One chronicler contended": Richard, vol. 1, p. 478. Ralph of Diceto asserts that young William's rebellion began in 1112. At that time, however, he was only thirteen, and furthermore, William had not yet met Dangereuse.

17 Portrait of Aenor: In fairness to Eleanor's mother, we know virtually nothing of her life or feelings. As the Bulloughs point out in *The Subordinate Sex* (p. 3): "About the only way a woman managed to appear as an individual in the historical record was when she scandalized her contemporaries." Unlike both her mother and her daughter, Aenor did nothing shocking. Thus even though she appears colorless, this may not have been the case.

17 "There is a story": Bregy, p. 91. Author does not cite source of this quote. However, I have included it because it is typical of the kind of thing said about Eleanor.

17 Eleanor's date of birth: Some chroniclers give the date as 1120, but since her age was recorded as eighty-two when she died in 1204, the year 1122 must be correct.

18 "She was named": Geoffrey of Vigeois, Delisle, vol. 12, pp. 434–435.

20 "How much I tupped them": Creekmore, p. 41.

20 William IX's Spanish Crusade: Marks, p. 86.

20 "My friends": *Ibid.*, p. 87.

21 Description of Eleanor's education and training are entirely inferential: Holmes, pp. 227–228; Evans, pp. 116–120; Rowling, p. 84.

24 "Her name first appeared": Richard, vol. 2, pp. 10–11, 18.

25 Life of Radegonde: *Encyclopedia of Catholic Saints*, Aug., pp. 69–72; Marks, pp. 1–10.

26 "Meeting at the Abbey of Montierneuf": James, *Letters*, p. 199.

27 "Once, some fifteen years earlier": *Ibid.*, p. 8.

27 "We have petitioned you": Williams, p. 132.

27 "The bishop of Poitiers": *Ibid.*, p. 133.

28 William's betrothal: Richard, vol. 2, p. 51. Geoffrey of Vigeois claimed that William actually married Emma, but subsequent events do not bear out this allegation.

31 "Throughout Aquitaine": Geoffrey of Vigeois, Delisle, vol. 12, p. 435.

32 William X's death: Ordericus Vitalis, vol. 4, p. 175.

The Devil and the Monk

33 Louis the Fat at Béthizy: Suger, *Vie*, pp. 280–282; Richard, vol. 2, pp. 57–58.

34 "The boy, says Walter": Walter Map, p. 285.

34 "The fall 'so dreadfully' ": Ordericus Vitalis, vol. 4, p. 129.

35 Louis's journey to Bordeaux: Geoffrey of Vigeois, Delisle, vol. 12, p. 435; Richard, vol. 2, pp. 59–60.

36 "Ringing in his ears": Molinier, p. 128.

37 "A great crowd": Geoffrey of Vigeois, Delisle, vol. 12, p. 435.

38 "The Franks to battle": Kelly, p. 13, citing Raoul of Caen.

39 "Scarcely the tongue": *Chronique de Morigny*, p. 68.

39 Wedding menu is inferential: Holmes, pp. 87–88, 93.

39 "Saint James": Flores, *Anthology,* p. 13.

39 "Perhaps Marcabru": *Ibid.,* pp. 15–25.

39 "The French clerks": Briffault, p. 53.

40 Eleanor and Louis's wedding: Ordericus Vitalis, vol. 4, p. 181; Richard, vol. 2, p. 61.

41 Trip to Poitiers: Suger, *Vie,* p. 283; Richard, vol. 2, pp. 60–61.

42 "With no father": Dangereuse lived a long and full life; she did not die until 1151.

42 "In a holiday mood": Ordericus Vitalis, vol. 4, p. 182.

43 Death of Louis the Fat: Suger, *Vie,* p. 285; Ordericus Vitalis, vol. 4, p. 181.

43 Troubles with the dowager queen: Molinier, p. 150.

44 "For the first time within memory": Briffault, p. 247, n. 77. Briffault and others agree that the introduction of Provençal poetry and "courtly" ideas into northern France was largely due to Eleanor and, later, to her daughters, Marie and Alix.

45 "In his personal routine": The Notre Dame referred to was a church dating back to Merovingian times. The cathedral we know today was not begun until 1163.

45 "Odo de Deuil": Odo de Deuil, p. 3. From a letter written to Suger in the winter of 1148 while on the Second Crusade.

46 "In sex Louis": Richard, vol. 2, p. 90.

46 Description of Paris: Holmes, pp. 77–107.

48 "Peter Abélard blazed": John of Salisbury, *Metalogicon,* p. 95.

48 "It seems inconceivable": Abélard, p. 15.

49 "He would always remain": Suger, *Vie,* p. 267.

49 "The queen Suger": *Ibid.,* p. 280.

49 "He had such a great knowledge": Suger, *Oeuvres,* p. 382.

49 "In recent years": James, *Letters,* p. 112.

50 Political situation in Orléans and Poitiers: Richard, vol. 2, pp. 61–68.

51 "His demands were positively": Molinier, p. 151.

53 "Unlike previous French queens": Facinger, pp. 28–29.

53 Toulouse expedition: Ordericus Vitalis, vol. 4, p. 221.

54 "Eleanor's private feelings": Her ideal man was not very different from that of most women in the twelfth century.

54 "Still, perhaps from pity": Later Louis gave the vase to Suger. It can be seen today in the Louvre with the following inscription:

> Hoc vas Sponsa dedit Aenor Regi Ludovici,
> Mitadolus avo, mihi Rex, sanctisque Sugerus.

> Eleanor, his wife, gave this vase to King Louis,
> Mitadolus gave it to her grandfather, the king gave it to me, I, Suger give it to the Saints.

54 "She would make a holiday": Richard, vol. 2, p. 77.

55 "That year the archbishopric": James, *Saint,* p. 153.

56 "Like Eleanor": John of Salisbury, *Hist. Pont.,* p. 14.

56 Marriage of Ralph and Petronilla: Richard, vol. 2, pp. 78–79.
57 "Innocent's response": James, *Letters,* p. 361.
57 "In January 1143": Richard, vol. 2, p. 79.

Behind the Red Cross

59 "But Louis, feeling his soul": Gervaise, vol. 3, p. 94.
60 Bernard's letters to Pope Innocent and Louis VII: James, *Letters,* pp. 362–365.
61 "In early 1144": Richard, vol. 2, p. 81.
63 Suger's Gothic cathedral: Heer, p. 397.
64 "No one would have taken": Gervaise, vol. 3, p. 98.
64 "His whole body": Alan, bishop of Auxerre, trans. in Coulton, *Life in the Middle Ages,* p. 162.
65 "His hostility": James, *Saint,* p. 40. Bernard succeeded in shaming his sister; two years later she entered a convent.
65 "It is ironic": James, *Letters,* pp. 174–177.
65 "Bernard remembered the queen": *Ibid.,* p. 175.
66 "By the time she had finished": James, *Saint,* p. 159; Williams, p. 215; Richard, vol. 2, p. 81.
66 "My child": Migne, vol. 185, pp. 332 and 527.
67 "The papal bans": John of Salisbury, *Hist. Pont.,* pp. 12, 14; Molinier, p. 150, n. 4.
67 "Following the havoc": Richard, vol. 2, p. 82.
68 "That year of 1145": *Ibid.,* p. 84.
68 "Then in the closing days": Oldenbourg, p. 319.
69 "Although rumors of disturbances": Runciman, vol. 2, p. 247.
69 **"At Christmas court": Odo de Deuil, p. 7;** *Chronique de Morigny,* p. 85.
70 "Among those who voiced disapproval": Odo de Deuil, p. 7, n. 6.
71 "And since there was no place": *Ibid.,* p. 9. Other chroniclers claim that the platform, except for the portion Louis stood on, collapsed, but no one was injured. Odo fails to mention the incident.
71 "Soon Bernard's supply": *Ibid.*
72 "Later, after the newly blessed *cruciati*": It is a dramatic story but probably not true. The tale is mentioned in Gervaise, vol. 3, p. 118, and has been repeated by numerous writers, including some fairly modern ones. "This band of mad-women practiced Amazonian exercises and performed a thousand follies in public" (Strickland, vol. 1, p. 246).
72 "William of Newburgh": William of Newburgh, vol. 1, pp. 92–93.
73 "To him, taking the cross": Oldenbourg, p. 324.
74 "William of Tyre relates": William of Tyre, vol. 2, p. 179.
74 "At Fontevrault": Richard, vol. 2, p. 85.
75 "Finally, at Christmas": Williams, p. 274.
75 "For this purpose": Roger of Wendover, vol. 1, p. 498.
76 Étampes conference: Odo de Deuil, pp. 13–15.
76 "Suger was only slightly": *Ibid.,* p. 15, n. 36.
77 "The crowds and the king's wife": *Ibid.,* p. 19.
80 "Somewhere in that unruly torrent": Marks, pp. 138–143. Rudel did not return. Either he was killed or he may have entered a monastery in Antioch and died there.

To Jerusalem

82 "Her critics": William of Tyre, vol. 2, p. 180.

83 "Odo de Deuil": Odo de Deuil, p. 21.

84 "Resigning herself": Odo includes only four brief references to Eleanor, and in not one of them does he call her by name. It has been suggested that Odo's work may have been subsequently revised, and all extensive references to Eleanor excised. For example, in the following passage, it would seem that a lacuna occurs: "Occasionally the empress wrote to the queen. And then the Greeks degenerated into women; putting aside all manly vigor, both of words and of spirit, they lightly swore whatever they thought would please us, but they neither kept faith with us nor maintained respect for themselves." Odo de Deuil, p. 57.

84 "The bishop of Langres": *Ibid.*, p. 27.

85 "To the thirteen-year-old": Anna Comnena, p. 248.

86 "Odo, having nothing": Odo de Deuil, p. 33.

86 "In a mood": Delisle, vol. 15, p. 487.

86 "For the other countries": Odo de Deuil, p. 41.

87 "Instead, in some bewilderment": *Ibid.*, p. 45.

87 "The only Greeks": *Ibid.*

87 "Because of this": *Ibid.*, p. 57.

87 "In other words": John of Salisbury, *Hist. Pont.*, p. 54.

87 "Since the bodies": Odo de Deuil, p. 47.

88 "While Rome had sunk": *Ibid.*, p. 63.

89 "Even Eleanor and Louis": *Ibid.*, p. 61, n. 5. Odo is vague about their accommodations. Some historians have concluded that they were lodged in Manuel's palace, the Blachernae, but I believe that if they had been invited to share the royal residence, Odo would have mentioned it. Probably he avoided doing so because he wished to gloss over the snub.

89 "Touring the Blachernae": Odo de Deuil, p. 65.

90 "Her fortunes transformed": William of Tyre, vol. 2, p. 174.

91 "Conscientiously she organized": Odo de Deuil, p. 67.

93 "Odo tells us": *Ibid.*, p. 67.

93 "One day": *Ibid.*, p. 75

94 "It was feared": *Ibid.*, p. 83.

94 "The victorious Turks": William of Tyre, vol. 2, p. 168.

95 "Louis, nevertheless": Odo de Deuil, p. 91.

96 "Most likely Conrad": *Ibid.*, p. 99.

96 "Although you do not fear": *Ibid.*, p. 105.

96 "Eventually he came across": *Ibid.*

96 "Perchance": William of Tyre, vol. 2, p. 174.

97 "Filled with joy": *Ibid.*, p. 175.

98 "Harassed at every step": Odo de Deuil, p. 111.

99 "At noon": William of Tyre, vol. 2, p. 175.

99 "Although there was no avenue": Odo de Deuil, p. 119.

99 "William of Tyre": William of Tyre, vol. 2, p. 176.

100 "His royal bodyguard": Odo de Deuil, p. 119.

100 "No aid came": *Ibid.*, p. 117.

100 "With tremulous voice": William of Tyre, vol. 2, p. 177.

100 "By many of the Franks": These charges would pursue Eleanor down to modern times. "The freaks of Queen Eleanor and her female warriors were the cause of all the misfortunes that befell King Louis and his army, especially in the defeat at Laodicea." Strickland, vol. 1, p. 246.

101 "With this food": Odo de Deuil, p. 129.

102 "Let us, the king insisted": *Ibid.*, p. 131.

102 "It is not difficult": *Ibid.*, p. 133.

103 "It was more like": Hill, *Gesta Francorum*, p. 76; Munro, p. 19.

104 "Thirteen years earlier": Runciman, vol. 2, p. 199.

104 Raymond's reception of the Crusaders: William of Tyre, vol. 2, p. 180.

107 "While Louis had been": In justice to Louis, it should be noted that as a rule the Capetian kings were faithful husbands; only two bastards were recorded for the fourteen kings of their dynasty (Fawtier, p. 52).

108 "Undoubtedly he recalled": John of Salisbury, *Hist. Pont.*, p. 52.

108 "How Louis initially reacted": *Ibid.*, p. 53.

108 "So when Louis objected": *Ibid.*

108 "Five years earlier": James, *Letters*, p. 371.

109 "Louis could not deny": Their kinship was extremely complicated. Another way of reckoning was that Eleanor's great-grandmother Aldeardis was an aunt of Louis's mother, Adelaide.

109 "However deeply moved": John of Salisbury, *Hist. Pont.*, p. 53.

109 "He boldly persuaded": *Ibid.*

110 "The archbishop would say": William of Tyre, vol. 2, p. 180.

110 "The anonymous chronicle": Minstrel of Reims, p. 258.

111 "The chronicles provide": John of Salisbury, *Hist. Pont.*, p. 53.

111 "Louis's arrival in Syria": William of Tyre, vol. 2, p. 181.

The Unwanted Crown

112 "At the Jaffa Gate": William of Tyre, vol. 2, p. 183.

113 "John of Salisbury": John of Salisbury, *Hist. Pont.*, p. 53.

114 "At this time, Frankish Syria": William of Tyre, vol. 2, p. 182.

114 "In mid-May": *Ibid.*, p. 185.

114 "Among the Crusaders": *Ibid.*, p. 181.

115 "This was, to put it mildly": Runciman, vol. 2, p. 281.

115 "On Saturday, July 24": William of Tyre, vol. 2, pp. 187–190.

116 "Arab historian": ibn-al-Qalanisi, trans. in Gabrieli, p. 59.

117 "On both sides": William of Tyre, vol. 2, p. 194.

117 "Slowly the crusading army": John of Salisbury, *Hist. Pont.*, p. 58.

118 "Thinly disguised": Delisle, vol. 15, pp. 509–510.

118 "O eternal God": Hill, *Gesta Francorum*, p. 102.

118 "She had climbed": *Ibid.*, p. 99.

119 "Many thinking men": John of Salisbury, *Hist. Pont.*, p. 11.

119 "Less charitable chroniclers": Delisle, vol. 12, p. 88.

121 "Nevertheless, Eleanor's determination": *Ibid.*, p. 53.

121 "The king was appealed": *Ibid.*, p. 60.

121 "Whatever adventures": Delisle, vol. 15, p. 513.

121 "After we were welcomed": *Ibid.*

122 "As William of Tyre": William of Tyre, vol. 2, p. 197.

122 "Wearied by killing": Ibid.

123 "According to one of Louis's letters": Delisle, vol. 15, p. 518.

124 Meeting at Tusculum: John of Salisbury, Hist. Pont., pp. 61–62, 81.

126 "Some miles southeast": Delisle, vol. 15, p. 518.

127 "To the king returning": Gervaise, vol. 3, p. 349.

128 "To her consternation": Some of Eleanor's recent interpreters have preferred to conclude that she was already pregnant when she arrived at
Tusculum (Kelly, p. 70). This seems unlikely because for several years,
and especially once the matter of a divorce was broached in Antioch,
abstinence from any physical relations between Eleanor and Louis was
certainly total. By then, Eleanor wanted nothing more to do with Louis
as a husband, and she would hardly have run the risk of another
pregnancy.

128 "To those who later recalled": Ralph of Diceto, vol. 1, p. 291.

130 "If luck failed": Fawtier, p. 50.

131 "With him at Barfleur": Henry of Huntingdon, p. 306.

131 "The king embarked": William of Malmesbury, vol. 2, p. 496.

132 "The small boat": Ibid., p. 497.

132 "Prince William": Henry of Huntingdon, p. 307.

132 "Most appalled": Ibid., p. 383.

133 "Two years after the birth": Roger of Wendover, vol. 1, p. 482.

134 "He was, wrote Walter": Walter Map, p. 296.

134 "Headstrong, intolerant": Gesta Stephani, p. 91.

134 "Men said": Anglo-Saxon Chronicle, p. 200.

134 "In the north country": Richard of Hexham, p. 152.

135 "In the Isle of Ely": Anglo-Saxon Chronicle, p. 199.

135 "The best description": Henry of Huntingdon, p. 400.

135 "Judging from a letter": James, Letters, p. 474.

136 "Once, he had met": Gerald of Wales, DPI, p. 309.

Stalking the Planta Genesta

138 "There were Frankish": Richard, vol. 2, p. 108.

142 "This appalling blasphemy": Robert of Torigni, p. 162.

142 "His close-cropped": Walter Map, pp. 297, 302.

143 "William of Newburgh tried": William of Newburgh, vol. 1, p. 93.

144 "On the other hand": Walter Map, p. 297.

146 "According to Gerald": Gerald of Wales, DPI, p. 300. After 1184, Gerald
became a royal chaplain at Henry's court and as such was an eyewitness
to the last years of his reign. Disappointed, however, over the king's
refusal to confirm his election to the see of St. David's, he took a belated
revenge by composing a lengthy tract, De Principis Instructione (For the
Instruction of Princes), viciously detailing the follies and vices of Henry
and his sons.

146 "That night, Geoffrey": Robert of Torigni, p. 163.

147 "In late September": Richard, vol. 2, p. 104.

147 "In Eleanor's lifetime": Migne, vol. 212, p. 1057.
147 "The Minstrel of Reims": Minstrel of Reims, p. 258.
148 "On March 21, 1152": Delisle, vol. 12, p. 127.
148 "A chronicler of a later century": Bouchet, p. 141.
149 "Near the city of Blois": Salmon, p. 135. Later that year, Theobald of Blois was betrothed to Eleanor's two-year-old daughter, Alix. They were married in 1164.
151 "Under the direction": Walter Map, p. 298.
151 "Anything he had once heard": Gerald of Wales, *DPI*, p. 215.
151 Map's description of Matilda and Henry: Walter Map, pp. 62, 298–299.
152 "Although fairly slender": Gerald of Wales, *DPI*, p. 214.
152 "Constantly in motion": Peter of Blois, in Migne, vol. 207, p. 66; Gerald of Wales, *DPI*, p. 160; Walter Map, pp. 213–214; Ralph Niger, p. 169.
153 "Since we know": Robert of Torigni, pp. 164–165; Richardson, p. 194.
153 "Burning with hatred": Gerald of Wales, *DPI*, p. 175.
154 "Backed by his brother": Robert of Torigni, p. 165.
154 "At a furious rate": *Ibid.*, pp. 169–170.
154 "Bereft of hope": *Gesta Stephani*, p. 149.
155 "At the Abbey of Saint-Maixent": Richard, vol. 2, p. 111.
155 "It was at Fontevrault": Round, *Cal. Doc.*, p. 375.
157 "In the midst": Richard, vol. 2, pp. 113–114.
157 "A man who detested": Henry of Huntingdon, p. 291.
158 "It has been suggested": Richard, vol. 2, p. 115.
159 "The castle of Angers": Marks, p. 156.
159 "The son of an archer": *Ibid.*, p. 161.
160 "The duchess of Aquitaine": Hill and Bergin, vol. 1, p. 38.
160 Bernard's view of Eleanor: *Ibid.*, pp. 42–43, 50–52.
160 "I am not one to scorn": *Ibid.*, p. 52; trans. by Marks, p. 166.
161 Henry's invasion: Henry of Huntingdon, pp. 290–291.
161 "It was, the chronicles tell us": *Gesta Stephani*, p. 157.
162 "On August 17": Gervase of Canterbury, vol. 1, p. 155.
162 Treaty of Winchester: Delisle and Berger, vol. 1, p. 61.
162 "He understood, too": Henry of Huntingdon, p. 296.
162 "Around Easter": *Ibid.*
163 "In the previous year": Walter Map, p. 299. Henry's other known illegitimate son, William Longspee or Longsword, may also have been born during his 1153–54 visit to England.
165 "Toward the end of October": Gervase of Canterbury, vol. 1, p. 159; Henry of Huntingdon, p. 296.
165 "Still, people hoped": Henry of Huntingdon, p. 297.
165 "The weatherbeaten youth": Gerald of Wales, *DPI*, p. 157.
166 "The royal vessel landed": Henry of Huntingdon, p. 296.
167 Description of London: William Fitz Stephen, pp. 2–13.
168 "There daily you may find": *Ibid.*, p. 5.
168 "Eleven days later": Gervase of Canterbury, vol. 1, p. 159.
168 "Immediately afterward": *English Historical Documents*, vol. 2, p. 407.
169 "Once Henry and Eleanor": Henry of Huntingdon, p. 296.
169 "As for Eleanor": Strickland, vol. 1, p. 255.

Queen of the English

170 "Some made sleds": William Fitz Stephen, p. 11.

170 "Around the entrance": In the twelfth century, the official language of England was Norman French. I presume that eventually Eleanor was able to understand something of what was said when subjects addressed her in English.

170 "Ever since Christmas": Gervase of Canterbury, vol. 1, p. 160.

171 "Otherwise the chronicles": Eyton, p. 85, n. 5. In addition to Emma, Henry had another illegitimate sister, Aldewide.

172 "Theobald had assured him": Brooke and Brooke, p. 88.

172 "Thomas was a slender": Icelandic Saga, trans. in *English Historical Documents*, vol. 2, p. 704, n. 6.

172 "Born in London": William Fitz Stephen, p. 14.

174 "The assignment": *Ibid.*, p. 19.

174 "In early June": Hall, *Court Life under the Plantagenets*, p. 57–59.

175 "Roger of Hovedon": Roger of Hovedon, vol. 1, p. 256.

175 "They became inseparable": William Fitz Stephen, p. 20.

175 "In contrast to his master": Migne, vol. 207, pp. 195–210.

175 "Various anecdotes": William Fitz Stephen, pp. 24–25.

176 "He ordered his hall": *Ibid.*, pp. 18–21.

176 "So sumptuous": *Ibid.*, p. 25.

177 "It was said that he adored": John of Salisbury, *Materials*, vol. 2, p. 302.

177 "And in a letter": *Materials*, vol. 7, p. 307.

179 "He delighted beyond measure": Gerald of Wales, *DPI*, p. 214.

180 "Whoever promises": Richard Fitzneale, p. 122.

181 "Working with Richard": Caenegem, p. 460.

182 "The pipe rolls show": Pipe Roll 2 Henry II, p. 4; Pipe Roll 3 Henry II, p. 71.

182 "During her first four years": Pipe Roll 2 Henry II, p. 34.

182 "Perhaps at this time": Holmes, p. 31.

182 "In the end": William of Newburgh, vol. 1, p. 114.

183 "In July": Eyton, p. 18.

183 "In England": William of Newburgh, vol. 1, p. 102.

184 "The various subdivisions": Richard, vol. 2, pp. 151–153.

184 "That fall, however": *Ibid.*, pp. 122–123.

186 "Owain's forces": William of Newburgh, vol. 1, p. 107.

187 "On September 8": Eyton, p. 30.

187 "A woman of Saint Albans": Norgate, *Richard*, p. 2. Richard's milk brother, Alexander Neckam, would become known as the author of a treatise on natural science.

187 "A prophecy attributed": Ralph of Diceto, vol. 2, p. 67.

188 "When Henry promised": Peter of Blois, Letter 14, in Migne, vol. 207, pp. 48–49.

189 "He was slow": Walter Map, p. 303.

189 "But even though the discomforts": *Ibid.*, p. 298.

189 "The meat, half-cooked": Peter of Blois, Letter 14, in Migne, vol. 207, pp. 48–49.

189 "By December": Eyton, pp. 29–41.
190 "A writ issued": Ibid., p. 40.
190 "According to the pipe rolls": Ibid., p. 42.
191 "The discipline": Labarge, p. 46.
191 "At the same time": Gerald of Wales, DPI, p. 215.
192 "Two hundred and fifty footmen": William Fitz Stephen, pp. 29–33.
194 "Now he proposed": Robert of Torigni, p. 196.
195 "Not only was it granted": Ibid., p. 198.
197 "Perhaps Walter Map": Walter Map, p. 303.
197 "Henry was not so crass": Robert of Torigni, p. 200.
198 "Not wishing to inconvenience": Ibid., p. 202.
198 "Nevertheless, some years later": Materials, vol. 5, p. 525.
199 "Within a week": Robert of Torigni, p. 203.
199 "Foolish superstition": William Fitz Stephen, p. 33.

Betrayals

203 "To judge from the pipe rolls": Eyton, p. 51.
203 "For the repair": Pipe Roll 6 Henry II, p. 49.
204 "After a difficult": Ralph of Diceto, vol. 1, p. 303.
204 "On November 2": Roger of Hovedon, vol. 1, p. 258.
204 "Having satisfactorily demonstrated": William of Newburgh, vol. 1, p. 159.
205 "In a last pathetic letter": John of Salisbury, Letters, p. 249.
206 "He strengthened": Robert of Torigni, p. 209.
206 "Taking advantage": Richard, vol. 2, p. 141.
207 "The fact that he had not": Migne, vol. 207, p. 221.
210 "The chancellor, however": Herbert Bosham, p. 180.
210 "Even though Eleanor": Pipe Roll 8, Henry II, p. 43.
210 "You do not yet fully comprehend": Herbert Bosham, pp. 180–181.
211 "According to Becket's close friend": John of Salisbury, Materials, vol. 2, p. 305.
211 "Richard, he demanded": Herbert Bosham, vol. 3, p. 182.
212 "Putting off the secular": William Fitz Stephen, pp. 37–39.
212 "By the eyes of God": Guernes, p. 23.
213 "Becket's tactless haste": According to Eyton, p. 174, n. 1, Henry did not appoint another chancellor until 1173, although the duties of the office were unofficially assigned to others.
213 "As Eleanor could have predicted": William Fitz Stephen, p. 43.
213 "Eleanor, too, was anxious": Ibid., p. 41.
214 "Judging from the pipe rolls": Pipe Roll 9 Henry II, p. 71.
214 "By this time": There is no trace of any writs issued in Eleanor's name after September 1163 (Richardson, p. 197).
214 "The king's courtiers": William Fitz Stephen, p. 41.
215 "By God's eyes": Edward Grim, p. 374.
215 "For some time now": William of Newburgh, vol. 1, p. 141.
216 "At Woodstock now": Edward Grim, p. 373.
217 "Before his listeners": Materials, vol. 4, p. 202.
217 "My lord of Canterbury": Ibid.

217 "Thomas pointed out": *Ibid.*
218 "He was not demanding": "Roger of Pontigny," p. 26.
218 "What was done": *Ibid.*
218 "By the eyes of God": *Ibid.*
218 "The behavior of some clerks": William of Newburgh, vol. 1, p. 141.
219 "The whole day passed": Herbert Bosham, p. 274.
219 "Meeting Thomas": "Roger of Pontigny," pp. 27–29.
220 "Eleanor and Henry celebrated": Eyton, p. 66.
221 "On January 25": *Ibid.*, p. 69.
221 "At which point": "Roger of Pontigny," p. 33.
222 "After the provisions": *Ibid.*, pp. 36–37.
222 "Becket's reaction": *Ibid.*
223 "He and Eleanor spent": Eyton, p. 71.
224 "Henry's taunts": Herbert Bosham, p. 294.
225 "One chronicler states": *Ibid.*, p. 299.
225 "At the castle doorway": William Fitz Stephen, p. 57.
226 "Where are you going?": William of Canterbury, p. 39.
226 "According to one chronicler": "Roger of Pontigny," p. 52.
226 "Others claim": William of Canterbury, p. 39; Edward Grim, p. 399.
226 "When Henry learned": "Roger of Pontigny," p. 55.
226 "Be it known to you": *English Historical Documents*, p. 734.
227 "Who *was* Archbishop": Herbert Bosham, p. 332.
227 "Then the king of France": "Roger of Pontigny," p. 59.
227 "Christmas 1164": *Materials*, vol. 6, p. 72.
228 "The next day": William of Newburgh, vol. 1, p. 142.
228 "In the dead of winter": Herbert Bosham, pp. 358–359.
229 "After Henry's departure": Eyton, p. 85.
230 "In July, the bishop": *Materials*, vol. 5, p. 197.
231 "In August 1165": Gerald of Wales, *DPI*, p. 290.
231 "Later it would be recalled": Roger of Hovedon, vol. 1, p. 267.
231 "In Angers, Eleanor": Ralph of Diceto, vol. 1, p. 329.
232 "The Poitevins": Gervase of Canterbury, vol. 1, p. 205.
232 "In fact, some Poitevin": *Materials*, vol. 6, p. 266.
232 "In early March": Eyton, p. 91.
232 "Once back on the Continent": *Ibid.*, pp. 92–97.
233 "Crossing the Channel": *Ibid.*, p. 108.
233 "There, on Christmas Eve": Ralph of Diceto, vol. 1, p. 325. Robert of Torigni (p. 233) places John's birth a year later, in 1167. This seems to be an error, because at the time that Eleanor would have had to conceive in order to give birth in December 1167, she was in England and Henry on the Continent.

The Court of Love

234 "Her crisped locks": *The Ballad of Fair Rosamond*, in Child, vol. 7, pp. 283–291.
234 "Rosamond Clifford": Archer, p. 531.
235 "In the densely forested park": Child, vol. 7, pp. 283–291.
235 "The first association": Heltzel, p. 100.

235 "Except for this particular chronicle": In a ballad written about 1685, *Queen Eleanor's Confession*, she makes a deathbed confession of Rosamond's murder to Henry and William Marshal, who have disguised themselves as friars.

235 "Gerald of Wales": Gerald of Wales, *DPI*, p. 165.

236 "A chronicler tells": Roger of Hovedon, vol. 2, p. 257.

236 "Rosamond was then interred": Ralph of Higden, p. 53.

238 "To that end": Pipe Roll 13 Henry II, pp. 2–3.

239 "One account claims": Eyton, p. 109.

239 "At Winchester": *Ibid.*, p. 112.

240 "Girding himself": Robert of Torigni, pp. 235–236.

241 "As a result": *Guillaume le Maréchal*, l. 1869–88.

243 "He opened the parley": William of Canterbury, p. 73.

245 "On the whole matter": Herbert Bosham, p. 418.

245 "Finally, he turned to Louis": Alan of Tewkesbury, p. 347.

245 "Turning to the archbishop": Herbert Bosham, p. 423.

247 "Life expectancy": Holmes, pp. 226–227.

247 "In the opinion of one chronicler": Gerald of Wales, *DPI*, p. 145.

249 "It is believed that John": Richard, vol. 2, p. 373.

250 "In her time": Creekmore, p. 40.

251 "The inferiority of the female": Adams, p. 199.

253 "There is little": Andreas Capellanus, pp. 81–82.

254 "The remnants of the royal family": Roger of Hovedon, vol. 1, p. 334.

255 "In early August": Stubbs, *Gesta Regis Henrici Secundi*, vol. 1, p. 6.

255 "And in that year": Edward Grim, p. 435.

255 "In July": *Materials*, vol. 7, pp. 326–333.

255 "In the end": *English Historical Documents*, p. 756.

256 "He would even ignore": William Fitz Stephen, p. 116.

256 "As he set out": Herbert Bosham, p. 478.

256 "He had brought with him": William Fitz Stephen, p. 122.

257 "Their evil accusations": *Ibid.*, p. 127.

257 "Exasperated, the king": William of Newburgh, vol. 1, p. 161.

257 "I have nourished": *Materials*, vol. 2, p. 429.

257 "Nor was it noticed": William of Newburgh, vol. 1, p. 162.

257 "Once admitted": Edward Grim, p. 431.

257 "Stop your threats": *Materials*, vol. 2, p. 432.

257 The murder of Becket: *Ibid.*, pp. 433–438.

259 "While the body": *Ibid.*, p. 15

259 "At the messenger's": Arnulf, bishop of Lisieux, Letter to Pope Alexander, in *English Historical Documents*, p. 770.

259 "At Winchester": William Fitz Stephen, p. 149.

260 "Almost everyone": William of Newburgh, vol. 1, p. 165.

261 "Once Marie's husband": Walter Map, p. 282.

261 "To Gerald of Wales": *Ibid.*, p. 281.

262 "Possibly she accepted": Ralph of Higden, p. 31.

262 "The Young King": *Guillaume le Maréchal*, l. 1956–8.

262 "He was beautiful": Walter Map, p. 178.

262 "On another occasion": Robert of Torigni, p. 253.
263 "He may have been noble": Walter Map, p. 179.
263 "Baseness of temper": *Ibid.*
263 "Foolishly liberal": Robert of Torigni, p. 305.
263 "He was a restless": William of Newburgh, vol. 1, p. 234.
263 "He was tall in stature": Itinerary of Richard I, trans. in Hassall, p. 100.
264 "Gerald of Wales"; Gerald of Wales, *DPI*, p. 177.
264 "Roger of Hovedon": Stubbs, *Gesta Regis Henrici Secundi*, vol. 1, p. 297.
264 "Afterwards between you and your son": Jordan Fantosme, p. 203.
265 "For those who kept track": Roger of Hovedon, vol. 1, p. 368.

The Wheel of Fortune Turns

266 "Anything that smacked": *Guillaume le Maréchal*, l. 2399.
267 "Henry did not care": *Ibid.*, l. 2637–95.
268 "Gervase of Canterbury": Gervase of Canterbury, vol. 1, p. 242.
268 "The anonymous chronicler": Stubbs, *Gesta Regis Henrici Secundi*, vol. 1, p. 42.
268 "William of Newburgh": William of Newburgh, vol. 1, p. 171.
268 "Richard Fitzneale": Richard Fitzneale, pp. 65–66.
271 "Louis replied": William of Newburgh, vol. 1, p. 170.
271 "Soon after": *Ibid.*
271 "Apparently undisturbed": Pipe Roll 19 Henry II, p. 55.
271 "Pious queen": Migne, vol. 207, pp. 448–449.
272 "In that spring of 1173": Gervase of Canterbury, vol. 1, p. 243.
273 "On the twenty-ninth": Roger of Hovedon, vol. 1, p. 368.
274 "Only a few months earlier": Richard le Poitevin, in Delisle, vol. 12, p. 419.
274 "The sole annalist": Gervase of Canterbury, vol. 1, p. 242.
275 "A twentieth-century historian": Richard, vol. 2, p. 170, n. 2.
275 "On Whitsunday": Ralph of Diceto, vol. 1, p. 379.
276 "Eleanor was carried": Roger of Hovedon, vol. 1, p. 380.
276 "Lord, if in my heart": Ralph of Diceto, vol. 1, p. 382.
277 "His footsteps": Gervase of Canterbury, vol. 1, p. 248.
277 "Brien, what news": Jordan Fantosme, p. 369.
278 "Furthermore, King Henry": Stubbs, *Gesta Regis Henrici Secundi*, vol. 1, pp. 77–79.
278 "The king and his four sons": Ralph of Diceto, vol. 1, p. 396.
279 "Tell me, Eagle": Richard le Poitevin, in Delisle, vol. 12, p. 420.
281 "During that year": Roger of Hovedon, vol. 1, p. 404.
281 "The winter was so severe": Robert of Torigni, p. 270.
281 "Entries in the Pipe Rolls": Pipe Roll 23 Henry II, p. 166.
281 "For 2 cloaks": Pipe Roll 24 Henry II, p. 128.
281 "In 1117, the chroniclers": Roger of Hovedon, vol. 1, p. 456.
282 "Gerald of Wales": Gerald of Wales, *DPI*, pp. 165–66, 232.
282 "Had he not publicly": Gerald of Wales, *De Vita Galfredi*, p. 368.

282 "Philip and his young friends": Stubbs, Gesta Regis Henrici, vol. 1,
p. 240; Robert of Torigni, pp. 282–83.

283 "Said the martyr": Robert of Torigni, pp. 282–83.

283 "The coronation was rescheduled": Roger of Hovedon, vol. 1, p. 518.

283 "On September 18": William of Tyre, vol. 2, p. 45.

283 "In perhaps a more impartial": William of Newburgh, vol. 1, p. 223.

284 "His imprisonment of Eleanor": Gerald of Wales, DPI, p. 282.

284 "Ralph of Diceto": Ralph of Diceto, vol. 1, p. 399.

285 "Henry the young king": Roger of Wendover, vol. 2, p. 43.

286 "The troubadour Bertran de Born": Clédat, p. 44.

287 "While Geoffrey expressed": Ralph of Diceto, vol. 2, pp. 18–19.

288 "War was in his heart": Walter Map, p. 180.

288 "Where is your filial": Peter of Blois, in Migne, vol. 207, p. 110.

288 "It was said that the Young King": Walter Map, p. 179.

289 "On Saturday, June 11": Roger of Hovedon, vol. 2, p. 26.

289 "What news": Geoffrey of Vigeois, in Delisle, vol. 18, pp. 218–219.

289 "Dismissing those who had crowded": Roger of Hovedon, vol. 2, p. 27.

289 "She asked Agnellus": Ralph of Coggeshall, pp. 272–273.

290 "In 1184, she received": Stubbs, Gesta Regis Henrici, vol. 1, p. 305.

290 "Apparently, her household": Pipe Roll 30 Henry II, p. 39.

290 "We know that she spent Easter": Pipe Roll 30 Henry II, p. 70.

290 "Reveling in her freedom": Ibid., p. 135.

291 "Ordered to attend": Stubbs, Gesta Regis Henrici, vol. 1, pp. 319–320.

291 "No expense": Pipe Roll 31 Henry II, p. 44.

292 "Arming his castles": Roger of Hovedon, vol. 2, pp. 50–51.

292 "Those who cast their eyes": Ibid., pp. 36–50.

292 "On his orders": Stubbs, Gesta Regis Henrici, vol. 1, p. 338.

293 "I wonder, he once mused": Gerald of Wales, DPI, p. 293.

294 "William of Newburgh claimed": William of Newburgh, vol. 1, p. 235.

294 "When he refused to yield": Stubbs, Gesta Regis Henrici, vol. 1, p. 350.

294 "His body was laid": William of Newburgh, vol. 1, p. 235.

294 "Overcome, Philip Augustus": Gerald of Wales, DPI, p. 176.

296 "Despite Henry's age": Ibid., pp. 256–257.

296 "Now, cried Richard": Gervase of Canterbury, vol. 1, p. 435.

297 "O God, he cried": Gerald of Wales, DPI, p. 283.

297 "By God's legs": Guillaume le Maréchal, l. 8837–47.

298 "Marshal, sweet gentle sir": Ibid., l. 8955–90.

298 "As Richard advanced": Gerald of Wales, DPI, p. 296.

298 "When Roger returned": Guillaume le Maréchal, l. 9051–2.

299 "Is it true": Ibid., l. 9083–4.

299 "Say no more": Gerald of Wales, DPI, p. 295.

299 "In the final hours": Ibid., p. 297.

299 "One could not tell": Guillaume le Maréchal, l. 9294–8.

299 "Then he knelt": Gerald of Wales, DPI, p. 305.

299 "At that moment": Ibid. There is no need to place any credence in this
detail. According to Broughton (p. 88) the belief that the wounds of a
slain man will bleed afresh at the approach of the murderer was widespread in the twelfth century, and by applying this belief to Richard, the

chroniclers were simply demonstrating the strained relations between father and son. Actually, it was not Richard who destroyed Henry but the Young King and John.

299 "It was, a chronicler said": Stubbs, *Gesta Regis Henrici*, vol. 2, p. 71.

Autumn and After

300 "But Eleanor, perhaps using": Ralph of Diceto, vol. 2, p. 67.

301 "With a sagacity": Roger of Hovedon, vol. 2, p. 112.

301 "Only William of Newburgh": William of Newburgh, vol. 1, p. 293.

302 "Roger of Wendover": Roger of Wendover, vol. 2, p. 77.

302 "In the midst of her journeying": Around this time she must have received news that her daughter Matilda had died on July 28.

302 "So complete was his security": Ralph of Diceto, vol. 2, p. 68.

302 "Briefly, Richard and Eleanor": John's betrothed, Princess Alice of Maurienne, had died.

302 "Through the nave": Roger of Hovedon, vol. 2, p. 117.

303 "Three days of festivities": Roger of Wendover, vol. 2, p. 81.

303 "When Abbot Samson": Jocelin of Brakelond, p. 46.

304 "The king, people said": William of Newburgh, vol. 1, p. 306.

304 "Although Gerald of Wales's": Gerald of Wales, *De Vita Galfredi*, p. 420.

305 "Already along the coast": Richard of Devizes, p. 394.

305 "Whoever shall kill": Stubbs, *Gesta Regis Ricardi*, vol. 1, pp. 110–111.

306 "To judge from the charters": Richard, vol. 2, p. 268.

306 "His contemporaries": Itinerary of Richard I, trans. in Hassall, p. 100.

306 "Already people called him": Hill and Bergin, vol. 1, p. 111. The practice of calling brave men lions was not limited to Richard Lionheart. His great-grandfather Henry I had been called the Lion of Justice; Duke Henry of Saxony was also known as the Lion, and so was King William of Scotland.

308 "Eleanor distrusted him": Gerald of Wales, *De Vita Galfredi*, p. 379.

309 "There was no fault": Richard of Devizes, p. 402; Ambrose, in Stone, p. 26.

310 "Many know what I wish": Richard of Devizes, p. 402.

310 "Declared Philip violently": Roger of Hovedon, vol. 2, p. 195.

311 "And as if all this": Roger of Wendover, vol. 2, p. 101.

312 "Calling together the bishops": Roger of Hovedon, vol. 2, p. 231.

312 "Pretending to be a woman": *Ibid.*, p. 236.

312 "Sitting on a rock": Roger of Wendover, vol. 2, p. 113.

313 "That day the crusading camp": Ambrose, in Stone, pp. 40–41.

314 "Grossly offended": Gervase of Canterbury, vol. 1, p. 514.

314 "Ten days after the fall": Stubbs, *Gesta Regis Henrici*, vol. 2, pp. 182–183.

315 "On January 20, 1192": Roger of Hovedon, vol. 2, p. 257.

315 "Fearing that the light-minded youth": Richard of Devizes, p. 432.

315 "All the great men": *Ibid.*

316 "Sweet Lord": Ambrose, in Stone, p. 159.

317 "On December 28": Roger of Hovedon, vol. 2, pp. 278–279.

317 Anselm's story: Ralph of Coggeshall, pp. 53–60.
320 "In the meantime, Eleanor": Gervase of Canterbury, vol. 1, p. 515.
320 "Her attitude was probably": Roger of Hovedon, vol. 2, p. 281.
320 "His death, it was decided": The mark was not a coin but a unit of account equivalent to eight ounces of silver or 120 silver pennies.
321 "The kingdom was stripped": William of Newburgh, vol. 1, p. 399.
321 "From Haguenau": Roger of Hovedon, vol. 2, pp. 290–291.
321 "It is said that I": Halliwell-Phillipps, pp. 7–9.
321 "He was always cheery": Ralph of Coggeshall, p. 58.
322 "Feeble the words": Richard Coeur de Lion, *Sirventes*, trans. in Norgate, *Richard the Lion Heart*, p. 278.
322 "I am all defiled": Wood, vol. 1, pp. 14–23.
323 "Quick to realize": Roger of Hovedon, vol. 2, p. 286.
324 "On February 4": *Ibid.*, p. 310.
324 "Her eldest son": Ralph of Diceto, vol. 2, p. 114.
324 "Once Richard's release": Roger of Hovedon, vol. 2, p. 297.
324 "With Richard, she made": *Ibid.*, p. 316.
324 "Not until May 12": Gervase of Canterbury, vol. 1, p. 527.
324 "Think no more of it": *Guillaume le Maréchal*, l. 10365–419.
325 According to the chronicles": Roger of Hovedon, vol. 2, p. 325.
326 "We know that on one occasion": Pipe Roll 9 Richard I, 98; Round, *Cal. Doc.*, p. 388.
327 "When finally Philip": Gerald of Wales, *DPI*, p. 290.
328 "A surgeon of sorts": Roger of Hovedon, vol. 2, p. 453.
328 "With an old friend": Round, *Cal. Doc.*, p. 472.
328 "He bequeathed": Nichols, p. 11.
328 "What evil": Roger of Hovedon, vol. 2, p. 453.
328 "On Tuesday, April 6": Ralph of Coggeshall, p. 96.
329 "For his greed": Roger of Hovedon, vol. 2, p. 454.

The Last Battle

330 "Ranulph de Glanville": *De Legibus et Consuetudinibus Angliae* and *Le Trés Ancien Coutumier de Normandie*, trans. in Warren, *King John*, p. 49.
331 "On the evening of April 10": *Guillaume le Maréchal*, l. 11877–908.
331 "*Hostis naturae*": William of Newburgh, vol. 1, p. 402.
331 "Henry had wanted": *Ibid.*, p. 235.
332 "During Richard's last hours": Richard, vol. 2, p. 334.
333 "While these matters": *Magna Vita*, pp. 288–291.
333 "Finally, on Easter Sunday": *Ibid.*, pp. 291–295.
334 "Unheeding of her age": Roger of Hovedon, vol. 2, p. 457.
335 "On May 27": Ralph of Coggeshall, p. 99; Roger of Hovedon, vol. 2, p. 458.
335 "Toward the end of April": Richard, vol. 2, p. 335.
335 "From her ducal inheritance": Round, *Cal. Doc.*, pp. 472–473.
336 "Justice was dispensed": *Ibid.*, p. 335.

336 "Petronilla": Neither Petronilla's later life nor the date of her death is recorded.

337 "At La Rochelle": Richard, vol. 2, p. 239.

337 "In July, she swallowed": *Oeuvres de Rigord*, vol. 1, p. 146; Richard, vol. 2, p. 353.

338 "Unable to stand": Roger of Hovedon, vol. 2, p. 463.

339 "At the conclusion": Gervase of Canterbury, vol. 2, p. 92.

339 "Eleanor's chests": Roger of Hovedon, vol. 2, p. 472.

341 "There was something about the child": Blanche of Castile, the mother of Saint Louis, became regent of France during her illustrious son's youth.

341 "While she was staying": Roger of Hovedon, vol. 2, p. 480.

342 "Early in 1200": Ralph of Diceto, vol. 2, p. 170.

342 "On seeing that the king": Roger of Hovedon, vol. 2, p. 483.

343 "At the beginning of October": Ralph of Diceto, vol. 2, p. 170.

344 "By the middle of March": Roger of Wendover, vol. 2, p. 201.

344 "But John had no such intention": Hardy, *Rotuli Chartarum*, pp. 102–103.

346 "It was not until July 19": Roger of Hovedon, vol. 2, p. 500.

346 "Using the Lusignans": Gervase of Canterbury, vol. 2, p. 93.

346 "John airily replied": Ralph of Coggeshall, p. 136.

347 "At Gournay": Round, *Cal. Doc.*, p. 475.

347 "Ever since his peace treaty": Gervase of Canterbury, vol. 2, p. 93.

348 "In the meantime, Arthur": Roger of Wendover, vol. 2, p. 203.

348 "But in the end": Ralph of Coggeshall, p. 137.

349 "By Monday, July 31": Roger of Wendover, vol. 2, pp. 203–204.

349 "With John came William": *Histoire des ducs de Normandie et des rois d'Angleterre*, p. 94.

349 "Dawn was breaking": Ralph of Coggeshall, pp. 137–138.

350 "Venting his frustration": Roger of Wendover, vol. 2, p. 205.

350 "Having secured his prisoners": *Ibid.*, p. 204.

351 "That year, John kept Christmas": *Ibid.*, p. 206.

351 "In November, John had released": Ralph of Coggeshall, p. 139.

351 "The king addressed him": Roger of Wendover, vol. 2, p. 205.

352 "Afterward, a chronicler said": Ralph of Coggeshall, pp. 140–141.

352 "In February": Roger of Wendover, vol. 2, p. 205.

353 "Opinion about the death": *Ibid.*, p. 206.

353 "The chronicler described": Luard, *Annals of Margam*, p. 27.

353 "We send to you brother John": Hardy, *Rotuli Litt. Pat.*, p. 28.

353 "It has been suggested": Richard, vol. 2, p. 424; Powicke, p. 476.

354 "Messengers came to John": Roger of Wendover, vol. 2, p. 207.

354 "In the meantime": *Ibid.*

354 "Whoso is afraid": *Guillaume le Maréchal*, l. 12721–42.

354 "On December 5": Roger of Wendover, vol. 2, p. 208.

355 "Those Norman barons": *Ibid.*, p. 214.

355 "She would not live": In 1259, Henry III, John's son and Eleanor's grandson, gave up all claims to Normandy, Anjou, Maine, Touraine, and Poitou. The southern portion of Aquitaine, however, continued to be a

source of discord between England and France for centuries. Not until the midfifteenth century would the last of Eleanor's inheritance be incorporated into France.

355 "The chroniclers were too busy": Peter of Blois, in Migne, vol. 207, p. 431.

355 "On April 1, 1204": Luard, *Annals of Waverley*, p. 256.

Bibliography

Abélard, Peter. *Historia Calamitatum.* Edited and translated by Henry A. Bellows. Saint Paul: T. A. Boyd, 1922.

Adams, Henry. *Mont-Saint-Michel and Chartres.* New York: Houghton Mifflin Co., 1913.

Alan of Tewkesbury. *Materials for the History of Thomas Becket.* Edited by J. C. Robertson. Rolls Series 67, vol. 2.

Ambrose. *L'Estoire de la guerre sainte.* In *Three Old French Chronicles of the Crusades.* Translated by Edward Noble Stone. Seattle: University of Washington, 1939.

Andreas Capellanus. *The Art of Courtly Love (De Amore).* Edited by J. J. Parry. New York: Columbia University Press, 1941.

The Anglo-Saxon Chronicle. Edited by Dorothy Whitelock. New Brunswick, N.J.: Rutgers University Press, 1961.

Anna Comnena. *The Alexiad of the Princess Anna Comnena.* Translated by Elizabeth Dawes. New York: Barnes & Noble, 1967.

Appleby, John T. *England Without Richard, 1189–1199.* London: G. Bell, 1965.

———. *Henry II: The Vanquished King.* New York: Macmillan Co., 1962.

Archer, T. A. "Clifford, Rosamond." In *The Dictionary of National Biography,* vol. 9, pp. 531–533.

Barber, Richard. *The Knight and Chivalry.* London: Longman Group Ltd., 1970.

Beard, Mary. *Woman as a Force in History.* New York: Macmillan Co., 1946.

Bouchet, Jean. *Les Annales d'Aquitaine.* Poitiers, 1644.

Bregy, Katherine. *From Dante to Jeanne D'Arc: Adventures in Medieval Life and Letters.* Port Washington, N.Y.: Kennikat Press, 1964.

Briffault, Robert. *The Mothers.* London: George Allen & Unwin Ltd., 1927.

———. *The Troubadours.* Bloomington, Ind.: Indiana University Press, 1965.

Brooke, Christopher. *From Alfred to Henry III.* Edinburgh: Thomas Nelson & Sons, 1961.

———. *The Twelfth Century Renaissance.* New York: Harcourt, Brace & World, 1969.

Brooke, Z. N., and Brooke, C. N. L. "Henry II, Duke of Normandy and Aquitaine." *English Historical Review* 61 (1946): 81–89.

Broughton, Bradford B. *The Legends of King Richard I Coeur De Lion.* The Hague: Mouton & Co., 1966.

Brundage, James A. *Richard Lion Heart.* New York: Charles Scribner's Sons, 1974.

Bryant, Arthur. *Makers of England.* Garden City, N.Y.: Doubleday & Co., 1962.

Bullough, Vern L., and Bullough, Bonnie. *The Subordinate Sex.* Urbana, Ill.: University of Illinois Press, 1973.

Caenegem, R. C. *Royal Writs in England from the Conquest to Glanvill.* London: Bernard Quaritch, 1959.

Cartellieri, Otto. *Abt Suger von Saint-Denis.* Berlin: Eberling, 1898.

Chambers, F. W. "Some Legends Concerning Eleanor of Aquitaine." *Speculum* 16 (1941): 459–468.

Chapman, Robert L. "Notes on the Demon Queen Eleanor." *Modern Language Notes,* June 1955, pp. 393–396.

Child, Francis James. *English and Scottish Ballads.* 8 vols. Boston: Little, Brown & Co., 1857–58.

La Chronique de Morigny. Edited by Leon Mirot. Paris: A. Picard et fils, 1912.

Clédat, Léon. *Du rôle historique de Bertrand de Born (1175–1200).* Paris, 1879.

Coulton, George Gordon. *Life in the Middle Ages (A Medieval Garner).* Cambridge, Eng.: University Press, 1967.

_____. *Social Life in Britain from the Conquest to the Reformation.* New York: Barnes & Noble, 1968.

Creekmore, Hubert, ed. *Lyrics of the Middle Ages.* New York: Grove Press, 1959.

Curtius, Ernest R. *European Literature in the Latin Middle Ages.* Translated by Willard R. Trask. New York: Pantheon Books, 1953.

De Beauvoir, Simone. *The Second Sex.* New York: Alfred A. Knopf, 1953.

Delisle, Leopold, ed. *Recueil des historiens des Gaules et de la France.* 24 vols. Paris, 1738–1904.

Delisle, Leopold, and Berger, Elie. *Recueil des actes de Henri II.* 2 vols. Paris: Imprimerie nationale, 1909–27.

De Loi, Raimon. *Trails of the Troubadours.* New York: Century Co., 1926.

deRiencourt, Amaury. *Sex and Power in History.* New York: David McKay, 1974.

Douglas, David C. *The Norman Achievement, 1050–1100.* Berkeley and Los Angeles: University of California Press, 1969.

Dronke, Peter. *Medieval Latin and the Rise of the European Love-Lyric.* 2 vols. Oxford: Clarendon Press, 1965–66.

Duggan, Alfred. *Devil's Brood.* New York: Coward-McCann, 1957.

Edward Grim. *Materials for the History of Thomas Becket.* Edited by J. C. Robertson. Rolls Series 67, vol. 2.

Encyclopedia of Catholic Saints. A project of Dimension Books. Philadelphia: Chilton Books, 1966.

English Historical Documents. Edited by David C. Douglas and George Greenaway. vol. 2. London: Eyre & Spottiswoode, 1953.

Evans, Joan. *Life in Medieval France.* London: Phaidon Press, 1925.

Eyton, Robert W. *Court, Household and Itinerary of King Henry II.* London, 1878.

Facinger, Marion. A Study of Medieval Queenship: Capetian France, 987–1237. Studies in Medieval and Renaissance History, vol. 5. Lincoln, Neb.: University of Nebraska Press, 1968.

Fawtier, Robert. The Capetian Kings of France. Translated by L. Butler and R. J. Adam. London: Macmillan & Co., 1960.

Florence of Worcester. The Chronicle of Florence of Worcester. Edited and translated by Thomas Forester. London: H. G. Bohn, 1854.

Flores, Angel, ed. An Anthology of Medieval Lyrics. New York: Modern Library, 1962.

_____. Medieval Age: Specimens of European Poetry from the 9th Century to the 15th Century. New York: Phoenix House, 1963.

Fowler, G. H. "Henry fitzHenry at Woodstock." English Historical Review 49 (1924): 240–241.

Gabrieli, Francesco, ed. and trans. Arab Historians of the Crusades. Berkeley: University of California Press, 1969.

Geoffrey of Vigeois. Chronicle. In Delisle, Recueil des historiens des Gaules et de la France, vols. 12 and 18. Paris, 1738–1904.

Gerald of Wales. The Autobiography of Giraldus Cambrensis. Edited and translated by H. E. Butler. London: Jonathan Cape, 1937.

_____. De Principis Instructione (For the Instruction of Princes). Edited by G. F. Warner. Rolls Series 21, vol. 8.

_____. De Vita Galfredi. Edited by J. S. Butler. Rolls Series 21, vol. 4.

Gervaise, F. A. Histoire de Suger. 3 vols. Paris, 1721.

Gervase of Canterbury. Opera Historica. Edited by William Stubbs. 2 vols. Rolls Series 73.

Gesta Francorum et Aliorum Hierosolimitanorum (The Deeds of the Franks and the Other Pilgrims to Jerusalem). Edited by Rosalind Hill. London: Thomas Nelson, 1962.

Gesta Regis Henrici Secundi (erroneously attributed to Benedict of Peterborough). Edited by William Stubbs. 2 vols. Rolls Series 49.

Gesta Regis Ricardi. Edited by William Stubbs. 2 vols. Rolls Series 49.

Gesta Stephani. Edited and translated by K. R. Potter. London: Thomas Nelson, 1955.

The Great Rolls of the Pipe for the Second, Third, and Fourth Years of the Reign of King Henry II, 1155–1158. Edited by Joseph Hunter. London: 1844.

The Great Rolls of the Pipe of the Reign of Henry the Second, 5th to 34th Years. 30 vols. London: Pipe Roll Society, 1884–1925.

The Great Rolls of the Pipe for the Reign of Richard I. London: Pipe Roll Society, 1925–33. (The roll for the first year of Richard's reign was published by the Record Commission in 1844.)

Guernes de Pont Sainte-Maxence. La Vie de Saint Thomas Becket. Edited by Emmanuel Walberg. Paris: Libraire Ancienne Honore Champion, 1936.

Guillaume le Maréchal, l'Histoire de. Edited and translated by Paul Meyer. 3 vols. Paris: Société de l'histoire de France, 1891–1901.

Hall, Hubert, Court Life under the Plantagenets. London: S. Sonnenschein & Co., 1899.

Halliwell-Phillipps, James O. Letters of the Kings of England. Vol. 1. London, 1848.

Hartley, Dorothy, and Elliot, Margaret M. *Life and Work of the People of England*. New York: G. P. Putnam's, 1929.

Harvey, John H. *The Plantagenets, 1154–1185*. London: B. T. Batsford, 1948.

Haskell, Daniel C. *Provençal Literature and Language, Including the Local History of Southern France*. New York: New York Public Library, 1925.

Haskins, Charles H. *The Renaissance of the Twelfth Century*. Cambridge, Mass.: Harvard University Press, 1927.

Hassall, W. O., ed. *They Saw It Happen: An Anthology of Eye-Witness Accounts of Events in British History, 55 B.C.–A.D. 1485*. Oxford: Basil Blackwell, 1957.

Hays, H. R. *The Dangerous Sex: The Myth of Feminine Evil*. New York: G. P. Putnam's, 1964.

Heer, Friedrich. *The Medieval World*. London: Weidenfeld & Nicolson, 1961.

Heltzel, Virgil B. *Fair Rosamund: A Study of the Development of a Literary Theme*. Evanston, Ill.: Northwestern University, 1947.

Henderson, Philip. *Richard Coeur De Lion*. New York: W. W. Norton, 1959.

Henry of Huntingdon. *The Chronicle of Henry of Huntingdon*. Translated and edited by Thomas Forester. London: H. G. Bohn, 1853.

Herbert Bosham. *Materials for the History of Thomas Becket*. Edited by J. C. Robertson. Rolls Series 67, vol. 3.

Hill, R. T., and Bergin, T. G. *Anthology of the Provençal Troubadours*. 2 vols. New Haven and London: Yale University Press, 1973.

Histoire des ducs de Normandie et des rois d'Angleterre. Edited by F. Michel. Paris, 1840.

Holmes, Urban Tigner. *Daily Living in the Twelfth Century*. Madison, Wis.: University of Wisconsin Press, 1964.

Howard, Philip. *The Royal Palaces*. Boston: Gambit, Inc., 1970.

James, Bruno Scott, ed. and trans. *The Letters of Saint Bernard of Clairvaux*. Chicago: Henry Regnery, 1953.

————. *Saint Bernard of Clairvaux*. New York: Harper & Bros., 1957.

Jocelin de Brakelond. *Chronicle*. Edited and translated by H. E. Butler. New York: Oxford University Press, 1949.

John of Salisbury. *The Historia Pontificalis*. Edited and translated by Marjorie Chibnall. London: Thomas Nelson, 1956.

————. *The Letters of John of Salisbury*. Edited by W. J. Millor and H. E. Butler. Revised by C. N. L. Brooke. Vol. 1. London: Thomas Nelson, 1955.

————. *Materials for the History of Thomas Becket*. Edited by J. C. Robertson. Rolls Series 67, vol. 2.

————. *The Metalogicon*. Translated by Daniel D. McGarry. Berkeley: University of California Press, 1955.

————. *Policraticus (The Statesman's Book of John of Salisbury)*. Translated by John Dickinson. New York: Alfred A. Knopf, 1927.

Jordan Fantosme. *Metrical Chronicle*. Edited by Richard Howlett. Rolls Series 82, vol. 3.

Kelly, Amy. *Eleanor of Aquitaine and the Four Kings*. Cambridge, Mass.: Harvard University Press, 1950.

Labarge, Margaret Wade. *A Baronial Household of the Thirteenth Century*. New York: Barnes & Noble, 1965.

Lees, Beatrice A. "The Letters of Queen Eleanor of Aquitaine to Pope Celestine III." *English Historical Review* 21 (1906): 78–93.

Lloyd, Alan. *The Maligned Monarch.* Garden City, N.Y.: Doubleday & Co., 1972.

Luchaire, Achille. *Social France at the Time of Philip Augustus.* Edited by E. B. Krehbiel. New York: Henry Holt, 1912.

Magna Vita Sancti Hugonis Episcopi Lincolniensis. Edited by James. F. Dimock. Rolls Series 37.

Mann, H. *The Lives of the Popes in the Middle Ages.* vol. 9. London: K. Paul, Trench, Trübner & Co., 1914.

Margam, Annals of (Annales Monastici). Edited by H. R. Luard. Rolls Series 36, vol. 1.

Marks, Claude. *Pilgrims, Heretics, and Lovers: A Medieval Journey.* New York: Macmillan Co., 1975.

Materials for the History of Thomas Becket. J. C. Robertson, ed. (vols. 1–6) and J. B. Sheppard, ed. (vol. 7). 7 vols. Rolls Series 67, 1875–85.

Maurois, André. *A History of France.* New York: Farrar, Straus & Cudahy, 1948.

Migne, J. P. *Patrologia Latina.* 221 vols. Paris: 1844–1864.

Minstrel of Reims. *Chronicle of Reims.* In *Three Old French Chronicles of the Crusades.* Translated by Edward Noble Stone. Seattle: University of Washington, 1939.

Molinier, Auguste. *Vie de Louis le Gros par Suger, suive de l'histoire du roi Louis VII.* Paris, 1887.

Moore, O. H. *The Young King Henry Plantagenet 1155–1183 in History, Literature and Tradition.* Columbus, Ohio: Ohio State University, 1925.

Munro, Dana Carleton. *The Kingdom of the Crusaders.* Port Washington, N.Y.: Kennikat Press, 1966.

Murray, Jane. *The Kings and Queens of England: A Tourist Guide.* New York: Charles Scribner's Sons, 1974.

National Geographic Society. *The Age of Chivalry.* Washington, D.C.: National Geographic Society, 1969.

Nicetae Choniatae Historia. Corpus Scriptorum Historiae Byzantinae. Edited by Emmanuel Bekker. Bonn, 1835.

Nichols, John. *A Collection of All the Wills of the Kings and Queens of England.* London, 1780.

Nitze, W. A. "The Exhumation of King Arthur of Glastonbury." *Speculum* 9 (1934): 355–361.

Norgate, Kate. *England under the Angevin Kings.* 2 vols. London: Macmillan & Co. 1887.

———. *John Lackland.* London: Macmillan & Co. 1902.

———. *Richard the Lion Heart.* London: Macmillan & Co. 1924.

Odo de Dueil. *De Prefectione Ludovici VII in Orientem.* Edited and translated by Virginia G. Berry. New York: Columbia University Press, 1948.

Oeuvres de Rigord et de Guillaume le Breton. Edited by H. F. Delaborde. 2 vols. Paris, 1882–85.

Oldenbourg, Zoe. *The Crusades.* Translated by Anne Carter. New York: Random House, 1966.

Ordericus Vitalis. *The Ecclesiastical History of England and Normandy.* Edited and translated by Thomas Forester. 4 vols. London: H. G. Bohn, 1853–56.

Pain, Nesta. *King and Becket.* New York: Barnes & Noble, 1967.

Painter, Sidney, *French Chivalry: Chivalric Ideas and Practices in Medieval France.* Baltimore: Johns Hopkins Press, 1949.

———. "The Houses of Lusignan and Châtellerault, 1150–1250." *Speculum* 30 (1955): 374–384.

———. *The Reign of King John.* Baltimore: Johns Hopkins Press, 1949.

———. *William Marshal, Knight-Errant, Baron and Regent of England.* Baltimore: Johns Hopkins Press, 1933.

Pernoud, Regine. *Eleanor of Aquitaine.* New York: Coward-McCann, 1968.

Peter of Blois. *Petri Blensis Archidiaconi Opera Omni.* Edited by J. A. Giles. 4 vols. Oxford, 1846–47. Letters in Migne, *Patrologia Latina*, vol. 207.

Petit-Dutaillis, Charles E. *Feudal Monarchy in France and England from the Tenth to the Thirteenth Century.* Translated by E. D. Hunt. New York: Barnes & Noble, 1964.

Poole, R. L. "Henry Plantagenet's Early Visits to England." *English Historical Review,* 47 (1932): 447–452.

Powicke, F. M. *The Loss of Normandy.* Manchester, Eng.: Manchester University Press, 1913.

Quennell, Marjorie, and Quennell, C. H. B. *History of Everyday Things in England—1066–1499.* London: B. T. Batsford, 1950.

Ralph of Coggeshall. *Chronicon Anglicanum.* Edited by Joseph Stevenson. Rolls Series 66.

Ralph of Diceto. *Opera Historica.* Edited by William Stubbs. 2 vols. Rolls Series 68.

Ralph of Higden. *Polychronicon.* Rolls Series 41, vol. 8.

Ralph Niger. *Chronica.* Edited by Robert Anstruther. London: Caxton Society, 1851.

The Receipt Roll of the Exchequer for Michaelmas Term 1185. Edited by Hubert Hall. London: London School of Economics and Political Science, 1899.

Richard, Alfred. *Histoire des comtes de Poitou, 778–1204.* 2 vols. Paris: A. Picard & Fils, 1903.

Richard of Devizes. *Chronicle.* In *Chronicles of the Reigns of Stephen, Henry II and Richard I,* vol. 3, edited by Richard Howlett. Rolls Series 82.

Richard Fitzneale. *The Course of the Exchequer by Richard, Son of Nigel.* Translated by Charles Johnson. London: Thomas Nelson, 1950.

Richard of Hexham. *Chronicle.* Edited by Richard Howlett. Rolls Series 82, vol. 3.

Richard le Poitevin. *Ex Chronico.* In Delisle, ed. *Recueil des historiens des Gaules et de la France,* vol. 12. Paris, 1738–1904.

Richardson, H. G. "Letters and Charters of Eleanor of Aquitaine." *English Historical Review,* April 1959, pp. 193–213.

Robert of Torigni. *Chronicle.* Edited by Richard Howlett. Rolls Series 82, vol. 4.

Roger of Hovedon. *Annals.* Edited and translated by Henry T. Riley. 2 vols. London: H. G. Bohn, 1853.

Roger of Pontigny (Pseud.). *Materials for the History of Thomas Becket.* Edited by J. C. Robertson. Rolls Series 67, vol. 4.

Roger of Wendover (formerly ascribed to Matthew Paris). *Flores Historiarum.* 2 vols., London, 1849.

Rosenberg, Melrich V. *Eleanor of Aquitaine: Queen of the Troubadours and of the Courts of Love.* Boston: Houghton Mifflin, 1937.

Rotuli Chartarum. Edited by T. D. Hardy. London, 1837.

Rotuli Litterarum Patentium. Edited by T. D. Hardy. vol. 1. London, 1835.

Round, John Horace, ed. *Calendar of Documents Preserved in France Illustrative of the History of Great Britain and Ireland.* vol. 1. London, 1899.

_____. *Ancient Charters, Royal and Private, Prior to* A.D. *1200.* London, 1888.

Rowling, Marjorie. *Life in Medieval Times.* New York: G. P. Putnam's, 1973.

Runciman, Steven. *A History of the Crusades.* 3 vols. New York: Harper & Row, 1965.

Rymer, Thomas. *Foedera, Conventiones, Litterae, et Acta Publica.* Edited by A. Clarke and F. Holbrooke. 7 vols. London, 1816–69.

Salmon, A., ed. *Recueil des Chroniques de Touraine.* Tours, 1854.

Schlight, John. *Henry II Plantagenet.* New York: Twayne Publishers, 1973.

Stenton, Doris Mary. *English Society in the Early Middle Ages.* Harmondsworth-Middlesex: Penguin Books, 1951.

_____. *The English Woman in History.* New York: Macmillan Co., 1957.

Stenton, Frank M. *Norman London.* London: G. Bell & Sons, 1934.

Stephenson, Carl, and Marcham, Frederick George, ed. and trans. *Sources of English Constitutional History.* New York: Harper & Row, 1937.

Stone, Edward Noble, trans. *Three Old French Chronicles of the Crusades.* Seattle: University of Washington, 1939.

Strickland, Agnes. *Lives of the Queens of England.* 8 vols. London, 1852.

Stubbs, William. *Seventeen Lectures on the Study of Medieval and Modern History.* Oxford: Clarendon Press, 1900.

_____. *Historical Introduction to the Rolls Series.* New York: Longmans, Green and Co., 1902.

Suger. *Oeuvres de Suger.* Edited by A. Lecoy de la Marche. Paris, 1867.

Suger. *Vie de Louis VI le Gros.* Edited by Henri Waquet. Paris: H. Champion, 1929.

Thurston, Herbert, and Attwater, Donald, eds. *Butler's Lives of the Saints.* New York: P. J. Kenedy & Sons, 1956.

Vaughan, Richard. *Matthew Paris.* Cambridge, Eng.: University Press, 1958.

Viorst, Milton. *The Great Documents of Western Civilization.* Philadelphia: Chilton, 1965.

Waddell, Helen. *The Wandering Scholars.* London: Constable & Co., 1927.

Walker, Curtis. *Eleanor of Aquitaine.* Richmond, Va.: University of North Carolina Press, 1950.

Walter Map. *De Nugis Curialium (Courtiers' Trifles).* Edited and translated by Frederick Tupper and M. B. Ogle. London: Chatto & Windus, 1924.

Warren, W. L. *King John.* New York: W. W. Norton, 1961.

_____. *Henry II.* Berkeley and Los Angeles: University of California Press, 1973.

Waverley, Annals of (Annales Monastici). Edited by H. R. Luard. Rolls Series 36, vol. 2.

White, Freda. *Ways of Aquitaine*. London: Faber, 1968.

William Fitz Stephen. *Materials for the History of Thomas Becket*. Edited by J. C. Robertson. Rolls Series 67, vol. 3.

William of Canterbury. *Materials for the History of Thomas Becket*. Edited by J. C. Robertson. Rolls Series 67, vol. 1.

William of Malmesbury. *Gesta Regum Anglorum*. Edited by William Stubbs. 2 vols. Rolls Series 90.

William of Newburgh. *Historia Rerum Anglicarum*. Edited by Richard Howlett. 2 vols. Rolls Series 82, vols. 1 and 2.

William of Tyre. *A History of Deeds Done Beyond the Sea*. Edited and translated by E. A. Babcock and A. C. Krey. 2 vols. New York: Columbia University Press, 1943.

Williams, Watkin. *Saint Bernard of Clairvaux*. Westminster, Md.: Newman Press, 1952.

Winston, Richard. *Thomas Becket*. New York: Alfred A. Knopf, 1967.

Wood, Mary Anne Everett, ed. *Letters of Royal and Illustrious Ladies of Great Britain*. 3 vols. London, 1846.

The Year 1200. The Cloisters Studies in Medieval Art. 2 vols. New York: Metropolitan Museum of Art, 1970.

Index